Other Books and Series by Jeff Bowen

Applications for Enrollment of Chickasaw Newborn Act of 1905
Volumes I thru VII

Cherokee Intermarried White 1906 Volume I thru X

Applications for Enrollment of Creek Newborn Act of 1905
Volumes I, II, III, IV, V, VI, VII, VIII, IX, X, XI & XII

Visit our website at **www.nativestudy.com** to learn more about these and other books and series by Jeff Bowen

APPLICATIONS FOR ENROLLMENT OF CREEK NEWBORN ACT OF 1905
VOLUME XIII

TRANSCRIBED BY
JEFF BOWEN
NATIVE STUDY
Gallipolis, Ohio
USA

Other Books and Series by Jeff Bowen

1901-1907 Native American Census Seneca, Eastern Shawnee, Miami, Modoc, Ottawa, Peoria, Quapaw, and Wyandotte Indians (Under Seneca School, Indian Territory)

1932 Census of The Standing Rock Sioux Reservation with Births And Deaths 1924-1932

Census of The Blackfeet, Montana, 1897-1901 Expanded Edition

Eastern Cherokee by Blood, 1906-1910, Volumes I thru XIII

Choctaw of Mississippi Indian Census 1929-1932 with Births and Deaths 1924-1931 Volume I
Choctaw of Mississippi Indian Census 1933, 1934 & 1937, Supplemental Rolls to 1934 & 1935 with Births and Deaths 1932-1938, and Marriages 1936-1938 Volume II

Eastern Cherokee Census Cherokee, North Carolina 1930-1939 Census 1930-1931 with Births And Deaths 1924-1931 Taken By Agent L. W. Page Volume I
Eastern Cherokee Census Cherokee, North Carolina 1930-1939 Census 1932-1933 with Births And Deaths 1930-1932 Taken By Agent R. L. Spalsbury Volume II
Eastern Cherokee Census Cherokee, North Carolina 1930-1939 Census 1934-1937 with Births and Deaths 1925-1938 and Marriages 1936 & 1938 Taken by Agents R. L. Spalsbury And Harold W. Foght Volume III

Seminole of Florida Indian Census, 1930-1940 with Birth and Death Records, 1930-1938

Texas Cherokees 1820-1839 A Document For Litigation 1921

Choctaw By Blood Enrollment Cards 1898-1914 Volumes I thru XVII

Starr Roll 1894 (Cherokee Payment Rolls) Districts: Canadian, Cooweescoowee, and Delaware Volume One
Starr Roll 1894 (Cherokee Payment Rolls) Districts: Flint, Going Snake, and Illinois Volume Two
Starr Roll 1894 (Cherokee Payment Rolls) Districts: Saline, Sequoyah, and Tahlequah; Including Orphan Roll Volume Three

Cherokee Intruder Cases Dockets of Hearings 1901-1909 Volumes I & II

Indian Wills, 1911-1921 Records of the Bureau of Indian Affairs Books One thru Seven;
Native American Wills & Probate Records 1911-1921

Other Books and Series by Jeff Bowen

Turtle Mountain Reservation Chippewa Indians 1932 Census with Births & Deaths, 1924-1932

Chickasaw By Blood Enrollment Cards 1898-1914 Volume I thru V

Cherokee Descendants East An Index to the Guion Miller Applications Volume I
Cherokee Descendants West An Index to the Guion Miller Applications Volume II (A-M)
Cherokee Descendants West An Index to the Guion Miller Applications Volume III (N-Z)

Applications for Enrollment of Seminole Newborn Freedmen, Act of 1905

Eastern Cherokee Census, Cherokee, North Carolina, 1915-1922, Taken by Agent James E. Henderson   Volume I (1915-1916)
Volume II (1917-1918)
Volume III (1919-1920)
Volume IV (1921-1922)

Complete Delaware Roll of 1898

Eastern Cherokee Census, Cherokee, North Carolina, 1923-1929, Taken by Agent James E. Henderson   Volume I (1923-1924)
Volume II (1925-1926)
Volume III (1927-1929)

Applications for Enrollment of Seminole Newborn Act of 1905 Volumes I & II

North Carolina Eastern Cherokee Indian Census 1898-1899, 1904, 1906, 1909-1912, 1914 Revised and Expanded Edition

1932 Hopi and Navajo Native American Census with Birth & Death Rolls (1925-1931) Volume 1 - Hopi
1932 Hopi and Navajo Native American Census with Birth & Death Rolls (1930-1932) Volume 2 - Navajo

Western Navajo Reservation Navajo, Hopi and Paiute 1933 Census with Birth & Death Rolls 1925-1933

Cherokee Citizenship Commission Dockets 1880-1884 and 1887-1889 Volumes I thru V

Copyright © 2012
by Jeff Bowen

ALL RIGHTS RESERVED
No part of this publication may be reproduced
or used in any form or manner whatsoever
without previous written permission from the
copyright holder or publisher.

Originally published:
Baltimore, Maryland
2012

Reprinted by:

Native Study LLC
Gallipolis, OH
www.nativestudy.com
2020

Library of Congress Control Number: 2020917992

ISBN: 978-1-64968-092-1

Made in the United States of America.

This series is dedicated to the descendants of the Creek newborn listed in these applications.

DEPARTMENT OF THE INTERIOR.

Commissioner to the Five Civilized Tribes.

NOTICE.

Opening of Land Office at Wewoka,
IN THE SEMINOLE NATION, INDIAN TERRITORY.

Notice is hereby given that on Monday, September 4, 1905, the Commissioner to the Five Civilized Tribes will establish a land office at Wewoka, in the Seminole Nation, Indian Territory, for the purpose of allowing citizens and freedmen of the Seminole Nation to select allotments of land for their minor children enrolled under the Act of Congress approved March 3, 1905 (33 Stat. L 1060), and for the further purpose of allowing citizens and freedmen of the Seminole Nation, whose allotments are incomplete, to select additional land in order to bring the value of their allotments up to the standard of $309.09, as nearly as may be practicable.

Each child whose enrollment in accordance with the Act of March 3, 1905, has been duly approved by the Secretary of the Interior, is entitled to receive an alllotment of forty acres without regard to the character or value of the land selected.

Selection of allotments for minor children must be made by their citizen or freedmen parents or by a duly appointed guardian, or curator, or by a duly appointed administrator.

TAMS BIXBY,
Commissioner.

Muskogee, Indian Territory,
July 29, 1905.

This particular notice makes mention of the Act of 1905. The Creek and Seminole were closely related tribes. Both tribes' notices were similar in nature.

DEPARTMENT OF THE INTERIOR,
Commission to the Five Civilized Tribes.

Closing of Citizenship Rolls
OF THE MUSKOGEE OR CREEK NATION.

WHEREAS, on June 13, 1904, the Secretary of the Interior, under the authority in him vested by the provisions of the act of Congress approved March 3, 1901, (31 Stat., 1058) ordered that September 1, 1904, be and the same is hereby fixed as the time when the rolls of the Muskogee or Creek Nation shall be closed:

Notice is hereby given that the Commission to the Five Civilized Tribes will, at its office in Muskogee, Indian Territory, up to and inclusive of September 1, 1904, receive applications for the enrollment of citizens and freedmen of the Muskogee or Creek Nation, and that after that date the application of no person whomsoever for enrollment as a citizen or freedman of said nation will be received by the Commission.

Commission to the Five Civilized Tribes,
TAMS BIXBY, Chairman,
T. B. NEEDLES,
C. R. BRECKINRIDGE,
Commissioners.

Muskogee, Indian Territory,
June 25, 1904.

A notice like this was printed in newspapers and posted throughout Indian Territory.

INTRODUCTION

This series concerns Applications for Enrollment of Creek Newborn, National Archive film M-1301 (Act of 1905), as described in the National Archives publication *American Indians*. It falls under the heading Applications for Enrollment of the Commission to the Five Civilized Tribes, 1898-1914, M-1301 and is transcribed from microfilm rolls 414-419. This shows the application forms filled out by individuals applying for enrollment in the Five Civilized Tribes under the Dawes Commission. These applications contain additional information that wasn't abstracted to the census cards that you find in series M-1186. This particular roll (Creek by Birth) contains its own series of numbers separate from M-1186. To find each party's roll number you would have to reference M-1186. On July 25, 1898, there was an Indian Territory Division created in the Office of the Department of Interior. This division was created because of the increased work caused by what was called the Curtis Act, named after Senator Charles Curtis. Basically, this law stated that the tribal rolls needed to be descriptive and pointed out that each tribal roll was without description and had to be redone. At this point there was such a struggle among the Creeks to accept that the Government was going to change their way of life, again, that their leaders were refusing to cooperate in handing over their census information. The Commission had found that enrolling the Creeks was a difficult task not only because the Creek feared what was coming but also because their tribal structure was consistent with being a confederacy with forty-four different bands whose tribesmen lived in different towns of which each had a king that was supposed to keep track of their citizenry. The Commission reported that there was very little evidence of any census that existed and what there was had been kept carelessly. There were attempts and tribal conflicts along the way, but the Curtis Act would make it so they had to do it again no matter what effort from the past. In 1899, Agent Wesley Smith educated Washington to the fact that it was difficult to verify Creek eligibility. The acts passed by the Creeks themselves concerning enrollment since 1893 had been strewn amongst the archives of the Creek Council in Muskogee, I.T., and there was no provision ever approved for the printing of the those enrollments. There was confusion and difficulty let alone the fact that surnames were practically unknown among the Creek. But there was no confusion on March 9, 1905, when the Commission stated they would come to seven towns in the Creek Nation and accept applications that had to be made on a standardized blank form and contain a notarized affidavit from the mother and the attending doctor or midwife. A few by mail, but most of them were offered to a field party led by Commissioner Needles. The Commission took in applications for 2,410 children by the deadline of midnight, May 2, 1905.

This series contains applications and correspondence from 1,171 of those claimants. Realizing there were over 2,400 applicants originally, it is understood that not all were accepted. Also included are names of doctors, lawyers, mid-wives, and others who attended to the Creek Nation before and during this time in history.

Jeff Bowen
Gallipolis, Ohio
NativeStudy.com

Applications for Enrollment of Creek Newborn
Act of 1905 Volume XIII

DEPARTMENT OF THE INTERIOR,
COMMISSIONER TO THE FIVE CIVILIZED TRIBES.
APRIL 24, 1905.

In the matter of the application for the enrollment of certain new borns as citizens of the Creek Nation.

Alex Posey, being duly sworn, testified as follow:

Statement: Freeland Lindsey, Tuckabatchee or Hillabee, Nancy Proctor, Tullahassoche, have a chil[sic] about two years old. Post Office, Hann[sic], Indian Territory.

2448 B

COPY. #10 C 1006

DEPARTMENT OF THE INTERIOR,
COMMISSION TO THE FIVE CIVILIZED TRIBES.
April 24, 1905.

In the matter of the application for the enrollment of certain new borns as citizens of the Creek Nation.

Alex Posey, being duly sworn, testified as follows:

By Commission:
Q What is your name, age and post office address? A Alex Posey, 31, Muskogee.
Q Are you a citizen of the Creek Nation? A Yes sir
Q Got your land, have you? A Yes sir.
Q You have been engaged recently in the field for the Dawes Commission securing evidence about Creek citizens or new borns? A Yes sir.
Q Have you a list of children for whom application could not be made and about whom you have succeeded in obtaining some information? A Yes sir.
Q You may state the conditions and the names of these children? You desire to make application for them? A Yes sir.
Q Name them.
A Jaly Proctor, Weogufky Town, Sukey Proctor, Weogufky Town, have two children -- one about three years old and one about six months old. Post office, Hanna, Indian Territory.
    Jacob Bullet, about three years old. Parents: Maxey Bullet, Seminole, and Hannah Bullet, Hillabee. Post Office, Hanna, Indian Territory.
    Connie Hawkins, Hillabee Town, Sabella Hawkins, Okchiye, have two children-- one about three years old and a younger child. Post Office, Hanna, Indian Territory.
    Willie Fisher, Hickory Ground Town, Lussee Fisher, Okfusky[sic] Canadian Town, have two children --one about three years old and a baby. Post Office, Slumpker, Indian Territory.

Applications for Enrollment of Creek Newborn
Act of 1905   Volume XIII

Lizzie Lasley, about three years old, Sam Lasley, born in either August or September, 1904. Parents: Sam Lasley, Okchiye, Wisey Lasley, Weogufky. Post Office, Hanna, Indian Territory.

Jim Haynes (or Sangee), Okchiye Town, Folotkokee, Weogufky Town have a male child about three years old named Joe. Post Office, Hanna, Indian Territory.

Taylor Foley, Weogufky, Melinda Foley, Okchiye, have a child about two years old. Post Office, Slumpker, Indian Territory.

Phillip Lindsey, Tuckabatchee, Cilla Lindsey, Hillabee, have a child about three years old. Post Office, Hanna, Indian Territory.

Big William (or William Thlocco), Okchiye Town, Cinda Williams, Weogufky Town, have two children -- one about three years old-- one born in February 1905. Post Office Hanna, Indian Territory.

✓ Freeland Lindsey, Tuckabatchee or Hillabee, Nancy Proctor, Tullahassoche, have a child about two years old. Post Office, Hanna, Indian Territory.

Timonthluppy George, Weogufky Town, Nellie George, Pukon Tullahassee, have a child about three years old. Post Office, Slumpker, Indian Territory.

Walter Simmons, Weogufky, Chippie Simmons, Pukon Tulahassee[sic], have a child about one years old. Post Office, Hannah, Indian Territory.

Jacob Larney (or Green), Arbeka Tulledega Town, Bettie Larney, (or Green), Hillabee Town, have a child. Post Office, Hanna, Indian Territory.

John Hill, Okchiye, Millie Hill, Weogufky, have a child about three months old. Post Office, Hanna, Indian Territory.

Jim Pigeon, Okchiye Town, Jennie Pigeon, Okchiye Town, have a child about five months old. Post Office, Hanna, Indian Territory.

Thomas Deo, Okchiye Town, Nancy Deo, Fish Pond Town, have a child about three months old. Post Office, Hanna, Indian Territory.

Jack Buckner, born December 17, 1904. Parents: Wiley Buckner, Okchiye, Susie Buckner, Cussehta. Post Office, Hanna, Indian Territory.

Q This is the information you received from relatives right around there on April 24, 1905? A Yes sir.
Q Were you informed that the parents of these children were unwilling to make application for their enrollment? A Yes sir.
Q This was the only way that the rights of these children would be saved? A Yes sir. I made every effort to obtain direct information from the parents but in every instance they refused to give their testimony.

Lona Merrick being duly sworn, states that the above and foregoing is a true and correct transcript of his stenographic notes as taken in said cause on said date.

(Signed) Lona Merrick

Subscribed and sworn to before me this 9th day of May, 1905.

(Signed) Edw C Griesel
Seal.   Notary Public.

Applications for Enrollment of Creek Newborn
Act of 1905   Volume XIII

I, Lona Merrick, solemnly swear that I copied the above testimony from the original, on the 18th day of July, 1905, and that the same is a true copy.

Lona Merrick

Subscribed and sworn to before me this 18th day of July, 1905.

Edw C Griesel
Notary Public.

NC 1006

DEPARTMENT OF THE INTERIOR,
COMMISSIONER TO THE FIVE CIVILIZED TRIBES.
Hanna, I. T., May 31?[sic] 1905.

In the matter of the application for the enrollment of Sarah Lindsey as a ctizen[sic] by blood of the Creek Nation.

LOUINA DEO, being duly sworn, testified as follows:

Through Alex Posey Official Interpreter:

BY COMMISSIONER:
Q What is your name? A Louina Deo.
Q How old are you? A About twenty-three.
Q What is your post office address? A Hanna.
Q Are you a citizen of the Creek Nation? A Yes, sir.
Q To what town do you belong? A Okchiye.
Q Do you make application for the enrollment of your minor child, Sarah Lindsey, as a citizen by blood of the Creek Nation? A Yes, sir.
Q Who is Sarah's father? A Freeland Lindsey.
Q Is Freeland Lindsey your lawful husband? A No, sir.
Q Were you ever married to him? A No, sir.
Q Does he acknowledge Sarah as his child? A Yes, sir.
Q Does he contribute towards the support of the child? A Yes, sir.
Q When was the child born? A The child was born in August and will be three years old next August.
Q Were you and Freeland Lindsey living together at the time the child was born? A No, sir.
Q You have never, at any time, lived together as man and wife? A No, sir.
Q Has Freeland Lindsey a lawful wife? A Yes, sir.
Q What is her name? A Sallie Lindsey.
Q Is he living with Sallie Lindsey at the present time? A Yes, sir.
Q Was he ever married to Nancy Proctor? A No, sir, but Nancy has a child by him.
Q What is the name of that child? A I do not know.

Applications for Enrollment of Creek Newborn
Act of 1905   Volume XIII

Q Do you know how old the child is? A I do not know when the child was born but it was born since the birth of my child.
Q Do you know whether or not Freeland Lindsey acknowledges Nancy's child as his own? A I do not know as to that but I suppose he does.
Q Where does Nancy Proctor live? A She lives near here? A[sic]
Q Who was present at the time your child Sallie was born? A Jennie Lasley.
Q Have you a lawful husband? A Thompson Deo is my lawful husband.

---oooOOOooo---

I, D. C. Skaggs, on oath state that the above and foregoing is a full and true transcript of my stenographic notes as taken in said cause on said date.

D. C. Skaggs

Subscribed and sworn to before me this 17th day of July 1905.

Edw C Griesel
Notary Public.

BIRTH AFFIDAVIT.

DEPARTMENT OF THE INTERIOR.
COMMISSION TO THE FIVE CIVILIZED TRIBES.

IN RE APPLICATION FOR ENROLLMENT, as a citizen of the Creek Nation, of Sarah Lindsey, born on the 24 day of August, 1902

Name of Father: Freeland Lindsey Tuckabatchee   a citizen of the   Creek   Nation.
Name of Mother: Lovina Deo (nee) Ahoyathlee or Gano   a citizen of the   Creek   Nation.

Postoffice   Hanna IT

AFFIDAVIT OF MOTHER.

UNITED STATES OF AMERICA, Indian Territory, ⎫
    Western   DISTRICT.   ⎬

I, Lovina Deo, on oath state that I am about 23 years of age and a citizen by blood , of the Creek Nation; that I am not the lawful wife of Freeland Lindsey , who is a citizen, by blood of the Creek Nation; that a female child was born to me on 24 day of August , 1902 , that said child has been named Sarah Lindsey , and was living March 4, 1905.

Applications for Enrollment of Creek Newborn
Act of 1905   Volume XIII

Witnesses To Mark:
{ DC Skaggs
  Alex Posey

her
Lovina x Deo
mark

Subscribed and sworn to before me this 31 day of May, 1905.

Drennan C Skaggs
Notary Public.

AFFIDAVIT OF ATTENDING PHYSICIAN OR MID-WIFE.

UNITED STATES OF AMERICA, Indian Territory,
     Western   DISTRICT.

I, Jennie Lasley, a Midwife, on oath state that I attended on Mrs. Lovina Deo, ~~wife of~~ *(blank)* on the about 3 years ago day of *(blank)*, 1*(blank)*; that there was born to her on said date a female child; that said child was living March 4, 1905, and is said to have been named Sarah Lindsey

her
Jennie x Lasley
mark

Witnesses To Mark:
{ DC Skaggs
  Alex Posey

Subscribed and sworn to before me this 31 day of May, 1905.

Drennan C Skaggs
Notary Public.

(The above Birth Affidavit given again.)

BIRTH AFFIDAVIT.

DEPARTMENT OF THE INTERIOR.
COMMISSION TO THE FIVE CIVILIZED TRIBES.

IN RE APPLICATION FOR ENROLLMENT, as a citizen of the Creek Nation, of Sarah Lindsey, born on the 24 day of August, 1902

Name of Father: Freeland Lindsey	a citizen of the	Creek Nation.
Name of Mother: Lovina Arsoyalee	a citizen of the	Creek Nation.
Roll #7084		

Postoffice   Hanna IT

Applications for Enrollment of Creek Newborn
Act of 1905 Volume XIII

Illegitimate Child

AFFIDAVIT OF MOTHER.

UNITED STATES OF AMERICA, Indian Territory, }
Western DISTRICT.

I, Lovina Arsoyalee, on oath state that I am about 24 years of age and a citizen by blood , of the Creek Nation; that I am not the lawful wife of Freeland Lindsey , who is a citizen, by blood of the Creek Nation; that a female child was born to me on 24" day of August , 1902 , that said child has been named Sarah Lindsey , and was living March 4, 1905 and is now living her
              Louina x Arsoyalee

Witnesses To Mark: mark
{ J McDermott
 R B Selvidge

Subscribed and sworn to before me this 7" day of December , 1906.
My Commission
Expires July 25" 1907   J McDermott
              Notary Public.

BIRTH AFFIDAVIT.

DEPARTMENT OF THE INTERIOR.
COMMISSION TO THE FIVE CIVILIZED TRIBES.

IN RE APPLICATION FOR ENROLLMENT, as a citizen of the Creek Nation, of Sarah Lindsey, born on the 24th day of Aug, 1902

Name of Father: Freeland Lindsey a citizen of the Creek Nation.
Name of Mother: Lovina Arsoyalee a citizen of the Creek Nation.

         Post office Hanna IT

AFFIDAVIT OF ATTENDING PHYSICIAN OR MID-WIFE.

UNITED STATES OF AMERICA, Indian Territory, }
Western DISTRICT.

I, Jennie Lasley , a midwife , on oath state that I attended on Mrs. Lovina Arsoyalee, not the wife of Freeland Lindsey on the 24" day of Aug , 1902 ; that there was born to her on said date a female child; that said child was living March 4, 1905, and is said to have been named Sarah Lindsey   her
            Jennie x Lasley
             mark

Applications for Enrollment of Creek Newborn
Act of 1905   Volume XIII

Witnesses To Mark:
{ J McDermott
  Jim Cantrell

Subscribed and sworn to before me this 18 day of December, 1906.
My Commission
Expires July 25" 1907   J McDermott
                                          Notary Public.

NC
~~NV~~ 100<u>6</u>.

Muskogee, Indian Territory, October 23, 1905.

Louina Deo,
    Hanna, Indian Territory.

Dear Madam:

In the matter of the application for the enrollment of your minor child, Sarah Lindsey, born August 24, 1902, as a citizen by blood of the Creek Nation, this office is unable to identify you on its final roll of citizens by blood of the Creek Nation under the name Louina Deo or under the names of Ahoyathlee or Gano, by which name it is stated in the caption of the affidavit in said case your[sic] were formerly known.

You are requested to state if you were ever known by the name of Lobina[sic] Arsoy, also state all the names by which you have been known, the Creek Indian town to which you belong, the names of your parents, and your roll number as the same appears on your deeds and allotment certificate.

                        Respectfully,
                                Commissioner.

                                                                JWH
NC 1006
                Muskogee, Indian Territory, March 1, 1907.

Louina Deo,
    % Freeland Lindsey,
        Hanna, Indian Territory.

Dear Madam :--

You are hereby advised that on February 15, 1907, the Secretary of the Interior approved the enrollment of your minor child, Sarah Lindsey, as a citizen by blood of the Creek Nation, and that the name of said child appears upon the roll of New Born citizens

Applications for Enrollment of Creek Newborn
Act of 1905 Volume XIII

by blood of the Creek Nation, enrolled under the Act of Congress approved March 3, 1905, as number 1191.

    This child is now entitled to allotment and application therefor should be made without delay at the Creek Land Office, Muskogee, Indian Territory.

                        Respectfully,

                                    Commissioner.

BIRTH AFFIDAVIT.

DEPARTMENT OF THE INTERIOR.
COMMISSION TO THE FIVE CIVILIZED TRIBES.

IN RE APPLICATION FOR ENROLLMENT, as a citizen of the Creek Nation, of Caesar King, born on the 7 day of February, 1902

Name of Father: Jackson King Tuskegee Town	a citizen of the	Creek Nation.
Name of Mother: Jennie King Tulwa Thlocco Town	a citizen of the	Creek Nation.

                      Postoffice   Hitchita, Ind. Ter.

AFFIDAVIT OF MOTHER.

UNITED STATES OF AMERICA, Indian Territory,
    Western   **DISTRICT.**   Child is present

    I, Jennie King, on oath state that I am about 36 years of age and a citizen by blood, of the Creek Nation; that I am the lawful wife of Jackson King, who is a citizen, by blood of the Creek Nation; that a male child was born to me on 7 day of February, 1902, that said child has been named Caesar King, and was living March 4, 1905.

                                        her
                                Jennie x King
Witnesses To Mark: mark
   { Alex Posey
   { DC Skaggs

Applications for Enrollment of Creek Newborn
Act of 1905   Volume XIII

Subscribed and sworn to before me this 11 day of April , 1905.

                         Drennan C Skaggs
                         Notary Public.

AFFIDAVIT OF ATTENDING PHYSICIAN OR MID-WIFE.

UNITED STATES OF AMERICA, Indian Territory,
     Western   DISTRICT.

     I, Sukey Kelly, a midwife , on oath state that I attended on Mrs. Jennie King , wife of Jackson King on the 7 day of February , 1902 ; that there was born to her on said date a male child; that said child was living March 4, 1905, and is said to have been named Caesar King

                                         her
Witnesses To Mark: Sukey x Kelly
     Alex Posey   mark
     DC Skaggs

Subscribed and sworn to before me this 11 day of April , 1905.

                         Drennan C Skaggs
                         Notary Public.

(Note on small piece of paper.)

The mother of this child May be enrolled as Chippie Fixico or Chippie Lunisey.

                         Posey

Applications for Enrollment of Creek Newborn
Act of 1905   Volume XIII

#11 C
COPY.

DEPARTMENT OF THE INTERIOR,
COMMISSION TO THE FIVE CIVILIZED TRIBES.
April 24, 1905.

In the matter of the application for the enrollment of certain new borns as citizens of the Creek Nation.

Alex Posey, being duly sworn, testified as follows:

By Commission:
Q   What is your name, age and post office address?   A   Alex Posey, 31, Muskogee.
Q   Are you a citizen of the Creek Nation?   A   Yes sir
Q   Got your land, have you?   A   Yes sir.
Q   You have been engaged recently in the field for the Dawes Commission securing evidence about Creek citizens or new borns?   A   Yes sir.
Q   Have you a list of children for whom application could not be made and about whom you have succeeded in obtaining some information?   A   Yes sir.
Q   You may state the conditions and the names of these children?   You desire to make application for them?   A   Yes sir.
Q   Name them.
A   Jaly Proctor, Weogufky Town, Sukey Proctor, Weogufky Town, have two children -- one about three years old and one about six months old.   Post office, Hanna, Indian Territory.

Jacob Bullet, about three years old.   Parents: Maxey Bullet, Seminole, and Hannah Bullet, Hillabee.   Post Office, Hanna, Indian Territory.

Connie Hawkins, Hillabee Town, Sabella Hawkins, Okchiye, have two children-- one about three years old and a younger child.   Post Office, Hanna, Indian Territory.

Willie Fisher, Hickory Ground Town, Lussee Fisher, Okfusky[sic] Canadian Town, have two children --one about three years old and a baby.   Post Office, Slumpker, Indian Territory.

Lizzie Lasley, about three years old, Sam Lasley, born in either August or September, 1904.   Parents: Sam Lasley, Okchiye, Wisey Lasley, Weogufky.   Post Office, Hanna, Indian Territory.

Jim Haynes (or Sangee), Okchiye Town, Folotkokee, Weogufky Town have a male child about three years old named Joe.   Post Office, Hanna, Indian Territory.

Taylor Foley, Weogufky, Melinda Foley, Okchiye, have a child about two years old.   Post Office, Slumpker, Indian Territory.

Phillip Lindsey, Tuckabatchee, Cilla Lindsey, Hillabee, have a child about three years old.   Post Office, Hanna, Indian Territory.

Big William (or William Thlocco), Okchiye Town, Cinda Williams, Weogufky Town, have two children -- one about three years old-- one born in February 1905.   Post Office Hanna, Indian Territory.

Freeland Lindsey, Tuckabatchee cr Hillabee, Nancy Proctor, Tullahassoche, have a child about two years old.   Post Office, Hanna, Indian Territory.

Applications for Enrollment of Creek Newborn
Act of 1905   Volume XIII

Timonthluppy George, Weogufky Town, Nellie George, Pukon Tullahassee, have a child about three years old. Post Office, Slumpker, Indian Territory.

✓ Walter Simmons, Weogufky, Chippie Simmons, Pukon Tulahassee[sic], have a child about one years old. Post Office, Hannah, Indian Territory.

Jacob Larney (or Green), Arbeka Tulledega Town, Bettie Larney, (or Green), Hillabee Town, have a child. Post Office, Hanna, Indian Territory.

John Hill, Okchiye, Millie Hill, Weogufky, have a child about three months old. Post Office, Hanna, Indian Territory.

Jim Pigeon, Okchiye Town, Jennie Pigeon, Okchiye Town, have a child about five months old. Post Office, Hanna, Indian Territory.

Thomas Deo, Okchiye Town, Nancy Deo, Fish Pond Town, have a child about three months old. Post Office, Hanna, Indian Territory.

Jack Buckner, born December 17, 1904. Parents: Wiley Buckner, Okchiye, Susie Buckner, Cussehta. Post Office, Hanna, Indian Territory.

Q This is the information you received from relatives right around there on April 24, 1905? A Yes sir.

Q Were you informed that the parents of these children were unwilling to make application for their enrollment? A Yes sir.

Q This was the only way that the rights of these children would be saved? A Yes sir. I made every effort to obtain direct information from the parents but in every instance they refused to give their testimony.

Lona Merrick being duly sworn, states that the above and foregoing is a true and correct transcript of his stenographic notes as taken in said cause on said date.

(Signed) Lona Merrick

Subscribed and sworn to before me this 9th day of May, 1905.

Seal.

(Signed) Edw C Griesel
Notary Public.

I, Lona Merrick, solemnly swear that I copied the above testimony from the original, on the 18th day of July, 1905, and that the same is a true copy.

Lona Merrick

Subscribed and sworn to before me this 18th day of July, 1905.

Edw C Griesel
Notary Public.

Applications for Enrollment of Creek Newborn
Act of 1905   Volume XIII

BIRTH AFFIDAVIT.

DEPARTMENT OF THE INTERIOR.
COMMISSION TO THE FIVE CIVILIZED TRIBES.

IN RE APPLICATION FOR ENROLLMENT, as a citizen of the Creek Nation, of Emma Simmons, born in on the day of June, 1904

Name of Father: Walter Simmons   a citizen of the   Creek   Nation.
(Illegible)   (nee Fixico)
Name of Mother: Chippie Simmons   a citizen of the   Creek   Nation.
Pukkon Tulahassee[sic]
                            Postoffice   Hanna, Ind. Terr.

AFFIDAVIT OF ATTENDING PHYSICIAN OR MID-WIFE.

UNITED STATES OF AMERICA, Indian Territory, }
   Western   DISTRICT.

                                           are personally acquainted with
We, the undersigned   , a *(blank)* , on oath state that I we attended on Mrs. Chippie Simmons , wife of Walter Simmons on the day of , 1 ; that there was born to her in June on said date a female child; that said child was living March 4, 1905, and is said to have been named Emma Simmons   her
                                         Meleya x Tish
Witnesses To Mark: mark
  { DC Skaggs   her
    Alex Posey   x Tahakee
                                   mark
Subscribed and sworn to before me 7 day of October, 1905.

                                              Drennan C Skaggs
                                              Notary Public.

BIRTH AFFIDAVIT.

DEPARTMENT OF THE INTERIOR.
COMMISSION TO THE FIVE CIVILIZED TRIBES.

IN RE APPLICATION FOR ENROLLMENT, as a citizen of the Creek Nation, of Emma Simmons , born on the *(blank)* day of June, 1904

Name of Father: Walter Simmons   a citizen of the   Creek   Nation.
Weogufke
Name of Mother: Chippie Simmons   a citizen of the   Creek   Nation.
Pukkon Tallahassee   Slumpker
                         Postoffice   Selumker, I.T.

Applications for Enrollment of Creek Newborn
Act of 1905 Volume XIII

AFFIDAVIT OF MOTHER.

UNITED STATES OF AMERICA, Indian Territory, }   Child present
   Western   DISTRICT.

     I, Chippie Simmons , on oath state that I am about 26 years of age and a citizen by blood , of the Creek Nation; that I am the lawful wife of Walter Simmons , who is a citizen, by blood of the Creek Nation; that a female child was born to me on *(blank)* day of June , 1904 , that said child has been named Emma Simmons , and is now living. and was living March 4, 1905. That no one attended on me at the birth of the child

                                                her
Witnesses To Mark: Chippie x Simmons
   { DC Skaggs   mark
   { Alex Posey

     Subscribed and sworn to before me this 29 day of May , 1905.

                                              Drennan C Skaggs
                                              Notary Public.

                                    #11   C 1010
                              COPY.

DEPARTMENT OF THE INTERIOR,
COMMISSION TO THE FIVE CIVILIZED TRIBES.
April 24, 1905.

     In the matter of the application for the enrollment of certain new borns as citizens of the Creek Nation.

     Alex Posey, being duly sworn, testified as follows:

By Commission:
Q What is your name, age and post office address? A Alex Posey, 31, Muskogee.

Applications for Enrollment of Creek Newborn
Act of 1905   Volume XIII

Q Are you a citizen of the Creek Nation? A Yes sir
Q Got your land, have you? A Yes sir.
Q You have been engaged recently in the field for the Dawes Commission securing evidence about Creek citizens or new borns? A Yes sir.
Q Have you a list of children for whom application could not be made and about whom you have succeeded in obtaining some information? A Yes sir.
Q You may state the conditions and the names of these children? You desire to make application for them? A Yes sir.
Q Name them.
A Jaly Proctor, Weogufky Town, Sukey Proctor, Weogufky Town, have two children -- one about three years old and one about six months old. Post office, Hanna, Indian Territory.
    Jacob Bullet, about three years old. Parents: Maxey Bullet, Seminole, and Hannah Bullet, Hillabee. Post Office, Hanna, Indian Territory.
    Connie Hawkins, Hillabee Town, Sabella Hawkins, Okchiye, have two children-- one about three years old and a younger child. Post Office, Hanna, Indian Territory.
    Willie Fisher, Hickory Ground Town, Lussee Fisher, Okfusky[sic] Canadian Town, have two children --one about three years old and a baby. Post Office, Slumpker, Indian Territory.
    Lizzie Lasley, about three years old, Sam Lasley, born in either August or September, 1904. Parents: Sam Lasley, Okchiye, Wisey Lasley, Weogufky. Post Office, Hanna, Indian Territory.
    Jim Haynes (or Sangee), Okchiye Town, Folotkokee, Weogufky Town have a male child about three years old named Joe. Post Office, Hanna, Indian Territory.
    Taylor Foley, Weogufky, Melinda Foley, Okchiye, have a child about two years old. Post Office, Slumpker, Indian Territory
    Phillip Lindsey, Tuckabatchee, Cilla Lindsey, Hillabee, have a child about three years old. Post Office, Hanna, Indian Territory.
    Big William (or William Thlocco), Okchiye Town, Cinda Williams, Weogufky Town, have two children -- one about three years old-- one born in February 1905. Post Office Hanna, Indian Territory.
    Freeland Lindsey, Tuckabatchee or Hillabee, Nancy Proctor, Tullahassoche, have a child about two years old. Post Office, Hanna, Indian Territory.
    Timonthluppy George, Weogufky Town, Nellie George, Pukon Tullahassee, have a child about three years old. Post Office, Slumpker, Indian Territory.
    Walter Simmons, Weogufky, Chippie Simmons, Pukon Tulahassee[sic], have a child about one years old. Post Office, Hannah, Indian Territory.
    ✓ Jacob Larney (or Green), Arbeka Tulledega Town, Bettie Larney, (or Green), Hillabee Town, <u>have a child</u>. Post Office, Hanna, Indian Territory.
    John Hill, Okchiye, Millie Hill, Weogufky, have a child about three months old. Post Office, Hanna, Indian Territory.
    Jim Pigeon, Okchiye Town, Jennie Pigeon, Okchiye Town, have a child about five months old. Post Office, Hanna, Indian Territory.
    Thomas Deo, Okchiye Town, Nancy Deo, Fish Pond Town, have a child about three months old. Post Office, Hanna, Indian Territory.
    Jack Buckner, born December 17, 1904. Parents: Wiley Buckner, Okchiye, Susie Buckner, Cussehta. Post Office, Hanna, Indian Territory.

Applications for Enrollment of Creek Newborn
Act of 1905   Volume XIII

Q This is the information you received from relatives right around there on April 24, 1905? A Yes sir.
Q Were you informed that the parents of these children were unwilling to make application for their enrollment? A Yes sir.
Q This was the only way that the rights of these children would be saved? A Yes sir. I made every effort to obtain direct information from the parents but in every instance they refused to give their testimony.

Lona Merrick being duly sworn, states that the above and foregoing is a true and correct transcript of his stenographic notes as taken in said cause on said date.

(Signed) Lona Merrick

Subscribed and sworn to before me this 9th day of May, 1905.

(Signed) Edw C Griesel
Seal.   Notary Public.

I, Lona Merrick, solemnly swear that I copied the above testimony from the original, on the 18th day of July, 1905, and that the same is a true copy.

Lona Merrick
Subscribed and sworn to before me this 18th day of July, 1905.

Edw C Griesel
Notary Public.

DEPARTMENT OF THE INTERIOR,
COMMISSIONER TO THE FIVE CIVILIZED TRIBES.
MUSKOGEE, INDIAN TERRITORY.
FEBRUARY 16, 1907.

In the matter of the application for the enrollment of Cheparney Larney, as a citizen by blood of the Creek Nation.

ALEX POSEY, being duly sworn, by O. C. Hinkle, a Notary Public, testified as follows:

Examination by Commissioner.
Q What is your name, age and post office address? A Alex Posey, age 33, Muskogee.
Q Did you on July 19, 1905 go to the home of Jacob and Bettie Larney, for the purpose of obtaining information with reference to a child of theirs? A Yes sir.
Q Did you see that child? A Yes sir.
Q Was that child a boy or girl? A I am under the impression he was a boy.
Q What is your best opinion with reference to the age of that child? A The child appeared at that time to be about a year old.

Applications for Enrollment of Creek Newborn
Act of 1905   Volume XIII

Q The parents of that child refused to give any information concerning that child?
A They wouldn't give any information whatever.
Q Do you know whether they are members of the Snake or disaffected faction of Creeks? A The father of the child's mother very much opposed the work of this Commission.
Q Do you know if the child is now living? A I made inquiries about this child a short time ago and I am informed that the child is still living.

------------oOo------------

Lona Merrick, being duly sworn, states that the above and foregoing is a true and correct transcript of her stenographic notes as taken in said cause on said date.

Lona Merrick

Subscribed and sworn to before me this 18th day of February, 1907.

(Name Illegible)
Notary Public.

NC 1010.   OCH
   CM

DEPARTMENT OF THE INTERIOR,
COMMISSIONER TO THE FIVE CIVILIZED TRIBES.

In the matter of the application for the enrollment of Cheparney Larney as a citizen by blood of the Creek Nation.

DECISION

It appears from the records of this office that on April 24, 1905 testimony was offered "In the matter of the application for the enrollment of certain new borns, as citizens of the Creek Nation" which embraced a child of Jacob Larney (or Green) and Bettie Larney (or Green), which is herein considered as an original application for the enrollment of said person as a citizen by blood of the Creek Nation. Furthere[sic] proceedings were had February 16, 1907.

It appears from the testimony that about July 19, 1905 a Creek field party went to the home of said child for the purpose of obtaining information with reference to the right to enrollment of said child, and that the parents refused to give such information because of the influence over them of the Snake or disaffected faction of the Creeks; that the clerk in charge is under the impression that said child is a male but states that he could not learn the name of said child. In view of the fact that the full name of said child could not be ascertained, and that it is believed that said child is a male, reference to said person will hereinafter be made under the name of Cheparney Larney, the Creek word, "Cheparney" is signifying "little boy".

Applications for Enrollment of Creek Newborn
Act of 1905   Volume XIII

The evidence and the records of this office show that said Cheparney Larney is the child of Jacob Larney and Bettie Larney, whose names appear as "Big Jack" and "Bettie" on a schedule of citizens by blood of the Creek Nation, approved by the Secretary of the Interior March 28, 1902, opposite Nos. 8291 and 8292 respectively.

The evidence shows that about July 19, 1905, said Cheparney Larney appeared to be about one year old.

Although the evidence herein is not as full and complete as has heretofore been required by this office to establish the right of a person to be enrolled as a citizen of the Creek Nation, in view of the provisions of the Act of Congress approved April 26, 1906, (34 Stat. L. 137), fixing March 4, 1907 as the date after which the Secretary of the Interior shall have no jurisdiction to approve the enrollment of any person as a citizen of said Nation, it is believed that the evidence herein should be considered sufficient to establish the facts necessary to enrollment.

It is, therefore, ordered and adjudged that said Cheparney Larney is entitled to be enrolled as a citizen by blood of the Creek Nation, under the provisions of the Act of Congress approved March 3, 1905 (33 Stat. L. 1048), and the application for his enrollment as such is accordingly granted.

Tams Bixby   COMMISSIONER.

Muskogee, Indian Territory,
    FEB 23 1907

Cr. 2448-B
DEPARTMENT OF THE INTERIOR,
COMMISSIONER TO THE FIVE CIVILIZED TRIBES.

Muskogee, Indian Territory, July 19, 1905.

Commissioner to the Five Civilized Tribes,
    Muskogee, Indian Territory.

Sir:

In the matter of the application for the enrollment of an unnamed child of Jacob and Bettie Larney (2448-B), as a citizen by blood of the Creek Nation, I have the honor to report that the parents of said child refuse to execute affidavits or to testify in the case; nor can any evidence be secured from relatives and neighbors about said child. Said child appears to be about a year old, but I am unable to ascertain its name or sex.

Respectfully,
(Signed) Alex Posey,
Clerk in Charge Creek
Field Party.

Applications for Enrollment of Creek Newborn
Act of 1905   Volume XIII

NC 1010.

Muskogee, Indian Territory, March 18, 1907.

Bettie Larney,
    c/o Jacob Larney,
        Hanna, Indian Territory.

Dear Madam:

    You are hereby advised that the Secretary of the Interior under date of March 4, 1907, approved the enrollment of your minor child, Cheparney Larney, as a citizen by blood of the Creek Nation, and that the name of said child appears upon the roll of new born citizens by blood of the Creek Nation, enrolled under the act of Congress approved March 3, 1905, as number 1287.

    This child is now entitled to allotment and application therefor should be made without delay at the Creek Land Office, Muskogee, Indian Territory.

                Respectfully,
                          Commissioner.

DEPARTMENT OF THE INTERIOR,
COMMISSIONER TO THE FIVE CIVILIZED TRIBES.
MUSKOGEE, OKLAHOMA, MARCH 19, 1910.

    In the matter of the application for the enrollment of Cheparney Larney as a New Born Creek citizen, who is enrolled opposite approved Roll number 1287.

    Examination conducted on behalf of the Commissioner to the Five Civilized Tribes, by W. H. Angell.

    Jacob Larney, being first duly sworn by George A. Lowell, notary public, testified, through Jesse McDermott, interpreter, as follows:

Q What is your name? A I have two named; Jacob Larney and Jacob Tiger.
Q Under what name are you enrolled? A Jacob Tiger.
Q How old are you? A I do not know; I was a young man at the opening of the Civil War.
Q What is your post office address? A Hanna.
Q Under what name are you generally known in the vicinity in which you reside? A I am generally known as Jacob Larney, although some know me by the name of Jacob Tiger.
Q What is the name of your father? A Cotcha Homatka, which means Tiger.
Q How did you acquire the name of Larney? A I am unable to tell you just why they named me that, but it is more of a nick name given me when a small boy.
Q Have you any other children besides Cheparney Larney? A I have a small one.

Applications for Enrollment of Creek Newborn
Act of 1905   Volume XIII

Q What is the name of that child? A Joe.
Q Any other name? A Joe Tiger.
Q When was Cheparney Larney born? A He is now about six years old.
Q Has he got any other name? A No; there have been a number of names given him but we never called him by either ot[sic] those names.
Q Is he living? A Yes sir.
Q Does he live with you? A Yes sir.
Q Did Alex Posey appear at your house in April, 1905, to ascertain whether or not you had any children that were entitled to enrollment? A Yes sir.
Q Did you tell him that you had a child that ought to be enrolled at that time? A Yes sir.
Q Did y tell him who the mother of that child was? A Yes sir.
Q Who did you tell him was the mother of the child? A I did not tell him the name of the mother, because she was present herself and Mr. Posey knew her.
Q What is the name of the mother of the child? A Peetie.
Q Under what other name is she known? A None.
Q Who is Lucy Green? A I am unable to tell you who Lucy Green is just now.
Q Under what name is your wife, Peetie, enrolled? A She ought to be enrolled under the name of Peetie.
Q Have you received allotment certificates and patents covering the land allotted to her? A No, not yet. I understand that her land is located near the town of Paden.
Q Has your wife any brothers and sisters living? A Jennetta, Siah and George Hutkey or White.
Q What are the english[sic] names of your wife's father and mother? A Bennie is the name of the father. I do not know her mother's name.
Q Did your wife ever go by the name of Green? A Yes sir, if she was called according to my Indian name, she would be called Green
Q What is your Indian name? A Jacob Larney is my boy name.
Q What is the word for Green in the Creek language? A Larney.
Q Was your wife ever known by the name of Lucy Green? A I never did hear any body call her by that name, but it seems from the records here that she is enrolled as Lucy Green.
Q How old is she? A About thirty years old.
Q Do you know Big Jack? A Yes sir.
Q Has he got a wife by the name of Bettie? A Yes sir. It appears from the records of this office that one Cheparney Larney is enrolled as a New Born Creek citizen opposite No. 1287; that the names of the parents are given as Jacob Larney and Bettie Larney and that they were identified on the approved roll as Big Jack and Bettie, respectively.
Q Have you any reason to believe that this identification is incorrect? A To my knowledge Big Jack and his wife have never had a child by the name of Cheparney.
Q Have they any ale children under ten years of age? A They lost a male child about two years ago; they have one living at the present time and his name is Okchunpulla.
Q Cheparney means little boy, in Creek, does it not? A Yes sir.
Q Do you know whether or not Alex Posey went to the house of Big Jack to see whether or not he had any children to enroll in 1905? A No sir, I do not.
Q Was Big Jack ever known by the name of Larney? A No.
Q Is Peetie the only wife you ever had? A Yes sir.
Q And Cheparney is your only child? A Excepting the one that I have now.

Applications for Enrollment of Creek Newborn
Act of 1905 Volume XIII

Q Did you ever execute an affidavit relative to the birth of Cheparney Larney? A No, I did not. I was talking to him on the train about the child at another time and he told me that it would not be necessary for me to make an affidavit of any kind about the enrollment of the child.
Q How long was that after he appeared at your house on April 24, 1905? A I don't remember.
Q Did he tell you that Cheparney Larney had already been enrolled at the time he saw you on the train? A No, he told me that he was going to have him enrolled himself.
Q Did you ever receive a notice from the Commissioner to the Five Civilized Tribes to appear at the Creek Land Office and select land for Cheparney Larney? A Yes sir.
Q Were you ever notified that the Commissioner had made an arbitrary allotment to Cheparney? A Yes sir.
Q Did you ever receive allotment certificates covering the land allotted to Cheparney? A No; that is why I came in to make inquiry about the child's land
Q Has your wife a Creek name? A No, the only name that she has is Peetie.
Q What town does she belong to? A Hillabee Canadian.

Mattie P. Shanafelt, being first duly sworn, states that as stenographer to the Commissioner to the Five Civilized Tribes, she reported the proceedings had in the above entitled cause, and that the above and foregoing is a true and correct transcript of her stenographic notes taken in said cause on said date.

Mattie P. Shanafelt

Subscribed and sworn to before me this March 24' 1910.

Edward Merrick
Notary Public.

LAW OFFICE
CLARK NICHOLS
EUFAULA, OKLA.

MISCELLANEOUS.
R E C E I V E D
MAR 26 1920
No. **26214**
SUPT. FIVE CIVILIZED TRIBES

March 24 1920

Gabe E. Parker,
Supt. Five Civilized Tribes,
Muskogee Okla.
Dear Sir:

Applications for Enrollment of Creek Newborn
Act of 1905   Volume XIII

There seems to be a controversy between Heneha Fixico and Bettie the wife of Big Jack, about the parentage and family of one Cheparney Larney.

I saw a letter wherein your Mr. Keith had made an investigation of the records of your office, and made a report of his effort to Heneha Fixico or Bennie Green as he is sometimes known, to which report the said Bennie Green takes very violent exceptions.

After going over the matter very carefully I drew the enclosed affidavit, which he and Mr. Hill say is correct. I submit it to you for the information therein contained. I wish to suggest that on behalf of Bennie Green and the boy Cheparney Larney for whom Bennie Green is guardian, this affidavit be considered and the seeming errors in the records of your office be corrected, or if you so desire we can furnish further witnesses at any time their testimony could be taken in the neighborhood of Hanna.

My information is that some one taking the information found in your records is about to get Bettie to sell the land of Lucy Green the mother of Cheparney Larney, or perhaps it is some other land, but at any rate she is about to set toward some property in a manner which would be wrong if our contention is right.

May I hear from you after you have formed an opinion in the matter.

Yours very truly,
Clark Nichols

MISCELLANEOUS.
RECEIVED
MAR 26 1920
No. 26214
SUPT. FIVE CIVILIZED TRIBES

STATE OF OKLAHOMA)
) SS
MCINTOSH COUNTY   )

AFFIDAVIT

Henneha Fixico first being duly sworn on his oath deposes and says: that he is a full Blood Creek Indian and enrolled as such opposite Roll No. 8215 and that he is 57 years of age. That his wife was Sally, that of the marriage with Sally there was born one child named Bittie. That afterwards Sally died and he married Lucy and that there was born to them two children, Siah Fixico and Jenetta Fixico. That Bittie married Jacob Larney, some times known as Jacob Tiger, in the uear[sic] 1902 or 1903. That of the marriage between Jacob Larney enrolled as Jacob Tiger and Bettie there was born one child named Cheparney Larney who was enrolled on the Creek New Born Rolls at No. 1287.

Applications for Enrollment of Creek Newborn
Act of 1905   Volume XIII

That the affian[sic] is known by two names and was so known at the time of enrollment. That his Creek name was Heneha Fixico and that under this name he was enrolled at No 8215. That his english[sic] name was Bennie Green, and that he is known today by these two names and has two guardianship cases in the County Court of McIntosh County one under the name of Heneha Fixico and one under the name of Bennie Green.

That when his daughter Bittie was enrolled at Roll No. 8361 she was put on under the name of Lucy Green, and this affiant shown on same card as Bennie Green and he motner[sic] as Sally Green.

That he is the father of Lucy Green enrolled at Roll No. 8361 and Sally Green sometimes known as Sally was the mother. That Bittie Larney shown as the mother of Cheparney Larney at Roll No N.B.C. 12£7 is one and the same person as Lucy Green enrolled on the Creek Rolls at No 8361.

That Bettie enrolled opposite No. 8292 is no relation and in no way connected with Bittie Larney above mentioned. That Bettie at No 8292 was never married to Jacob Larney enrolled as Jacob Tiger and is not the mother of Cheparney Larney. That this affiant has known Bettie and Big Jack her husband for a long time, and has lived neighbor to them for a period extending from many years before enrolment[sic] until Now[sic], and known that Big Jack and Bettie have been married since some twenty years before enrollment and that Bettie never lived with anyone but Big Jack during that time.

Henneha Fixico

Subscribed and sworn to before me tis[sic] the 20th day of March 1920.

CNichols
Notary Public.

My Commission Expires Nov. 20, 1920.

J.H. Hill being duly sworn states that he has read the foregoing affidavit of Bennie Green sometimes known as Henneha Fixico and states that the facts contained therein are true.

James Hill

Subscribed and sworn to before me this the 20th day of March, 1920.

CNichols
Notary Public.

My Commission Expires Nov. 20, 1920.

Applications for Enrollment of Creek Newborn
Act of 1905   Volume XIII

DEPARTMENT OF THE INTERIOR,
COMMISSION TO THE FIVE CIVILIZED TRIBES.
April 24, 1905.

In the matter of the application for the enrollment of certain new borns as citizens of the Creek Nation.

Alex Posey, being duly sworn, testified as follows:

By Commission:
Q What is your name, age and post office address? A Alex Posey, 31, Muskogee.
Q Are you a citizen of the Creek Nation? A Yes sir
Q Got your land, have you? A Yes sir.
Q You have been engaged recently in the field for the Dawes Commission securing evidence about Creek citizens or new borns? A Yes sir.
Q Have you a list of children for whom application could not be made and about whom you have succeeded in obtaining some information? A Yes sir.
Q You may state the conditions and the names of these children? You desire to make application for them? A Yes sir.
Q Name them.
A Jaly Proctor, Weogufky Town, Sukey Proctor, Weogufky Town, have two children -- one about three years old and one about six months old. Post office, Hanna, Indian Territory.

Jacob Bullet, about three years old. Parents: Maxey Bullet, Seminole, and Hannah Bullet, Hillabee. Post Office, Hanna, Indian Territory.

Connie Hawkins, Hillabee Town, Sabella Hawkins, Okchiye, have two children-- one about three years old and a younger child. Post Office, Hanna, Indian Territory.

Willie Fisher, Hickory Ground Town, Lussee Fisher, Okfusky[sic] Canadian Town, have two children --one about three years old and a baby. Post Office, Slumpker, Indian Territory.

Lizzie Lasley, about three years old, Sam Lasley, born in either August or September, 1904. Parents: Sam Lasley, Okchiye, Wisey Lasley, Weogufky. Post Office, Hanna, Indian Territory.

Jim Haynes (or Sangee), Okchiye Town, Folotkokee, Weogufky Town have a male child about three years old named Joe. Post Office, Hanna, Indian Territory.

Taylor Foley, Weogufky, Melinda Foley, Okchiye, have a child about two years old. Post Office, Slumpker, Indian Territory.

Phillip Lindsey, Tuckabatchee, Cilla Lindsey, Hillabee, have a child about three years old. Post Office, Hanna, Indian Territory.

Big William (or William Thlocco), Okchiye Town, Cinda Williams, Weogufky Town, have two children -- one about three years old-- one born in February 1905. Post Office Hanna, Indian Territory.

Freeland Lindsey, Tuckabatchee or Hillabee, Nancy Proctor, Tullahassoche, have a child about two years old. Post Office, Hanna, Indian Territory.

Timonthluppy George, Weogufky Town, Nellie George, Pukon Tullahassee, have a child about three years old. Post Office, Slumpker, Indian Territory.

Applications for Enrollment of Creek Newborn
Act of 1905   Volume XIII

Walter Simmons, Weogufky, Chippie Simmons, Pukon Tulahassee[sic], have a child about one years old. Post Office, Hannah, Indian Territory.

Jacob Larney (or Green), Arbeka Tulledega Town, Bettie Larney, (or Green), Hillabee Town, have a child. Post Office, Hanna, Indian Territory.

✓John Hill, Okchiye, Millie Hill, Weogufky, have a child about three months old. Post Office, Hanna, Indian Territory.

Jim Pigeon, Okchiye Town, Jennie Pigeon, Okchiye Town, have a child about five months old. Post Office, Hanna, Indian Territory.

Thomas Deo, Okchiye Town, Nancy Deo, Fish Pond Town, have a child about three months old. Post Office, Hanna, Indian Territory.

Jack Buckner, born December 17, 1904. Parents: Wiley Buckner, Okchiye, Susie Buckner, Cussehta. Post Office, Hanna, Indian Territory.

Q This is the information you received from relatives right around there on April 24, 1905? A Yes sir.

Q Were you informed that the parents of these children were unwilling to make application for their enrollment? A Yes sir.

Q This was the only way that the rights of these children would be saved? A Yes sir. I made every effort to obtain direct information from the parents but in every instance they refused to give their testimony.

Lona Merrick being duly sworn, states that the above and foregoing is a true and correct transcript of his stenographic notes as taken in said cause on said date.

Lona Merrick

Subscribed and sworn to before me this 9th day of May, 1905.

Edw C Griesel
Notary Public.

---oooOOOooo---

I, D. C. Skaggs, on oath state that the above and foregoing is a full and true copy of the original now on file in the office of the Commissioner.

D. C. Skaggs

Subscribed and sworn to before me this 7th day of February, 1906.

J McDermott
Notary Public.

Applications for Enrollment of Creek Newborn
Act of 1905   Volume XIII

DEPARTMENT OF THE INTERIOR,
COMMISSION TO THE FIVE CIVILIZED TRIBES.
April 24, 1905.

In the matter of the application for the enrollment of certain new borns as citizens of the Creek Nation.

Alex Posey, being duly sworn, testified as follows:

Statement: John Hill, Okchiye, Millie Hill, Weogufky, have a child about three months old. Post Office, Hanna, Indian Territory.

BIRTH AFFIDAVIT.

DEPARTMENT OF THE INTERIOR.
COMMISSION TO THE FIVE CIVILIZED TRIBES.

IN RE APPLICATION FOR ENROLLMENT, as a citizen of the Creek Nation, of Lunisey Hill, (Deceased) born on the 31 day of January, 1905

Name of Father: John Hill Okchiye   a citizen of the   Creek   Nation.
Name of Mother: Millie Hill Weo   a citizen of the   Creek   Nation.

Postoffice   Hanna IT

AFFIDAVIT OF MOTHER.

UNITED STATES OF AMERICA, Indian Territory,
    Western   DISTRICT.

I, Millie Hill, on oath state that I am *(blank)* years of age and a citizen by blood, of the Creek Nation; that I am the lawful wife of John Hill, who is a citizen, by blood of the Creek Nation; that a male child was born to me on or about the 31 day of January, 1905, that said child has been named Lunisey Hill, and was living March 4, 1905. That said child died Apr 30, 1905

                                     Millie Hill
Witnesses To Mark:
    DC Skaggs

Subscribed and sworn to before me this 30" day of May, 1905.

                                Drennan C Skaggs
                                Notary Public.

Applications for Enrollment of Creek Newborn
Act of 1905   Volume XIII

AFFIDAVIT OF ATTENDING PHYSICIAN OR MID-WIFE.

UNITED STATES OF AMERICA, Indian Territory, }
Western   DISTRICT.

I, John Hill , a ~~(blank)~~ , on oath state that I attended on ^ my wife Mrs. Millie Hill , ~~wife of~~ *(blank)* on the 31 day of January , 1905 ; that there was born to her on said date a   male   child; that said child was living March 4, 1905, and is said to have been named Lunisey Hill That said child died Apr. 30, 1905

                                     his
                               John x Hill

Witnesses To Mark: mark
  { DC Skaggs
    Alex Posey

Subscribed and sworn to before me this 29 day of May, 1905.

                         Drennan C Skaggs
                               Notary Public.

BIRTH AFFIDAVIT.

DEPARTMENT OF THE INTERIOR.
COMMISSION TO THE FIVE CIVILIZED TRIBES.

IN RE APPLICATION FOR ENROLLMENT, as a citizen of the Creek Nation, of Lumsey Hill , born on the 31 day of January , 1905

Name of Father: John Hill	a citizen of the	Creek	Nation.
Name of Mother: Millie Hill	a citizen of the	Creek	Nation.

                       Postoffice   Hanna IT

AFFIDAVIT OF MOTHER.

UNITED STATES OF AMERICA, Indian Territory, }
Western   DISTRICT.

I, Millie Hill , on oath state that I am 20 years of age and a citizen by blood , of the Creek   Nation; that I am the lawful wife of John Hill , who is a citizen, by blood of the Creek   Nation; that a male   child was born to me on or about the 31 day of January , 1905 , that said child has been named Lumsey Hill , and ~~was living March 4, 1905~~. is now dead

                         Millie Hill

Applications for Enrollment of Creek Newborn
Act of 1905 Volume XIII

Witnesses To Mark:

{

Subscribed and sworn to before me this *(blank)* day of *(blank)*, 190___.

(blank)
Notary Public.

AFFIDAVIT OF ATTENDING PHYSICIAN OR MID-WIFE.

UNITED STATES OF AMERICA, Indian Territory, }
Western DISTRICT. }

I, Huston Harjo, a *(blank)*, on oath state that I attended on Mrs. Millie, wife of John Hill on the 31 day of January, 1905; that there was born to her on said date a male child; that said child was living March 4, 1905 and died, and is said to have been named Lumsey Hill

                                                      her
Witnesses To Mark: Huston x Harjo
{ D.D. Anderson   mark
{ Joe Smith

Subscribed and sworn to before me 8 day of Dec., 1905.

                                           DM Crawford
Sept. 19-07   Notary Public.

NC 1011

DEPARTMENT OF THE INTERIOR,
COMMISSIONER TO THE FIVE CIVILIZED TRIBES.
MUSKOGEE, INDIAN TERRITORY.
October 26, 1906.

In the matter of the application for the enrollment of Lumsey Hill, deceased, as a citizen by blood of the Creek Nation.

John Hill, being duly sworn by H.G. Hains, a Notary Public, testified as follows, through Official Interpreter, Lona Merrick.

Examination by Commissioner.

Q What is your name? A John Hill.
Q What is your age? [sic] I don't know, about fifty I guess.
Q What is your post office address? A Hanna.
Q Was it ever Eufaula, Indian Territory[sic] A Yes sir.

Applications for Enrollment of Creek Newborn
Act of 1905   Volume XIII

Q What Creek Indian town do you belong to? A Okchiye.
Q What is the name of your father? A Coxey.
Q Do you belong to any other town? A No sir.
Q What is the name of your mother? A Soma.
Q Is Jacob Hill a brother of yours? A No sir, he is my first cousin.
Q Name some of your brothers and sisters? [sic] Culler---
Q Who is Austin Barnett? A He is my first cousin.
Q What is the name of his father? A Martin.
Q What is the name of his mother? A Millie.
Q Is Soma living? A No sir.
Q Did she ever go by any other name? A No sir.
Q Did you go by any other name than John Hill? A No sir. I was called John Cox after my father but it was changed to Hill.
Q Did you know a sister of Austin Barnett by the name of Susanna? A Yes sir.
Q Susanna Riley, is that her name now? A She is married but I don't know her husband's name.
Q Did Susanna ever go by any other name besides Riley? A Not that I know of.
Q When did Soma die? A She died over a year ago.
Q Are you married? A Yes sir.
Q Have you been married before you were married to your present wife? A No sir.
Q Did you ever have a child by another woman before you did by your wife? A I have one child by another woman by the name of Sallie Hill.
Q What is its name? A Sallie Hill.
Q What is the name of its mother? A Malinda Deere, she was my first wife.
Q Was Malinda ever known by the name of Ludie Polokee? A Yes sir.
Q What was the name of the father of Malinda? Johnson or Tom Polokee.
Q And was the mother of your child Sallie? A Yes sir.
Q Is that the only child you ever had by Malinda Hill? A Yes sir.
Q Then you married Millie Hill your present wife? A Yes sir.
Q What was the name of Millie's father? A I can't recall his name just now.
Q Do you know what tonw[sic] he belongs to A Okchiye.
Q What is the name of Millie's mother? A Houston Harjo.
Q What town does she belong to? A Weogufkee.

Witness is identified as John Hill, opposite Creek Indian roll number 8319, and Millie Hill, his wife, is identified as Millie Hill, opposite Creek Indian Roll number 9135.

Q Have you had a child by Millie? A I have two, one is dead.
Q What are their names? A Sampson and Lumsey Hill, Sampson is not enrolled.
Q Which was born first? A Lumsey.
Q When was Sampson born? A August 18, this year.
Q Well, he is too late to be enrolled? A Yes sir, I know that.
Q Is Lumsey a boy? A Yes sir.
Q When was he born? A January 31, 1905.
Q Is he living? A No sir, he is dead.
Q How old was he when he died? A About four months old.
Q Have you a record of his birth and death with you? A Yes sir.

Applications for Enrollment of Creek Newborn
Act of 1905   Volume XIII

The record is in Creek and is handed to the interpreter for translation:
"Child born January 31, 1905, and died on the 30th day of April, 1905."

Q Where did that record come from? A A man by the name of Soloman wrote it for me.
Q Did you make a record of the date after the child was born? A Yes, I recorded the date the next day afte[sic] the birth of the child, but I haven't that record with me.
Q Where did this man get the record to write in this book that you have here? A I told him to write it.
Q Are you sure that the record you have here is the exact copy of the date of the birth you made after the child was born? A It was copied from the record I made.
Q Did you make a record of the death? A Yes sir. Soloman wrote it in this book.
Q Where did he get of[sic] the date from? A I just told him the date of the death of said child.
Q Did you make a record at the time it died? A No sir.
Q Well how do you know that is the correct date tht[sic] you told Soloman---the correct date of death that he wrote in that book? A I remembered when the child died.
Q How do you remember that? A I looked at the calendar and knew when it died.
Q Are you sure that your boy Lumsey was born in the first month of last year that is January 1905 and lived as much as three or four months? A Yes sir.
Q Who was present when Lumsey died? A The child's mother, and grandmother.
Q What is the grandmother's name? A Houston.
Q What is her post office address? A Hanna.
Q Was Houston also present when the child was born? A Yes sir.
Q Was she the midwife who attended on Millie when this child was born? A She was the midwife.
Q We will give blank form of birth affidavit to show whether this child was living March 4, 1905, and you must have Houston the midwife properly executed before a Notary Public, and you must return it to this office. The affidavit we have here simply Q[sic] state that it was dead at the time the affidavit was made out which was on December 8, 1905. The affidavit must show whether the child was living March 4, 1905.
Q Did you have a doctor when this child died? A Yes sir.
Q What is his name? A Keeley Proctor, an Indian doctor.
Q What is his post office address? A Hanna.
Q Where is this child buried? A In my yard.
Q Is there any mark on the grave to show when it died? A No sir, there is a little grave house on it but no writing on it.
Q Is there anything on that little house to show when that child died and was buried?
A No sir, there is no writing in it at all.
Q In your affidavit we have on file here it is stated that you attended on your wife, how does it come--you say now that your wife's mother, Houston Harjo atteneded[sic] on her?
A We both attended on her.
Q You didn't make application for this child yourself, did you? A No sir.
Q Why didn't you? A Because I didn't [sic] how to go about it, I can't take english[sic] and I couldn't get an interpreter--I didn't know who to go before to make application.
Q Haven't you belong to the so called snake[sic] faction? A No sir.

Applications for Enrollment of Creek Newborn
Act of 1905   Volume XIII

Lona Merrick, being duly sworn, states that the above and foregoing is a true and correct transcript of her stenographic notes as taken in said cause on said date.

Lona Merrick

Subscribed and sworn to before me this 31st day of October, 1906.

Edward Merrick
Notary Public.

BIRTH AFFIDAVIT.

DEPARTMENT OF THE INTERIOR.
COMMISSION TO THE FIVE CIVILIZED TRIBES.

IN RE APPLICATION FOR ENROLLMENT, as a citizen of the Creek Nation, of Lumsey Hill, born on the 31 day of January, 1905

Name of Father: John Hill	a citizen of the	Creek	Nation.
Name of Mother: Millie Hill	a citizen of the	Creek	Nation.

Postoffice   Hanna I.T.

AFFIDAVIT OF MOTHER.

UNITED STATES OF AMERICA, Indian Territory, }
Western   DISTRICT.

I, Millie Hill, on oath state that I am 20 years of age and a citizen by blood, of the Creek Nation; that I am the lawful wife of John Hill, who is a citizen, by blood of the Creek Nation; that a male child was born to me on 31 day of January, 1905, that said child has been named Lumsey Hill, and is now ~~living~~. dead

Millie Hill

Witnesses To Mark:
{

Subscribed and sworn to before me this *(blank)* day of *(blank)*, 190....

(No Signature)
Notary Public.

Applications for Enrollment of Creek Newborn
Act of 1905   Volume XIII

AFFIDAVIT OF ATTENDING PHYSICIAN OR MID-WIFE.

UNITED STATES OF AMERICA, Indian Territory,　}
　　Western　　　DISTRICT.

  I, Huston Harjo , a am , on oath state that I attended on Mrs. Millie Hill , wife of John Hill on the 31 day of January , 1905 ; that there was born to her on said date a male child; that said child is now living and is said to have been named Lumsey Hill

her
Houston x Harjo
mark

Witnesses To Mark:
 { D.D. Anderson
   Joe Smith

  Subscribed and sworn to before me this 8 day of Dec, 1905.

Sept 19 1907　　　　　　　　　　　　　DM Crawford
　　　　　　　　　　　　　　　　　　　　Notary Public.

BIRTH AFFIDAVIT.

DEPARTMENT OF THE INTERIOR.
COMMISSION TO THE FIVE CIVILIZED TRIBES.

  IN RE APPLICATION FOR ENROLLMENT, as a citizen of the Creek Nation, of Lumsey Hill (deceased) , born on the 31 day of January, 1905

Name of Father: John Hill　　　　　a citizen of the　　Creek　　Nation.
Okchiye
Name of Mother: Millie Hill　　　　a citizen of the　　Creek　　Nation.
Weogufke Town

      Postoffice　　Hanna I.T.

AFFIDAVIT OF MOTHER.

UNITED STATES OF AMERICA, Indian Territory,　}
　　Western　　　DISTRICT.

  I, Millie Hill , on oath state that I am 20 years of age and a citizen by blood , of the Creek Nation; that I am the lawful wife of John Hill , who is a citizen, by blood of the Creek Nation; that a male child was born to me on or about the 31 day of January, 1905 , that said child has been named Lumsey Hill , and is now was living. on March 4, 1905 That said child died April 30, 1905.

her
Millie x Hill
mark

Applications for Enrollment of Creek Newborn
Act of 1905   Volume XIII

Witnesses To Mark:
{ DC Skaggs

    Subscribed and sworn to before me this 30 day of May , 1905.

                            Drennan C Skaggs
                            Notary Public.

AFFIDAVIT OF ATTENDING PHYSICIAN OR MID-WIFE.

UNITED STATES OF AMERICA, Indian Territory,
    Western   DISTRICT.

                                    my wife
    I, John Hill, a———, on oath state that I attended on ^ Mrs. Millie Hill, ~~wife of~~ *(blank)* on the 31 day of January , 1905 ; that there was born to her on said date a male child; that said child ~~is now~~ was living on March 4, 1905 and is said to have been named Lumsey Hill. That said child died April 30, 1905.

                                his
                           John x Hill
Witnesses To Mark: mark
{ DC Skaggs
  Alex Posey

    Subscribed and sworn to before me this 29 day of May , 1905.

                            Drennan C Skaggs
                            Notary Public.

AFFIDAVIT OF ATTENDING PHYSICIAN OR MID-WIFE.

UNITED STATES OF AMERICA, Indian Territory,
.... District.

    I, Houston Harjo , a midwife , on oath state that I attended on Millie Hill , wife of John Hill ~~on~~ about the 31" day of January , 1905 ; that there was born to her on said date a male child; that said child ~~was~~ living March 4, ~~1906~~ 1905, and is said to have been named Lumsey Hill

                            ....

WITNESSES TO MARK:
{ ....
  ....

Subscribed and sworn to before me this...................day of............................., 1906.

                           ....
                            Notary Public.

Applications for Enrollment of Creek Newborn
Act of 1905 Volume XIII

Nov. 12th, 1906
Hanna, Ind. T

This is to inform you that Miss Houston Harjo was living on the 4th day of March.
As translated by the Official Interpreter

L.M.

NC 1011.

Muskogee, Indian Territory, October 23, 1905.

Millie Hill,
    Care John Hill,
        Hanna, Indian Territory/[sic]

Dear Madam:

    In the matter of the application for the enrollment of your minor child, Lumsey Hill, born January 31, 1905, as a citizen by blood of the Creek Nation, this office desires affidavit of the midwife or physician in attendance at the birth of said child and a blank for that purpose is enclosed herewith.

    In the event that there was no physician or midwife in attendance when said child was born, it will be necessary for you to furnish this office with the affidavits of two disinterested witnesses relative to his birth. Said affidavits must set forth said child's name, the date of his birth, the names of his parents and whether or not he was living on March 4, 1905.

    This office is unable to identify you on its final roll of citizens by blood of the Creek Nation; you are requested to state your maiden name, the names of your parents, the Creek Indian town to which you belong and the roll number which appears on your deeds and allotment certificate.

                        Respectfully,
                                      Commissioner.

NC 1011.

Muskogee, Indian Territory, December 19, 1905.

Millie Hill,
    Care John Hill,
        Hanna, Indian Territory.

Dear Madam:

Applications for Enrollment of Creek Newborn
Act of 1905   Volume XIII

In the matter of the application for the enrollment of your minor child, Lumsey Hill, born January 31, 1905, as a citizen by blood of the Creek Nation, this office is unable to identify you on its final roll of citizens by blood of the Creek Nation; you are requested to state your maiden name, the names of your parents, the Creek Indian town to which you belong and your roll number as the same appears on your deeds and llotment[sic] certificate.

Respectfully,
Commissioner.

(The letter below typed as given.)

1011
COPY

Hanna, I. T.
Jan. 26-1906.

Hon. Tams Bixby:

Sir: I got your letter here while back. You are further Requested me about Ralation. this is my Ralation. I have got two brothers But different fathers Charlie Simmons that one different father. Barney Beaver that one different father. I have a sister one sister. But that is Different father. I millie Hill. My father. that is Sorbe. But others They Different fathers. But those people got one mother. Her name Hasty Harjo. 2 boys 2 girls. this is we h have got Just one mother. that is all that is all I we have to say.

Yours truly,
Signed   Millie Hill.

(The letter below typed as given.)

Hanna, Ind. Ter.
August 10th, 1906.

to the Hon. Dawes Commission
For the Five Civilized Tribes,
   Muskogee, Indian Territory.

Sirs:

I write to you in regard to land matters, and about My Minor child, his name Lumsey Hill and my Maiden name is Millie Harjo, and I belong to Weogufkee Town, and my mother her name or Indian Name (Indian Name Yosta) and English Houster Harjo, and she belongs Weogufkee Town. and my father his name Sarbe, he belongs to Okchiye Town, and I made further information about the my Minor child has been taken up by the Alex Posey & D.C. Skaggs, in 1905, in May, for the enrollment of Lumsey or Ramsey Hill; he was born January 31st, 1905, and he died in April 30th, 1905, and I

Applications for Enrollment of Creek Newborn
Act of 1905   Volume XIII

clearly understand that enrolled by the Posey and Skaggs. This is all I can make a statement of my minor child, and I hoping and trusting to hear my request as soon as possible.

I remain, Yours Respectfully,
Millie Hill,
Hanna, I.T.

P.S. My sister her name Sallie Harjo, and my brothers names Charley Simmon, and Barney Beaver, but these two Bro's different fathers.

Yours respct. M.H.

N.C. 1011

Muskogee, Indian Territory, February 7, 1906.

Millie Hill,
    Hanna, Indian Territory.

Dear Madam:

    Receipt is acknowledged of your letter of January 26, 1906, in which you give the names of certain members of your family.

    You are advised that the information contained in your said letter is not sufficient to identify you on the rolls of the Creek Nation.

    You are requested to write this office giving the name of the Creek Indian town to which you belong and your name and roll number as same appear[sic] on your deeds and allotment certificates to land in the Creek Nation.

Respectfully,
Acting Commissioner.

JWH

N C 1011

Muskogee, Indian Territory, March 1, 1907.

Millie Hill,
    % John Hill,
        Hanna, Indian Territory.

Dear Madam :--

    You are hereby advised that on February 15, 1907, the Secretary of the Interior approved the enrollment of your minor child, Lumsey Hill, as a citizen by blood of the

Applications for Enrollment of Creek Newborn
Act of 1905 Volume XIII

Creek Nation, and that the name of said child appears upon the roll of New Born citizens by blood of the Creek Nation, enrolled under the Act of Congress approved March 3, 1905, as number 1192.

This child is now entitled to allotment and application therefor should be made without delay at the Creek Land Office, Muskogee, Indian Territory.

Respectfully,
Commissioner.

N.C. 1012.
DEPARTMENT OF THE INTERIOR,
COMMISSIONER TO THE FIVE CIVILIZED TRIBES,
NEAR DUSTIN, INDIAN TERRITORY,
December 6, 1906.

In the matter of the application for the enrollment of Nache Pigeon, as a citizen by blood of the Creek Nation.

JIM PIGEON, being first duly sworn by and examined through Alex Posey, a Notary Public and Official Interpreter, testified as follows:

BY THE COMMISSIONER:

Q What is your name? A Jim Pigeon.
Q How old are you? A About 27 or '8.
Q What is your postoffice address? A Hanna.
Q Are you a citizen of the Creek Nation? A Yes sir, I belong to Okchiye town.
Q Under what name are you enrolled? A As Cemelane Pigeon.
Q Who are your parents? A John and Mattie Pigeon.
Q To what Creek towns do they belong? A My mother belongs to Okchiye and my father to Hillabee.
Q Are you married? A Yes sir.
Q What is the name of your wife? A Jennie Pigeon. My wife's maiden name was Jennie Deo, she also belongs to Okchiye.
Q Have you a daughter named Nache Pigeon? A Yes sir.
Q Is she living? A No sir, she is now dead.
Q When did she die? A September 11, 1905.
Q When was she born? A November 21, 1904.

Applications for Enrollment of Creek Newborn
Act of 1905   Volume XIII

This testimony is taken for the purpose of identifying the parents of the said Nache Pigeon, deceased, whose application for enrollment is now pending.

J.B. Myers, being first duly sworn, states, that as stenographer to the Commissioner to the Five Civilized Tribes, he recorded the testimony in the foregoing proceedings, and that the above is a true and correct transcript of his stenographic notes thereof.

J.B. Myers

Subscribed and sworn to before me, this 13 day of   Dec   , 1906.

BIRTH AFFIDAVIT.

Copy
DEPARTMENT OF THE INTERIOR.
COMMISSION TO THE FIVE CIVILIZED TRIBES.

IN RE APPLICATION FOR ENROLLMENT, as a citizen of the Creek Nation, of Nache Pigeon, born on the 21 day of Nov , 1904

Name of Father: Jim Pigeon	a citizen of the	Creek	Nation.
Name of Mother: Jennie Pigeon	a citizen of the	Creek	Nation.

Postoffice   Hanna IT

AFFIDAVIT OF ATTENDING PHYSICIAN OR MID-WIFE.

UNITED STATES OF AMERICA, Indian Territory,
   Western   DISTRICT.

                                                                         are personally acquainted with We, the undersigned   , a—, on oath state that I we attended on Mrs. Jennie Pigeon , wife of Jim Pigeon on the   day of   , 1 —; that there was born to her on said Nov 21, 1904 date a female child; that said child was living March 4, 1905, and is said to have been named Nache Pigeon

Thomas Deo
his
Wilson x Gibson
mark

Witnesses To Mark:
 { DC Skaggs
   Alex Posey

Subscribed and sworn to before me 7 day of October, 1905.

Drennan C Skaggs
Notary Public.

Applications for Enrollment of Creek Newborn
Act of 1905   Volume XIII

(The above Birth Affidavit of Disinterested Witnesses given again.)

Copy

BIRTH AFFIDAVIT.

DEPARTMENT OF THE INTERIOR.
COMMISSION TO THE FIVE CIVILIZED TRIBES.

IN RE APPLICATION FOR ENROLLMENT, as a citizen of the Creek Nation, of Nache Pigeon, born on the 21 day of November, 1904

Name of Father: Jim Pigeon　　　　a citizen of the　Creek　Nation.
Okchiye
Name of Mother: Jennie Pigeon　　　a citizen of the　Creek　Nation.
Okchiye

Postoffice　　Hanna IT

AFFIDAVIT OF MOTHER.

Child present

UNITED STATES OF AMERICA, Indian Territory,　}
　　Western　　　　　DISTRICT.

I, Jennie Pigeon, on oath state that I am about 20 years of age and a citizen by blood, of the Creek Nation; that I am the lawful wife of Jim Pigeon, who is a citizen, by blood of the Creek Nation; that a female child was born to me on 21 day of November, 1904, that said child has been named Nache Pigeon, and is now living. and was living March 4, 1905.

　　　　　　　　　　　　　　　her
　　　　　　　　　　Jennie x Pigeon
Witnesses To Mark:　　　mark
　{ D C Skaggs
　 Alex Posey

Subscribed and sworn to before me this 1 day of June, 1905.

　　　　　　　　Drennan C Skaggs
　　　　　　　　Notary Public.

AFFIDAVIT OF ATTENDING PHYSICIAN OR MID-WIFE.

UNITED STATES OF AMERICA, Indian Territory,　}
　　Western　　　　　DISTRICT.

　　　　　　　　　　　　　　　　　　my wife
　I, Jim Pigeon, a ~~(blank)~~, on oath state that I attended on ^ Mrs. Jennie Pigeon, wife of *(blank)* on the 21 day of November, 1904 ; that there was born to

Applications for Enrollment of Creek Newborn
Act of 1905   Volume XIII

her on said date a   female   child; that said child is now living and was living Mch 4, 1905, and is said to have been named Nache Pigeon

                                  Jim Pigeon

Witnesses To Mark:
{

    Subscribed and sworn to before me this 1 day of June , 1905.

                                  Drennan C Skaggs
                                  Notary Public.

DEPARTMENT OF THE INTERIOR.
COMMISSION TO THE FIVE CIVILIZED TRIBES.

In the matter of the death of   Nache Pigeon   a citizen of the Creek Nation, who formerly resided at or near   Hanna , Ind. Ter., and died on the   11th day of   September , 1905

AFFIDAVIT OF RELATIVE.

UNITED STATES OF AMERICA, Indian Territory, }
    Western   DISTRICT.

I, Jim Pigeon , on oath state that I am about 28 years of age and a citizen by blood , of the Creek Nation; that my postoffice address is   Hanna , Ind. Ter.; that I am   the father   of   Nache Pigeon   who was a citizen, by blood , of the Creek   Nation and that said   Nache Pigeon   died on the   11th day of September , 1905

                                  Jim Pigeon

Witnesses To Mark:
{

    Subscribed and sworn to before me this 5th day of December, 1905.

                                  Alex Posey
                                  Notary Public.

Applications for Enrollment of Creek Newborn
Act of 1905   Volume XIII

BIRTH AFFIDAVIT.

DEPARTMENT OF THE INTERIOR.
COMMISSION TO THE FIVE CIVILIZED TRIBES.

IN RE APPLICATION FOR ENROLLMENT, as a citizen of the Creek Nation, of Nache Pigeon, born on the 21 day of November, 1904

Name of Father: Jim Pigeon   a citizen of the   Creek   Nation.
Okchiye Town
Name of Mother: Jennie Pigeon (nee Deo)   a citizen of the   Creek   Nation.
Okchiye Town

Postoffice   Hanna IT

AFFIDAVIT OF MOTHER. Child present

UNITED STATES OF AMERICA, Indian Territory,
    Western   DISTRICT.

    I, Jennie Pigeon, on oath state that I am about 20 years of age and a citizen by blood, of the Creek Nation; that I am the lawful wife of Jim Pigeon, who is a citizen, by blood of the Creek Nation; that a female child was born to me on 21 day of November, 1904, that said child has been named Nache Pigeon, and is now living. and was living March 4, 1905.

                                           her
                                 Jennie x Pigeon
Witnesses To Mark: mark
   { D C Skaggs
     Alex Posey

Subscribed and sworn to before me this 1 day of June, 1905.

                                 Drennan C Skaggs
                                    Notary Public.

AFFIDAVIT OF ATTENDING PHYSICIAN OR MID-WIFE.

UNITED STATES OF AMERICA, Indian Territory,
    Western   DISTRICT.

                                                                            my wife
    I, Jim Pigeon, a *(blank)*, on oath state that I attended on ^ Mrs. Jennie Pigeon, wife of *(blank)* on the 21 day of November, 1904 ; that there was born to her on said date a female child; that said child is now living and was living Mch 4, 1905, and is said to have been named Nache Pigeon

                                       Jim Pigeon

Applications for Enrollment of Creek Newborn
Act of 1905 Volume XIII

Witnesses To Mark:

{

Subscribed and sworn to before me this 1 day of June, 1905.

Drennan C Skaggs
Notary Public.

NC 1012

Muskogee, Indian Territory, October 23, 1905.

Jennie Pigeon,
    Care Jim Pigeon,
        Hanna, Indian Territory.

Dear Madam:

In the matter of the application for the enrollment of your minor child, Nache Pigeon, born November 21, 1904, as a citizen by blood of the Creek Nation, this office is unable to identify you or your husband, Jim Pigeon, on its final roll of citizens by blood of the Creek Nation.

You are requested to state your maiden name, the names of the parents of yourself and of your said husband, the Creek Indian town to which you each belong, also the roll number of yourself and husband as the same appear on your deeds and allotment certificate.

Respectfully,

Commissioner.

N.C. 1012

Muskogee, Indian Territory, December 18, 1905.

Jim Pigeon,
    Hanna, Indian Territory.

Dear Sir:

In the matter of the application for the enrollment of your minor child, Nache Pigeon, born November 21, 1904, as a citizen by blood of the Creek Nation, this office is unable to identify you on its final roll of citizens by blood of the Creek Nation; you are requested to state the names of your parents, the Creek Indian town to which you belong and your roll number as the same appears on your deeds and allotment certificate.

This matter should receive your immediate attention.

Applications for Enrollment of Creek Newborn
Act of 1905   Volume XIII

Respectfully,

Commissioner.

NC 1012

T.E. Proctor   Geo. Simmons

Proctor & Company
T.E. Proctor Manager
Dealers in
General Merchandise

Trenton, I.T. Jan. 13, 1906.

Commissioner to the five civilized tribes[sic],
Muskogee, I.T.

Dear Sir:

I wish to inform you that my maiden name was Jennie Deo Creek Indian town (Okchieyee[sic]) parent (Nasa Deo) husband (Jim Pigeon my roll number is 6204 I received your letter I enclosed names and roll number

reply early
Jennie Pigeon

Copy

Muskogee I T Jan 16 06

Jennie Pigeon
    Trenton I T

Dear Madam:

Receipt is acknowledged of your letter of January 13, 1906, containing information which enables this office to identify you as a citizen of the Creek Nation.

You are advised that this office desires to identify Jim Pigeon, the father of your minor child, Nache Pigeon, and for this purpose you are requested to write at once giving the names of his parents and other members of his family, any name, other than Jim Pigeon by which he May have been carried on the Creek tribal rolls the Creek Indian town to which he belongs and if possible his name and roll number as same appear upon his deeds to land in the Creek Nation

This matter should receive your prompt attention.

Applications for Enrollment of Creek Newborn
Act of 1905   Volume XIII

            Respt
                  Comr

                                                                                    JWH

N C 1012

                  Muskogee, Indian Territory, March 1, 1907.

Jennie Pigeon,
    % Jim Pigeon,
        Hanna, Indian Territory.

Dear Madam :--

    You are hereby advised that on February 15, 1907, the Secretary of the Interior approved the enrollment of your minor child, Nache Pigeon, as a citizen by blood of the Creek Nation, and that the name of said child appears upon the roll of New Born citizens by blood of the Creek Nation, enrolled under the Act of Congress approved March 3, 1905, as number 1193.

    This child is now entitled to allotment and application therefor should be made without delay at the Creek Land Office, Muskogee, Indian Territory.

                            Respectfully,
                                          Commissioner.

(The Birth Affidavit of Disinterested Witnesses is typed as given.)

Eufaula I T

We the undersigned do testify that Selina Raiford, is the Legal or Lawful wife of Ossie Raiford. That Pearl Raiford was borned[sic] about Jan. 6, 1903 and Lena Raiford was borned[sic] about March 8, 1904 and both and living on March 4, 1905 --

                              AE Raiford
                              Wesley Thomas his x mark
Witness to mark

                              L.G. McIntosh
                                Ossie Raiford

Applications for Enrollment of Creek Newborn
Act of 1905   Volume XIII

582

    A. E. Raiford
&   Wesley Thomas

Came before me, a Notary Public of Western District and swear that the affidavit of Salina Raiford is correct, is correct to the best of their knoledge[sic]

                A E Raiford
                Wesley Thomas by x

Sworn and subscribed to before me this subscribed before me this 4 day of Jan. 1906

                L.G. McIntosh
                Notary Public

My Commission Expires April 10th 1907

(The above Affidavit given again.)

My town is Eufaula *(Illegible)* - Seminole - Selina Raiford

    We desire that our children take their allotments in the Creek Nation -

                Selina Raiford
                Ossie Raiford

Indian Territory, I
          I ss:
Western District.I

    I   my
We, the undersigned, do hereby elect to have our child,   Lena Raiford   , born on the 8" day of March , 1904 , enrolled as a citizen of the   Creek   Nation, and to have said child receive   her   allotment of land and distribution of moneys in said nation.

Witnesses to mark: Ossie Raiford

_____
_____   _____
_____

    Subscribed and sworn to before me this 28" day of Dec ,1906.

                Edward Merrick
                Notary Public.

N.B.   The mother of Lena Raiford is dead.

Applications for Enrollment of Creek Newborn
Act of 1905 Volume XIII

NC 1013

United States of America,
    Western District,
    Indian Territory.

We, the undersigned, on oath state that we are personally acquainted with Selina Raiford the wife of Ossie Raiford ; that there was born to her a female child on or about 8 day of March 190 4 ; that the said child has been named Lena Raiford and was living March 4, 1905.

We further state that we have no interest in this case.

Witness to mark   Charter Givens   his x ma
L.G. McIntosh   John Francis   his x ma
W.T. Fears

Subscribed and sworn to before me this 14 day of Apr. 1906

                 L.G. McIntosh
                 Notary Public.

My Com expires
Apr 10, 1907

BIRTH AFFIDAVIT.

DEPARTMENT OF THE INTERIOR.
COMMISSION TO THE FIVE CIVILIZED TRIBES.

IN RE APPLICATION FOR ENROLLMENT, as a citizen of the Creek Nation, of Lena Rayford, born on the 8 day of March, 1904

Name of Father: Ossie Rayford   a citizen of the   Creek   Nation.
Coweta Town
Name of Mother: Selina Rayford   a citizen of the   Creek   Nation.
Artussee Town

               Postoffice   Eufaula, I. T.

Applications for Enrollment of Creek Newborn
Act of 1905   Volume XIII

AFFIDAVIT OF MOTHER.   Child present

UNITED STATES OF AMERICA, Indian Territory, }
   Western   DISTRICT.

I, Selina Rayford , on oath state that I am about 27 years of age and a citizen by blood , of the Creek Nation; that I am the lawful wife of Ossie Rayford , who is a citizen, by blood of the Creek Nation; that a female child was born to me on 8 day of March , 1904 , that said child has been named Lena Rayford , and was living March 4, 1905.

Selina Raiford

Witnesses To Mark:
{

Subscribed and sworn to before me this 11 day of April , 1905.

Drennan C Skaggs
Notary Public.

father
AFFIDAVIT OF ~~ATTENDING PHYSICIAN OR MID-WIFE~~.

UNITED STATES OF AMERICA, Indian Territory, }
   Western   DISTRICT.

I, Ossie Rayford , ~~a~~——— , on oath state that I assisted the midwife who attended on my wife Mrs. Selina Rayford , ~~wife of~~— on the 8 day of March , 1904 ; that there was born to her on said date a   female   child; that said child was living March 4, 1905, and is said to have been named Lena Rayford

Ossie Raiford

Witnesses To Mark:
{

Subscribed and sworn to before me this 11 day of April, 1905.

Drennan C Skaggs
Notary Public.

Applications for Enrollment of Creek Newborn
Act of 1905   Volume XIII

BIRTH AFFIDAVIT.

DEPARTMENT OF THE INTERIOR.
COMMISSION TO THE FIVE CIVILIZED TRIBES.

IN RE APPLICATION FOR ENROLLMENT, as a citizen of the Creek Nation, of Pearl Rayford, born on the 6 day of January, 1903

Name of Father: Ossie Rayford   a citizen of the   Creek   Nation.
Coweta Town
Name of Mother: Selina Rayford   a citizen of the   Creek   Nation.
Artussee Town
                    Postoffice   Eufaula, I. T.

AFFIDAVIT OF MOTHER.   Child present

UNITED STATES OF AMERICA, Indian Territory, ⎫
    Western   DISTRICT.   ⎭

I, Selina Rayford, on oath state that I am about 27 years of age and a citizen by blood, of the Creek Nation; that I am the lawful wife of Ossie Rayford, who is a citizen, by blood of the Creek Nation; that a female child was born to me on 6 day of January, 1903, that said child has been named Pearl Rayford, and was living March 4, 1905.

                                Selina Raiford
Witnesses To Mark:
{

Subscribed and sworn to before me this 11 day of April, 1905.

                                Drennan C Skaggs
                                    Notary Public.

---
                            father
AFFIDAVIT OF ~~ATTENDING PHYSICIAN OR MID-WIFE~~.

UNITED STATES OF AMERICA, Indian Territory, ⎫
    Western   DISTRICT.   ⎭

I, Ossie Rayford, ~~a~~————, on oath state that I assisted the midwife who attended on my wife Mrs. Selina Rayford, ~~wife of~~ on the 6 day of January, 1903; that there was born to her on said date a   female   child; that said child was living March 4, 1905, and is said to have been named Pearl Rayford

                                Ossie Raiford
Witnesses To Mark:
{

47

Applications for Enrollment of Creek Newborn
Act of 1905 Volume XIII

Subscribed and sworn to before me this 11 day of April, 1905.

                              Drennan C Skaggs
                              Notary Public.

BIRTH AFFIDAVIT.

Department of the Interior,
COMMISSION TO THE FIVE CIVILIZED TRIBES.

IN RE APPLICATION FOR ENROLLMENT, as a citizen of the Creek Nation, of Lena Raiford, born on the 8 day of March, 1904

Name of Father: Ossie Raiford   a citizen of the   Creek   Nation.
Name of Mother: Selina Raiford   a citizen of the   Creek   Nation.

                    Post-Office: Senora I.T.

AFFIDAVIT OF MOTHER.

UNITED STATES OF AMERICA,
    INDIAN TERRITORY,
    Western   District.

I, Selina Raiford, on oath state that I am 30 years of age and a citizen by blood, of the Creek Nation; that I am the lawful wife of Osie Raiford, who is a citizen, by blood of the Creek Nation; that a Female child was born to me on 8 day of March, 1904, that said child has been named Lena Raiford, and is now living.

                                Selina Raiford

WITNESSES TO MARK:

{

Subscribed and sworn to before me this 4 *day of* Jan., *1906.*

                              L.G. McIntosh
My Commission Expires April 10th 1907.   *Notary Public.*

DEPARTMENT OF THE INTERIOR.
COMMISSION TO THE FIVE CIVILIZED TRIBES.

In the matter of the death of Selina Raiford a citizen of the Creek Nation, who formerly resided at or near Eufaula, Ind. Ter., and died on the 26" day of February, 1906

Applications for Enrollment of Creek Newborn
Act of 1905 Volume XIII

AFFIDAVIT OF RELATIVE.

UNITED STATES OF AMERICA, Indian Territory, }
    Western   DISTRICT.

    I, Ossie Raiford, on oath state that I am 34 years of age and a citizen by blood, of the Creek Nation; that my postoffice address is Eufaula, Ind. Ter.; that I am Husband of Selina Raiford who was a citizen, by blood, of the Seminole Nation and that said Selina Raiford died on the 26" day of February, 1906.

                              Ossie Raiford

Witnesses To Mark:
{

    Subscribed and sworn to before me this 28" day of December, 1906.

                              Edward Merrick
                              Notary Public.

AFFIDAVIT OF ACQUAINTANCE.

UNITED STATES OF AMERICA, Indian Territory, }
    Western   DISTRICT.

    I, Major Wesley, on oath state that I am 26 years of age, and a citizen by blood of the Creek Nation; that my postoffice address is Eufaula, Ind. Ter.; that I was personally acquainted with Selina Raiford who was a citizen, by blood, of the Seminole Nation; and that said Selina Raiford died on the 26" day of February, 1906

                                  his
                            Major x Wesley

Witnesses To Mark: mark
    { Edward Merrick
      Ira S. *(Illegible)*

    Subscribed and sworn to before me this 28" day of December, 1906.

                              Edward Merrick
                              Notary Public.

Applications for Enrollment of Creek Newborn
Act of 1905   Volume XIII

Indian Territory, I
       I ss:
Western District. I
    I   my

~~We~~, the undersigned, do hereby elect to have ~~our~~ child, Pearl Raiford , born on the 6" day of January , 1903 , enrolled as a citizen of the Creek Nation, and to have said child receive her allotment of land and distribution of moneys in said nation.

Witnesses to mark: Ossie Raiford

_____

_____   _____

_____

Subscribed and sworn to before me this 28" day of Dec , 1906.

                           Edward Merrick
                            Notary Public.

   N.B.   The mother of Pearl is dead.

                             NC 1013

United States of America,
    Western District,
    Indian Territory.

We, the undersigned, on oath state that we are personally acquainted with Selina Raiford the wife of Ossie Raiford ; that there was born to her a female child on or about 6 day of Jan. 1903 ; that the said child has been named Pearl Raiford and was living March 4, 1905.

We further state that we have no interest in this case.

Witness to mark   Charter Givens his x ma
L.G. McIntosh   John Francis   his x ma
W.T. Fears

    Subscribed and sworn to before me this 14 day of Apr. 1906

                           L.G. McIntosh
                           Notary Public.

My Com expires
Apr 10, 1907

Applications for Enrollment of Creek Newborn
Act of 1905   Volume XIII

DEPARTMENT OF THE INTERIOR.
COMMISSION TO THE FIVE CIVILIZED TRIBES.

In the matter of the death of   Lena Raiford   a citizen of the Creek Nation, who formerly resided at or near   Eufaula   , Ind. Ter., and died on the   9" day of July   , 1905

AFFIDAVIT OF RELATIVE.

UNITED STATES OF AMERICA, Indian Territory,
Western   DISTRICT.

I, Ossie Raiford , on oath state that I am about 33 years of age and a citizen by blood , of the Creek Nation; that my postoffice address is Eufaula , Ind. Ter.; that I am father of Lena Raiford who was a citizen, by blood , of the Creek Nation and that said Lena Raiford died on the 9" day of July , 1905

Ossie Raiford

Witnesses To Mark:
{

Subscribed and sworn to before me this 20" day of June, 1906.

HGHains
Notary Public.

BIRTH AFFIDAVIT.

Department of the Interior,
COMMISSION TO THE FIVE CIVILIZED TRIBES.

IN RE APPLICATION FOR ENROLLMENT, as a citizen of the Creek Nation, of Pearl Raiford , born on the 6th day of Jan , 1903

Name of Father: Ossie Raiford   a citizen of the   Creek   Nation.
Name of Mother: Selina Raiford   a citizen of the   Creek   Nation.

Post-Office: Senora I.T.

Applications for Enrollment of Creek Newborn
Act of 1905   Volume XIII

AFFIDAVIT OF MOTHER.

UNITED STATES OF AMERICA,
    INDIAN TERRITORY,
    Western   District.

    I, Selina Raiford , on oath state that I am 30 years of age and a citizen by Blood , of the Creek Nation; that I am the lawful wife of Ossie Raiford , who is a citizen, by Blood of the Creek Nation; that a Female child was born to me on 6th day of Jan. , 1903 , that said child has been named Pearl Raiford , and is now living.

                                       Selina Raiford

WITNESSES TO MARK:

{

    Subscribed and sworn to before me this 4 *day of* Jan, 1906.

                                   L.G. McIntosh
                                      Notary Public.

AFFIDAVIT OF ATTENDING PHYSICIAN OR MID-WIFE.

UNITED STATES OF AMERICA,
    INDIAN TERRITORY,
    Western   District.

    I, The midwife is dead , a   , ~~on oath state that I attended on Mrs~~. Who attended on , ~~wife of~~   me on the *(blank)* day of *(blank)* , 190*(blank)* ; that there was born to her on said date a *(blank)* child; that said child is now living and is said to have been named Whose name was Lena McIntosh
           Ossie Raiford was present, Husband --

~~WITNESSES TO MARK:~~

{   Ossie Raiford

    Subscribed and sworn to before me this 4 *day of* Jan., 1906.

                                   LG McIntosh
My Commission Expires April 10th 1907.   Notary Public.

Applications for Enrollment of Creek Newborn
Act of 1905 Volume XIII

W^mO.B

COMMISSIONERS:
TAMS BIXBY,
THOMAS B. NEEDLES,
C.R. BRECKINRIDGE.

WM. O. BEALL
Secretary

DEPARTMENT OF THE INTERIOR,
COMMISSIONER TO THE FIVE CIVILIZED TRIBES.

REFER IN REPLY TO THE FOLLOWING:
Seminole NB
81.

ADDRESS ONLY THE
COMMISSION TO THE FIVE CIVILIZED TRIBES.

Muskogee, Indian Territory June 20, 1905.

Commission to the Five Civilized Tribes,
    Creek Enrollment Division.

Gentlemen:

    On May 31, 1905 Thomas Palmer, band chief, appeared before the Commission and made application for the enrollment of Pearl Raiford, born January 6, 1903, and Lena Raiford, born March 8, 1904, as citizens by blood of the Seminole Nation. He stated that the father of said children was Sosa Raiford, a citizen of the Creek Nation, and that the mother was Selina Raiford, a citizen by blood of the Seminole Nation.

    You are requested to inform the Seminole Enrollment Division as to whether or not any application has been made to the Commission for the enrollment of said children as citizens of the Creek Nation and if so what disposition, if any, has been made of said application.

                           Respectfully,
                           Tams Bixby Chairman.

NC 1013.

Muskogee, Indian Territory, June 23, 1905.

Commission to the Five Civilized Tribes,
    Seminole Enrollment Division.

Gentlemen:

    Receipt is acknowledged of your letter of June 20, 1905, (Sem. NC 81), in which you state that application has been made for the enrollment of Pearl and Lena Raiford, as citizens of the Seminole Nation. You state that the father of said children is Sosa Raiford, a citizen of the Creek Nation, and the mother is Salina Raiford, a citizen by blood of the Seminole Nation. You ask to be informed whether or not application has been made to the Commission for the enrollment of said children as citizens of the Creek Nation, and if so, what disposition if any has been made of said application.

    In reply you are advised that on April 13, 1905, Ossie and Selina Rayford made application for the enrollment of their children, Pearl Rayford, born January 6, 1903, and

Applications for Enrollment of Creek Newborn
Act of 1905   Volume XIII

Lena Rayford, born March 8, 1904, as citizens by blood of the Creek Nation. It is stated in said application that both the mother and father of said children are citizens by blood of the Creek Nation, but the Commission has been unable to identify Salina Rayford on its rolls. When said application is finally disposed of you will be duly notified.

Respectfully,
Chairman.

(The above letter given again.)

NC. 1012[sic]

Muskogee, Indian Territory, October 23, 1905.

Selina Raiford,
    Eufaula, Indian Territory.

Dear Madam:

    In the matter of the application for the enrollment of your minor children, Pearl Raiford, born January 6, 1903, and Lena Raiford, born March 8, 1904, as citizens by blood of the Creek Nation, your surname, the surname of the father of said children, and the surnames of said children are spelled, in your affidavit relative to their births, executed April 11, 1905, Rayford.

    The father of said children has been identified on the final roll of citizens by blood of the Creek Nation as Ossie Raiford.

    If you are, as stated, the lawful wife of said Ossie Raiford, it necessarily follows that your correct surname is Raiford and is also the correct name of your said children, they having been born in lawful wedlock.

    There is herewith enclosed a blank affidavit which you are requested to execute before a notary public, care being taken that all names are spelled correctly and that the notary affix his name and notarial seal to same, and return to this office in the enclosed envelope.

    This office is unable to identify you on its final roll of citizens by blood of the Creek Nation; you are requested to state your maiden name, the names of your parents, the Creek Indian town to which you belong, and your roll number as the same appears on your deeds and allotment certificate.

    You are further requested to inform this office whether you are not in fact a citizen of the Seminole Nation and if so under what name you are enrolled in said Seminole Nation.

Applications for Enrollment of Creek Newborn
Act of 1905   Volume XIII

In the event that you are a citizen of the Seminole Nation, this office requires the joint affidavit of yourself and the father of said children electing in which nation you desire to have them enrolled and receive their allotment of land.

This office requires proof of you marriage to said Ossie Raiford, such proof may consist of either the original or a certified copy of your marriage license and certificate.

It will be necessary for you to furnish this office with the affidavits of two disinterested witnesses relative to the birth of said children. Said affidavits must set forth the names of said children, the dates of their birth, the names of their parents, and whether or not they were living on March 4, 1905.

Respectfully,

BC
Env.

Commissioner.

NC 1013

REFER IN REPLY TO THE FOLLOWING:

DEPARTMENT OF THE INTERIOR,
COMMISSIONER TO THE FIVE CIVILIZED TRIBES.

Muskogee, Indian Territory, November 16, 1905.

Chief Clerk,
   Creek Enrollment Division.

Dear Sir:

In compliance with your verbal request, you are advised that the name of Selina Raiford appears upon the approved roll of Seminole citizens by blood opposite No. 110. She is further identified as the mother of Pearl and Lena Raiford, who are applicants for enrollment as citizens of the Creek Nation under the Act of Congress approved March 3, 1905.

Respectfully,
                Tams Bixby   Commissioner.

Applications for Enrollment of Creek Newborn
Act of 1905 Volume XIII

W^mO.B.

REFER IN REPLY TO THE FOLLOWING:
Sem. N.B. 81
NBC 1013

DEPARTMENT OF THE INTERIOR,
COMMISSIONER TO THE FIVE CIVILIZED TRIBES.

Muskogee, Indian Territory, December 29, 1905.

Chief Clerk,
    Creek Enrollment Division.

Dear Sir:

    On May 31, 1905, application was made for the enrollment as citizens of the Seminole Nation under the act of Congress of March 3, 1905, of Pearl and Lena Raiford, born January 6, 1903 and March 9, 1904, respectively, children of Sosa Raiford, a citizen of the Creek Nation and Selina Raiford, a Seminole citizen.

    It appears from the record in this case that application has also been made for the enrollment of the above named children as citizens of the Creek Nation and you are requested to advise the Seminole Enrollment Division whether the names of these children have been placed upon a schedule of new born citizens of the Creek Nation which has been forwarded the Department, and whether or not their enrollment has been approved by the Secretary, if so, giving the date of their approval and their roll numbers.

                  Respectfully,
                          Tams Bixby   Commissioner.

Sem. NB-81.
NBC-1013.

Muskogee, Indian Territory, January 2, 1906.

Chief Clerk of Seminole Enrollment Division.
    Muskogee, Indian Territory.

Dear Sir:

    Receipt is acknowledged of your letter of December 29, 1905, in which you ask to be advised whether the names of Pearl and Lena Raiford, born January 6, 1903, and March 8, 1905, respectively, have been placed upon a schedule of new born citizens of the Creek Nation which has been forwarded to the Department, and whether or not their enrollment has been approved by the Secretary.

    In reply you are advised that the matter of the enrolment of said children is pending in this office.

                  Respectfully,
                                Commissioner.

Applications for Enrollment of Creek Newborn
Act of 1905   Volume XIII

N.C. 1013.

Muskogee, Indian Territory, April 9, 1906.

Ossie Raiford,
    Eufaula, Indian Territory.

Dear Sir:

    Receipt is acknowledged of your letter of April 6, 1906, in which you ask if your minor children, Pearl and Lena Raiford are enrolled in the Creek Nation.

    You are advised that this office requires an affidavit of the midwife or physician in attendance at the birth of said children; in the event that same cannot be procured, the affidavits of two dis-interested witness, relative to the birth of each of said children should be furnished this office at your earliest convenience.

                         Respectfully,

                                    Acting Commissioner.

                                                  JWH

N C 1013

Muskogee, Indian Territory, March 1, 1907.

Ossie Raiford,
    Eufaula, Indian Territory.

Dear Sir :--

    You are hereby advised that on February 18, 1907, the Secretary of the Interior approved the enrollment of your minor children, Pearl and Lena Raiford, as citizens by blood of the Creek Nation, and that the names of said children appear upon the roll of New Born citizens by blood of the Creek Nation, enrolled under the Act of Congress approved March 3, 1905, as numbers 1194 and 1195, respectively.

    These children are now entitled to allotment and application therefor should be made without delay at the Creek Land Office, Muskogee, Indian Territory.

                         Respectfully,

                                    Commissioner.

Applications for Enrollment of Creek Newborn
Act of 1905   Volume XIII

REFER IN REPLY TO THE FOLLOWING:

Sem. NB-81

DEPARTMENT OF THE INTERIOR,
COMMISSIONER TO THE FIVE CIVILIZED TRIBES.

Muskogee, Indian Territory, March 6, 1907.

Chief Clerk,
    Creek Enrollment Division.

Dear Sir:-

You are hereby advised that the Commissioner to the Five Civilized Tribes on February 20, 1907, rendered his decision, dismissing the application for the enrollment of Pearl Raiford and Lena Raiford as citizens of the Seminole Nation.

                  Respectfully,
                          Tams Bixby   Commissioner.

BIRTH AFFIDAVIT.

DEPARTMENT OF THE INTERIOR.
COMMISSION TO THE FIVE CIVILIZED TRIBES.

IN RE APPLICATION FOR ENROLLMENT, as a citizen of the Creek Nation, of Roman Randall , born on the 17" day of November, 1904

Name of Father: Sam Randall   a citizen of the   Creek   Nation.
Name of Mother: Dicey Randall   a citizen of the   Creek   Nation.

                Postoffice   Henryetta Ind. Ter.

AFFIDAVIT OF MOTHER.

UNITED STATES OF AMERICA, Indian Territory, }
    Western   DISTRICT.

I, Dicey Randall , on oath state that I am about Thirty years of age and a citizen by blood , of the Creek Nation; that I am the lawful wife of Sam Randall , who is a

Applications for Enrollment of Creek Newborn
Act of 1905 Volume XIII

citizen, by blood of the Creek Nation; that a male child was born to me on 17" day of November, 1904, that said child has been named Roman Randall, and is now living.

her
Dicey x Randall
mark

Witnesses To Mark:
{ John W. Sullins Henryetta I.T.
{ James R Vallyhon

Subscribed and sworn to before me this 6th day of November, 1905.

MY COMMISSION EXPIRES Julia B. Sullins
JULY 14th, 1906. Notary Public.

AFFIDAVIT OF ATTENDING PHYSICIAN OR MID-WIFE.

UNITED STATES OF AMERICA, Indian Territory,
Western DISTRICT.

I, Lena Johnson, a Midwife, on oath state that I attended on Mrs. Dicey Randall, wife of Sam Randall on the 17" day of November, 1904; that there was born to her on said date a male child; that said child is now living and is said to have been named Roman Randall

her
Lena x Johnson
mark

Witnesses To Mark:
{ John W. Sullins Henryetta I.T.
{ JR Vallyhon

Subscribed and sworn to before me this 6th day of November, 1905.

MY COMMISSION EXPIRES Julia B. Sullins
JULY 14th, 1906. Notary Public.

BIRTH AFFIDAVIT.

DEPARTMENT OF THE INTERIOR.
COMMISSION TO THE FIVE CIVILIZED TRIBES.

IN RE APPLICATION FOR ENROLLMENT, as a citizen of the Creek Nation, of Roman Randall, born on the 17 day of Nov., 1904

Name of Father: Sam Randall a citizen of the Creek Nation.
Nuyaka Town
Name of Mother: Dicey Randall (nee Fields) a citizen of the Creek Nation.
Hutche chuppa Town

Postoffice Henryetta, Ind. Ter.

Applications for Enrollment of Creek Newborn
Act of 1905 Volume XIII

AFFIDAVIT OF MOTHER.

UNITED STATES OF AMERICA, Indian Territory, }
Western   DISTRICT.

Child is present

I, Dicey Randall , on oath state that I am about 30 years of age and a citizen by blood , of the Creek Nation; that I am the lawful wife of Sam Randall , who is a citizen, by blood of the Creek Nation; that a male child was born to me on 17 day of November , 1904 , that said child has been named Roman Randall , and was living March 4, 1905.

                                        her
                                   Dicey x Randall

Witnesses To Mark: mark
{ Alex Posey
{ DC Skaggs

Subscribed and sworn to before me this 11 day of April , 1905.

                                   Drennan C Skaggs
                                   Notary Public.

AFFIDAVIT OF ATTENDING PHYSICIAN OR MID-WIFE.

UNITED STATES OF AMERICA, Indian Territory, }
Western   DISTRICT.

                                    my wife

I, Sam Randall , a~~ (blank)~~ , on oath state that I attended on ^ Mrs. Dicey Randall , ~~wife of~~ on the 17 day of Nov , 1904 ; that there was born to her on said date a male child; that said child was living March 4, 1905, and ~~is said to have~~ has been named Roman Randall

                                   his
                                   Sam x Randall

Witnesses To Mark: mark
{ Alex Posey
{ DC Skaggs

Subscribed and sworn to before me this 11 day of April , 1905.

                                   Drennan C Skaggs
                                   Notary Public.

Applications for Enrollment of Creek Newborn
Act of 1905   Volume XIII

BIRTH AFFIDAVIT.

DEPARTMENT OF THE INTERIOR.
COMMISSION TO THE FIVE CIVILIZED TRIBES.

IN RE APPLICATION FOR ENROLLMENT, as a citizen of the Creek Nation, of Willie Randall, born on the 6 day of March., 1902 and died March 10, 1902

Name of Father: Sam Randall   a citizen of the   Creek   Nation.
Nuyaka Town
Name of Mother: Dicey Randall   a citizen of the   Creek   Nation.
Hutche chuppa Town

           Postoffice   Henryetta, Ind. Ter.

AFFIDAVIT OF MOTHER.

UNITED STATES OF AMERICA, Indian Territory, }
    Western   DISTRICT.

     I, Dicey Randall , on oath state that I am about 30 years of age and a citizen by blood , of the Creek Nation; that I am the lawful wife of Sam Randall , who is a citizen, by blood of the Creek Nation; that a male child was born to me on 6 day of March , 1902 , that said child ~~has been~~ was named Willie Randall , and was living March 4, 1905.

                                   her
                            Dicey x Randall
Witnesses To Mark: mark
   { Alex Posey
   { DC Skaggs

     Subscribed and sworn to before me this 11 day of April , 1905.

                               Drennan C Skaggs
                                   Notary Public.

AFFIDAVIT OF ATTENDING PHYSICIAN OR MID-WIFE.

UNITED STATES OF AMERICA, Indian Territory, }
    Western   DISTRICT.

                                                      my wife
     I, Sam Randall , ~~a (blank)~~ , on oath state that I attended on ^ Mrs. Dicey Randall , ~~wife of~~ on the 6 day of March , 1902 ; that there was born to her on said date a male child; that said child ~~was living March 4, 1905~~ died March 10, 1905[sic], and is said to have been named Roman Randall

                                  his
                             Sam x Randall
                                 mark

Applications for Enrollment of Creek Newborn
Act of 1905 Volume XIII

Witnesses To Mark:
{ Alex Posey
{ DC Skaggs

Subscribed and sworn to before me this 11 day of April, 1905.

Drennan C Skaggs
Notary Public.

N.C. 1015.

DEPARTMENT OF THE INTERIOR,
COMMISSIONER TO THE FIVE CIVILIZED TRIBES.
NEAR HENRYETTA, I. T., JAN. 30, 1907.

In the matter of the application for the enrollment of Willie Randall, deceased, as a citizen by blood of the Creek Nation.

SAM RANDALL, being first duly sworn by and examined through Alex Posey, a Notary Public and official interpreter, testified as follows:

BY THE COMMISSIONER:

Q What is your name? A Sam Randall.
Q How old are you? A Between 34 and 35 years old.
Q What is your postoffice address? A Henryetta.
Q Are you a citizen of the Creek Nation? A Yes sir, I belong to Nuyaka town.
Q Are you married? A Yes sir.
Q To whom? A Dicy[sic] Randall.
Q Is Dicy your lawful wife? A Yes sir
Q To what Creek town does she belong? A Hutchechuppa.
Q Have you and Dicy a deceased minor child named Willie Randall? A Yes sir.
Q When was the child born? A Either in March or April, 1902. I am unable to fix the exact date of its birth.
Q When did the child die? A Either in March or April, 1902, it only lived four years after it was born.
Q Are you positive that the child was born in either March or April, 1902, and lived only four days? A Yes sir.
Q According to a joint affidavit executed by yourself and wife April 11, 1905, your deceased minor child, Willie Randall, was born March 6, 1902, and died March 10, 1905. Are the dates as given in said affidavit as to the birth and death of your child correct, or not? A The date of its birth is probably correct, but the date of its death is not. The child only lived four days, and was born in either March or April, 1902. I had a record showing the dates of the child's birth and death but have lost it since making application for its enrollment and I am unable at this time to state exactly when it was born or when it

Applications for Enrollment of Creek Newborn
Act of 1905   Volume XIII

died, but I can swear positively the child was born in either March or April, 1902, and living~~ed~~ only four days.

Q Then the only proof that either yourself or wife can furnish as to the ~~death of this child~~ birth and death of this child is that it was born either in March or April, 1902 and that it lived only four days after it was born? A Yes sir; since losing the record we had we are unable to fix the exact dates of its birth and death. My wife knows less about it than I do.

- - - -

J.B. Myers, being first duly sworn, states, that as stenographer to the Commissioner to the Five Civilized Tribes, he recorded the testimony in the foregoing proceedings, and that the above is a true and correct transcript of his stenographic notes thereof.

JB Myers

Subscribed and sworn to before me,
this 31st day of January, 1907.

Alex Posey
JBM   Notary Public.

N.F. 1015   FHW
                                                                                       AG

DEPARTMENT OF THE INTERIOR,
COMMISSIONER TO THE FIVE CIVILIZED TRIBES.

In the matter of the application for the enrollment of Willie Randall, deceased, as a citizen by blood of the Creek Nation.

STATEMENT AND ORDER.

The record in this case shows that an application was filed in affidavit form on April 13, 1905, for the enrollment of Willie Randall, deceased, as a citizen by blood of the Creek Nation. Further proceedings were had before a Creek enrollment field party, near Henrietta[sic], Indian Territory, January 30, 1907.

The evidence in this case shows that a clerical error was made in the affidavit as to the date of the death of the applicant but the same is corrected in the testimony taken January 30, 1907, which fully warrants the conclusion that the applicant was born March 6, 1902 and died March 10, 1902.

In view of the foregoing, I am of the opinion that there is no authority of law for the enrollment of Willie Randall, deceased, as a citizen by blood of the Creek Nation and the application for his enrollment as such is accordingly dismissed.

Tams Bixby   COMMISSIONER.

Muskogee, Indian Territory,
FEB 7- 1907

Applications for Enrollment of Creek Newborn
Act of 1905   Volume XIII

NC 1015

Muskogee, Indian Territory, October 23, 1905.

Dicey Randall,
    Care Sam Randall,
        Henryetta, Indian Territory.

Dear Madam:

    In the matter of the application for the enrollment of your minor child, Roman Randall, born November 17, 1904, as a citizen by blood of the Creek Nation, this office desires affidavit of the midwife or physician in attendance at the birth of said child and a blank for that purpose is enclosed herewith.

    In the event that there was no physician or midwife in attendance when said child was born, it will be necessary for you to furnish this office with the affidavits of two disinterested witnesses relative to his birth. Said affidavits must set forth said child's name, the date of his birth, the names of his parents and whether or not he was living on March 4, 1905.

                            Respectfully,

                                            Commissioner.

BA
Env.

N.C. 1015

Muskogee, Indian Territory, November 24, 1906.

Dicy Randall,
    Care of Sam Randall,
        Henryetta, Indian Territory.

Dear Madam:

    In the matter of the application for the enrollment of your minor child Willie Randall, deceased, as a citizen by blood of the Creek Nation you are advised that this office requires further proof of his death.

    For this purpose there is herewith inclosed blank form of birth affidavit, and in executing same care should be exercised to see that all blanks are properly filled, all names written in full and in the event that either of the persons signing the affidavit is unable to, which you and the father of said child should have properly executed and returned to this office at an early date in the inclosed envelope.

                            Respectfully,

                                            Commissioner.

Inc. D.C. Env.

Applications for Enrollment of Creek Newborn
Act of 1905   Volume XIII

N.C. 1015

Muskogee, Indian Territory, ~~November 24, 1906~~.
Jan 22 - 07

Dicy Randall,
    Care of Sam Randall,
        Henryetta, Indian Territory.

Dear Madam:

In the matter of the application for the enrollment of your minor child Willie Randall, deceased, as a citizen by blood of the Creek Nation you are advised that this office requires further proof of his death.

For this purpose there is herewith inclosed blank form of birth affidavit, and in executing same care should be exercised to see that all blanks are properly filled, all names written in full and in the event that either of the persons signing the affidavit is unable to, which you and the father of said child should have properly executed ad returned to this office at an early date in the inclosed envelope.

                Respectfully,
                Commissioner.

Inc D C Skaggs Env

N.C. 1015.

Muskogee, Indian Territory, January 22, 1907.

Alex Posey,
    Clerk in Charge Creek Field Party.

Dear Sir:

In the matter of the application for the enrollment of Willie Randall, deceased, as a citizen by blood of the Creek Nation, there is enclosed herewith a copy of a letter from this office addressed to Dicy Randall, the mother of the applicant, also a copy of the birth affidavit.

You are directed to procure a death affidavit executed in accordance with our letter to Dicy Randall.

                Respectfully,
                Commissioner.

AG-22-1

Applications for Enrollment of Creek Newborn
Act of 1905   Volume XIII

REFER IN REPLY TO THE FOLLOWING:
N.C. 1015.

DEPARTMENT OF THE INTERIOR,
COMMISSIONER TO THE FIVE CIVILIZED TRIBES.

Stidham, Indian Territory, January 31, 1907.

Commissioner to the Five Civilized Tribes,
      Muskogee, Indian Territory.

Sir:

    In the matter of the application for the enrollment of Willie Randall, deceased, as a citizen by blood of the Creek Nation, there is herewith inclosed the testimony of Sam Randall, taken by the Creek Field PARTY January 30, 1907, relative to the death of said Willie Randall. Said testimony was taken in lieu of a death affidavit for the reason that the parents of said child are unable to fix the exact date of its death.

                Respectfully,
                          Alex Posey
                          In Charge
                          Creek Field Party.

JBM

                                              JWH

NF-1015

                Muskogee, Indian Territory, February 8, 1907.

Dicy Randall,
    % Sam Randall,
        Henryetta, Indian Territory.

Dear Madam :--

    There is enclosed herewith copy of statement and order of the Commissioner to the Five Civilized Tribes, dated February 7, 1907, dismissing the application made by you for the enrollment of your deceased minor child, Willie Randall, as a citizen by blood of the Creek Nation.

                Respectfully,
                            Commissioner.

Registered.
JWH 8-7

Applications for Enrollment of Creek Newborn
Act of 1905   Volume XIII

2448 B

DEPARTMENT OF THE INTERIOR,
COMMISSION TO THE FIVE CIVILIZED TRIBES.
April 24, 1905.

In the matter of the application for the enrollment of certain new borns as citizens of the Creek Nation.

Alex Posey, being duly sworn, testified as follows:

By Commission:
Q What is your name, age and post office address? A Alex Posey, 31, Muskogee.
Q Are you a citizen of the Creek Nation? A Yes sir
Q Got your land, have you? A Yes sir.
Q You have been engaged recently in the field for the Dawes Commission securing evidence about Creek citizens or new borns? A Yes sir.
Q Have you a list of children for whom application could not be made and about whom you have succeeded in obtaining some information? A Yes sir.
Q You may state the conditions and the names of these children? You desire to make application for them? A Yes sir.
Q Name them. Jaly Proctor, Weogufky Town, Sukey Proctor, Weogufky Town, have two children --one about three years old and one about six months old. Post office, Hanna, Indian Territory.

Jacob Bullet, about three years old. Parents: Maxey Bullet, Seminole, and Hannah Bullet, Hillabee. Post Office, Hanna, Indian Territory.

Connie Hawkins, Hillabee Town, Sabella Hawkins, Okchiye, have two children-- one about three years old and a younger child. Post Office, Hanna, Indian Territory.

Willie Fisher, Hickory Ground Town, Lussee Fisher, Okfusky[sic] Canadian Town, have two children --one about three years old and a baby. Post Office, Slumpker, Indian Territory.

Lizzie Lasley, about three years old, Sam Lasley, born in either August or September, 1904. Parents: Sam Lasley, Okchiye, Wisey Lasley, Weogufky. Post Office, Hanna, Indian Territory.

Jim Haynes (or Sangee), Okchiye Town, Folotkokee, Weogufky Town have a male child about three years old named Joe. Post Office, Hanna, Indian Territory.

Taylor Foley, Weogufky, Melinda Foley, Okchiye, have a child about two years old. Post Office, Slumpker, Indian Territory.

Phillip Lindsey, Tuckabatchee, Cilla Lindsey, Hillabee, have a child about three years old. Post Office, Hanna, Indian Territory.

Big William (or William Thlocco), Okchiye Town, Cinda Williams, Weogufky Town, have two children -- one about three years old-- one born in February 1905. Post Office Hanna, Indian Territory.

Freeland Lindsey, Tuckabatchee or Hillabee, Nancy Proctor, Tullahassoche, have a child about two years old. Post Office, Hanna, Indian Territory.

Timonthluppy George, Weogufky Town, Nellie George, Pukon Tullahassee, have a child about three years old. Post Office, Slumpker, Indian Territory.

Applications for Enrollment of Creek Newborn
Act of 1905 Volume XIII

~~Willi~~ Walter Simmons, Weogufky, Chippie Simmons, Pukon Tulahassee[sic], have a child about one years old. Post Office, Hannah, Indian Territory.

Jacob Larney (or Green), Arbeka Tulledega Town, Bettie Larney, (or Green), Hillabee Town, have a child. Post Office, Hanna, Indian Territory.

John Hill, Okchiye, Millie Hill, Weogufky, have a child about three months old. Post Office, Hanna, Indian Territory.

Jim Pigeon, Okchiye Town, Jennie Pigeon, Okchiye Town, have a child about five months old. Post Office, Hanna, Indian Territory.

Thomas Deo, Okchiye Town, Nancy Deo, Fish Pond Town, have a child about three months old. Post Office, Hanna, Indian Territory.

Jack Buckner, born December 17, 1904. Parents: Wiley Buckner, Okchiye, Susie Buckner, Cussehta. Post Office, Hanna, Indian Territory.

Q This is the information you received from relatives right around there on April 24, 1905? A Yes sir.
Q Were you informed that the parents of these children were unwilling to make application for their enrollment? A Yes sir.
Q This was the only way that the rights of these children would be saved? A Yes sir. I made every effort to obtain direct information from the parents but in every instance they refused to give their testimony.

Lona Merrick being duly sworn, states that the above and foregoing is a true and correct transcript of his stenographic notes as taken in said cause on said date.

Lona Merrick

Subscribed and sworn to before me this 9th day of May, 1905.

Edw C Griesel
Notary Public.

BIRTH AFFIDAVIT.

DEPARTMENT OF THE INTERIOR.
COMMISSION TO THE FIVE CIVILIZED TRIBES.

IN RE APPLICATION FOR ENROLLMENT, as a citizen of the Creek Nation, of Jack Buckner, born on the 17 day of December, 1904

Name of Father: Wiley Buckner   a citizen of the   Creek   Nation.
  Okchiye Town
Name of Mother: Susie Buckner   a citizen of the   Creek   Nation.
  Cussehta

Postoffice   Hanna, I. T.

Applications for Enrollment of Creek Newborn
Act of 1905   Volume XIII

AFFIDAVIT OF MOTHER.

UNITED STATES OF AMERICA, Indian Territory, }
    Western   DISTRICT.

Child is present

I, Susie Buckner, on oath state that I am about 40 years of age and a citizen by blood, of the Creek Nation; that I am the lawful wife of Wiley Buckner, who is a citizen, by blood of the Creek Nation; that a male child was born to me on 17 day of December, 1904, that said child has been named Jack Buckner, and is now living. and was living March 4, 1905.

                                    her
                           Susie x Buckner
Witnesses To Mark: mark
  { DC Skaggs
    Alex Posey

Subscribed and sworn to before me this 29 day of May, 1905.

                                Drennan C Skaggs
                                Notary Public.

AFFIDAVIT OF ATTENDING PHYSICIAN OR MID-WIFE.

UNITED STATES OF AMERICA, Indian Territory, }
    Western   DISTRICT.

I, Lizzie Buckner, a mid-wife, on oath state that I attended on Mrs. Susie Buckner, wife of Wiley Buckner on or about the 17 day of December, 1904; that there was born to her on said date a male child; that said child is now living and was living March 4, 1905, and is said to have been named Jack Buckner

                                  her
                         Lizzie x Buckner
Witnesses To Mark: mark
  { DC Skaggs
    Alex Posey

Subscribed and sworn to before me this 30 day of May, 1905.

                                Drennan C Skaggs
                                Notary Public.

Applications for Enrollment of Creek Newborn
Act of 1905 Volume XIII

DEPARTMENT OF THE INTERIOR,
COMMISSION TO THE FIVE CIVILIZED TRIBES.
EUFAULA, I.T. April 19, 1905.

In the matter of the application for the enrollment of certain new born children concerning whom no application could be obtained except through testimony.

Jimsey Fish and William Givens, being duly sworn, testified as follows testified as follows, through Official Interpreter, Alex Posey.

Examination by the Commission:
Q What is your name? A Jimsey Fish.
Q How old are you? A I have never been able to determine my age. (Witness appears to be about 48).
Q What is our post office? A Mellette, I.T.
Q Do you know of some new born children whose parents are unwilling to have them enrolled? A Yes sir.
Q Those about whom you and Mr. Givens are testifying are children all born since May 25, 1901? And for whom application could only be made in this way? A Yes sir.

Q What is your name? A William Givens.
Q How old are you? A I am 25.
Q What is your post office address? A Mellette.

Statement: Nocus Ela has two children--his white name is Jim Davis--he belongs to Kialigee Town--I don't know the name of his wife, but she belongs to Kialigee town; one of them is walking and the other is younger. The one that is walking is a <u>boy</u>, don't know the sex of the other. The oldest is named <u>Johnny</u>, don't know the other's name. Both are living. They are both new born children and Nocus said the other day that he had never enrolled them-the post office is Hanna.

Bob and Mahala Bender have two children--these people belong to Tuckabatchee and Hillabee Towns respectively--one of the children is <u>Thomas</u> and the other is <u>Easma</u>--Thomas is just beginning to talk and Easma is older than Thomas. Their post office is Mellette. These children are new borns also.

Josie and Mahala Roberts have two children--the parents belong to Hutchechuppa and Kialigee respectively-- I don't [sic] the names of the children-- one is walking and the other is a baby yet a small child.
Q Were both of them born since May 25, 1901? A Yes sir. The oldest is a girl and I don't know the sex of the youngest. Both are living. Their post office is Indianola.

Thompson Fields and Susie Fields--he is of Okchiye or Fish Pond, I don't know which, and Susie belongs to Hutchechuppa; they have one <u>child</u> born since May 25, 1901, I don't know but I think the gi child is a girl. It is living, the child is not able to crawl but can sit up.

Applications for Enrollment of Creek Newborn
Act of 1905 Volume XIII

Earnest and Nicey <u>Gouge</u>, of Hickory Ground and Hillabee Towns respectively----had <u>two</u> children the last time I was at their house--both were born since May 25, don't know the names, <u>both boys</u> I think, both living, post office, Hanna.

Conn<u>ie Hawkins</u> of Hillabee Town and Sybilla Hawkins of Fish Pong (?) I don't know her town' they had one child at the time I was at their house; I was at their house last summer 1904, don't know whether a boy or girl, born after May 25, 1901, it was a small child at that time, it is living. Post Office, Hanna.

Micco Emarthla, his white name is Neddie Walker, and Sallie Emarthla, both parents belong to Kialigee, have one child names <u>Walter</u> born since May 25, 1901, and living. Post Office, Indianola.

Wiley <u>Fish</u> of Tuckabatchee and Hettie Fish of Kialigee, post office, Mellette, Indian Territory have two children, but one is probably too old being about seven years old, but the field party last year failed to get that old one. The youngest was probably born since May 25, 1901. It is a boy and living. The oldest one is named <u>John</u> I don't know the other.

Noah <u>Roberts</u> of Kialigee and Hannah <u>Roberts</u> of Hillabee post office, Mellette, Indian Territory have one child name not known, born since May 25, 1901. Don't now the sex, it is living. Noah also has a step-son about seven years old that has never been enrolled named <u>Walter Starr</u>.

Questions addressed to both witnesses:
Q These statements which you have made are for the purpose of getting enrolled the new born children of parents belonging to the Snake Faction? A Yes sir.
Q Neither of you are related to them? A I Jimsey am related to Wiley Fish, who is the son of my brother and that's all.

Henry G. Hains, being duly sworn, on his oath, states that the above and foregoing is a true and correct transcript of his stenographic notes as taken in said cause on said date.

Henry G. Hains

Subscribed and sworn to before me this 11th day of May, 1905.

Drennan C Skaggs
Notary Public.

Applications for Enrollment of Creek Newborn
Act of 1905 Volume XIII

2461 B
#1 - C 1048

DEPARTMENT OF THE INTERIOR,
COMMISSION TO THE FIVE CIVILIZED TRIBES.
EUFAULA, I.T. April 19, 1905.

In the matter of the application for the enrollment of certain new born children concerning whom no application could be obtained except through testimony.

Jimsey Fish and William Givens, being duly sworn, testified as follows testified as follows, through Official Interpreter, Alex Posey.

Examination by the Commission:
Q What is your name? A Jimsey Fish.
Q How old are you? A I have never been able to determine my age. (Witness appears to be about 48).
Q What is our post office? A Mellette, I.T.
Q Do you know of some new born children whose parents are unwilling to have them enrolled? A Yes sir.
Q Those about whom you and Mr. Givens are testifying are children all born since May 25, 1901? And for whom application could only be made in this way? A Yes sir.

Q What is your name? A William Givens.
Q How old are you? A I am 25.
Q What is your post office address? A Mellette.

Statement: Nocus Ela has two children--his white name is Jim Davis--he belongs to Kialigee Town--I don't know the name of his wife, but she belongs to Kialigee town; one of them is walking and the other is younger. The one that is walking is a <u>boy</u>, don't know the sex of the other. The oldest is named <u>Johnny</u>, don't know the other's name. Both are living. They are both new born children and Nocus said the other day that he had never enrolled them--the post office is Hanna.

Bob and Mahala Bender have two children--these people belong to Tuckabatchee and Hillabee Towns respectively--one of the children is <u>Thomas</u> and the other is <u>Easma</u>--Thomas is just beginning to talk and Easma is older than Thomas. Their post office is Mellette. These children are new borns also.

Josie and Mahala Roberts have two children--the parents belong to Hutchechuppa and Kialigee respectively-- I don't [sic] the names of the children-- one is walking and the other is a baby yet a small child.
Q Were both of them born since May 25, 1901? A Yes sir. The oldest is a girl and I don't know the sex of the youngest. Both are living. Their post office is Indianola.

Thompson Fields and Susie Fields--he is of Okchiye or Fish Pond, I don't know which, and Susie belongs to Hutchechuppa; they have one <u>child</u> born since May 25,

Applications for Enrollment of Creek Newborn
Act of 1905 Volume XIII

1901, I don't know but I think the ~~gi~~ child is a girl. It is living, the child is not able to crawl but can sit up.

Earnest and Nicey <u>Gouge</u>, of Hickory Ground and Hillabee Towns respectively----had <u>two</u> children the last time I was at their house--both were born since May 25, don't know the names, <u>both boys</u> I think, both living, post office, Hanna.

Conn<u>ie Hawkin</u>s of Hillabee Town and Sybilla Hawkins of Fish Pong (?) I don't know her town' they had one child at the time I was at their house; I was at their house last summer 1904, don't know whether a boy or girl, born after May 25, 1901, it was a small child at that time, it is living. Post Office, Hanna.

Micco Emarthla, his white name is Neddie Walker, and Sallie Emarthla, both parents belong to Kialigee, have one child names <u>Walter</u> born since May 25, 1901, and living. Post Office, Indianola.

Wiley <u>Fish</u> of Tuckabatchee and Hettie Fish of Kialigee, post office, Mellette, Indian Territory have two children, but one is probably too old being about seven years old, but the field party last year failed to get that old one. The youngest was probably born since May 25, 1901. It is a boy and living. The oldest one is named <u>John</u> I don't know the other.

Noah <u>Roberts</u> of Kialigee and Hannah <u>Roberts</u> of Hillabee post office, Mellette, Indian Territory have one child name not known, born since May 25, 1901. Don't now the sex, it is living. Noah also has a step-son about seven years old that has never been enrolled named <u>Walter Starr</u>.

Questions addressed to both witnesses:
Q These statements which you have made are for the purpose of getting enrolled the new born children of parents belonging to the Snake Faction? A Yes sir.
Q Neither of you are related to them? A I Jimsey am related to Wiley Fish, who is the son of my brother and that's all.

Henry G. Hains, being duly sworn, on his oath, states that the above and foregoing is a true and correct transcript of his stenographic notes as taken in said cause on said date.

(signed) Henry G. Hains

Subscribed and sworn to before me this 11th day of May, 1905.

(Signed) Drennan C Skaggs
Notary Public.

I, Anna Garrigues, on oath state that I copied the above testimony from the original on the 18th day of July, 1906 and that it is a true and correct copy of same.

Anna Garrigues

Applications for Enrollment of Creek Newborn
Act of 1905 Volume XIII

Subscribed and sworn to before me this 18th day of July 1905.

                         Edw C Griesel
                         Notary Public.

DEPARTMENT OF THE INTERIOR,
COMMISSIONER TO THE FIVE CIVILIZED TRIBES.
DUSTIN, INDIAN TERRITORY,
APRIL 22, 1905.

In the matter of the application for the enrollment of certain new borns as citizens of the Creek Nation.

Alex Posey, being duly sworn, testified as follows:

By Commission:

Q: What is your name, age and post office address?
A: Alex Posey, 31 and Muskogee.
Q: Are you a citizen of the Creek Nation? A: Yes sir.
Q: Got any land, have you? A: Yes sir.
Q: You have been engaged recently in the field for the Dawes Commission securing evidence about Creek citizens or new borns? A: Yes sir.
Q: Have you a list of children for whom application could not be made and about whom you have succeeded in obtaining some information? A: Yes sir.
Q: You May state the conditions and the names of these children You[sic] desire to make application for them? A: Yes sir.
Q: Name them? A: Span Hopiye, Tuckabatchee, Jennie Hopiye (or Barnett), Tuckabatchee have a female child about two years old. Post Office, Wetumka, Indian Territory.
Jim Davis, Kialigee, has two new born children--one about two years old (boy); another (a girl) about one year old. Post Office, Mellette, Indian Territory.
Sam Butler, about three years old. Parents: Myron Butler U.S. Citizen and Lydia Fields, Quassarte No. 2. Post Office Dustin, Indian Territory.
Billy Barlow, Quassarte No. 2 and Lydia Fields, Quassarte No. 2 have a child about a year old. Post Office, Dustin, Indian Territory.
Q: This is the information you received from relatives right around Dustin, on April 22, 1905? A Yes sir.
Q: Were you informed that the parents of these children were unwilling to make application for their enrollment? A Yes sir.
Q: This was the only way that the rights of these children would be saved? A Yes, sir. I made every effort to obtain direct information from the parents but in every instance they refused to give their testimony.

Lona Merrick, being duly sworn, states that the above and foregoing is a true and correct transcript of her stenographic notes as taken in said cause on said date.

Applications for Enrollment of Creek Newborn
Act of 1905 Volume XIII

(Signed) Lona Merrick

Subscribed and sworn to before me this 9 day of May, 1905.

(Signed) Edw C Griesel
(SEAL) Notary Public.

I, Julia C. Laval on my oath state that the above and foregoing is a true and correct copy of the original.

Julia C. Laval

Subscribed and sworn to before me this 23 day of January 1907.

Edward Merrick
Notary Public.

NC-1017. OCH.
JCL.

DEPARTMENT OF THE INTERIOR, COMMISSIONER TO THE FIVE CIVILIZED TRIBES.

In the matter of the application for the enrollment of Johnnie Gray and Mandy Gray as citizens by blood of the Creek Nation.

DECISION.

The records in the possession of the Commissioner show that on April 19, 1905, application was made for the enrollment of certain children as citizens by blood of the Creek Nation, which said application embraced the names of Johnny Davis, and one other, children of Jim Davis. Further proceedings were had in said cause, April 22, 1905.

Said records further show that on May 29, 1905, application was made, in affidavit form for the enrollment of Johnnie Gray and Mandy Gray as citizens by blood of the Creek Nation. Supplemental affidavits were filed October 3, 1905. It appears from the record in these cases and the records in the possession of the Commissioner that said Johnny Davis, and one other, are the same persons for whom application was made, in affidavit form, as above stated. Said children will hereafter be known in this cause as Johnnie Gray and Mandy Gray.

The evidence shows that said Johnnie Gray and Mandy Gray, are the children of Nancy Gray and Jimmy Gray.

The evidence and the records in the possession of the Commissioner show that said Nancy Gray and said Jimmy Gray are identified as Nancy Starr and Nocus Elle, respectively, upon wa schedule of citizens by blood of the Creek Nation approved by the Secretary of the Interior, March 28, 1902, opposite numbers 6552 and 8243, respectively.

The evidence further shows that said Johnnie Gray was born April 2, 1902; that said Mandy Gray was born June 15, 1904; and that both of said children were living March 4, 1905.

Applications for Enrollment of Creek Newborn
Act of 1905   Volume XIII

It is, therefore, ordered and adjudged that the said Johnnie Gray and Mandy Gray are entitled to be enrolled as citizens by blood of the Creek Nation under the provisions of the Act of Congress approved March 3, 1905 (33 Stats. L. 1048) and the application for their enrollment as such is accordingly granted.

Tams Bixby   COMMISSIONER.

Muskogee, Indian Territory.
FEB 2- 1907

BIRTH AFFIDAVIT.

DEPARTMENT OF THE INTERIOR.
COMMISSION TO THE FIVE CIVILIZED TRIBES.

IN RE APPLICATION FOR ENROLLMENT, as a citizen of the Creek Nation, of Mandy Gray, born on the 15 day of June, 1904

Name of Father: Jimmy Gray   a citizen of the   Creek   Nation.
Kialigee Town
Name of Mother: Nancy Gray   a citizen of the   Creek   Nation.
Kialigee Town

Postoffice   Hanna, I.T.

AFFIDAVIT OF MOTHER.

UNITED STATES OF AMERICA, Indian Territory,
   Western   DISTRICT.

I, Nancy Gray, on oath state that I am about 25 years of age and a citizen by blood, of the Creek Nation; that I am the lawful wife of Jimmy Gray, who is a citizen, by blood of the Creek Nation; that a female child was born to me on 15 day of June, 1904, that said child has been named Mandy Gray, and ~~is now~~ was living. on March 4, 1905

                          her
                      Nancy x Gray

Witnesses To Mark: mark
  { DC Skaggs
    Alex Posey

Subscribed and sworn to before me this 25 day of May, 1905.

                      Drennan C Skaggs
                      Notary Public.

Applications for Enrollment of Creek Newborn
Act of 1905   Volume XIII

AFFIDAVIT OF ATTENDING PHYSICIAN OR MID-WIFE.

UNITED STATES OF AMERICA, Indian Territory, ⎱
    Western   DISTRICT.   ⎰

    I, Fannie Bear , a mid-wife , on oath state that I attended on Mrs. Nancy Gray , wife of Jimmy Gray on the 15 day of June , 1904 ; that there was born to her on said date a female child; that said child ~~is now~~ was living on March 4, 1905 and is said to have been named Mandy Gray

                                                                her
Witnesses To Mark: Fannie x Bear
  ⎧ DC Skaggs   mark
  ⎩ Alex Posey

    Subscribed and sworn to before me this 25 day of May , 1905.

                                        Drennan C Skaggs
                                        Notary Public.

BIRTH AFFIDAVIT.
DEPARTMENT OF THE INTERIOR.
COMMISSION TO THE FIVE CIVILIZED TRIBES.

    IN RE APPLICATION FOR ENROLLMENT, as a citizen of the Creek Nation, of Johnnie Gray , born on the 2 day of April , 1902

Name of Father: Jimmy Gray (Nocus Ela)   a citizen of the   Creek   Nation.
Kialigee Town
Name of Mother: Nancy Gray (nee Starr)   a citizen of the   Creek   Nation.
Kialigee Town
                          Postoffice   Hanna, I.T.

AFFIDAVIT OF MOTHER.

UNITED STATES OF AMERICA, Indian Territory, ⎱
    Western   DISTRICT.   ⎰

    I, Nancy Gray , on oath state that I am about 25 years of age and a citizen by blood , of the Creek Nation; that I am the lawful wife of Jimmy Gray , who is a citizen, by blood of the Creek Nation; that a male child was born to me on 2 day of April , 1902 , that said child has been named Johnnie Gray , and ~~is now~~ was living. on March 4, 1905
                                        her
                                Nancy x Gray
                                   mark

Applications for Enrollment of Creek Newborn
Act of 1905   Volume XIII

Witnesses To Mark:
{ DC Skaggs
{ Alex Posey

Subscribed and sworn to before me this   25 day of May , 1905.

Drennan C Skaggs
Notary Public.

AFFIDAVIT OF ATTENDING PHYSICIAN OR MID-WIFE.

UNITED STATES OF AMERICA, Indian Territory,
   Western   DISTRICT.

my wife
I, Jimmy Gray , a (blank) , on oath state that I attended on ^ Mrs. Nancy Gray, wife of *(blank)* on the 2 day of April , 1902 ; that there was born to her on said date a   male   child; that said child is now was living on March 4, 1905 and is said to have been named Johnnie Gray
                                    his
                              Johnny x Gray
Witnesses To Mark: mark
{ DC Skaggs
{ Alex Posey

Subscribed and sworn to before me this   25 day of May , 1905.

Drennan C Skaggs
Notary Public.

BIRTH AFFIDAVIT.

DEPARTMENT OF THE INTERIOR.
COMMISSION TO THE FIVE CIVILIZED TRIBES.

IN RE APPLICATION FOR ENROLLMENT, as a citizen of the Creek Nation, of Johnnie Gray, born on the 2" day of April , 1902

Name of Father: Jimmie Gray   a citizen of the   Creek   Nation.
Kialigee Town
Name of Mother: Nancy Gray   a citizen of the   Creek   Nation.
Kialigee Town
                         Postoffice   Hanna, Ind. Terr.

Applications for Enrollment of Creek Newborn
Act of 1905   Volume XIII

AFFIDAVIT OF ATTENDING PHYSICIAN OR MID-WIFE.

UNITED STATES OF AMERICA, Indian Territory,
Western   DISTRICT.

we are personally acquainted with We, the undersigned , a—, on oath state that I attended on Mrs. Nancy Gray , wife of Jimmie Gray on the day of , 1—; that there was born to her on April 2, 1902 said date a male child; that said child was living March 4, 1905, and is said to have been named Johnnie Gray

                        her
                    x Syokigee

Witnesses To Mark: mark
  { DC Skaggs   his
  { Alex Posey   George x Fields
                                      mark

Subscribed and sworn to before me 28   day of Sept. , 1905.

                                 Drennan C Skaggs
                                      Notary Public.

BIRTH AFFIDAVIT.

DEPARTMENT OF THE INTERIOR.
COMMISSION TO THE FIVE CIVILIZED TRIBES.

IN RE APPLICATION FOR ENROLLMENT, as a citizen of the Creek Nation, of Mandy Gray, born on the 15" day of June , 1904

Name of Father: Jimmie Gray   a citizen of the   Creek   Nation.
Kialigee
Name of Mother: Nancy Gray   a citizen of the   Creek   Nation.
Kialigee
                          Postoffice   Hanna, Ind. Terr.

AFFIDAVIT OF ATTENDING PHYSICIAN OR MID-WIFE.

UNITED STATES OF AMERICA, Indian Territory,
Western   DISTRICT.

we are personally acquainted with We, the undersigned   , a—, on oath state that I attended on Mrs. Nancy Gray , wife of   Jimmie Gray on the day of , 1—; that there was born to her on said date a female child; that said child was living March 4, 1905, and is said to have been named Mandy Gray

                        her
                    x Syokigee
                    mark

Applications for Enrollment of Creek Newborn
Act of 1905 Volume XIII

Witnesses To Mark:
   { DC Skaggs
    Alex Posey   his
                                  George x Fields
                                        mark
    Subscribed and sworn to before me 28 day of Sept. , 1905.

                                       Drennan C Skaggs
                                           Notary Public.

(Mandy Gray's Birth Affidavit given again.)

(Johnnie Gray's Birth Affidavit given again.)

(Disinterested Witnesses' Affidavit for Johnnie Gray given again.)

(Disinterested Witnesses' Affidavit for Mandy Gray given again.)

NC 1017.
                        Eufaula, Indian Territory, October 2, 1905.

Commissioner to the Five Civilized Tribes,
    Muskogee, Indian Territory.

Sir:

    There is enclosed herewith supplemental proof in the matter of the application for the eneollment[sic] of Johnnie and Mandy Gray, as citizens by blood of the Creek Nation, together with other papers in connection with said case.

                                   Respectfully,
                                   Alex Posey

NC 1017.
                        Muskogee, Indian Territory, October 23, 1905.

Nancy Gray,
    Care Jimmie Gray (or Nocus Elle),
        Hanna, Indian Territory.

Dear Madam:

Applications for Enrollment of Creek Newborn
Act of 1905   Volume XIII

    In the matter of the application for the enrollment of your minor children, Johnnie Gray, born April 2, 1902, and Mandy Gray, born June 15, 1904, as citizens by blood of the Creek Nation, this office is unable to identify you on its roll of citizens by blood of the Creek Nation; you are requested to state your maiden name, the names of your parents, the Creek Indian town to which you belong and your roll number as the same appears on your deeds and allotment certificate.

    Your husband, Jimmie Gray, is identified on the final roll of citizens by blood of the Creek Nation, as Nocus Elle; if this is his correct name and you are his lawful wife, it necessarily follows that your correct surname is Elle and that it is also the correct name of your said children, they having been born in lawful wedlock.

                  Respectfully,

                                Commissioner.

NC 1017.

                    Muskogee, Indian Territory, Dec. 18, 1905.

Nancy Gray,
    Care Jimmie Gray (or Nocus Elle),
        Hanna, Indian Territory.

Dear Madam:

    In the matter of the application for the enrollment of your minor children, Johnnie Gray, born April 2, 1902, and Mandy Gray, born June 15, 1904, as citizens by blood of the Creek Nation, this office is unable to identify you on its roll of citizens by blood of the Creek Nation; you are requested to state your maiden name, the names of your parents, the Creek Indian town to which you belong and your roll number as the same appears on your deeds and allotment certificate.

    Your husband, Jimmie Gray, is identified on the final roll of citizens by blood of the Creek Nation, as Nocus Elle.

    If you are, as stated, his lawful wife, it necessarily follow that your name and the names of said children, they having been born in lawful wedlock, are Elle and not Gray.

    There are herewith enclosed blank forms of birth affidavit which you are requested to execute, being careful to give your correct name, the correct name of your said husband, and the correct names of your said children and return to this office in the enclosed envelope.

    This matter should receive your prompt attention.

                  Respectfully,

                                Commissioner.

Applications for Enrollment of Creek Newborn
Act of 1905   Volume XIII

NC 1017.

Muskogee, Indian Territory, March 18, 1907.

Nancy Gray,
  c/o Jimmy Gray,
    Hanna, Indian Territory.

Dear Madam:

You are hereby advised that the Secretary of the Interior under date of March 4, 1907, approved the enrollment of your minor children, Johnnie and Mandy Gray, as citizens by blood of the Creek Nation, and that the names of said children appear upon the roll of new born citizens by blood, enrolled under the act of Congress approved March 3, 1905, as numbers 1288 and 1289, respectively.

These children are now entitled to allotment and application therefor should be made without delay at the Creek Land Office, Muskogee, Indian Territory.

                    Respectfully,
                              Commissioner.

BIRTH AFFIDAVIT.

DEPARTMENT OF THE INTERIOR.
COMMISSION TO THE FIVE CIVILIZED TRIBES.

IN RE APPLICATION FOR ENROLLMENT, as a citizen of the Creek Nation, of Willie B. Ryal, born on the 7 day of Sept, 1901

Name of Father: L.B. Ryal	a citizen of the U.S.	Nation.
Name of Mother: Annie Ryal	a citizen of the Creek	Nation.
(Tulwathlocco)		

                    Postoffice   ~~Sen~~ Henryetta

Applications for Enrollment of Creek Newborn
Act of 1905   Volume XIII

Child Present - Gr.

AFFIDAVIT OF MOTHER.

UNITED STATES OF AMERICA, Indian Territory,
Western   DISTRICT.

I, Annie Ryal , on oath state that I am 40 years of age and a citizen by blood , of the Creek   Nation; that I am the lawful wife of L. B. Ryal , who is a citizen, by ----- of the U. S. Nation; that a male   child was born to me on 7 day of Sept , 1901 , that said child has been named Willie B. Ryal , and was living March 4, 1905.

Annie Ryal

Witnesses To Mark: (Seal)

Subscribed and sworn to before me this 11 day of April , 1905.

Edw C Griesel
Notary Public.

BIRTH AFFIDAVIT.

DEPARTMENT OF THE INTERIOR.
COMMISSION TO THE FIVE CIVILIZED TRIBES.

IN RE APPLICATION FOR ENROLLMENT, as a citizen of the Creek Nation, of Willie Ryal , born on the 9 day of Sep, 1901

	non	
Name of Father: L.B. Ryal	a citizen of the	Nation.
Name of Mother: Annie Ryal	a citizen of the Creek	Nation.
Tulwa Thlocco Town		

Postoffice   Henryetta I.T.

AFFIDAVIT OF MOTHER.

UNITED STATES OF AMERICA, Indian Territory,
Western   DISTRICT.

I, Annie Ryal , on oath state that I am 40 years of age and a citizen by Blood , of the Creek   Nation; that I am the lawful wife of ~~Willie Ryal~~ L. B. Ryal , who is a citizen, by marriage of the Creek   Nation; that a male   child was born to me on 9 day of September , 1901 , that said child has been named Willie Ryal , and was living March 4, 1905.

Annie Ryal

Witnesses To Mark:

Applications for Enrollment of Creek Newborn
Act of 1905 Volume XIII

Subscribed and sworn to before me this 1 day of May, 1905.

My Commission expires 11/17/06 W.H. Harrison
                                  Notary Public.

AFFIDAVIT OF ATTENDING PHYSICIAN OR MID-WIFE.

UNITED STATES OF AMERICA, Indian Territory,
  Western   DISTRICT.

I, Emerline Lucus, a midwife, on oath state that I attended on Mrs. Annie Ryal, wife of L.B. Ryal on the 9 day of Sep, 1901; that there was born to her on said date a male child; that said child was living March 4, 1905, and is said to have been named Willie Ryal   her
                                                  Emerline x Lucus
Witnesses To Mark: mark
  { (Illegible) Smith
  { Wilson Harrison

Subscribed and sworn to before me this 1 day of May, 1905.

My Commission expires 11/17/06 W.H. Harrison
                                  Notary Public.

BIRTH AFFIDAVIT.

DEPARTMENT OF THE INTERIOR.
COMMISSION TO THE FIVE CIVILIZED TRIBES.

IN RE APPLICATION FOR ENROLLMENT, as a citizen of the Creek Nation, of Mary Ryal, born on the 1 day of Jan, 1904

Name of Father: L.B. Ryal   a citizen of the U.S.   Nation.
Name of Mother: Annie "   a citizen of the Creek   Nation.

                    Postoffice   Henryetta

Child Present - Gr.
AFFIDAVIT OF MOTHER.

UNITED STATES OF AMERICA, Indian Territory,
  Western   DISTRICT.

I, Annie Ryal, on oath state that I am 40 years of age and a citizen by blood, of the Creek Nation; that I am the lawful wife of L. B. Ryal, who is a citizen, by -----

Applications for Enrollment of Creek Newborn
Act of 1905 Volume XIII

of the U. S. Nation; that a female child was born to me on 1 day of Jan , 1904 , that said child has been named Mary Ryal , and ~~was living March 4, 1905~~. died Jan 1-1904

Annie Ryal

Witnesses To Mark: (Seal)

{

Subscribed and sworn to before me this 1 day of Jan , 1905.

Edw C Griesel
Notary Public.

NC 1018   JLD
DEPARTMENT OF THE INTERIOR,
COMMISSIONER TO THE FIVE CIVILIZED TRIBES.

In the matter of the application for the enrollment of Mary Ryal, deceased, as a citizen by blood of the Creek Nation.

. . . .

STATEMENT AND ORDER.

The record in this case shows that on April 13, 1905, application was made in affidavit form, for the enrollment of Mary Ryal, deceased, as a citizen by blood of the Creek Nation, under the provisions of the act of Congress approved March 3, 1905.

It appears from the affidavit filed in this matter that said Mary Ryal, deceased, was born January 1, 1904 and died January 1, 1904.

The Act of Congress approved March 3, 1905, (33 Stats. 1048) provides:

"That the Commission to the Five Civilized Tribes is authorized for sixty days after the date of the approval of this act to receive and consider applications for enrollment, of children, <u>born subsequent to May twenty-fifth, nineteen hundred and one, and prior to March fourth, nineteen hundred and five, and living on said latter date,</u> to citizens of the Creek tribe of Indians whose enrollment has been approved by the Secretary of the Interior prior to the approval of this act; and to enroll and make allotments to such children."

It is, therefore, ordered that the application for the enrollment of said Mary Ryal, deceased, as a citizen by blood of the Creek Nation, be, and the same is, hereby dismissed.

Tams Bixby   Commissioner.

Muskogee, Indian Territory.
JAN 4- 1907

Applications for Enrollment of Creek Newborn
Act of 1905   Volume XIII

C 1019

(Copy)   Cr 2449-B
DEPARTMENT OF THE INTERIOR,
COMMISSION TO THE FIVE CIVILIZED TRIBES.
Near Weleetka, I. T. April 25, 1905.

In the matter of the application for new born children concerning whose enrollment no affidavits could be obtained in time.

James Spaniard, being duly sworn, testified as follows through Alex Posey, Official Interpreter.

Examination by the Commission:
Q What is your name? A James Spaniard.
Q How old are you? A About 42.
Q What is your postoffice address? A Carson.

✓ Statement: Tommie Lott of Cheyarhar Town and Tena Lott of Tulmochuss Town, have two children both girls, the oldest Lucy, and the other Jennie. They are both living. I don't know their ages exactly, but they are new borns. Their post office is Carson

Ceasar Johnson, of Tookpufka and Eliza John, probably of Eufaula Canadian, have two children. I don't know their names or ages, but they are new borns. Both are living and boys. Their Post office is Carson, Indian Territory and I think the oldest is names Wesley and the youngest Hotulke.

Boley and Kizzie----of Thlewarthle and Tulmochuss respectively--I just know they have a child, whose name or sex I am unfamiliar with. Don't know it age. It's a young child something over a year old I think.

Dave Hullie of Tookpufka and Eliza Hullie, deceased, of Kialigee, have a boy about three or under and living, names Tarpie. Their post office is Carson.

Thomas Wilson of Hickory Ground and Bettie Wilson oft Tulmochuss have two children both girls. The oldest is named Wisey and the youngest Minnie. Wisey is three or nearly so and Minnie is about two years old. Both living. Post office, Carson.

Timmie Stidham of Cheyarhar and Liza Stidham of Weogufky have two children. The oldest a girl named Mattie, and the youngest a boy, don't know the name. Both living, the youngest about a year old and the other over two years old. Post Office, Carson.

Henry G. Hains, being duly sworn, on his oath, states that the above and foregoing is a true and correct transcript of his stenographic notes as taken in said cause on said date.

Applications for Enrollment of Creek Newborn
Act of 1905 Volume XIII

(signed) HENRY G. HAINS.

Subscribed and sworn to before me this 10th day of May, 1905.

(SEAL)

(signed) DRENNAN C. SKAGGS
Notary Public.

C 1019

(Copy)   Cr 2449-B

DEPARTMENT OF THE INTERIOR,
COMMISSION TO THE FIVE CIVILIZED TRIBES.
Near Weleetka, I. T. April 25, 1905.

In the matter of the application for new born children concerning whose enrollment no affidavits could be obtained in time.

James Spaniard, being duly sworn, testified as follows through Alex Posey, Official Interpreter.

Examination by the Commission:
Q What is your name? A James Spaniard.
Q How old are you? A About 42.
Q What is your postoffice address? A Carson.

✓ Statement: Tommie Lott of Cheyarhar Town and Tena Lott of Tulmochuss Town, have two children both girls, the oldest Lucy, and the other Jennie. They are both living. I don't know their ages exactly, but they are new borns. Their post office is Carson

Ceasar Johnson, of Tookpufka and Eliza John[sic], probably of Eufaula Canadian, have two children. I don't know their names or ages, but they are new borns. Both are living and boys. Their Post office is Carson, Indian Territory and I think the oldest is names Wesley and the youngest Hotulke.

Boley and Kizzie----of Thlewarthle and Tulmochuss respectively--I just know they have a child, whose name or sex I am unfamiliar with. Don't know its age. It's a young child something over a year old I think.

Dave Hullie of Tookpufka and Eliza Hullie, deceased, of Kialigee, have a boy about three or under and living, names Tarpie. Their post office is Carson.

Thomas Wilson of Hickory Ground and Bettie Wilson oft Tulmochuss have two children both girls. The oldest is named Wisey and the youngest Minnie. Wisey is three or nearly so and Minnie is about two years old. Both living. Post office, Carson.

Applications for Enrollment of Creek Newborn
Act of 1905 Volume XIII

Timmie Stidham of Cheyarhar and Liza Stidham of Weogufky have two children. The oldest a girl named Mattie, and the youngest a boy, don't know the name. Both living, the youngest about a year old and the other over two years old. Post Office, Carson.

Henry G. Hains, being duly sworn, on his oath, states that the above and foregoing is a true and correct transcript of his stenographic notes as taken in said cause on said date.

(signed) HENRY G. HAINS.

Subscribed and sworn to before me this 10th day of May, 1905.

(signed) DRENNAN C. SKAGGS
(SEAL) Notary Public.

INDIAN TERRITORY, Western District.

I, J. Y. Miller, a stenographer in the office of the Commissioner to the Five Civilized Tribes, do hereby certify that the above and foregoing is a true and correct copy of its original to be found in the records of the aforesaid office.

JY Miller

Sworn to and subscribed before
me this the 18th day of
July, 1905.

Edw C Griesel
Notary Public.

N.C. 1019
DEPARTMENT OF THE INTERIOR,
COMMISSIONER TO THE FIVE CIVILIZED TRIBES.
Muskogee, Indian Territory, February 16, 1906.

In the matter of the application for the enrollment of Lucy and Jennie Lott as citizens by blood of the Creek Nation.

THOMAS LOTT, being duly sworn, testified as follows through Alex Posey official interpreter.

Q What is your name? A Thomas Lott.
Q What is your age? A About forty four.
Q What is your post office address? A Carson.
Q Are you a citizen of the Creek Nation? A Yes, sir.
Q Have you two new born children? A Yes, sir.
Q What are their names? A Jennie and Lucy.
Q Are they living or dead[sic] A Both living.

Applications for Enrollment of Creek Newborn
Act of 1905   Volume XIII

Q Which one is older? A Lucy.
Q How old is she? A A little over three years
Q How old is the other one? A Two years old.
Q Do you know the date of their birth? The day, month and year? A Lucy was born in December, don't know the year.
Q We have an affidavit executed by you in which you state that Lucy was born December 10, 1901, a little over five years ago? A Yes, that's right.
Q Then your child Lucy is five instead of three; between 4 and 5[sic] A Yes, sir.
Q We have your affidavit that Jennie was born March 1, 1903, is that correct? A Yes, sir.
Q That would make her about three years old? A Yes, sir. I remember now that I gave you those dates and they are correct

I, Anna Garrigues, on oath state that the above and foregoing is a true and correct transcript of my stenographic notes as taken in said cause on said date.

                                        Anna Garrigues
Subscribed and sworn to before me
this 20 day of February 1906.
                                        J McDermott
                                        Notary Public.

Indian Territory)
)
Western District) SS

We, the undersigned, on oath state that we are personally acquainted with Lena Lott   wife of   Thomas Lott   and that on or about the --- day of Dec. 1901, a female   child was born to them and has been named   Lucy Lott ; that said child was living March 4, 1905.

We further state that we have no interest in the above case.

                                        W.H. Oxford
                                            her
                                        Hannah x Jones
Witnesses to mark: mark
HG Hains
Alex Posey

Subscribed and sworn to before me this 16 day of Feb 1906.

                                        HGHains
                                        Notary Public.

Applications for Enrollment of Creek Newborn
Act of 1905   Volume XIII

(The above Disinterested Witnesses' Affidavit given again.)

BIRTH AFFIDAVIT.

DEPARTMENT OF THE INTERIOR.
COMMISSION TO THE FIVE CIVILIZED TRIBES.

IN RE APPLICATION FOR ENROLLMENT, as a citizen of the Creek Nation, of Jennie Lott, born on the 1 day of March, 1903

Name of Father: Tommie Lott   a citizen of the   Creek   Nation.
 Cheyaha Town
Name of Mother: Lena Lott   a citizen of the   Creek   Nation.
 Tulcachussee
                        Postoffice   Carson, I.T.

AFFIDAVIT OF MOTHER.

UNITED STATES OF AMERICA, Indian Territory, ⎱
    Western   DISTRICT.   ⎰

I, Lena Lott, on oath state that I am about 38 years of age and a citizen by blood, of the Creek Nation; that I am the lawful wife of Tommie Lott, who is a citizen, by blood of the Creek Nation; that a female child was born to me on 1st day of March, 1903, that said child has been named Jennie Lott, and is now living. and was living March 4, 1905.
                                    her
                            Lena x Lott
Witnesses To Mark: mark
 ⎰ DC Skaggs
 ⎱ Alex Posey

Subscribed and sworn to before me this 10 day of June, 1905.

                        Drennan C Skaggs
                            Notary Public.

Applications for Enrollment of Creek Newborn
Act of 1905   Volume XIII

AFFIDAVIT OF ATTENDING PHYSICIAN OR MID-WIFE.

UNITED STATES OF AMERICA, Indian Territory, }
     Western   DISTRICT.

Child present.

I, Tommie Lott , a (blank) , on oath state that I attended on ^ Mrs. Lena Lott , wife of *(blank)* on the 1 day of March , 1903 ; that there was born to her on said date a   female   child; that said child is now living and was living March 4, 1905 and is said to have been named Jennie Lott

(^ my wife)

                                    his
                            Tommie x Lott
Witnesses To Mark: mark
  { DC Skaggs
  { Alex Posey

Subscribed and sworn to before me this 9 day of   June   , 1905.

                            Drennan C Skaggs
                            Notary Public.

BIRTH AFFIDAVIT.

DEPARTMENT OF THE INTERIOR.
COMMISSION TO THE FIVE CIVILIZED TRIBES.

IN RE APPLICATION FOR ENROLLMENT, as a citizen of the Creek Nation, of Lucy Lott , born on the 10 day of December , 1901

Name of Father: Tommie Lott   a citizen of the   Creek   Nation.
Name of Mother: Lena Lott   a citizen of the   Creek   Nation.

                Postoffice   Carson, I.T.

AFFIDAVIT OF MOTHER.

UNITED STATES OF AMERICA, Indian Territory, }
     Western   DISTRICT.

I, Lena Lott , on oath state that I am   about 38   years of age and a citizen by blood , of the Creek   Nation; that I am the lawful wife of Tommie Lott , who is a citizen, by blood of the Creek   Nation; that a   female   child was born to me on   10" day of December , 1901 , that said child has been named Lucy Lott , and was living March 4, 1905.

                                    her
                            Lena x Lott
Witnesses To Mark: mark
  { DC Skaggs
  { Alex Posey

Applications for Enrollment of Creek Newborn
Act of 1905   Volume XIII

Subscribed and sworn to before me this 10 day of June , 1905.

         Drennan C Skaggs
         Notary Public.

AFFIDAVIT OF ATTENDING PHYSICIAN OR MID-WIFE.

UNITED STATES OF AMERICA, Indian Territory,
  Western   **DISTRICT.**

                  my wife
 I, Tommie Lott , a *(blank)* , on oath state that I attended on ^ Mrs. Lena Lott , wife of *(blank)* on the 10" day of December , 1901 ; that there was born to her on said date a   female   child; that said child was living March 4, 1905 and is said to have been named Lucy Lott

             his
        Tommie x Lott
Witnesses To Mark: mark
 { DC Skaggs
   Alex Posey

Subscribed and sworn to before me this 9 day of June , 1905.

         Drennan C Skaggs
         Notary Public.

         Near Weleetka I T April 25, 1905

In the matter of the application for new born children concerning whose enrollment no affidavits could be obtained.

James Spaniard being duly sworn testified as follows through Alex Posey official interpreter

Q What is your name? A James Spaniard
Q How old are you? A About 42
Q What is your post office address? A Carson

Statement   Tommie Lott of Cheyarhar town and Tena Lott of Tulmochuss town, have two children both girls, the oldest Lucy and the other Jennie. They are both living. I dont[sic] know their ages exactly but they are new borns. Their post office is Carson.

Applications for Enrollment of Creek Newborn
Act of 1905   Volume XIII

NC 1019.

Muskogee, Indian Territory, October 23, 1905

Lena Lott,
    Care Thomas Lott,
        Carson, Indian Territory.

Dear Madam:

    In the matter of the application for the enrollment of your minor children, Lucy Lott, born December 10, 1901, and Jennie Lott, born March 1, 1903, as citizens by blood of the Creek Nation, this office desires the affidavits of two disinterested witnesses relative to the birth of each child. Said affidavits must set forth the names of said children, the dates of their birth, the names of their parents and whether or not they were living on March 4, 1905.

                Respectfully,
                            Commissioner.

NC 1019.

Muskogee, Indian Territory, December 19, 1905

Lena Lott,
    Care of Thomas Lot[sic],
        Carson, Indian Territory.

Dear Madam:

    In the matter of the application for the enrollment of your minor children, Lucy Lott, born December 10, 1901, and Jennie Lott, born March 1, 1903, as citizens by blood of the Creek Nation, this office desires the affidavit of the physician or midwife in attendance at the birth of said children, and blanks for that purpose are herewith enclosed. In the event there was no midwife or physician present at the birth of said children, it will be necessary for you to furnish this office with the affidavits of two disinterested persons relative to the birth of each of said children. Said affidavits must set forth the names of the children, the names of their parents, the dates of the births of said children, and whether or not they were living March 4, 1905, and blanks for that purpose are herewith enclosed.

    This matter should receive your prompt attention.

                Respectfully,
                            Commissioner.

Applications for Enrollment of Creek Newborn
Act of 1905 Volume XIII

#2 C 1020

(Copy) Cr 2449-B
DEPARTMENT OF THE INTERIOR,
COMMISSION TO THE FIVE CIVILIZED TRIBES.
Near Weleetka, I. T. April 25, 1905.

In the matter of the application for new born children concerning whose enrollment no affidavits could be obtained in time.

James Spaniard, being duly sworn, testified as follows through Alex Posey, Official Interpreter.

Examination by the Commission:
Q What is your name? A James Spaniard.
Q How old are you? A About 42.
Q What is your postoffice address? A Carson.

Statement: Tommie Lott of Cheyarhar Town and Tena Lott of Tulmochuss Town, have two children both girls, the oldest Lucy, and the other Jennie. They are both living. I don't know their ages exactly, but they are new borns. Their post office is Carson

✓Coasar[sic] Johnson, of Tookpufka and Eliza John[sic], probably of Eufaula Canadian, have two children. I don't know their names or ages, but they are new borns. Both are living and boys. Their Post office is Carson, Indian Territory and I think the oldest is names Wesley and the youngest Hotulke.

Boley and Kizzie----of Thlewarthle and Tulmochuss respectively--I just know they have a child, whose name or sex I am unfamiliar with. Don't know its age. It's a young child something over a year old I think.

Dave Hullie of Tookpufka and Eliza Hullie, deceased, of Kialigee, have a boy about three or under and living, names Tarpie. Their post office is Carson.

Thomas Wilson of Hickory Ground and Bettie Wilson oft Tulmochuss have two children both girls. The oldest is named Wisey and the youngest Minnie. Wisey is three or nearly so and Minnie is about two years old. Both living. Post office, Carson.

Timmie Stidham of Cheyarhar and Liza Stidham of Weogufky have two children. The oldest a girl named Mattie, and the youngest a boy, don't know the name. Both living, the youngest about a year old and the other over two years old. Post Office, Carson.

Henry G. Hains, being duly sworn, on his oath, states that the above and foregoing is a true and correct transcript of his stenographic notes as taken in said cause on said date.

Applications for Enrollment of Creek Newborn
Act of 1905 Volume XIII

(signed) HENRY G. HAINS.

Subscribed and sworn to before me this 10th day of May, 1905.

(signed) DRENNAN C. SKAGGS
(SEAL) Notary Public.

INDIAN TERRITORY, Western District.

I, J. Y. Miller, a stenographer in the office of the Commissioner to the Five Civilized Tribes, do hereby certify that the above and foregoing is a true and correct copy of its original to be found in the records of the aforesaid office.

JY Miller

Sworn to and subscribed before
me this the 18th day of
July, 1905.

Edw C Griesel
Notary Public.

DEPARTMENT OF THE INTERIOR,
COMMISSIONER TO THE FIVE CIVILIZED TRIBES.
Carson, I. T., June 10, 1905.

In the matter of the application for the enrollment of Wesley Johnson as a citizen by blood of the Creek Nation.

ELIZA JOHNSON, being duly sworn, testified as follows:

Through Alex Posey Official Interpreter:

BY COMMISSION:
Q What is your name? A Eliza Johnson.
Q How old are you? A Twenty-nine.
Q What is your post office address? A Carson.
Q Are you a citizen of the Creek Nation? A Yes, sir.
Q To what town do you belong? A Eufaula Deep Fork.
Q Have you a child named Wesley Johnson? A Yes, sir.
Q What is the name of the child's father? A Jim Pigeon, but the child was named after its step-father, Ceasar Johnson.
Q When was the child born? A It was born in August, about the time the Creek Council met at Okmulgee, and is over five years old.
Q Have you made application for the enrollment of Wesley? A I made application for the child before the Commission at Okmulgee and he has been allotted land.
Q Have you received a certificate and deed to the child's allotment? A Yes, sir.

Applications for Enrollment of Creek Newborn
Act of 1905   Volume XIII

Q Have you that certificate now? A I deposited the certificate at Wetumka for safe-keeping.

---oooOOOooo---

    I, D. C. Skaggs, on oath state that the above and foregoing is a full and true transcript of my stenographic notes as taken in said cause on said date.

    Subscribed and sworn to before me this___day of_____1905.

Notary Public.

BIRTH AFFIDAVIT.

DEPARTMENT OF THE INTERIOR.
COMMISSION TO THE FIVE CIVILIZED TRIBES.

IN RE APPLICATION FOR ENROLLMENT, as a citizen of the Creek Nation, of Hotulke Johnson, born on the 7 day of August, 1902

Name of Father: Ceasar Johnson	a citizen of the Creek	Nation.
(Illegible) Town		
Name of Mother: Eliza Johnson	a citizen of the Creek	Nation.
Eufaula Deep Fork		

                        Postoffice   Carson, Ind. Terr.

AFFIDAVIT OF MOTHER.   Child present.

UNITED STATES OF AMERICA, Indian Territory, ⎫
    Western   DISTRICT.   ⎭

    I, Eliza Johnson, on oath state that I am 29 years of age and a citizen by blood, of the Creek Nation; that I am the lawful wife of Ceasar Johnson, who is a citizen, by blood of the Creek Nation; that a male child was born to me on 7 day of August, 1902, that said child has been named Hotulke Johnson, and is now living. and was living March 4, 1905.

her
Eliza x Johnson
mark

Witnesses To Mark:
  { DC Skaggs
    Alex Posey

    Subscribed and sworn to before me this 10 day of June, 1905.

Drennan C Skaggs
Notary Public.

Applications for Enrollment of Creek Newborn
Act of 1905   Volume XIII

AFFIDAVIT OF ATTENDING PHYSICIAN OR MID-WIFE.

UNITED STATES OF AMERICA, Indian Territory, }
  Western   DISTRICT.

I, Leah Tiger, a mid-wife, on oath state that I attended on Mrs. Eliza Johnson, wife of Ceasar Johnson on the 7 day of August, 1902; that there was born to her on said date a male child; that said child is now living and was living on March 4, 1905, and is said to have been named Hotulke Johnson

                                                  her
Witnesses To Mark: Leah x Tiger
  { DC Skaggs   mark
  { Alex Posey

Subscribed and sworn to before me this 10 day of June, 1905.

                                          Drennan C Skaggs
                                               Notary Public.

UNITED STATES OF AMERICA,)
)
WESTERN JUDICIAL DISTRICT,) ss.
)
INDIAN TERRITORY.   )

C. R. Bruster being first duly sworn says that he is personally acquainted with the minor child, Lucreesey Rentie, and the childs[sic] parents, Louis Rentie, the father, and Peggie Rentie, the mother, and I am entirely a disinterested person and that I know of my own knowledge that said child, Lucreesey Rentie, was born November 9th, 1903, and that said child was living March 4th, 1905 and is still living.

                                          CR Bruster

Subscribed and sworn to before me this 28th day of October, 1905.

                                          Harry E. Breese
                                              Notary Public.
My commission expires July 7-1907.

Applications for Enrollment of Creek Newborn
Act of 1905 Volume XIII

NC. 1022

Muskogee, Indian Territory, October 23, 1905.

Peggie Rentie,
    Care Lewis Rentie,
        Henryetta, Indian Territory.

Dear Madam:

    In the matter of the application for the enrollment of your minor child, Lucreesey Rentie, born November 9, 1903, this office desires the affidavits of two disinterested witnesses relative to her birth. Said affidavits must set forth said child's name, the date of her birth, the names of her parents and whether or not she was living on March 4, 1905.

                Respectfully,

                            Commissioner.

UNITED STATES OF AMERICA,)
)
WESTERN JUDICIAL DISTRICT,) ss.
)
INDIAN TERRITORY.   )

    E.A. Cobbs being first duly sworn says that he is personally acquainted with the minor child, Lucreesey Rentie, and the childs[sic] parents, Louis Rentie, the father, and Peggie Rentie, the mother, and I am entirely a disinterested person and that I know of my own knowledge that said child, Lucreesey Rentie, was born November 9th, 1903, and that said child was living March 4th, 1905 and is still living.

                              E. A. Cobbs

Subscribed and sworn to before me this 28th day of October, 1905.

                              Harry E. Breese
                              Notary Public.

My commission expires July 7-1907.

Applications for Enrollment of Creek Newborn
Act of 1905   Volume XIII

BIRTH AFFIDAVIT.

DEPARTMENT OF THE INTERIOR.
COMMISSION TO THE FIVE CIVILIZED TRIBES.

IN RE APPLICATION FOR ENROLLMENT, as a citizen of the Creek Nation, of Lucreesey Rentie, born on the 9 day of November, 1903

Name of Father: Lewis Rentie   a citizen of the   Creek   Nation.
Canadian Colored Town
Name of Mother: Peggie Rentie (nee Harry)   a citizen of the   Creek   Nation.
Tuskegee Town

                       Postoffice   Henryetta, I.T.

                                        Child present.

AFFIDAVIT OF MOTHER.

UNITED STATES OF AMERICA, Indian Territory,
   Western   DISTRICT.

     I, Peggie Rentie, on oath state that I am 25 years of age and a citizen by adoption, of the Creek Nation; that I am the lawful wife of Lewis Rentie, who is a citizen, by adoption of the Creek Nation; that a female child was born to me on 9 day of November, 1903, that said child has been named Lucreesey Rentie, and was living March 4, 1905.

                                     Peggie Rentie

Witnesses To Mark:

     Subscribed and sworn to before me this 11 day of April, 1905.

                                     Drennan C Skaggs
                                        Notary Public.

AFFIDAVIT OF ATTENDING PHYSICIAN OR MID-WIFE.

UNITED STATES OF AMERICA, Indian Territory,
   Western   DISTRICT.

     I, Martha Grisholm, a mid wife, on oath state that I attended on Mrs. Peggie Rentie, wife of Lewis Rentie ~~on the day of , 1~~; that there was born to her on said date a female child; that said child was living March 4, 1905, and is said to have been named Lucreesey Rentie
                                           her
                                    Martha x Grisholm
Witnesses To Mark: mark
    DC Skaggs
    Lewis Rentie

Applications for Enrollment of Creek Newborn
Act of 1905   Volume XIII

Subscribed and sworn to before me this 11 day of April , 1905.

>Drennan C Skaggs
>Notary Public.

N.C. 1023.

>DEPARTMENT OF THE INTERIOR,
>COMMISSIONER TO THE FIVE CIVILIZED TRIBES.
>CALVIN, I. T., SEPTEMBER 4, 1906.

In the matter of the application for the enrollment of Tarpie Herrod as a citizen by blood of the Creek Nation.

>SAM HELLETT being duly sworn testified as follows:
>Through Alex Posey Official Interpreter.

BY THE COMMISSIONER:

Q What is your name? A Sarnie Herrod.
Q Are you enrolled under that name? A No sir, I am enrolled as Sam Hellet.
Q How old are you? A 26.
Q What is your postoffice address? A Calvin.
Q Are you a citizen of the Creek Nation? A Yes sir.
Q Are you acquainted with David and Eliza Herrod? A Yes sir, they are my parents.
Q Do you know a child of theirs named Tarpie? A Yes sir, that is the child out there in the yard.
Q When was the child born? A The child was born in December, 1901.
Q Are both parents living? A The father is living, but the mother is dead; she died about a week after the child was born.
Q Was there a mid-wife present at the birth of Tarpie? A No sir.

The father of the child is present but refuses to give any evidence whatever about the child.

James B. Myers, being first duly sworn, states, that as stenographer to the Commissioner to the Five Civilized Tribes, he recorded the testimony in the foregoing proceedings, and that the above is a true, and correct transcript of his stenographic notes thereof.

Applications for Enrollment of Creek Newborn
Act of 1905 Volume XIII

James B. Myers

Subscribed and sworn to before me this 27 day of September, 1906.

Alex Posey
Notary Public.

DEPARTMENT OF THE INTERIOR,
COMMISSIONER TO THE FIVE CIVILIZED TRIBES.
Near Weeletka[sic], I.T. April 25, 1905.

In the matter of the application for new born children concerning whose enrollment no affidavit could be obtained in time.

Charlie Wilson, being duly sworn, testified as follows:
Through Alex Posey Official Interpreter:

Examination by the Commission:
Q What is your name? A Charlie Wilson.
Q What is your age? A 31.
Q What is your post office address? A Carson.

Statement: Davis Harred of Tookpafka, and Liza Harred of Kialigee, have a boy who is nearly three years old. The child was born in December, 1901. I was present when he was born. Name Tarpie Harred, and he is living. This is the same as Hullie. Right name Harred. (See Testimony of James Spaniard, taken this day).
Tokpafka
Sarah Harred of Weogufky and Sarney Harred identified as Sam Hellet of C.T.R. No. 3326 of Okchiye have a child just beginning to walk. A boy named Adam. It is living. Post Office Calvin.
Tokpafka
Willie Bruner of Tookpafka, and Addie Bruner of Little River Tulsa, have a girl who is known as both Susie and Mary, about two years old. Child was born July 1, 1902. I was at his house ane[sic] happened to see the record on the door facing. Their post office is Calvin. Tokpafka

Henry G. Hains, being duly sworn, on his oath, states that the above and foregoing is a true and correct transcript of his stenographic notes as taken in said cause on said date.

Henry G Hains

Subscribed and sworn to before me this 10th day of May, 1905.

Drennan C Skaggs
Notary Public.

Applications for Enrollment of Creek Newborn
Act of 1905   Volume XIII

#4 C 1023

(Copy)   Cr 2449-B
DEPARTMENT OF THE INTERIOR,
COMMISSION TO THE FIVE CIVILIZED TRIBES.
Near Weleetka, I. T. April 25, 1905.

In the matter of the application for new born children concerning whose enrollment no affidavits could be obtained in time.

James Spaniard, being duly sworn, testified as follows through Alex Posey, Official Interpreter.

Examination by the Commission:
Q What is your name? A James Spaniard.
Q How old are you? A About 42.
Q What is your postoffice address? A Carson.

Statement: Tommie Lott of Cheyarhar Town and Tena Lott of Tulmochuss Town, have two children both girls, the oldest Lucy, and the other Jennie. They are both living. I don't know their ages exactly, but they are new borns. Their post office is Carson

Ceasar Johnson, of Tookpufka and Eliza John[sic], probably of Eufaula Canadian, have two children. I don't know their names or ages, but they are new borns. Both are living and boys. Their Post office is Carson, Indian Territory and I think the oldest is names Wesley and the youngest Hotulke.

Boley and Kizzie----of Thlewarthle and Tulmochuss respectively--I just know they have a child, whose name or sex I am unfamiliar with. Don't know its age. It's a young child something over a year old I think.

Dave Hullie of Tookpufka and Eliza Hullie, deceased, of Kialigee, have a boy about three or under and living, names Tarpie. Their post office is Carson.

Thomas Wilson of Hickory Ground and Bettie Wilson oft Tulmochuss have two children both girls. The oldest is named Wisey and the youngest Minnie. Wisey is three or nearly so and Minnie is about two years old. Both living. Post office, Carson.

Timmie Stidham of Cheyarhar and Liza Stidham of Weogufky have two children. The oldest a girl named Mattie, and the youngest a boy, don't know the name. Both living, the youngest about a year old and the other over two years old. Post Office, Carson.

Henry G. Hains, being duly sworn, on his oath, states that the above and foregoing is a true and correct transcript of his stenographic notes as taken in said cause on said date.

Applications for Enrollment of Creek Newborn
Act of 1905   Volume XIII

       (signed) HENRY G. HAINS.

Subscribed and sworn to before me this 10th day of May, 1905.

       (signed) DRENNAN C. SKAGGS
(SEAL)   Notary Public.

INDIAN TERRITORY, Western District.

  I, J. Y. Miller, a stenographer in the office of the Commissioner to the Five Civilized Tribes, do hereby certify that the above and foregoing is a true and correct copy of its original to be found in the records of the aforesaid office.

       JY Miller

Sworn to and subscribed before
 me this the 18th day of
 July, 1905.

       Edw C Griesel
         Notary Public.

Western District
Indian Territory SS

        were
  We, the undersigned, on oath state that we ~~are~~ personally acquainted with Eliza Herrod (deceased) wife of David Herrod and that ~~on or about the~~ sometime in ~~day of~~ December 1901 , a male child was born to them and has been named Tarpie Herrod ; that said child was living March 4, 1905. and is now living

  We further state that we have no interest in the above case.

          her
       Lucy x Anderson
         mark
Witness to mark: his
 Alex Posey   Barney x Lender
 JB Myers   mark
 Alex Posey
 JB Myers

Subscribed and sworn to before
me this 4 day of Sept 1906.   Alex Posey
         Notary Public.

Applications for Enrollment of Creek Newborn
Act of 1905   Volume XIII

BIRTH AFFIDAVIT.

DEPARTMENT OF THE INTERIOR,
COMMISSIONER TO THE FIVE CIVILIZED TRIBES.

ENROLLMENT OF MINORS.   ACT OF CONGRESS, APPROVED APRIL 26, 1906.

IN RE APPLICATION FOR ENROLLMENT, as a citizen of the Creek Nation, of Tarpie Herrod, born ~~on the~~ in ~~day of~~ December, 1901

Name of Father: David Herrod   a citizen of the   Creek   Nation.
Name of Mother: Eliza Herrod (deceased)   a citizen of the   Creek   Nation.

Tribal enrollment of father   Tokpafka   Tribal enrollment of mother   Kialigee

Postoffice   Calvin, Indian Territory

AFFIDAVIT OF MOTHER.

UNITED STATES OF AMERICA, Indian Territory,
Western District.

I, Sam Hellet, on oath state that I am 26 years of age and a citizen by blood, of the Creek Nation; that I am the ~~lawful wife~~ son of Eliza Herrod (deceased), who ~~is~~ was a citizen, by blood of the Creek Nation; that a male child was born to her ~~me on~~ in ~~day of~~ December, 1901, that said child has been named Tarpie Herrod, and was living March 4, 1906. and is now living.

                             his
                      Sam x Hellet
WITNESSES TO MARK: mark
    { Alex Posey
      JB Myers

Subscribed and sworn to before me this 4 day of September, 1906.

                             Alex Posey
                             Notary Public.

NC-1023

                     Muskogee, Indian Territory, October 23, 1905.

Eliza Herrod,
     Care David Herrod (or Hullie),
         Carson, Indian Territory.

Dear Madam:

Applications for Enrollment of Creek Newborn
Act of 1905   Volume XIII

In the matter of the application for the enrollment of your minor child, Tarpie Herrod, said to have been born subsequent to May 25, 1901, as a citizen by blood of the Creek Nation, this office desires your affidavit and affidavit of the midwife or physician in attendance at the birth of said child and a blank for that purpose is enclosed herewith.

In the event that there was no physician or midwife in attendance when said child was born, it will be necessary for you to furnish this office with the affidavits of two disinterested witnesses relative to his birth. Said affidavits must set forth said child's name, the date of his birth, the names of his parents and whether or not he was living on March 4, 1905.

Respectfully,

Commissioner.

AG-10-23

N C 1023

JWH

Muskogee, Indian Territory, March 1, 1907.

Eliza Herrod,
  % David Herrod,
    Calvin, Indian Territory.

Dear Madam :--

You are hereby advised that on February 15, 1907, the Secretary of the Interior approved the enrollment of your minor child, Tarpie Herrod, as a citizen by blood of the Creek Nation, and that the name of said child appears upon the roll of New Born citizens by blood of the Creek Nation, enrolled under the Act of Congress approved March 3, 1905, as number 1196.

This child is now entitled to allotment and application therefor should be made without delay at the Creek Land Office, Muskogee, Indian Territory.

Respectfully,

Commissioner.

Applications for Enrollment of Creek Newborn
Act of 1905 Volume XIII

#6- C 1025

(Copy) Cr 2449-B
DEPARTMENT OF THE INTERIOR,
COMMISSION TO THE FIVE CIVILIZED TRIBES.
Near Weleetka, I. T. April 25, 1905.

In the matter of the application for new born children concerning whose enrollment no affidavits could be obtained in time.

James Spaniard, being duly sworn, testified as follows through Alex Posey, Official Interpreter.

Examination by the Commission:
Q What is your name? A James Spaniard.
Q How old are you? A About 42.
Q What is your postoffice address? A Carson.

Statement: Tommie Lott of Cheyarhar Town and Tena Lott of Tulmochuss Town, have two children both girls, the oldest Lucy, and the other Jennie. They are both living. I don't know their ages exactly, but they are new borns. Their post office is Carson

Ceasar Johnson, of Tookpufka and Eliza John[sic], probably of Eufaula Canadian, have two children. I don't know their names or ages, but they are new borns. Both are living and boys. Their Post office is Carson, Indian Territory and I think the oldest is names Wesley and the youngest Hotulke.

Boley and Kizzie----of Thlewarthle and Tulmochuss respectively--I just know they have a child, whose name or sex I am unfamiliar with. Don't know its age. It's a young child something over a year old I think.

Dave Hullie of Tookpufka and Eliza Hullie, deceased, of Kialigee, have a boy about three or under and living, names Tarpie. Their post office is Carson.

Thomas Wilson of Hickory Ground and Bettie Wilson oft Tulmochuss have two children both girls. The oldest is named Wisey and the youngest Minnie. Wisey is three or nearly so and Minnie is about two years old. Both living. Post office, Carson.

✓Timmie Stidham of Cheyarhar and Liza Stidham of Weogufky have two children. The oldest a girl named Mattie, and the youngest a boy, don't know the name. Both living, the youngest about a year old and the other over two years old. Post Office, Carson.

Henry G. Hains, being duly sworn, on his oath, states that the above and foregoing is a true and correct transcript of his stenographic notes as taken in said cause on said date.

Applications for Enrollment of Creek Newborn
Act of 1905 Volume XIII

(signed) HENRY G. HAINS.

Subscribed and sworn to before me this 10th day of May, 1905.

(signed) DRENNAN C. SKAGGS
(SEAL) Notary Public.

INDIAN TERRITORY, Western District.

I, J. Y. Miller, a stenographer in the office of the Commissioner to the Five Civilized Tribes, do hereby certify that the above and foregoing is a true and correct copy of its original to be found in the records of the aforesaid office.

JY Miller

Sworn to and subscribed before
me this the 18th day of
July, 1905.

Edw C Griesel
Notary Public.

AFFIDAVIT OF DISINTERESTED WITNESS.

UNITED STATES OF AMERICA,
Western DISTRICT, SS
INDIAN TERRITORY.

We, the undersigned, on oath state that we are personally acquainted with Eliza Stidham wife of Tommy Stidham ; that there was born to her a male child on or about the 12 day of September - 1904 ; that the said child has been named Johnny Stidham , and was living March 4, 1905, and is now living.

We further state that we have no interest in this case.

Witnesses:
J McDermott

H L Fairfield

his
Sam x Mitchell
mark
her
Nellie x Mitchell
mark

Subscribed and sworn to before me this 24 day of November, 1906.

My Commission   J McDermott
Expires July 25" 1907   Notary Public.

Applications for Enrollment of Creek Newborn
Act of 1905   Volume XIII

BIRTH AFFIDAVIT.

DEPARTMENT OF THE INTERIOR.
COMMISSION TO THE FIVE CIVILIZED TRIBES.

IN RE APPLICATION FOR ENROLLMENT, as a citizen of the Creek Nation, of Johnny Stidham, born on the 12 day of September, 1904

Name of Father: Timmy Stidham   a citizen of the   Creek   Nation.
Big Spring Town
Name of Mother: Eliza Stidham   a citizen of the   Creek   Nation.
Weogufky
                       Postoffice   Carson I.T.

AFFIDAVIT OF MOTHER.

UNITED STATES OF AMERICA, Indian Territory, }
   Western   DISTRICT.

    I, Eliza Stidham , on oath state that I am 32 years of age and a citizen by blood, of the Creek Nation; that I am the lawful wife of Timmy Stidham , who is a citizen, by blood of the Creek Nation; that a male child was born to me on 12" day of September , 1904 , that said child has been named Johnny Stidham , and was living March 4, 1905.
                                       her
                                Eliza x Stidham
Witnesses To Mark: mark
   { DC Skaggs
     Alex Posey

    Subscribed and sworn to before me this 12" day of   June   , 1905.

                                Drennan C Skaggs
                                Notary Public.

AFFIDAVIT OF ATTENDING PHYSICIAN OR MID-WIFE.

UNITED STATES OF AMERICA, Indian Territory, }
   Western   DISTRICT.

                                                        my wife
    I, Timmy Stidham , a (blank) , on oath state that I attended on ^ Mrs. Eliza Stidham , wife of (blank) on the 12 day of September , 1904 ; that there was born to her on said date a   male   child; that said child was living March 4, 1905, and is said to have been named Johnny Stidham   his
                                Timmy x Stidham
                                mark

Applications for Enrollment of Creek Newborn
Act of 1905 Volume XIII

Witnesses To Mark:
{ DC Skaggs
{ Alex Posey

    Subscribed and sworn to before me this 12" day of   June   , 1905.

                              Drennan C Skaggs
                              Notary Public.

BIRTH AFFIDAVIT.

DEPARTMENT OF THE INTERIOR.
COMMISSION TO THE FIVE CIVILIZED TRIBES.

IN RE APPLICATION FOR ENROLLMENT, as a citizen of the Creek Nation, of Mattie Stidham, born on the 2 day of March, 1902

Name of Father: Timmy Stidham   a citizen of the   Creek   Nation.
Big Spring Town
Name of Mother: Eliza Stidham   a citizen of the   Creek   Nation.
Weogufke Town
                      Postoffice   Carson I.T.

AFFIDAVIT OF MOTHER.

UNITED STATES OF AMERICA, Indian Territory, }
    Western   **DISTRICT.** }

    I, Eliza Stidham , on oath state that I am 32 years of age and a citizen by blood, of the Creek Nation; that I am the lawful wife of Timmy Stidham , who is a citizen, by blood of the Creek Nation; that a female child was born to me on 2 day of March , 1902 , that said child has been named Mattie Stidham , and was living March 4, 1905.   her
                              Eliza x Stidham
Witnesses To Mark: mark
{ DC Skaggs
{ Alex Posey

    Subscribed and sworn to before me this 12 day of   June   , 1905.

                              Drennan C Skaggs
                              Notary Public.

Applications for Enrollment of Creek Newborn
Act of 1905   Volume XIII

AFFIDAVIT OF ATTENDING PHYSICIAN OR MID-WIFE.

UNITED STATES OF AMERICA, Indian Territory,
    Western   DISTRICT.

I, Suckey Washington , a mid-wife , on oath state that I attended on Mrs. Eliza Stidham , wife of Timmy Stidham ~~on the   day of~~ sometime in March , 1902 ; that there was born to her on said date a female child; that said child was living March 4, 1905, and is said to have been named Mattie Stidham

her
Suckey x Washington
mark

Witnesses To Mark:
{ DC Skaggs
{ Alex Posey

Subscribed and sworn to before me 14 day of June , 1905.

Drennan C Skaggs
Notary Public.

(The Birth Affidavit of Johnny Stidham given again.)

NC 1o25[sic]

Muskogee, I T October 23 1905

Eliza Stidham,
    Care Timmy,
        Carson, I.T.

Dear Madam:

In the matter of the application for the enrollment of your minor child, Johnny Stidham, born September 12, 1904, as a citizen by blood of the Creek Nation, this office desires affidavit of the midwife or physician in attendance at the birth of said child and a blank for that purpose is inclosed herewith.

In the event that there was no physician or midwife in attendance when said child was born, it will be necessary for you to furnish this office with the affidavits of two disinterested witnesses relative to his birth. Said affidavits must set forth said child's name, the date of his birth, the names of his parents and whether or not he was living on March 4, 1905.

Respectfully,

Commissioner.

BC Env

Applications for Enrollment of Creek Newborn
Act of 1905   Volume XIII

NC 1o25[sic]   Muskogee, I.T. July 5 1906

Eliza Stidham
        Care Timmie Stidham
           Carson, I T

Dear Madam:

    In the matter of the application for the enrollment of your minor child, Johnny Stidham, born September 12, 1904, as a citizen by blood of the Creek Nation, this office desires affidavit of the midwife or physician in attendance at the birth of said child and a blank for that purpose is inclosed herewith. In the event that there was no midwife or physician in attendance, this office desires the affidavits of two disinterested witnesses relative to its birth. Said affidavits should set forth the name of said child, the names of its parents, the date of its brth[sic] and whether or not it was living March 4, 1905.

                                    Respectfully,
                                          Commissioner.

                                                                                JWH
N C 1023
                        Muskogee, Indian Territory, March 1, 1907.

Eliza Stidham,
      % Timmy Stidham,
            Carson, Indian Territory.

Dear Madam :--

    You are hereby advised that on February 15, 1907, the Secretary of the Interior approved the enrollment of your minor child, Johnny Stidham, as a citizen by blood of the Creek Nation, and that the name of said child appears upon the roll of New Born citizens by blood of the Creek Nation, enrolled under the Act of Congress approved March 3, 1905, as number 1197.

    This child is now entitled to allotment and application therefor should be made without delay at the Creek Land Office, Muskogee, Indian Territory.

                                    Respectfully,
                                          Commissioner.

Applications for Enrollment of Creek Newborn
Act of 1905   Volume XIII

DEPARTMENT OF THE INTERIOR,
COMMISSIONER TO THE FIVE CIVILIZED TRIBES.
Near Weeletka[sic], I.T. April 25, 1905.

In the matter of the application for new born children concerning whose enrollment no affidavit could be obtained in time.

Charlie Wilson, being duly sworn, testified as follows:
Through Alex Posey Official Interpreter:

Examination by the Commission:
Q What is your name? A Charlie Wilson.
Q What is your age? A 31.
Q What is your post office address? A Carson.

Statement: Davis Harred of Tookpafka, and Liza Harred of Kialigee, have a boy who is nearly three years old. The child was born in December, 1901. I was present when he was born. Name Tarpie Harred, and he is living. This is the same as Hullie. Right name Harred. (See Testimony of James Spaniard, taken this day).

Sarah Harred of Weogufky and Sarney Harred identified as Sam Hellet of C.T.R. No. 3326 of Okchiye have a child just beginning to walk. A boy named Adam. It is living. Post Office Calvin.

Willie Bruner of Tookpafka, and Addie Bruner of Little River Tulsa, have a girl who is known as both Susie and Mary, about two years old. Child was born July 1, 1902. I was at his house ane[sic] happened to see the record on the door facing. Their post office is Calvin.

Henry G. Hains, being duly sworn, on his oath, states that the above and foregoing is a true and correct transcript of his stenographic notes as taken in said cause on said date.

Henry G Hains

Subscribed and sworn to before me this 10th day of May, 1905.

Drennan C Skaggs
Notary Public.

Applications for Enrollment of Creek Newborn
Act of 1905   Volume XIII

N.C. 485
N.C. 1026.

DEPARTMENT OF THE INTERIOR,
COMMISSIONER TO THE FIVE CIVILIZED TRIBES.
CALVIN, I.T. SEPTEMBER 4, 1906.

In the matter of the application for the enrollment of Adam Hellet as a citizen by blood of the Creek Nation.

SAM HELLET being duly sworn testified as follows:
Through Alex Posey Official Interpreter.

BY THE COMMISSIONER:

Q What is your name? A Sarnie Herrod, but I am enrolled as Sam Hellet.
Q How old are you? A 26.
Q What is your postoffice address? A Calvin.
Q Are you a citizen of the Creek Nation? A Yes sir.
Q To what Creek town do you belong? A Okchiye.
Q Have you a child named Adam? A Yes sir, but the child is now dead.
Q When was Adam born? A September 22, 1904.
Q When did the child die? A August 12, 1905.
Q Who was the mother of the child? A Sarah.
Q Is Sarah your lawful wife? A According to Indian custom.
Q To what town does Sarah belong? A Weogusky[sic].
Q How long have you and Sarah been married? A Between three and four years.
Q What was Sarah's name before you were married to her? A Sarah Bear.
Q Who were her parents? A Maggie Bruner and Nocus Elle Bearfoot.
Q Who are your parents? A David and Eliza Herrod. My mother is now dead.
Q Is your wife Sarah living? A Yessir[sic], she is present, but refuses to testify or make affidavits.
Q Have you and Sarah another new born child besides Adam? A Yes sir.
Q Is the it a boy or girl? A It is a boy.
Q What is its name? A Aman.
Q When was the child born? A January 8, 1906.
Q Is the child now living? A Yes sir.
Q Who attended on your wife at the birth of Adam? A Nicey Bruner.
Q Who attended on her at the birth of Aman? A She had no midwife, and no one was present except myself.

8326

Sarnie Herrod is identified opposite Creek Indian Roll No. 823, as Sam Hullet. Sarah Herrod is identified opposite Creek Indian Roll No. 820. 6857

James B. Myers, being first duly sworn, states, that as stenographer to the Commissioner to the Five Civilized Tribes, he recorded the testimony in the foregoing

Applications for Enrollment of Creek Newborn
Act of 1905   Volume XIII

proceedings, and that the above is a true, and correct transcript of his stenographic notes thereof.

James B. Myers

Subscribed and sworn to before me this 27 day of September, 1906.

Alex Posey
Notary Public.

Western District
Indian Territory   SS

We, the undersigned, on oath state that we are personally acquainted with Sarah Herrod   wife of   Sam Hellet   ; and that on or about the 22 day of September 1904, a   male   child was born to them and has been named   Adam Hellet ; that said child was living March 4, 1905. and died on or about August 12, 1905.

We further state that we have no interest in the above case.

her
Lucy x Anderson
mark
his
Barney x Lender
mark

Witness to mark:
 Alex Posey
 JB Myers
 Alex Posey
 JB Myers
Subscribed and sworn to before
me this 4" day of Sept 1906.

Alex Posey
Notary Public.

BIRTH AFFIDAVIT.

DEPARTMENT OF THE INTERIOR,
COMMISSIONER TO THE FIVE CIVILIZED TRIBES.

ENROLLMENT OF MINORS.   ACT OF CONGRESS, APPROVED APRIL 26, 1906.

IN RE APPLICATION FOR ENROLLMENT, as a citizen of the Creek Nation, of   Adam Hellet (deceased), born on the 22 day of September, 1904

Name of Father: Sam Hellet (C.I. Roll No 8326)   a citizen of the   Creek   Nation.
Name of Mother: Sarah Herrod (C.I. Roll No 6857) a citizen of the   Creek   Nation.

Applications for Enrollment of Creek Newborn
Act of 1905 Volume XIII

Tribal enrollment of father   Okchiye   Tribal enrollment of mother   Weogufky

Postoffice   Calvin, Indian Territory

Father
AFFIDAVIT OF ~~MOTHER~~.

UNITED STATES OF AMERICA, Indian Territory, }
Western   District.

I, Sam Hellet , on oath state that I am 26 years of age and a citizen by blood , of the Creek Nation; that I am the lawful ~~wife~~ husband according to Indian custom of Sarah Herrod , who is a citizen, by blood of the Creek Nation; that a male child was born to ~~me~~ her on 22 day of September , 1904 , that said child has been named Adam Hellet , and was living March 4, 1906. (and died August 12, 1905

                                            his
                                  Sam x Hellet
WITNESSES TO MARK: mark
{ Alex Posey
{ JB Myers

Subscribed and sworn to before me this 4 day of September , 1906.

                                      Alex Posey
                                      Notary Public.

NC 1026

                         Muskogee, Indian Territory, December 19, 1905.

Sarah Harred,
    Care of Sarney Harred,
        Calvin, Indian Territory.

Dear Madam:

    In the matter of the application for the enrollment of your minor child, Adam Harjo[sic], as a citizen by blood of the Creek Nation, it will be necessary for you to furnish this Office with your affidavit and the affidavit of the physician or midwife in attendance at the birth of said child, relative to its birth. In the event there was no midwife or physician present at the birth of said child, it will be necessary for you to furnish this Office with the affidavits of two disinterested persons relative to said child's birth. Blanks for both purposes are herewith enclosed. In having the blanks executed, care should be taken to see that all blanks are properly filled, all names written in full, and in the event that the person signing an affidavit is unable to write, his or her mark must be attested by two witnesses who are able to write. The notary public must date, sign and seal each separate affidavit.

Applications for Enrollment of Creek Newborn
Act of 1905   Volume XIII

    In the event you have in your possession certificates of allotment or deeds to land in the Creek Nation of yourself and husband, you are requested to consult same before executing the affidavits in this case, and be careful to see that the surname of said child corresponds with the surname of his father as given in his allotment certificate or deed, and that your given name and the given name of the father of said child correspond with your respective given names as the same appear in your allotment certificates or deeds to land in the Creek Nation.

    This matter should receive your prompt attention.

                          Respectfully,

                                        Commissioner.

1 BA
Dis

                                                JWH

N C 1026

                   Muskogee, Indian Territory, March 1, 1907.

Sarah Harred,
    % Sarney Harred,
        Calvin, Indian Territory.

Dear Madam :--

    You are hereby advised that on February 15, 1907, the Secretary of the Interior approved the enrollment of your minor child, Adam Hellet, as a citizen by blood of the Creek Nation, and that the name of said child appears upon the roll of New Born citizens by blood of the Creek Nation, enrolled under the Act of Congress approved March 3, 1905, as number 1198.

    This child is now entitled to allotment and application therefor should be made without delay at the Creek Land Office, Muskogee, Indian Territory.

                          Respectfully,

                                        Commissioner.

Applications for Enrollment of Creek Newborn
Act of 1905 Volume XIII

DEPARTMENT OF THE INTERIOR,
COMMISSIONER TO THE FIVE CIVILIZED TRIBES.
Near Weeletka[sic], I.T. April 25, 1905.

In the matter of the application for new born children concerning whose enrollment no affidavit could be obtained in time.

Charlie Wilson, being duly sworn, testified as follows:
Through Alex Posey Official Interpreter:

Examination by the Commission:
Q What is your name? A Charlie Wilson.
Q What is your age? A 31.
Q What is your post office address? A Carson.

Statement: Davis Harred of Tookpafka, and Liza Harred of Kialigee, have a boy who is nearly three years old. The child was born in December, 1901. I was present when he was born. Name Tarpie Harred, and he is living. This is the same as Hullie. Right name Harred. (See Testimony of James Spaniard, taken this day).

Sarah Harred of Weogufky and Sarney Harred identified as Sam Hellet of C.T.R. No. 3326 of Okchiye have a child just beginning to walk. A boy named Adam. It is living. Post Office Calvin.

Willie Bruner of Tookpafka, and Addie Bruner of Little River Tulsa, have a girl who is known as both Susie and Mary, about two years old. Child was born July 1, 1902. I was at his house ane[sic] happened to see the record on the door facing. Their post office is Calvin.

Henry G. Hains, being duly sworn, on his oath, states that the above and foregoing is a true and correct transcript of his stenographic notes as taken in said cause on said date.

Henry G Hains

Subscribed and sworn to before me this 10th day of May, 1905.

Drennan C Skaggs
Notary Public.

(No other information given.)

Applications for Enrollment of Creek Newborn
Act of 1905   Volume XIII

BIRTH AFFIDAVIT.

DEPARTMENT OF THE INTERIOR.
COMMISSION TO THE FIVE CIVILIZED TRIBES.

IN RE APPLICATION FOR ENROLLMENT, as a citizen of the Creek Nation, of Wiley Sampson, born on the 13 day of August, 1904

Name of Father: Wash Sampson   a citizen of the   Creek   Nation.
Cussehta Town
Name of Mother: Cindy Sampson (nee Hill)   a citizen of the   Creek   Nation.
Tulwa Thlocco Town
                         Postoffice   Naudack, Ind. Ter.

AFFIDAVIT OF MOTHER.

UNITED STATES OF AMERICA, Indian Territory,
   Western   DISTRICT.   Child is present

I, Cindy Sampson , on oath state that I am 19 years of age and a citizen by blood , of the Creek Nation; that I am the lawful wife of Wash Sampson , who is a citizen, by blood of the Creek Nation; that a male child was born to me on 13 day of August , 1904 , that said child has been named Wiley Sampson , and was living March 4, 1905.
                                         her
                              Cindy x Sampson
Witnesses To Mark: mark
  { Alex Posey
  { DC Skaggs

   Subscribed and sworn to before me this 11 day of   April   , 1905.

                              Drennan C Skaggs
                              Notary Public.

AFFIDAVIT OF ATTENDING PHYSICIAN OR MID-WIFE.

UNITED STATES OF AMERICA, Indian Territory,
   Western   DISTRICT.

I, Louisa Tiger , a—, on oath state that I attended on Mrs. Cindy Sampson , wife of Wash Sampson on the 13 day of August , 1904 ; that there was born to her on said date a male child; that said child was living March 4, 1905, and is said to have been named Wiley Sampson   her
                              Louisa x Tiger
                                   mark

Applications for Enrollment of Creek Newborn
Act of 1905   Volume XIII

Witnesses To Mark:
{ Alex Posey
{ DC Skaggs

Subscribed and sworn to before me this 11 day of   April   , 1905.

Drennan C Skaggs
Notary Public.

DEPARTMENT OF THE INTERIOR,
COMMISSIONER TO THE FIVE CIVILIZED TRIBES.
NEAR WETUMKA, I.T. April 26, 1905.

In the matter of the application for new born children concerning whose enrollment no affidavits could be obtained in time.

Felix Canard, being duly sworn, testified as follows:
Through Official Interpreter, Alex Posey:

Examination by the Commission:
Q What is your name? A Felix Canard.
Q What is your age? A 25.
Q What is your post office address? A Wetumka.

Statement: Willie Parnoske of L.R. Tulsa, Indian Territory and Selina Parnoske of Thlewarthle, have a boy-- the mother herself is a Snake and has never been enrolled-- about a little over a year old; she also has an older one about four years old that has not yet been enrolled. The boy is called nicknames of Bunkie and Nuskey. Their post office is Wetumka.

Nettie Fife of Thlopthlocco, the daughter of Nixie, has a child --father unknown. I believe it is a boy --don't know its name. Its[sic] about eight months old, its[sic] living. Post Office, Wetumka.

Henry G. Hains, being duly sworn, on his oath, states that the above and foregoing is a true and correct transcript of his stenographic notes as taken in said cause on said date.

Henry G. Hains

Applications for Enrollment of Creek Newborn
Act of 1905   Volume XIII

Subscribed and sworn to before me this 10th day of May, 1905.

Drennan C Skaggs
Notary Public.

N.C. 1029.

DEPARTMENT OF THE INTERIOR,
COMMISSIONER TO THE FIVE CIVILIZED TRIBES.
Wetumka, I. T., April 10, 1906.

In the matter of the application for the enrollment of two unnamed minor children of Willie and Selina Panoske as citizens by blood of the Creek Nation.

SELINA PANOSKE, being duly sworn, testified as follows

Through Alex Posey Official Interpreter:

BY THE COMMISSIONER:
Q What is your name? A Selina Panoske.
Q How old are you? A About thirty.
Q What is your post office address? A Wetumka.
Q Are you a citizen of the Creek Nation? A Yes, sir.
Q To what town do you belong? A Alabama.
Q Who are your parents? A My father was Suntulle Harjo. He belonged to Thlopthlocco Town. My mother was Eliza Harjo or Alabama Town.
Q Are you[sic] parents living? A No, sir, they are both dead.
Q Under what name are you enrolled? A I think I am enrolled as Selina Harjo.
Q Have you received certificates or deeds to you[sic] allotment? A No, sir.
Q Is Willie Pancake your lawfull[sic] husband? A Yes, sir, but we are now separated.
Q To what town does he belong? A Little River Tulsa.
Q Is he known by any other name? A His town name is Tummie Fixico.
Q Have you and Willie Pancake two new born children? A Yes, sir.
Q What are their names? A Cindy and Cheparne Pancake.
Q When was Cindy born? A September the 5th, 1901.
Q Who attended on you at the birth of Cindy? A Louina Harjo, my sister.
Q When was Cheparney born? A February 7, 1904.
Q Who attended on you at the birth of Cheparney? A Jennie Hopiye.
Q Are both of these children living? A Cheparney is dead.
Q When did he die? A he[sic] died last September, but I do not know what day.

---oooOOOooo---

I, D. C. Skaggs, on oath state that the above and foregoing is a full and true transcript of my stenographic notes as taken in said cause on said date.

D. C. Skaggs

Applications for Enrollment of Creek Newborn
Act of 1905   Volume XIII

Subscribed and sworn to before me this 17th day of April, 1906.

                                              Alex Posey
                                              Notary Public.

BIRTH AFFIDAVIT.

DEPARTMENT OF THE INTERIOR.
COMMISSION TO THE FIVE CIVILIZED TRIBES.

IN RE APPLICATION FOR ENROLLMENT, as a citizen of the Creek Nation, of Cheparney Panoske, born on the 7 day of February, 1904

Name of Father: Willie Panoske   a citizen of the Creek Nation.
Name of Mother: Selina Panoske   a citizen of the Creek Nation.

                          Postoffice   Wetumka, I.T.

AFFIDAVIT OF MOTHER.

UNITED STATES OF AMERICA, Indian Territory,
    Western   **DISTRICT.**

    I, Selina Panoske, on oath state that I am about 30 years of age and a citizen by blood, of the Creek Nation; that I am the lawful wife of Willie Panoske, who is a citizen, by blood of the Creek Nation; that a male child was born to me on the 7th day of February, 1904, that said child has been named Cheparney Panoske, and was living March 4, 1905.

                                            her
Witnesses To Mark: Selina x Panoske
   { DC Skaggs   mark
   { Alex Posey

    Subscribed and sworn to before me this 10 day of   April   , 1906.

                                      Drennan C Skaggs
                                      Notary Public.

Applications for Enrollment of Creek Newborn
Act of 1905   Volume XIII

AFFIDAVIT OF ATTENDING PHYSICIAN OR MID-WIFE.

UNITED STATES OF AMERICA, Indian Territory,
Western   DISTRICT.

I, Jennie Hopiye , a mid- wife , on oath state that I attended on Mrs. Selina Panoske , wife of Willie Panoske on the 7" day of Feb , 1904 ; that there was born to her on said date a male child; that said child was living March 4, 1905, and is said to have been named Cheparney Panoske

                             her
Witnesses To Mark: Jennie x Hopiye
  { DC Skaggs   mark
    Alex Posey

Subscribed and sworn to before me 10 day of   April   , 1906.

                     Drennan C Skaggs
                     Notary Public.

DEPARTMENT OF THE INTERIOR.
COMMISSION TO THE FIVE CIVILIZED TRIBES.

In the matter of the death of   Cheparney Panoske   a citizen of the Creek Nation, who formerly resided at or near   Wetumka   , Ind. Ter., and died on the ----- day of September , 1905

AFFIDAVIT OF RELATIVE.

UNITED STATES OF AMERICA, Indian Territory,
Western   DISTRICT.

I, Selina Panoske , on oath state that I am   about 30   years of age and a citizen by blood , of the Creek Nation; that my postoffice address is   Wetumka   , Ind. Ter.; that I am the mother   of   Cheparney Panoske   who was a citizen, by blood   , of the Creek   Nation and that said   Cheparney Panoske   died on the ----- day of September   , 1905

                           her
                     Selina x Panoske
Witnesses To Mark: mark
  { DC Skaggs
    Alex Posey

Applications for Enrollment of Creek Newborn
Act of 1905   Volume XIII

Subscribed and sworn to before me this 10" day of April, 1906.

                        Drennan C Skaggs
                        Notary Public.

BIRTH AFFIDAVIT.

DEPARTMENT OF THE INTERIOR.
COMMISSION TO THE FIVE CIVILIZED TRIBES.

IN RE APPLICATION FOR ENROLLMENT, as a citizen of the Creek Nation, of Cindy Panoske, born on the 5 day of September, 1901

Name of Father: Willie Panoske   a citizen of the   Creek   Nation.
Name of Mother: Selina Panoske   a citizen of the   Creek   Nation.

                  Postoffice   Wetumka, I.T.

AFFIDAVIT OF MOTHER.

UNITED STATES OF AMERICA, Indian Territory,
    Western   DISTRICT.

I, Selina Panoske, on oath state that I am about 30 years of age and a citizen by blood, of the Creek Nation; that I am the lawful wife of Willie Panoske, who is a citizen, by blood of the Creek Nation; that a female child was born to me on 5th day of September, 1901, that said child has been named Cindy Panoske, and was living March 4, 1905.

                                  her
                          Selina x Panoske
Witnesses To Mark: mark
  { DC Skaggs
     Alex Posey

Subscribed and sworn to before me this 10 day of   April   , 1906.

                        Drennan C Skaggs
                        Notary Public.

AFFIDAVIT OF ATTENDING PHYSICIAN OR MID-WIFE.

UNITED STATES OF AMERICA, Indian Territory,
    Western   DISTRICT.

I, Louina Harjo, a mid-wife, on oath state that I attended on Mrs. Selina Panoske, wife of Willie Panoske on the 5 day of Sept, 1901; that there was born to

Applications for Enrollment of Creek Newborn
Act of 1905   Volume XIII

her on said date a female child; that said child was living March 4, 1905, and is said to have been named Cindy Panoske

her
Louina x Harjo
mark

Witnesses To Mark:
  { DC Skaggs
   Alex Posey

    Subscribed and sworn to before me 11 day of   April   , 1906.

Drennan C Skaggs
Notary Public.

NC-1029

                    Muskogee, Indian Territory, December 19, 1905.

Selina Parnoske[sic],
    Care of Willie Parnoske,
        Wetumka, Indian Territory

Dear Madam:

    In the matter of the application for the enrollment of your minor children, Bunkie (or Nuskey) Parnoskey[sic] and his older brother[sic] whose given name is to this Office unknown, as citizens by blood of the Creek Nation, it will be necessary for you to furnish this Office with your affidavits and the affidavits of the physician or midwife in attendance at the births of said children, relative to their births. In the event there was no midwife or physician present at the births of said children, it will be necessary for you to furnish this Office with the affidavits of two disinterested persons relative to each of said children's birth. Blanks for both purposes are herewith enclosed. In having the blanks executed, care should be taken to see that all blanks are properly filled, all names written in full, and in the event that a party signing an affidavit is unable to write, his or her mark must be attested by two witnesses who are able to write. The notary public must date, sign and seal each separate affidavit.

    In the event you have in your possession certificate of allotment or deeds to land in the Creek Nation of yourself and husband, you are requested to consult same before executing the affidavits in this case, and be careful to see that the surname of said children corresponds with the surname of their father, and that your given name and the given name of the father of said children corresponds with your respective given names as the same appear in your allotment certificates or deeds to land in the Creek Nation.

    These matters should receive your immediate attention.

Respectfully,

2 B A   Commissioner.
2 Dis

Applications for Enrollment of Creek Newborn
Act of 1905   Volume XIII

HGH

REFER IN REPLY TO THE FOLLOWING:

**DEPARTMENT OF THE INTERIOR,
COMMISSIONER TO THE FIVE CIVILIZED TRIBES.**

Muskogee, Indian Territory, October 24, 1906.

Salina Parnosky[sic],
 c/o Willie Parnosky,
  Wetumka, Indian Territory.

Dear Madam:

You are hereby advised that the names of your minor children, Cindy and Cheparney Parnosky, are contained in the partial list of citizens by blood of the Creek Nation, approved by the Secretary of the Interior October 15, 1906, and that selections of land in the Creek Nation May now be made for said children at the Creek Land Office in Muskogee, Indian Territory.

This matter should receive your prompt attention.

Respectfully,
Tams Bixby Commissioner.

DEPARTMENT OF THE INTERIOR,
COMMISSIONER TO THE FIVE CIVILIZED TRIBES.
NEAR WETUMKA, I.T. April 26, 1905.

In the matter of the application for new born children concerning whose enrollment no affidavits could be obtained in time.

Felix Canard, being duly sworn, testified as follows:
Through Official Interpreter, Alex Posey:

Examination by the Commission:
Q What is your name? A Felix Canard.
Q What is your age? A 25.
Q What is your post office address? A Wetumka.

Applications for Enrollment of Creek Newborn
Act of 1905   Volume XIII

Statement: Willie Parnoske of L.R. Tulsa, Indian Territory and Selina Parnoske of Thlewarthle, have a boy-- the mother herself is a Snake and has never been enrolled-- about a little over a year old; she also has an older one about four years old that has not yet been enrolled. The boy is called nicknames of Bunkie and Nuskey. Their post office is Wetumka.

Nettie Fife of Thlopthlocco, the daughter of Nixie, has a child --father unknown. I believe it is a boy --don't know its name. Its[sic] about eight months old, its[sic] living. Post Office, Wetumka.

Henry G. Hains, being duly sworn, on his oath, states that the above and foregoing is a true and correct transcript of his stenographic notes as taken in said cause on said date.

Henry G. Hains

Subscribed and sworn to before me this 10th day of May, 1905.

Drennan C Skaggs
Notary Public.

(COPY)

Muskogee, Indian Territory, January 28, 1907.

The Commissioner
    to the Five Civilized Tribes
        Muskogee, Indian Territory.

Sir:

On December 24, 1906, I reported in the matter of the application for the enrollment of an unnamed minor child of Nettie Fife, as a citizen by blood of the Creek Nation, relative to the parentage of said child, but failed to state whether or not said child was living.

I have the honor to further report that said child was living on the date above referred to.

Respectfully,
(Signed) Jesse M. McDermott.

Applications for Enrollment of Creek Newborn
Act of 1905 Volume XIII

NC 1030.   OCH.
DEPARTMENT OF THE INTERIOR,
COMMISSIONER TO THE FIVE CIVILIZED TRIBES.

In the matter of the application for the enrollment of Della Yaholar, as a citizen by blood of the Creek Nation.

DECISION.

The record in this case shows that on April 26, 1905, testimony was offered "In the matter of the application for new born children concerning whose enrollment no affidavit could be obtained in time", which embraced a child of Nettie Fife. Attached hereto and made part of this record are letters addressed to the Commissioner to the Five Civilized Tribes under dates of December 24, 1906 and January 28, 1907, which show that said child is known as Della Yaholar. The testimony above mentioned is herein considered as an official application for the enrollment of said Della Yaholar, as a citizen by blood of the Creek Nation under the provisions of the act of Congress approved March 3, 1905 (33 Stats. L., 1048).

The evidence and the records of this office show that said Della Yaholar is the daughter of Nettie Fife, whose name appears as "Nellie Fife" upon a schedule of citizens by blood of the Creek Nation approved by the Secretary of the Interior March 13, 1902, opposite number 4701.

The letters which are part of the record tend to show that the father of said Della Yaholar is Roman Yaholar, whose name appears upon a schedule of citizens by blood of the Creek Nation approved by the Secretary of the Interior March 28, 1902, opposite number 6370.

The evidence and the letters above referred to show that said Della Yaholar was born prior to March 4, 1905, and was living on December 4, 1906.

It is, therefore, ordered and adjudged that said Della Yaholar is entitled to be enrolled as a citizen by blood of the Creek Nation under the provisions of the act of Congress approved March 3, 1905 (33 Stats. L., 1048), and the application for her enrollment as such is accordingly granted.

Tams Bixby   COMMISSIONER.

Muskogee, Indian Territory.
FEB 2- 1907

Applications for Enrollment of Creek Newborn
Act of 1905 Volume XIII

(COPY)

Beggs, Indian Territory, December 24, 1906.

Commissioner to the Five Civilized Tribes,
    Muskogee, Indian Territory.

Sir:

    I have the honor to report in the matter of the application for the enrollment of an unnamed minor child of Nettie Fife, as a citizen by blood of the Creek Nation, that the mother, Nettie Fife, refuses to testify or to execute affidavit relative to the birth of her said minor child. I have indirect information that the name of said child is Della Yahola; that the date of her birth is April 27, 1904; that the name of her father is Roman Yahola, of Fentress, Indian Territory; and that the mother is Nettie Fife.

    Copies of record in said case are herewith enclosed.

                     Respectfully,
                     (Signed) Jesse McDermott.

N C 1030.

                 Muskogee, Indian Territory, March 7, 1907.

Nellie[sic] Fife,
    Care of Roman Yahola,
        Wetumka, Indian Territory.

Dear Madam:

    You are hereby advised that on March 2, 1907 the Secretary of the Interior approved the enrollment of your minor child, Della Yaholar, as a citizen by blood of the Creek Nation, and that the name of said child appears upon the roll of new born citizens by blood of the Creek Nation, enrolled under the Act of Congress approved March 3, 1905, as number 1245.

    This child is now entitled to allotment and application therefor should be made without delay at the Creek Land Office, Muskogee, Indian Territory.

                     Respectfully,
                           Commissioner.

Applications for Enrollment of Creek Newborn
Act of 1905   Volume XIII

DEPARTMENT OF THE INTERIOR,
COMMISSIONER TO THE FIVE CIVILIZED TRIBES.
Near Bearden, I.T. April 27, 1905.

In the matter of the application for a new born children concerning whose enrollment no affidavits could be obtained in time.

Simmer being duly sworn, testified as follows: Through Official Interpreter, Alex Posey.

Examination by the Commission:
Q What is your name? A Simmer.
Q What is your age? A About 46.
Q What is your post office address? A Bearden.

N C 1031
Statement: I am Town King of Quassarte No. 2. Henry King of Fish Pond and Sallie King of Okchiye, have a child names Janelle-- a girl--about three years old, and the youngest child is unnamed. It is a little over a month old--don't know what time in last it was born--it is a boy. Both are living. Post Office Bearden.

NC 1032
Moser and Arlie Bunny both of Fish Pond Town have a child I think is a girl-- about a year old and living. Post Office Bearden.

NC 1033
Jasper Hill and Maggie Hill Maychick, both of Fish Pond, have a boy about a year old or a little over a year old--Billie Hill is its name--he is living. Post Office, Bearden.

NC 1034
Isparney and Sophy Deere, both of Fish Pond, have two children--the oldest a girl named Minnie, about two years old--the other is about a year old--don't know the sex or the name.

NC 1035
Cobler Wolf, deceased, a Seminole, and Annie Yahola of Hillabee, have a girl child named Matilda Wolf--about three years old and living. Post Office, Bearden.

Henry G. Hains, being duly sworn, on his oath, states that the above and foregoing is a true and correct transcript of his stenographic notes as taken in said cause on said date.

Henry G. Hains

Subscribed and sworn to before me this 10th day of May, 1905.

Drennan C Skaggs
Notary Public.

Applications for Enrollment of Creek Newborn
Act of 1905   Volume XIII

2452-B.

DEPARTMENT OF THE INTERIOR,
COMMISSIONER TO THE FIVE CIVILIZED TRIBES.
Bearden, I. T., November 1, 1905.

In the matter of the application for the enrollment of two minor children of Henry and Sallie King as citizens by blood of the Creek Nation.

HEPSEY KING, being duly sworn, testified as follows:

Through Alex Posey Official Interpreter:

BY THE COMMISSIONER:
Q What is your name? A Hepsey King.
Q How old are you? A I do not know how old I am.

Witness appears to be about twenty years of age.

Q What is your post office address? A Bearden.
Q Are you a citizen of the Creek Nation? A Yes, sir.
Q To what town do you belong? A Fish Pond.
Q Do you know Henry and Sallie King? A Yes, sir. Henry is my brother.
Q Are they both living? A No, sir, Sallie is dead.
Q When did she die? A She died in the early summer.
Q Have they a child named Janelly? A Yes, sir.
Q That child is a girl is it? A Yes, sir.
Q Do you know when she was born? A I do not know.
Q How old is the child? A I do not know.
Q Is the child living? A Yes, sir. The child is present.

Janelly is present and appears to be about three years of age.

Q Have they another child? A They had a child that died.
Q What was its name? A The child died unnamed.
Q Do you know when it was born? A No, sir.
Q When did the child die? A It died in the summer of this year.
Q How old was the child when it died? A It was about four months old. I know nothing about the ages of the children. If the father was here he could give you all the information you want but he has gone to Muskogee.

---oooOOOooo---

I, D. C. Skaggs, on oath state that the above and foregoing is a full and true transcript of my stenographic notes as taken in said cause on said date.

Applications for Enrollment of Creek Newborn
Act of 1905   Volume XIII

D. C. Skaggs

Subscribed and sworn to before me this 4 day of Jan 1906.

J McDermott
Notary Public.

2452-B.

DEPARTMENT OF THE INTERIOR,
COMMISSIONER TO THE FIVE CIVILIZED TRIBES.
Bearden, I. T., November 1, 1905.

In the matter of the application for the enrollment of two minor children of Henry and Sallie King as citizens by blood of the Creek Nation.

ISPARNEY DEERE, being duly sworn, testified as follows

Through Alex Posey Official Interpreter:

BY THE COMMISSIONER:
Q What is your name? A Isparney Deere.
Q How old are you? A About twenty-nine.
Q What is your post office address? A Butner.
Q Are you a citizen of the Creek Nation? A Yes, sir.
Q To what town do you belong? A Fish Pond.
Q Did you know Henry and Sallie King? A Yes, sir.
Q Do you know a child of theirs named Janelly? A Yes, sir.
Q Do you know when she was born? A I do not know.
Q How old do you judge her to be? A She is about two months younger than my daughter, Minnie, who was born February 12, 1902.
Q Have they a younger child than Janelly? A They had a younger child but it is dead.
Q What was that child's name? A I do not think the child had been named when it died.
Q Do you know when it was born? A On the eighth or nineth[sic] of March, this year, and it died on August 25 or 26, this year.
Q Is the mother of these children living? A No, sir, she is dead.
Q Do you know when she died? A I think she died April 30, this year.

---oooOOOooo---

I, D. C. Skaggs, on oath state that the above and foregoing is a full and true transcript of my stenographic notes as taken in said cause on said date.

D. C. Skaggs

Applications for Enrollment of Creek Newborn
Act of 1905   Volume XIII

Subscribed and sworn to before me this 4 day of Jan 1906.

                                      J McDermott
                                      Notary Public.

N.C. 1031

DEPARTMENT OF THE INTERIOR,
COMMISSIONER TO THE FIVE CIVILIZED TRIBES.
Okemah, Indian Territory, September 22, 1906.

In the matter of the application for the enrollment of Janelly King as a citizen by blood of the Creek Nation.

HENRY KING, being duly sworn, testified as follows (through Jesse McDermott official interpreter):

BY COMMISSIONER:

Q What is your name? A Henry King.
Q What is your age? A I am 31.
Q What is your postoffice address? A Bearden, I.T.
Q Have you a child for whom you applied to have enrolled in the Creek Nation? A Yes.
Q What is the name [sic] that child? A Janelly King.
Q When was Janelly born? A April 9, 1902.
Q Is she living? A Yes sir.
Q What is the name of the mother of this child? A Sallie. She is dead.
Q When did she die? A May 6, 1904.
Q Were you lawfully married to Sallie when Janelly was born? A No, according to the Indian custom, we were.
Q What was her name before you married her? A Sallie Little.

The witness presents deeds issued to Sallie Little Creek Roll No. 6928. He also presents deeds issued to himself and he is identified as Haney King.

---oooOOOooo---

I, Jesse McDermott, on oath state that the above and foregoing is a full and true transcript of my notes as taken in said cause on said date.

                                      Jesse McDermott

Subscribed and sworn to before me this 7th day of November, 1906.

                                      Frank J. Smith
                                      Notary Public.

Applications for Enrollment of Creek Newborn
Act of 1905 Volume XIII

BIRTH AFFIDAVIT.

DEPARTMENT OF THE INTERIOR.
COMMISSION TO THE FIVE CIVILIZED TRIBES.

IN RE APPLICATION FOR ENROLLMENT, as a citizen of the Creek Nation, of Janelly King, born on the 9 day of April, 1902

Name of Father: Haney King   a citizen of the   Creek   Nation.
Roll #6565
Name of Mother: Sallie King   a citizen of the   Creek   Nation.
Okchiye Town

Postoffice   Bearden Ind Ter

AFFIDAVIT OF MOTHER.

UNITED STATES OF AMERICA, Indian Territory, }
   Western   DISTRICT.

I, Haney King, on oath state that I am 31 years of age and a citizen by blood, of the Creek Nation; that I am the lawful ~~wife~~ husband of Sallie King, who is a citizen, by blood of the Creek Nation; that a female child was born to ~~me~~ her on 9" day of April, 1902, that said child has been named Janelly King, and was living March 4, 1905. and is now living   his
                                         Haney x King
Witnesses To Mark: mark
  { Jesse McDermott
  { Alex Harjo

Subscribed and sworn to before me this 22 day of September , 1906.

My Commission   J McDermott
Expires July 25" 1907   Notary Public.

BIRTH AFFIDAVIT.

DEPARTMENT OF THE INTERIOR.
COMMISSION TO THE FIVE CIVILIZED TRIBES.

IN RE APPLICATION FOR ENROLLMENT, as a citizen of the Creek Nation, of Janelly King, born ~~on~~ the month day of April, 1902

Name of Father: Haney King   a citizen of the   Creek   Nation.
Name of Mother: Sallie " (nee Little)   a citizen of the   "   Nation.

Postoffice   Bearden IT

Applications for Enrollment of Creek Newborn
Act of 1905 Volume XIII

AFFIDAVIT OF ATTENDING ~~PHYSICIAN OR~~ MID-WIFE.

UNITED STATES OF AMERICA, Indian Territory,
Western DISTRICT.

I, Keepsey Harjo , a midwife , on oath state that I attended on Mrs. Sallie King, wife of Haney King ~~on~~ in the month ~~day~~ of April , 1902 ; that there was born to her on said date a female child; that said child was living March 4, 1905, and is said to have been named Janelly King

                              her
                          Keepsey x Harjo

Witnesses To Mark: mark
  { Jesse McDermott
    J.E. Guy

Subscribed and sworn to before me 4th day of October , 1906.

My Commission   J McDermott
Expires July 25" 1907   Notary Public.

N C 1031.

Sallie King (or Sallie Little),
     Care of Haney King,
         Bearden, Indian Territory.

Dear Madam:

You are hereby advised that on March 2, 1907 the Secretary of the Interior approved the enrollment of your minor child, Janelly King, as a citizen by blood of the Creek Nation, and that the name of said child appears upon the roll of new born citizens by blood of the Creek Nation enrolled under the Act of Congress approved March 3, 1905, as number 1246.

This child is now entitled to allotment and application therefor should be made without delay at the Creek Land Office, Muskogee, Indian Territory.

                        Respectfully,
                                  Commissioner.

Applications for Enrollment of Creek Newborn
Act of 1905 Volume XIII

DEPARTMENT OF THE INTERIOR,
COMMISSIONER TO THE FIVE CIVILIZED TRIBES.
Near Bearden, I.T. April 27, 1905.

In the matter of the application for a new born children concerning whose enrollment no affidavits could be obtained in time.

Simmer being duly sworn, testified as follows: Through Official Interpreter, Alex Posey.

Examination by the Commission:
Q What is your name? A Simmer.
Q What is your age? A About 46.
Q What is your post office address? A Bearden.

Statement: I am Town King of Quassarte No. 2. Henry King of Fish Pond and Sallie King of Okchiye, have a child names Janelle-- a girl--about three years old, and the youngest child is unnamed. It is a little over a month old--don't know what time in last it was born--it is a boy. Both are living. Post Office Bearden.

X Moser and Arlie Bunny both of Fish Pond Town have a child I think is a girl-- about a year old and living. Post Office Bearden.

Jasper Hill and Maggie Hill Maychick, both of Fish Pond, have a boy about a year old or a little over a year old--Billie Hill is its name--he is living. Post Office, Bearden.

Isparney and Sophy Deere, both of Fish Pond, have two children--the oldest a girl named Minnie, about two years old--the other is about a year old--don't know the sex or the name.

Cobler Wolf, deceased, a Seminole, and Annie Yahola of Hillabee, have a girl child named Matilda Wolf--about three years old and living. Post Office, Bearden.

Henry G. Hains, being duly sworn, on his oath, states that the above and foregoing is a true and correct transcript of his stenographic notes as taken in said cause on said date.

Henry G. Hains

Subscribed and sworn to before me this 10th day of May, 1905.

Drennan C Skaggs
Notary Public.

Applications for Enrollment of Creek Newborn
Act of 1905 Volume XIII

NC 1032. F.H.W.
DEPARTMENT OF THE INTERIOR,
COMMISSIONER TO THE FIVE CIVILIZED TRIBES.

In the matter of the application for the enrollment of Susie Bunner, as a citizen by blood of the Creek Nation.

DECISION.

The record in this case shows that on April 27, 1905, Simmer, the Town King of Quassarte No. 2, appeared before a Creek Enrollment Field Party near Bearden, Indian Territory, and testified "in the matter of the application for new born children concerning whose enrollment no affidavit could be obtained in time", and in the said testimony appeared the following statement: "Moser and Arlie Bunny, both of Fish Pond town, have a child, I think a girl about a year old and living, postoffice Bearden." The said statement herein is considered as an original application for enrolment of Susie Bunner, as a citizen by blood of the Creek Nation. The supplemental affidavit filed November 11, 1905, is attached to and mad a part of the record herein.

The evidence shows that there is a discrepancy in the spelling of the names of the applicant and the parents of said Susie Bunner.

It is, however, established from the evidence and the records in this office that said Susie Bunner is the child of Mosey Bunner and Ollie Bunner. Said Mosey Bunner is identified in a partial schedule of citizens by blood of the Creek Nation, approved by the Secretary of the Interior March 13, 1902, opposite number 18, and said Ollie Bunner is identified as Ollie Hale, whose name appears in a partial schedule of citizens by blood of the Creek Nation, approved March 28, 1902, opposite number 8046. Inasmuch as the father of the applicant appears on the roll as above stated, applicant is herein considered as Susie Bunner.

It further appears from the evidence that said Susie Bunner was born August 18, 1904, and was living March 4, 1905.

The Act of Congress approved March 3, 1905, (33 Stats. 1048) provides in part as follows:

"That the Commission to the Five Civilized Tribes is authorized for sixty days after the date of the approval of this act to receive and consider applications for enrollment, of children, born subsequent to May twenty-five, nineteen hundred and one, and prior to March fourth, nineteen hundred and five, and living on said latter date, to citizens of the Creek tribe of Indians whose enrollment has been approved by the Secretary of the Interior prior to the approval of this act; and to enroll and make allotments to such children."

It is, therefore, ordered and adjudged that the said Susie Bunner is entitled to be enrolled as a citizen by blood of the Creek Nation under the provisions of the act of Congress above quoted, and the application for her enrollment as such is accordingly granted.

Tams Bixby Commissioner.

Muskogee, Indian Territory.
JAN 25 1907

Applications for Enrollment of Creek Newborn
Act of 1905 Volume XIII

BIRTH AFFIDAVIT.

DEPARTMENT OF THE INTERIOR.
COMMISSION TO THE FIVE CIVILIZED TRIBES.

IN RE APPLICATION FOR ENROLLMENT, as a citizen of the Creek Nation, of Susie Bunner, born on the 18 day of August , 1904

Name of Father: Mosey Bunner   a citizen of the Creek Nation.
Fish Pond
Name of Mother: Ollie Bunner (nee Hill)   a citizen of the Creek Nation.
Fish Pond

Postoffice   Butner, I.T.

AFFIDAVIT OF MOTHER.

UNITED STATES OF AMERICA, Indian Territory, }
    Western   DISTRICT.

    I, Ollie Bunner , on oath state that I am about 26 years of age and a citizen by blood , of the Creek Nation; that I am the lawful wife of Mosey Bunner , who is a citizen, by blood of the Creek Nation; that a female child was born to me on 18 day of August , 1904 , that said child has been named Susie Bunner , and was living March 4, 1905.

                             Ollie Bunner
Witnesses To Mark:
   {

    Subscribed and sworn to before me this 1st day of November , 1905.

                             Drennan C Skaggs
                             Notary Public.

AFFIDAVIT OF ATTENDING PHYSICIAN OR MID-WIFE.

UNITED STATES OF AMERICA, Indian Territory, }
....DISTRICT.

    I, Sophy Deere , a mid-wife , on oath state that I attended on Mrs. Ollie Bunner, wife of Mosey Bunner on the 18 day of Aug , 1904 ; that there was born to her on said date a female child; that said child was living March 4, 1905, and is said to have been named Susie Bunner
                                  her
                            Sophy x Deere
Witnesses To Mark: mark
   { DC Skaggs
     Alex Posey

Applications for Enrollment of Creek Newborn
Act of 1905   Volume XIII

Subscribed and sworn to before me 1ˢᵗ day of   Nov   , 1905.

Drennan C Skaggs
Notary Public.

NC 1032

Muskogee, Indian Territory, October 23, 1905.

Arlie Bunner,
    Care Mosey Bunner,
        Bearden, Indian Territory.

Dear Madam:

    In the matter of the application for the enrollment of your minor child, name unknown, said to have been born subsequent to May 25, 1901, as a citizen by blood of the Creek Nation, this office desires your affidavit and affidavit of the midwife or physician in attendance at the birth of said child and a blank for that purpose is enclosed herewith.

    In the event that there was no physician or midwife in attendance when said child was born, it will be necessary for you to furnish this office with the affidavits of two disinterested witnesses relative to its birth. Said affidavits must set forth said child's name, the date of its birth, the names of its parents and whether or not it was living on March 4, 1905.

    This office is unable to identify you on its roll of citizens by blood of the Creek Nation; you are requested to state if you were ever known by the name of Ollie Hall, also state your maiden name, the names of your parents, the Creek Indian town to which you belong, and your roll number as the same appears on your deeds to lands in the Creek Nation.

Respectfully,
Commissioner.

AG-1032

Applications for Enrollment of Creek Newborn
Act of 1905   Volume XIII

NC 1032.

Muskogee, Indian Territory, October 3, 1906.

Ollie Bunner,
    c/o Mosey Bunner,
        Butner, Indian Territory.

Dear Madam:

In the matter of the application for the enrollment of your minor child, Susie Bunner, as a citizen of the Creek Nation, there is on file in this office your affidavit to which signature is very illegible. To correct same there is herewith enclosed a blank form of birth affidavit which you are requested to have properly executed and returned to this office at an early date.

                Respectfully,

1 BA   Commissioner.

N C 1032.

Muskogee, Indian Territory, March 7, 1907.

Ollie Bunner,
    Care of Mosey Bunner,
        Bearden, Indian Territory.

Dear Madam:

You are hereby advised that on March 2, 1907 the Secretary of the Interior approved the enrollment of your minor child, Susie Bunner, as a citizen by blood of the Creek Nation, and that the name of said child appears upon the roll of new born citizens by blood of the Creek Nation enrolled under the Act of Congress approved March 3, 1905, as number 1247.

This child is now entitled to allotment and application therefor should be made without delay at the Creek Land Office, Muskogee, Indian Territory.

                Respectfully,
                                        Commissioner.

Applications for Enrollment of Creek Newborn
Act of 1905   Volume XIII

DEPARTMENT OF THE INTERIOR,
COMMISSIONER TO THE FIVE CIVILIZED TRIBES.
Near Bearden, I.T. April 27, 1905.

In the matter of the application for a new born children concerning whose enrollment no affidavits could be obtained in time.

Simmer being duly sworn, testified as follows: Through Official Interpreter, Alex Posey.

Examination by the Commission:
Q What is your name? A Simmer.
Q What is your age? A About 46.
Q What is your post office address? A Bearden.

Statement: I am Town King of Quassarte No. 2. Henry King of Fish Pond and Sallie King of Okchiye, have a child names Janelly-- a girl--about three years old, and the youngest child is unnamed. It is a little over a month old--don't know what time in last it was born--it is a boy. Both are living. Post Office Bearden.

Moser and Arlie Bunny both of Fish Pond Town have a child I think is a girl-- about a year old and living. Post Office Bearden.

Jasper Hill and Maggie Hill Maychick, both of Fish Pond, have a boy about a year old or a little over a year old--Billie Hill is its name--he is living. Post Office, Bearden.

Isparney and Sophy Deere, both of Fish Pond, have two children--the oldest a girl named Minnie, about two years old--the other is about a year old--don't know the sex or the name.

Cobler Wolf, deceased, a Seminole, and Annie Yahola of Hillabee, have a girl child named Matilda Wolf--about three years old and living. Post Office, Bearden.

Henry G. Hains, being duly sworn, on his oath, states that the above and foregoing is a true and correct transcript of his stenographic notes as taken in said cause on said date.

(Signed) Henry G. Hains

Subscribed and sworn to before me this 10th day of May, 1905.

(Signed) Drennan C Skaggs
Notary Public.

Lona Merrick, being duly sworn, states that she copied the above and foregoing and that the same is a true and correct copy.

Lona Merrick

Applications for Enrollment of Creek Newborn
Act of 1905 Volume XIII

Subscribed and sworn to before me this 18th day of August, 1906.

J McDermott
Notary Public.

AFFIDAVIT OF DISINTERESTED WITNESS.

UNITED STATES OF AMERICA,
Western DISTRICT,   SS
INDIAN TERRITORY.

We, the undersigned, on oath state that we are personally acquainted with Maggie Hale   wife of   Jasper Hale   ; that there was born to her a   male child on or about the 4 day of   November, 1904   ; that the said child has been named   Billy Hale   and was living March 4, 1905.

Witnesses:

Jesse McDermott	his Pinkey x Deere
J.E. Guy	mark her Linda x Deere mark

Subscribed and sworn to before me this 4 day of   October   190 6

My Com
Ex July 25" 1907

J McDermott
Notary Public.

BIRTH AFFIDAVIT.

DEPARTMENT OF THE INTERIOR.
COMMISSION TO THE FIVE CIVILIZED TRIBES.

IN RE APPLICATION FOR ENROLLMENT, as a citizen of the Creek Nation, of   Billy Hale , born on the 4 day of Nov , 1904

Name of Father: Jasper Hale   a citizen of the   Creek   Nation.
  Fish Pond
Name of Mother: Maggie Hale (nee Cheek)   a citizen of the   Creek   Nation.
  Fish Pond

Postoffice   Butner, I.T.

Applications for Enrollment of Creek Newborn
Act of 1905   Volume XIII

AFFIDAVIT OF MOTHER.

UNITED STATES OF AMERICA, Indian Territory,
   Western   DISTRICT.

I, Maggie Hale, on oath state that I am about 23 years of age and a citizen by blood, of the Creek Nation; that I am the lawful wife of Jasper Hale, who is a citizen, by blood of the Creek Nation; that a male child was born to me on 4th day of Nov, 1904, that said child has been named Billy Hale, and was living March 4, 1905.

Maggie Hale

Witnesses To Mark:

Subscribed and sworn to before me this 1" day of November, 1905.

Drennan C Skaggs
Notary Public.

BIRTH AFFIDAVIT.

DEPARTMENT OF THE INTERIOR,
COMMISSION TO THE FIVE CIVILIZED TRIBES.

In Re Application for Enrollment, as a citizen of the Creek Nation, of Billy Hale, born on the 4 day of Nov, 1904

Name of Father: Jasper Hale   a citizen of the   Creek   Nation.
Fish Pond
Name of Mother: Maggie Hale (nee Cheek)   a citizen of the   Creek   Nation.
Fish Pond

Post-office   Butner, I.T.

AFFIDAVIT OF MOTHER.

UNITED STATES OF AMERICA,
   INDIAN TERRITORY,
   Western   District.

I, Maggie Hale, on oath state that I am about 23 years of age and a citizen by blood, of the Creek Nation; that I am the lawful wife of Jasper Hale, who is a citizen, by blood, of the Creek Nation; that a male child was born to me on 4th day of Nov, 1904, that said child has been named Billy Hale, and ~~is now~~ was living. March 4, 1905.

Maggie Hale

Applications for Enrollment of Creek Newborn
Act of 1905   Volume XIII

WITNESSES TO MARK:

{

Subscribed and sworn to before me this 1" day of November , 1905.

Drennan C Skaggs
NOTARY PUBLIC.

NC 1033.

Muskogee, Indian Territory, October 23, 1905.

Maggie Hale,
    Care of Jasper Hale,
        Bearden, Indian Territory.

Dear Madam:

In the matter of the application for the enrollment of your minor child, Billie Hale, said to have been born subsequent to May 25, 1901, as a citizen by blood of the Creek Nation, this office desires your affidavit and affidavit of the midwife or physician in attendance at the birth of said child and a blank for that purpose is enclosed herewith.

In the event that there there[sic] was no physician or midwife in attendance when said child was born, it will be necessary for you to furnish this office with the affidavits of two disinterested witnesses relative to his birth. Said affidavits must set forth said child's name, the date of his birth, the names of his parents and whether or not he was living on March 4, 1905.

This office is unable to identify you on its roll of citizens by blood of the Creek Nation; you are requested to state if you were ever known as Maggie Arholokoche, also state your maiden name, the names of your parents, the Creek Indian town to which you belong and your roll number as the same appears on your deeds and allotment certificate.

                      Respectfully,

BC. Env.   Commissioner.

Applications for Enrollment of Creek Newborn
Act of 1905 Volume XIII

2452-B.

Okemah, Indian Territory, November 9, 1905.

Commissioner to the Five Civilized Tribes,
    Muskogee, Indian Territory.

Sir:

There is enclosed herewith the affidavit of Maggie Hale in the matter of the application for the enrollment of Billy Hale as a citizen by blood of the Creek Nation.

I am unable to secure further evidence in said case.

                Respectfully,
                Alex Posey,
                Clerk in Charge Field Party.

                                            JWH

N C 1033

              Muskogee, Indian Territory, March 1, 1907.

Maggie Hale,
    % Jasper Hale,
        Bearden, Indian Territory.

Dear Madam :--

You are hereby advised that on February 15, 1907, the Secretary of the Interior approved the enrollment of your minor child, Billy Hale, as a citizen by blood of the Creek Nation, and that the name of said child appears upon the roll of New Born citizens by blood of the Creek Nation, enrolled under the Act of Congress approved March 3, 1905, as number 1199.

This child is now entitled to allotment and application therefor should be made without delay at the Creek Land Office, Muskogee, Indian Territory.

                Respectfully,
                                    Commissioner.

Applications for Enrollment of Creek Newborn
Act of 1905   Volume XIII

DEPARTMENT OF THE INTERIOR,
COMMISSIONER TO THE FIVE CIVILIZED TRIBES.
Near Bearden, I.T. April 27, 1905.

In the matter of the application for a new born children concerning whose enrollment no affidavits could be obtained in time.

Simmer being duly sworn, testified as follows: Through Official Interpreter, Alex Posey.

Examination by the Commission:
Q What is your name? A Simmer.
Q What is your age? A About 46.
Q What is your post office address? A Bearden.

Statement: I am Town King of Quassarte No. 2. Henry King of Fish Pond and Sallie King of Okchiye, have a child names Janelly-- a girl--about three years old, and the youngest child is unnamed. It is a little over a month old--don't know what time in last it was born--it is a boy. Both are living. Post Office Bearden.

Moser and Arlie Bunny both of Fish Pond Town have a child I think is a girl--about a year old and living. Post Office Bearden.

Jasper Hill and Maggie Hill Maychick, both of Fish Pond, have a boy about a year old or a little over a year old--Billie Hill is its name--he is living. Post Office, Bearden.

1034   Isparney and Sophy Deere, both of Fish Pond, have two children--the oldest a girl named Minnie, about two years old--the other is about a year old--don't know the sex or the name.

Cobler Wolf, deceased, a Seminole, and Annie Yahola of Hillabee, have a girl child named Matilda Wolf--about three years old and living. Post Office, Bearden.

Henry G. Hains, being duly sworn, on his oath, states that the above and foregoing is a true and correct transcript of his stenographic notes as taken in said cause on said date.

Henry G. Hains

Subscribed and sworn to before me this 10th day of May, 1905.

Drennan C Skaggs
Notary Public.

Applications for Enrollment of Creek Newborn
Act of 1905   Volume XIII

BIRTH AFFIDAVIT.

DEPARTMENT OF THE INTERIOR,
COMMISSION TO THE FIVE CIVILIZED TRIBES.

In Re Application for Enrollment, as a citizen of the Creek Nation, of Edmund Deere, born on the 13" day of March , 1905

Name of Father: Isparney Deere   a citizen of the   Creek   Nation.
Fish Pond
Name of Mother: Sophy Deere   a citizen of the   Creek   Nation.
Fish Pond
                              Post-office   Butner, I.T.

AFFIDAVIT OF MOTHER.

UNITED STATES OF AMERICA,
   INDIAN TERRITORY,
   Western   District.

I, Sophy Deere , on oath state that I am about 25" years of age and a citizen by blood , of the Creek Nation; that I am the lawful wife of Isparney Deere , who is a citizen, by blood of the Creek Nation; that a male child was born to me on the 13th day of March , 1905 , that said child has been named Edmund Deere , and is now was living. March 4, 1905
                                    her
                            Sophy x Deere
WITNESSES TO MARK: mark
   DC Skaggs
   Alex Posey

Subscribed and sworn to before me this 1st day of Nov , 1905.

                        Drennan C Skaggs
                              NOTARY PUBLIC.

AFFIDAVIT OF ATTENDING PHYSICIAN OR MID-WIFE.

UNITED STATES OF AMERICA,
   INDIAN TERRITORY,
   Western   District.

                                                we are personally acquainted with
I, We the undersigned , a (blank) , on oath state that I attended on Mrs. Sophy Deere , wife of Isparney Deere on the (blank) day of (blank) , 1(blank) ; that there was born to her on or about March 13, 1905 said date a male child; that

Applications for Enrollment of Creek Newborn
Act of 1905 Volume XIII

said child is now was living March 4, 1905 and is said to have been named Edmund Deere

WITNESSES TO MARK:
{ DC Skaggs
  Alex Posey

Wicey x Wilson
    mark
her
Katy x Sampson
    mark

Subscribed and sworn to before me this 1st day of Nov , 1905.

Drennan C Skaggs
NOTARY PUBLIC.

(The above Birth Affidavit given again.)

BIRTH AFFIDAVIT.

DEPARTMENT OF THE INTERIOR.
COMMISSION TO THE FIVE CIVILIZED TRIBES.

IN RE APPLICATION FOR ENROLLMENT, as a citizen of the Creek Nation, of Edmund Hale, born on the 13 day of March , 1904

Name of Father: Isparney Deere	a citizen of the	Creek	Nation.
Name of Mother: Sophy Deere (nee Hale)	a citizen of the	Creek	Nation.

Postoffice   Butner IT.

AFFIDAVIT OF MOTHER.

UNITED STATES OF AMERICA, Indian Territory,
    Western   DISTRICT.

I, Sophy Deere , on oath state that I am 26 years of age and a citizen by blood, of the Creek Nation; that I am the lawful wife of Isparney Deere , who is a citizen, by blood of the Creek Nation; that a male child was born to me on 13" day of March , 1904 , that said child has been named Edmund Deere , and was living March 4, 1905. that the child died last March

Witnesses To Mark:
{ Jesse McDermott
  J.E. Guy

her
Sophy x Deere
mark

Applications for Enrollment of Creek Newborn
Act of 1905   Volume XIII

Subscribed and sworn to before me this 4ᵗʰ day of   October   , 1906.

                         J McDermott
                         Notary Public.

AFFIDAVIT OF ATTENDING PHYSICIAN OR MID-WIFE.

UNITED STATES OF AMERICA, Indian Territory,
     Western   DISTRICT.

I, Ollie Hale , a midwife , on oath state that I attended on Mrs. Sophy Deere , wife of Isparney Deere on the 13" day of March , 1904 ; that there was born to her on said date a male child; that said child was living March 4, 1905, and is said to have been named Edmund Deere

                                     her
                              Ollie x Hale
Witnesses To Mark: mark
   { Jesse McDermott
   { J.E. Guy

Subscribed and sworn to before me this 4ᵗʰ day of   October   , 1906.

My Commission   J McDermott
Expires July 25" 1907   Notary Public.

BIRTH AFFIDAVIT.

DEPARTMENT OF THE INTERIOR.
COMMISSION TO THE FIVE CIVILIZED TRIBES.

IN RE APPLICATION FOR ENROLLMENT, as a citizen of the Creek Nation, of Minnie Deere, born on the 12ᵗʰ day of February, 1902

Name of Father: Isparney Deere   a citizen of the   Creek   Nation.
Fish Pond
Name of Mother: Sophy Deere   a citizen of the   Creek   Nation.
Fish Pond
                       Postoffice   Butner, Ind. Terr.

Applications for Enrollment of Creek Newborn
Act of 1905   Volume XIII

AFFIDAVIT OF MOTHER.

UNITED STATES OF AMERICA, Indian Territory, ⎫
    Western   DISTRICT.   ⎭

    I, Sophy Deere , on oath state that I am about 25 years of age and a citizen by blood , of the Creek Nation; that I am the lawful wife of Isparney Deere , who is a citizen, by blood of the Creek Nation; that a female child was born to me on the 12" day of February , 1902 , that said child has been named Minnie Deere , and was living March 4, 1905.

                                                      her
                                         Sophy x Deere
Witnesses To Mark: mark
   { DC Skaggs
     Alex Posey

    Subscribed and sworn to before me this 1st day of November , 1905.

                                              Drennan C Skaggs
                                              Notary Public.

AFFIDAVIT OF ATTENDING PHYSICIAN OR MID-WIFE.

UNITED STATES OF AMERICA, Indian Territory, ⎫
    Western   DISTRICT.   ⎭

                                                               are personally acquainted with We, the undersigned , a——, on oath state that I we attended on Mrs. Sophy Deere , wife of Isparney Deere on the day of , 1 ; that there was born to her on or about the 12th day of Feb 1902 said date a female child; that said child was living March 4, 1905, and is said to have been named Minnie Deere

                                                     her
                                         Wicey x Wilson
Witnesses To Mark: mark
   { D.C. Skaggs   her
     Alex Posey   Katy x Sampson
                                         mark
    Subscribed and sworn to before me this 1st day of November , 1905.

                                              Drennan C Skaggs
                                              Notary Public.

Applications for Enrollment of Creek Newborn
Act of 1905   Volume XIII

NC 1034

Muskogee, Indian Territory, October 23, 1905.

Sophia Deer,
    Care Sparny Deer,
        Bearden, Indian Territory.

Dear Madam:

    In the matter of the application for the enrollment of your minor children, Minnie Deer and _____ Deer, the given name of the latter being unknown to this office, both of whom are said to have been born subsequent to May 25, 1901, as citizens by blood of the Creek Nation, this office desires your affidavit and affidavit of the midwife or physician in attendance at the birth of said children and a blank for that purpose is enclosed herewith.

    In the event that there was no physician or midwife in attendance when said children were born, it will be necessary for you to furnish this office with the affidavits of two disinterested witnesses relative to the birth of each child. Said affidavits must set forth the names of said children, the date of their birth, the names of their parents and whether or not they was living on March 4, 1905.

                                      Respectfully,

AG-1034   Commissioner.

2452-B.

DEPARTMENT OF THE INTERIOR.
COMMISSION TO THE FIVE CIVILIZED TRIBES.

Okemah, Indian Territory, November 9, 1905.

Commissioner to the Five Civilized Tribes,
    Muskogee, Indian Territory.

Sir:

    There are enclosed herewith the affidavits of Sophy Deere, Wicey Wilson and Katy Sampson in the matter of the application for the enrollment of Minnie Deere as a citizen by blood of the Creek Nation.

                                      Respectfully,
                                                   Alex Posey
                                      Clerk in Charge Creek Field Party.

Applications for Enrollment of Creek Newborn
Act of 1905   Volume XIII

NC 1034.

Muskogee, Indian Territory, December 19, 1905

Sophie Deere,
    care[sic] Isparney Deere,
        Butner, Indian Territory.

Dear Madam:

In the matter of the application for the enrollment of your minor child, Edmund Deere, as a citizen by blood of the Creek Nation, it is stated in your affidavit and in the affidavits of Wicey Wilson and Katy Sampson relative to the birth of said Edmund Deere that he was born March 13, 1905, and that he was living March 4, 1905. This is obviously an error for the purpose of correcting which there is herewith enclosed blank form of birth affidavit for the mother which you are requested to execute, giving the correct date of the birth of said child and stating whether or not it was living on March 4, 1905.

There is also enclosed a blank form of affidavit for two disinterested witnesses which you are requested to have executed by said Wicey Wilson and Katy Sampson care being taken that all names are correctly spelled and dates given correctly.

This matter should have your immediate attention.

                Respectfully,

BA Dis.   Commissioner.

HGH

REFER IN REPLY TO THE FOLLOWING:

DEPARTMENT OF THE INTERIOR,
COMMISSIONER TO THE FIVE CIVILIZED TRIBES.

Muskogee, Indian Territory, December 19, 1905.

Alex Posey,
    Clerk in Charge Creek Field Party.

Dear Sir:

On April 27, 1905, Simmer appeared before the Commission to the Five Civilized Tribes at Bearden, Indian Territory, and gave the following testimony: "Isparney and Sophy Deere, both of Fish Pond have two children--the oldest a girl named Minnie, about two years old--the other is about a year old, don't know the sex or the name."

Applications for Enrollment of Creek Newborn
Act of 1905 Volume XIII

On November 9, 1905, you forwarded to this office, an affidavit in proper form relating to the birth of said Minnie Deere. you[sic] also forwarded an affidavit executed by Sophy Deere, the mother, and Wicey Wilson and Katy Sampson, two disinterested witnesses, relative to the birth of the other child referred to in the testimony whose name it appears is Edmund Deere. All the witnesses in said affidavit state that said Edmund Deere was born March 13, 1905 and that he was living on March 4, 1905. This is obviously an error and you are requested to secure new affidavits in said case, giving the correct date of the birth of said child and whether or not he was living on March 4, 1905.

      Respectfully,
          Tams Bixby
           Commissioner.

N.C. 1034

      Muskogee, Indian Territory, March 1, 1907.

Sophia Deer,
  Care Sparny Deer,
    Bearden, Indian Territory.

Dear Madam:

You are hereby advised that on February 15, 1907, the Secretary of the Interior approved the enrollment of your minor child, Edmund Deer, as a citizen by blood of the Creek Nation, and that the name of said child appears upon the roll of new born citizens by blood of the Creek Nation, enrolled under the Act of Congress approved March 3, 1905, as No. 1200.

This child is now entitled to allotment and application therefor should be made without delay at the Creek Land Office, Muskogee, Indian Territory.

      Respectfully,
          Commissioner.

Applications for Enrollment of Creek Newborn
Act of 1905   Volume XIII

N.C. 1035

Seminole Div.

Has appl. ever been made for Matilda Wolf as Sem?

No application for Matilda Wolf as a Seminole under Act of Mch 3, 1905.

AB

Mr. Bixby:

Possibly the testimony of July 16 1906 refers to another child of the same mother but there is so little ~~too~~ to it, and it is so probable that the witness on July 16 1906 did not give correct time of birth; together with the fact that we have no other evidence of there being two children and it being apparently impossible to get any evidence that I have ok'd the decision.

DEPARTMENT OF THE INTERIOR,
COMMISSIONER TO THE FIVE CIVILIZED TRIBES.
Near Bearden, I.T. April 27, 1905.

In the matter of the application for ~~a~~ new born children concerning whose enrollment no affidavits could be obtained in time.

Simmer being duly sworn, testified as follows: Through Official Interpreter, Alex Posey.

Examination by the Commission:
Q What is your name? A Simmer.
Q What is your age? A About 46.
Q What is your post office address? A Bearden.

Statement: I am Town King of Quassarte No. 2. Henry King of Fish Pond and Sallie King of Okchiye, have a child names Janelly-- a girl--about three years old, and the youngest child is unnamed. It is a little over a month old--don't know what time in last it was born--it is a boy. Both are living. Post Office Bearden.

Moser and Arlie Bunny both of Fish Pond Town have a child I think is a girl-- about a year old and living. Post Office Bearden.

Jasper Hill and Maggie Hill Maychick, both of Fish Pond, have a boy about a year old or a little over a year old--Billie Hill is its name--he is living. Post Office, Bearden.

Applications for Enrollment of Creek Newborn
Act of 1905   Volume XIII

1034   Isparney and Sophy Deere, both of Fish Pond, have two children--the oldest a girl named Minnie, about two years old--the other is about a year old--don't know the sex or the name.

Cobler Wolf, deceased, a Seminole, and Annie Yahola of Hillabee, <u>have a girl child named Matilda Wolf--about three years old and living</u>. Post Office, Bearden.

Henry G. Hains, being duly sworn, on his oath, states that the above and foregoing is a true and correct transcript of his stenographic notes as taken in said cause on said date.

(Signed)   Henry G. Hains
Subscribed and sworn to before me this 10th day of May, 1905.
(Signed)   Drennan C Skaggs
(SEAL)   Notary Public.

Lona Merrick, being duly sworn, states that the above and foregoing is a true and correct copy of the original testimony taken in said cause.

Lona Merrick

Subscribed and sworn to before me
this 13th day of February, 1907

(No Signature given)

DEPARTMENT OF THE INTERIOR,
COMMISSIONER TO THE FIVE CIVILIZED TRIBES.
Okemah, Indian Territory, July 16, 1906.

In the matter of the application for the enrollment, as citizens of the Creek Nation, of minor children born to duly enrolled citizens members of the so called Snake faction.

SIMMER, being duly sworn, testified as follows through Alex Posey official interpreter.

Q What is your name? A Simmer.
Q What is your age? A Forty six.
Q What is your post office address? A Bearden.
Q Are you a citizen of the Creek Nation? A Yes, sir
Q To what Creek Indian town do you belong? A Quassarte No. 2
Q Do you know of any minor children in your town or neighborhood for whose enrollment application has not been made? A Annie Smith of Hillabee town, a neighbor of mine, has a girl child born some time last winter but I don't know the child's name.
Q Do you know the father of the child? A Willie Yahola of Fish Pond.
Q It the child living? A Yes, sir

Applications for Enrollment of Creek Newborn
Act of 1905 Volume XIII

Q What is the post office address of the parents? A Bearden or Butner.

Annie Smith is identified opposite Creek Indian roll No. 8352.

Willie Yahola is identified opposite Creek Indian roll No. 8641.

I, Alex Posey, on oath state that the above and foregoing is a true and correct transcript of my notes as taken in said cause on said date.

Alex Posey

Subscribed and sworn to before me this 31 day of July 1906

Edward Merrick
Notary Public.

BIRTH AFFIDAVIT.

DEPARTMENT OF THE INTERIOR.
COMMISSION TO THE FIVE CIVILIZED TRIBES.

IN RE APPLICATION FOR ENROLLMENT, as a citizen of the Creek Nation, of Matilda Wolf, born on the 30 day of July , 1903

Name of Father: Cobley Wolf   a citizen of the Seminole   Nation.
Name of Mother: Annie Yahola   a citizen of the Creek   Nation.
Hillabee Town

Postoffice   Bearden IT

AFFIDAVIT OF MOTHER.

UNITED STATES OF AMERICA, Indian Territory, }
  Western   DISTRICT.

I, Annie Yahola , on oath state that I am about 34 years of age and a citizen by blood , of the Creek Nation; that I ~~am~~ was the lawful wife of Cobley Wolf , who is a citizen, by blood of the Seminole Nation; that a female child was born to me on the 30" day of July , 1903 , that said child has been named Matilda Wolf , and ~~is now~~ was living. March 4, 1905

her
Annie x Wolf
mark

Witnesses To Mark:
  { DC Skaggs
  { Alex Posey

155

Applications for Enrollment of Creek Newborn
Act of 1905   Volume XIII

Subscribed and sworn to before me this 1st day of   Nov.   , 1905.

Drennan C Skaggs
Notary Public.

(The above Birth Affidavit given again.)

NC 1035. OCH
EK

DEPARTMENT OF THE INTERIOR,
COMMISSIONER TO THE FIVE CIVILIZED TRIBES.

In the matter of the application for the enrollment of Matilda Wolf, as a citizen by blood of the Creek Nation.

DECISION.

The record in this case shows that on April 27, 1905, testimony was offered "in the matter of the application for new born children", which embraces Matilda Wolf, and is herein considered an original application for her enrollment as a citizen by blood of the Creek Nation, under the provisions of the Act of Congress approved March 3, 1905 (33 Stat., L. 1048). Further proceedings were had July 16, 1906. An affidavit, in the matter of the birth of said Matilda Wolf was filed November 11, 1905.

The evidence and the records of this office show that said Matilda Wolf is the child of Annie Yahola, whose name appears as Annie Smith upon a partial schedule of citizens by blood of the Creek Nation approved by the Secretary of the Interior March 28, 1902, opposite roll number 8352. The evidence does not establish the name of the father of said child.

The evidence shows that said Matilda Wolf was born July 30, 1903, and was living March 4, 1905.

The evidence and the records of this office fail to show that any application has ever been made for the enrollment of said Matilda Wolf, as a citizen of the Seminole Nation.

It is, therefore, ordered and adjudged that the said Matilda Wolf is entitled to be enrolled as a citizen by blood of the Creek Nation, under the provisions of the Act of Congress approved March 3, 1905 and the application for her enrollment as such is accordingly granted.

Tams Bixby   COMMISSIONER.

Muskogee, Indian Territory,
FEB 20 1907

Applications for Enrollment of Creek Newborn
Act of 1905   Volume XIII

NC. 1035.

Muskogee, Indian Territory, July 15, 1905.

Chief Clerk,
    Seminole Enrollment Division,
        Muskogee, Indian Territory.

Dear Sir:

    April 27, 1905, application was made to the Commission to the Five Civilized Tribes for the enrollment of Matilda Wolf, date of birth not given, as a citizen by blood of the Creek Nation. It is stated in said application that the father of said child was Cobler Wolf, deceased, a citizen of the Seminole Nation, and that the mother is Annie Yahola, a citizen of the Creek Nation.

    You are requested to inform the Creek Enrollment Division as to whether application has been made for the enrollment of said Matilda Wolf as a citizen of the Seminole Nation, and if so, what disposition has been made of the same.

                Respectfully,
                              Commissioner.

W.F.

DEPARTMENT OF THE INTERIOR.
COMMISSION TO THE FIVE CIVILIZED TRIBES.

Muskogee, Indian Territory, July 19, 1905.

Chief Clerk,
    Creek Enrollment Division.

Dear Sir:

    Receipt is acknowledged of your letter of July 15, 1905, (NC-1035) stating the application was made to the Commission to the Five Civilized Tribes for the enrollment of Matilda Wolf, date of birth not given, child of Cobler Wolf, deceased, a citizen of the Seminole Nation, and Annie Yahola, a citizen of the Creek Nation, as a citizen by blood of the Creek Nation and requesting to be informed as to whether application was made for the enrollment of said child as a citizen of the Seminole Nation. as to whether application has been made for the enrollment of said Matilda Wolf as a citizen of the Seminole Nation.

    In reply to your letter you are advised that it does not appear from an examination of the records of this office that application was made for the enrollment of said Matilda Wolf as a citizen of the Seminole Nation.

Applications for Enrollment of Creek Newborn
Act of 1905   Volume XIII

Respectfully,
Tams Bixby   Commissioner.

2452-B.

Okemah, Indian Territory, November 9, 1905.

Commissioner to the Five Civilized Tribes,
Muskogee, Indian Territory.

Sir:

There is enclosed herewith the affidavit of Annie Yahola in the matter of the application for the enrollment of Matilda Wolf, as a citizen by blood of the Creek Nation.

I am unable to secure further evidence in said case.

Respectfully,
Alex Posey,
Clerk in Charge Creek Field Party.

DEPARTMENT OF THE INTERIOR,
NC 1035.   COMMISSIONER TO THE FIVE CIVILIZED TRIBES.

Okemah, Indian Territory, January 15, 1907.

Commissioner to the Five Civilized Tribes,
Muskogee, Indian Territory.

Sir:

I have the honor to report in the matter of the application for the enrollment of Matilda Wolf, born July 30, 1903, as a citizen by blood of the Creek Nation, that, Annie Yahola, the mother, together with her neighbors refuse to testify or furnish any information relative to the birth of said child   Copies of record in said case are herewith enclosed.

Respectfully,
Jesse McDermott
Clerk in Charge.

Commissioner to the Five Civilized Tribes,
Number 2813--Received Jan. 16, 1907.

Applications for Enrollment of Creek Newborn
Act of 1905   Volume XIII

NC 1035.

Muskogee, Indian Territory, March 16, 1907.

Annie Yahola,
c/o Cobley Wolf,
Bearden, Indian Territory.

Dear Madam:

You are hereby advised that the Secretary of the Interior under date of March 4, 1907, approved the enrollment of your minor child, Matilda Wolf, as a citizen by blood of the Creek Nation, and that the name of said child appears upon the roll of new born citizens by blood, enrolled under the act of Congress approved March 3, 1905, as number 1290.

This child is now entitled to allotment and application therefor should be made without delay at the Creek Land Office, Muskogee, Indian Territory.

Respectfully,
Commissioner.

BIRTH AFFIDAVIT.

DEPARTMENT OF THE INTERIOR.
COMMISSION TO THE FIVE CIVILIZED TRIBES.

IN RE APPLICATION FOR ENROLLMENT, as a citizen of the Creek Nation, of Nora Thompson, born on the 21 day of September, 1903

Name of Father: Manuel Thompson   a citizen of the   Creek   Nation.
Tokpafka Town
Name of Mother: Cogee Thompson (nee King)   a citizen of the   Creek   Nation.
Tuskegee Town

Postoffice   Naudack, Ind. Ter.

Applications for Enrollment of Creek Newborn
Act of 1905   Volume XIII

AFFIDAVIT OF MOTHER.

UNITED STATES OF AMERICA, Indian Territory, } Child is present
Western   DISTRICT.

I, Cogee Thompson, on oath state that I am 20 years of age and a citizen by blood, of the Creek Nation; that I am the lawful wife of Manuel Thompson, who is a citizen, by blood of the Creek Nation; that a female child was born to me on 21 day of September, 1903, that said child has been named Nora Thompson, and was living March 4, 1905.

                                           her
                                   Cogee x Thompson

Witnesses To Mark: mark
{ Alex Posey
{ DC Skaggs

Subscribed and sworn to before me this 11 day of April, 1905.

                                   Drennan C Skaggs
                                   Notary Public.

AFFIDAVIT OF ATTENDING PHYSICIAN OR MID-WIFE.

UNITED STATES OF AMERICA, Indian Territory, }
Western   DISTRICT.

I, Louisa King, a midwife, on oath state that I attended on Mrs. Cogee Thompson, wife of Manuel Thompson on the 21 day of September, 1903 ; that there was born to her on said date a female child; that said child was living March 4, 1905, and is said to have been named Nora Thompson

                                   her
                                 Louisa x King

Witnesses To Mark: mark
{ Alex Posey
{ DC Skaggs

Subscribed and sworn to before me this 11 day of April, 1905.

                                   Drennan C Skaggs
                                   Notary Public.

Applications for Enrollment of Creek Newborn
Act of 1905   Volume XIII

DEPARTMENT OF THE INTERIOR,
COMMISSION TO THE FIVE CIVILIZED TRIBES.
Near ~~Morris~~, I.T. April 28, 1905.
Morse

In the matter of the application for new born children concerning whose enrollment no affidavits could be obtained in time.

William Yahola, being duly sworn, testified as follows:
Through Official Interpreter, Alex Posey.

Examination by the Commission.
Q What is your name? [sic] William Yahola.
Q What is your age? A About 32.
Q What is your post office address? [sic] Morse.

Statement: I am a member of the House of Warriros from Nuyaka Town. Yahdehka Harjoche of Okfusky[sic] and Losanna Harjo of Nuyaka, who is my sister and -----the oldest child is about four years old--can't find out when the child was born--<u>Lottie Harjos</u>[sic] it's[sic] name. The next to the oledest[sic] is <u>Martha</u> about two years old--and the youngest is named <u>Adam</u>, not quite a year old--about eight or nine months old, all living. Post Office, ~~Morris~~. Morse.

Dickey and Hunda Harjo, both of Nuyaka Town, have a child named <u>Leester</u>, about three years old and living--a girl-- post office, Morse, I.T.

Henry G. Hains, being duly sworn, on his oath, states that the above and foregoing is a true and correct transcript of his stenographic notes as taken in said cause on said date.   Henry G. Hains

Subscribed and sworn to before me this 10th day of May, 1905.

                              Drennan C Skaggs
                              NOTARY PUBLIC.

Applications for Enrollment of Creek Newborn
Act of 1905   Volume XIII

BIRTH AFFIDAVIT.

DEPARTMENT OF THE INTERIOR.
COMMISSION TO THE FIVE CIVILIZED TRIBES.

IN RE APPLICATION FOR ENROLLMENT, as a citizen of the Creek Nation, of Martha Harjochee, ~~born on the~~ in ~~day of~~ September, 1902

Name of Father: Yardeka Harjochee   a citizen of the Creek Nation.
Okfuskee Deep Fork Town
Name of Mother: Losanna Harjochee   a citizen of the Creek Nation.
Nuyaka Town
                    Postoffice   Morse, Ind. Terr.

AFFIDAVIT OF MOTHER.

UNITED STATES OF AMERICA, Indian Territory,
    Western   DISTRICT.

    I, Losanna Harjochee, on oath state that I am about 28 years of age and a citizen by blood, of the Creek Nation; that I am the lawful wife of Yardeka Harjochee, who is a citizen, by blood of the Creek Nation; that a female child was born to me ~~on   day of~~ in September, 1902, that said child has been named Martha Harjochee, and was living March 4, 1905.
                                            her
                          Losanna x Harjochee
Witnesses To Mark: mark
  { DC Skaggs
  { Alex Posey

    Subscribed and sworn to before me this 27 day of   October, 1905.

                          Drennan C Skaggs
                            Notary Public.

AFFIDAVIT OF ATTENDING PHYSICIAN OR MID-WIFE.

UNITED STATES OF AMERICA, Indian Territory,
    Western   DISTRICT.

                                                            are personally acquainted with We, the undersigned, ~~a~~ *(blank)*, on oath state that ~~I~~ we ~~attended on~~ Mrs. Losanna Harjochee, wife of Yardeka Harjochee ~~on the   day of   , 1~~ ; that there was born to her ~~on said date~~ in September, 1902, a female child; that said child was living March 4, 1905, and is said to have been named Martha Harjochee
                              her
                            x Kessetka
                              mark

Applications for Enrollment of Creek Newborn
Act of 1905 Volume XIII

Witnesses To Mark:
{ DC Skaggs
{ Alex Posey

                              her
                        Nettie x Lasah
                            mark

Subscribed and sworn to before me this 27 day of October, 1905.

                                          Drennan C Skaggs
                                          Notary Public.

BIRTH AFFIDAVIT.

DEPARTMENT OF THE INTERIOR.
COMMISSION TO THE FIVE CIVILIZED TRIBES.

IN RE APPLICATION FOR ENROLLMENT, as a citizen of the Creek Nation, of Adam Harjochee, ~~born on the~~ in ~~day of~~ April, 1904

Name of Father: Yardeka Harjochee   a citizen of the Creek Nation.
Okfuskee Deep Fork
Name of Mother: Losanna Harjochee   a citizen of the Creek Nation.
Nuyaka Town
                            Postoffice   Morse, Ind. Terr.

AFFIDAVIT OF MOTHER.

UNITED STATES OF AMERICA, Indian Territory, }
      Western   DISTRICT. }

    I, Losanna Harjochee, on oath state that I am about 28 years of age and a citizen by blood, of the Creek Nation; that I am the lawful wife of Yardeka Harjochee, who is a citizen, by blood of the Creek Nation; that a male child was born to me ~~on day of~~ in April, 1904, that said child has been named Adam Harjochee, and was living March 4, 1905.

                                              her
                                    Losanna x Harjochee
Witnesses To Mark: mark
{ DC Skaggs
{ Alex Posey

Subscribed and sworn to before me this 27 day of October, 1905.

                                          Drennan C Skaggs
                                          Notary Public.

Applications for Enrollment of Creek Newborn
Act of 1905   Volume XIII

AFFIDAVIT OF ATTENDING PHYSICIAN OR MID-WIFE.

UNITED STATES OF AMERICA, Indian Territory,
  Western   DISTRICT.

are personally acquainted with We, the undersigned , a *(blank)* , on oath state that ~~I~~ we ~~attended on~~ Mrs. Losanna Harjochee , wife of Yardeka Harjochee ~~on the   day of   , 1~~ ; that there was born to her on said date, a male child; that said child was living March 4, 1905, and is said to have been named Adam Harjochee

                her
               x Kessetka
                mark

Witnesses To Mark: her
  { DC Skaggs   Nettie x Lasah
    Alex Posey   mark

Subscribed and sworn to before me this 27 day of   October   , 1905.

                Drennan C Skaggs
                Notary Public.

N.C. 1037   Okemah, Indian Territory, September 28, 1906.

Commissioner to the Five Civilized Tribes,
      Muskogee, Indian Territory

Dear Sir:

    In the matter of the application for the enrollment of Adam Harjochee as a citizen by blood of the Creek Nation, I have the honor to report that the parents of said child refuse to execute affidavits relative to his birth or to testify in the case.

    There are on file affidavits of two dis-interested witnesses executed October 27, 1905, before Drennan C Skaggs, which appears to have been executed in compliance with your letter of October 23. 1905.

                Respectfully,
                Jesse McDermott

N.C. 1037.   F.H.W.
            DEPARTMENT OF THE INTERIOR,
     COMMISSIONER TO THE FIVE CIVILIZED TRIBES.

    In the matter of the application for the enrollment of Martha Harjochee and Adam Harjochee as citizens by blood of the Creek Nation.

                D E C I S I O N.

Applications for Enrollment of Creek Newborn
Act of 1905 Volume XIII

The record in this case shows that on April 28, 1905, William Yahola appeared before a Creek enrollment field party near Morse, Indian Territory, and testified "in the matter of the application for new born children, concerning whose enrollment no affidavits could be obtained in time", and in said testimony reference is made to Martha and Adam Harjoche[sic]. Said testimony will herein be considered an application for the said Martha and Adam Harjoche, in order that their citizenship rights be protected. Inasmuch as the father of said applicants is identified on the records of this office under the surname of Har-joc-che the said applicants are herein referred to as Martha and Adam Harjoche. Supplemental affidavits filed November 3, 1905, are attached to and made a part of the record herein.

The evidence and the records of this office show that the said Martha and Adam Harjoche are the children of Losana Harjochee and Yarteka Harjoche, whose names appear on a partial schedule of citizens by blood of the Creek Nation, approved by the Secretary of the Interior, March 13, 1902, opposite roll Nos. 4220 and 4343 respectively.

The evidence further shows that Martha Harjoche was born in September 1902, that Adam Harjoche was born in April 1904, and that both were living on March 4, 1905.

The Act of Congress approved March 3, 1905, (33 Stats. 1048) provides in part as follows:

"That the Commission to the Five Civilized Tribes is authorized for sixty days after the date of the approval of this act to receive and consider applications for enrollment, of children, born subsequent to May twenty-fifth, nineteen hundred and one, and prior to March fourth, nineteen hundred and five, and living on said latter date, to citizens of the Creek tribe of Indians whose enrollment has been approved by the Secretary of the Interior prior to the approval of this act; and to enroll and make allotments to such children."

It is, therefore, ordered and adjudged that the said Martha and Adam Harjoche are entitled to be enrolled as citizens by blood of the Creek Nation, in accordance with the provisions of law above quoted, and the application for their enrollment as such is accordingly granted.

Tams Bixby COMMISSIONER.

Muskogee, Indian Territory,
JAN 25 1907

BIRTH AFFIDAVIT.

DEPARTMENT OF THE INTERIOR,
COMMISSION TO THE FIVE CIVILIZED TRIBES.

In Re Application for Enrollment, as a citizen of the Creek Nation, of Adam Harjoche, born ~~on the~~ ~~day of~~ in April, 1904

Name of Father: Yardeka Harjochee   a citizen of the   Creek   Nation.
Okfuskee DF
Name of Mother: Losanna Harjochee   a citizen of the   Creek   Nation.

Applications for Enrollment of Creek Newborn
Act of 1905   Volume XIII

Post-office   Morse Ind. Ter

AFFIDAVIT OF MOTHER.

UNITED STATES OF AMERICA,
INDIAN TERRITORY,
Western   District.

I, Losanna Harjochee, on oath state that I am about 28 years of age and a citizen by blood, of the Creek Nation; that I am the lawful wife of Yardeka Harjochee, who is a citizen, by blood of the Creek Nation; that a male child was born to me ~~on day of~~ in April, 1904, that said child has been named Adam Harjochee, and ~~is now~~ was living. March 4, 1905

          her
Losanna x Harjochee
          mark

WITNESSES TO MARK:
{ DC Skaggs
  Alex Posey

Subscribed and sworn to before me this 27 day of October, 1905.

Drennan C Skaggs
NOTARY PUBLIC.

AFFIDAVIT OF ATTENDING PHYSICIAN OR MID-WIFE.

UNITED STATES OF AMERICA,
INDIAN TERRITORY,
Western   District.

we are personally [sic] with
~~I~~, We the undersigned, a *(blank)*, on oath state that ~~I attended~~ on Mrs. Losanna Harjochee, wife of Yardeka Harjochee ~~on the day of, 1~~; that there was born to her on said date a male child; that said child ~~is now~~ was living March 4, 1905 and is said to have been named Adam Harjochee

          her
    x Kessetka
WITNESSES TO MARK: mark
{ DC Skaggs   her
  Alex Posey   Nettie x Lasah
          mark

Subscribed and sworn to before me this 27 day of October, 1905.

Drennan C Skaggs
NOTARY PUBLIC.

Applications for Enrollment of Creek Newborn
Act of 1905 Volume XIII

BIRTH AFFIDAVIT.

DEPARTMENT OF THE INTERIOR.
COMMISSION TO THE FIVE CIVILIZED TRIBES.

IN RE APPLICATION FOR ENROLLMENT, as a citizen of the Creek Nation, of Lottie Harjochee, born on the 12 day of January, 1900

Name of Father: Yardeka Harjochee   a citizen of the Creek Nation.
Okfuskee Deep Fork Town
Name of Mother: Losanna Harjochee   a citizen of the Creek Nation.
Nuyaka Town
           Postoffice   Morse, Ind. Terr.

AFFIDAVIT OF MOTHER.

UNITED STATES OF AMERICA, Indian Territory,
     Western   DISTRICT.

     I, Losanna Harjochee, on oath state that I am about 28 years of age and a citizen by blood, of the Creek Nation; that I am the lawful wife of Yardeka Harjochee, who is a citizen, by blood of the Creek Nation; that a female child was born to me on 12 day of January, 1900, that said child has been named Lottie Harjochee, and was living March 4, 1905.
                                            her
                                  Losanna x Harjochee
Witnesses To Mark: mark
   { DC Skaggs
   { Alex Posey

Subscribed and sworn to before me this 27 day of   October, 1905.

                                    Drennan C Skaggs
                                        Notary Public.

AFFIDAVIT OF ATTENDING PHYSICIAN OR MID-WIFE.

UNITED STATES OF AMERICA, Indian Territory,
     Western   DISTRICT.

                                                      are personally acquainted with
    We, the undersigned, a̶, on oath state that I̶ we a̶t̶t̶e̶n̶d̶e̶d̶ ̶o̶n̶ Mrs. Losanna Harjochee, wife of Yardeka Harjochee o̶n̶ ̶t̶h̶e̶ ̶ ̶ ̶d̶a̶y̶ ̶o̶f̶ ̶ ̶,̶ ̶1̶ ; that there was born to her on s̶a̶i̶d̶ ̶d̶a̶t̶e̶ the 12" day of Jan, 1900, a female child; that said child was living March 4, 1905, and is said to have been named Lottie Harjochee
                                 her
                             x Kessetka
                               mark

Applications for Enrollment of Creek Newborn
Act of 1905 Volume XIII

Witnesses To Mark:
{ DC Skaggs
  Alex Posey

her
Nettie x Lasah
mark

Subscribed and sworn to before me this 27 day of October , 1905.

Drennan C Skaggs
Notary Public.

N.C. 1037.

F.H.W.

DEPARTMENT OF THE INTERIOR,
COMMISSIONER TO THE FIVE CIVILIZED TRIBES.

In the matter of the application for the enrollment of Lottie Harjochee as a citizen by blood of the Creek Nation.

DECISION.

The record in this case shows that William Yahola appeared before a Creek enrollment field party near Morse, Indian Territory, on April 28, 1905, and testified "in the matter of the application for new born children concerning whose enrollment no affidavits could be obtained in time." In the testimony above referred to reference is made to Lottie Harjo, and this reference will be considered an original application for the enrollment of the said Lottie Harjoche, inasmuch as the father of said applicant is identified on the approved Creek roll under the surname of Har-jo-che, in order that the citizenship rights of the applicant be protected. A supplemental affidavit filed November 3, 1905, is attached to and made a part of the record herein.

The evidence and the records of this office show that the parents of Lottie Harjoche were members of the Snake or disaffected faction of Creek Indians. The evidence further shows that the said Lottie Harjoche is the child of Yarteka Harjoche and Losana Harjochee, whose names appear on a partial schedule of citizens by blood of the Creek Nation, approved by the Secretary of the Interior March 13, 1902, opposite roll Nos. 4343 and 4220 respectively. It is also in evidence that the said Lottie Harjoche was born on January 12, 1900 and was living March 4, 1905.

Although the application herein was not made within the time designated by the Secretary of the Interior under the authority in him vested by the provisions of the Act of Congress approved March 3, 1901 (33 Stats., 1010), jurisdiction to consider the same under the Act of June 30, 1902, was given to this office and the Department by the provisions of Section One of the Act of Congress approved April 26, 1906, (34 Stats., 137).

It is, therefore, ordered and adjudged that the said Lottie Harjoche are entitled to be enrolled as citizens by blood of the Creek Nation, in accordance with the provisions of the Act of Congress approved June 30, 1902 (32 Stats. 500), and the application for her enrollment as such is accordingly granted.

Applications for Enrollment of Creek Newborn
Act of 1905   Volume XIII

Tams Bixby   COMMISSIONER.

Muskogee, Indian Territory,
JAN 26 1907

NC 1037.

Muskogee, Indian Territory, October 23, 1905.

Losana Harjochee,
    Care of Yarteka Harjochee,
        Morse, Indian Territory.

Dear Madam:

    In the matter of the application for the enrollment of your minor children, Lottie Harjochee, Martha Harjochee, and Adam Harjochee, all of whom are said to have been born subsequent to May 25, 1901, as citizens by blood of the Creek Nation, this office desires your affidavit and affidavit of the midwife or physician in attendance at the birth of said children and blanks for that purpose is herewith enclosed.

    In the event that there was no physician or midwife in attendance when said children were born, it will be necessary for you to furnish this office with the affidavits of two disinterested witnesses relative to the birth or each child. Said affidavits must set forth the names of said children, the dates of their birth, the names of their parents and whether or not they were living on March 4, 1905.

Respectfully,

AG-1037.

Commissioner.

2453-B.

Okemah, Indian Territory, November 1, 1905.

Commissioner to the Five Civilized Tribes,
    Muskogee, Indian Territory.

Sir:
    There is enclosed herewith supplemental proof in the matter of the application for the enrollment of Lottie, Martha and Adam, minor children of Yahdehka Harjochee and Losanna Harjo, as citizens by blood of the Creek Nation, together with a copy of the testimony heretofore taken in said case.

Respectfully,
        Alex Posey,
        Clerk in Charge Field Party.

Applications for Enrollment of Creek Newborn
Act of 1905   Volume XIII

NC 1037.

Muskogee, Indian Territory, August 27, 1906.

Losanna Harjochee,
    Care of Yarteka Harjochee,
        Morse, Indian Territory.

Dear Madam:

In the matter of the application for the enrollment of your minor child, Lottie Harjochee, as a citizen of the Creek Nation, you are advised that this office requires your affidavit in same; said affidavit should give the name of the child, the names of its parents, the date of its birth, and whether it was living March 4, 1906. This matter should receive your prompt attention.

Respectfully,

Acting Commissioner.

N C 1037.

Muskogee, Indian Territory, March 7, 1907.

Losana Harjochee,
    Care of Yahdehka Harjochee,
        Morse, Indian Territory.

Dear Madam:

You are hereby advised that on March 2, 1907 the Secretary of the Interior approved the enrollment of your minor children, Martha and Adam Harjoche, as citizens by blood of the Creek Nation, and that the names of said children appear upon the roll of new born citizens by blood of the Creek Nation enrolled under the Act of Congress approved March 3, 1905, as numbers 1248 and 1249, respectively.

These children are now entitled to allotment and application therefor should be made without delay at the Creek Land Office, Muskogee, Indian Territory.

Respectfully,

Commissioner.

Applications for Enrollment of Creek Newborn
Act of 1905 Volume XIII

NC-1038

Muskogee, Indian Territory, October 21, 1905.

Susan Tiger,
    Care George W. Tiger,
        Sharpe, Indian Territory.

Dear Madam:

In the matter of the application for the enrollment of Bryan Tiger, born June 7, 1904, as a citizen by blood of the Creek Nation, this office desires the affidavit of the physician in attendance at the birth of said child and a blank for that purpose is herewith enclosed.

In the event that you are unable to obtain the affidavit of the physician in attendance at the birth of said child, it will be necessary for you to furnish this office with the affidavits of two disinterested witnesses relative to his birth. Said affidavits must set forth said child's name, the date of his birth, the names of his parents and whether or not he was living on March 4, 1905.

                      Respectfully,
AG-1038   Commissioner.

DEPARTMENT OF THE INTERIOR.
COMMISSION TO THE FIVE CIVILIZED TRIBES.

In re application for enrollment as a Creek citizen
of Bryan Tiger, born on the 7th. day of June, 1904.

United States of America,)
   Indian Territory,   (SS.
Western Judicial District.)

J. M. Palmer and Sarah Palmer being first duly sworn upin[sic] their oaths state that they are neighbors of Susan H. Tiger and George W. Tiger and live about one quarter of a mile from them; that on the 7th. day of June, 1904, there was born to the said Susan H. Tiger a male child; that said child was named Bryan Tiger and was living on the 4th. day of March, 1905; that affiant Sarah Palmer was present with Susan H. Tiger at the time of the birth of the said child; that the attending physician, James Howard, is now deceased; that the name of the father of the said child id[sic] George W. Tiger and the name of the Mother of said child is Susan H. Tiger; and that affiants are wholly disinterested in this application for the enrollment of said child.

                                                         his
Witnesses to mark   J. M. x Palmer
W.R. Saunders   mark
H.L. Allen

Applications for Enrollment of Creek Newborn
Act of 1905   Volume XIII

her
Sarah x Palmer
mark

Subscribed in my presence and sworn to before me this 11th. day of November, 1905.

E.T. Noble
Notary Public.

My commission expires April 24th. 1907.

BIRTH AFFIDAVIT.   **COPY**
DEPARTMENT OF THE INTERIOR.
COMMISSION TO THE FIVE CIVILIZED TRIBES.

IN RE APPLICATION FOR ENROLLMENT, as a citizen of the Creek Nation, of Bryan Tiger, born on the 7th day of June , 1904

Name of Father: George W. Tiger	a citizen of the Creek	Nation.
Name of Mother: Susan H. Tiger	a citizen of the Creek	Nation.

Postoffice   Sharp, Indian Territory

AFFIDAVIT OF MOTHER.

UNITED STATES OF AMERICA, Indian Territory, }
   Western   DISTRICT.

I, Susan H. Tiger , on oath state that I am 35 ~~ye~~ years of age and a citizen by blood , of the Creek Nation; that I am the lawful wife of George W. Tiger , who is a citizen, by blood of the Creek Nation; that a male child was born to me on 7th day of June , 1904 , that said child has been named Bryan Tiger , and was living March 4, 1905.

Susan H. Tiger

Witnesses To Mark:
{

Subscribed and sworn to before me this 11th day of November   , 1905.

E. T. Noble
My Com Ex Apr 24, 1907   Notary Public.

Applications for Enrollment of Creek Newborn
Act of 1905   Volume XIII

AFFIDAVIT OF ATTENDING PHYSICIAN OR MID-WIFE.

UNITED STATES OF AMERICA, Indian Territory, }
Western   DISTRICT.

was present with
I, Sarah Palmer , a neighbor of Mrs Tiger , on oath state that I ~~attended on~~ Mrs. Susah H. Tiger, wife of George W. Tiger on the 7th day of June , 1904 ; that there was born to her on said date a male child; that said child was living March 4, 1905, and is said to have been named Bryan Tiger

                                                                    her
                                             Sarah x Palmer

Witnesses To Mark: mark
{ ET Noble
  WR Saunders

Subscribed and sworn to before me this 11" day of November , 1905.

                                      E. T. Noble
My Com Ex Apr 24, 1907   Notary Public.

BIRTH AFFIDAVIT.

DEPARTMENT OF THE INTERIOR.
COMMISSION TO THE FIVE CIVILIZED TRIBES.

IN RE APPLICATION FOR ENROLLMENT, as a citizen of the Creek Nation, of Bryan Tiger, born on the 7 day of June , 1904

Name of Father: George W. Tiger   a citizen of the   Creek   Nation.
Eufaula Deep Fork
Name of Mother: Susan Tiger   a citizen of the   Creek   Nation.
Osoche Town
                            Postoffice   Sharpe, I.T.

                                    Child present
AFFIDAVIT OF MOTHER.

UNITED STATES OF AMERICA, Indian Territory, }
Western   DISTRICT.

I, Susan Tiger , on oath state that I am 34 years of age and a citizen by blood , of the Creek Nation; that I am the lawful wife of George Tiger , who is a citizen, by blood of the Creek Nation; that a male child was born to me on 7 day of June , 1904 , that said child has been named Bryan Tiger , and was living March 4, 1905.

                                          Susie Tiger

Witnesses To Mark:
{

Applications for Enrollment of Creek Newborn
Act of 1905   Volume XIII

Subscribed and sworn to before me this 11 day of April , 1905.

Drennan C Skaggs
Notary Public.

father
AFFIDAVIT OF ~~ATTENDING PHYSICIAN OR MID-WIFE~~.

UNITED STATES OF AMERICA, Indian Territory,
Western   DISTRICT.

assisted the physician who
I, George W. Tiger , ~~a~~——, on oath state that I ^ attended my wife Mrs. Susan Tiger , ~~wife of~~——— on the   7 day of June , 1904 ; that there was born to her on said date a   male   child; that said child was living March 4, 1905, and is said to have been named Bryan Tiger

Geo W. Tiger

Witnesses To Mark:
{

Subscribed and sworn to before me this 11 day of April , 1905.

Drennan C Skaggs
Notary Public.

DEPARTMENT OF THE INTERIOR,
COMMISSION TO THE FIVE CIVILIZED TRIBES.
Near ~~Morris~~, I.T. April 28, 1905.
Morse

In the matter of the application for new born children concerning whose enrollment no affidavits could be obtained in time.

William Yahola, being duly sworn, testified as follows:
Through Official Interpreter, Alex Posey.

Examination by the Commission.
Q What is your name? [sic] William Yahola.
Q What is your age? A About 32.
Q What is your post office address? [sic] Morse.

Applications for Enrollment of Creek Newborn
Act of 1905   Volume XIII

Statement: I am a member of the House of Warriros from Nuyaka Town. Yahdehka Harjoche of Okfusky[sic] and Losanna Harjo of Nuyaka, who is my sister and -----the oldest child is about four years old--can't find out when the child was born--<u>Lottie Harjos</u>[sic] it's[sic] name. The next to the oledest[sic] is <u>Martha</u> about two years old--and the youngest is named <u>Adam</u>, not quite a year old--about eight or nine months old, all living. Post Office, ~~Morris~~. Morse.

Dickey and Hunda Harjo, both of Nuyaka Town, have a child named <u>Leester</u>, about three years old and living--a girl-- post office, Morse, I.T.

Henry G. Hains, being duly sworn, on his oath, states that the above and foregoing is a true and correct transcript of his stenographic notes as taken in said cause on said date.

Henry G. Hains

Subscribed and sworn to before me this 10th day of May, 1905.

Drennan C Skaggs
NOTARY PUBLIC.

C 1039

2453-B.

DEPARTMENT OF THE INTERIOR,
COMMISSIONER TO THE FIVE CIVILIZED TRIBES.
Okfuske, I. T., October 26, 1905.

In the matter of the application for the enrollment of Lesta Harjo as a citizen by blood of the Creek Nation.

DICKEY HARJO, being duly sworn, testified as follows:

Through Alex Posey Official Interpreter:

BY THE COMMISSIONER:
Q What is your name? A Dickey Harjo.
Q How old are you? A About thirty.
Q What is your post office address? A Morse.
Q Are you a citizen of the Creek Nation? A Yes, sir.
Q To what town do you belong? A Nuyaka.
Q Have you a child named Lesta? A Yes, sir
Q What is the name of the mother of the child? A Hunter Harjo. She was formerly Hunter Scott and is enrolled under that name.
Q Are you enrolled as Dickey Harjo? A I am enrolled simply as Teke.
Q When was your child, Lesta, born? A
   Witness presents a piece of paper on which the following record appears: "Jan. 1, 1902 Lesta"

Applications for Enrollment of Creek Newborn
Act of 1905   Volume XIII

Q Does this record refer to the birth of your daughter, Lesta Harjo? A Yes, sir.
Q Who made the record? A Chofolop Harjo, my Town King.
Q When did he make it? A On the same day the child was born.

---oooOOOooo---

    I, D. C. Skaggs, on oath state that the above and foregoing is a full and true transcript of my stenographic notes as taken in said cause on said date.

D. C. Skaggs

Subscribed and sworn to before me this 30 day of Dec 1905.

Edw C Griesel
Notary Public.

BIRTH AFFIDAVIT.

DEPARTMENT OF THE INTERIOR.
COMMISSION TO THE FIVE CIVILIZED TRIBES.

IN RE APPLICATION FOR ENROLLMENT, as a citizen of the Creek Nation, of Lesta Harjo, born on the 1st day of January, 1902

Name of Father: Dickey Harjo   a citizen of the   Creek   Nation.
Nuyaka Town
Name of Mother: Hunter Harjo   a citizen of the   Creek   Nation.
Nuyaka Town

Postoffice   Morse, I.T.

AFFIDAVIT OF MOTHER.

UNITED STATES OF AMERICA, Indian Territory,
    Western   **DISTRICT.**

    I, Hunter Harjo, on oath state that I am about 20 years of age and a citizen by blood, of the Creek Nation; that I am the lawful wife of Dickey Harjo, who is a citizen, by blood of the Creek Nation; that a female child was born to me on the 1st day of January, 1902, that said child has been named Lesta Harjo, and was living March 4, 1905.

her
Hunter x Harjo
mark

Witnesses To Mark:
    { DC Skaggs
      Alex Posey

Applications for Enrollment of Creek Newborn
Act of 1905   Volume XIII

Subscribed and sworn to before me this 26 day of October   , 1905.

                                        Drennan C Skaggs
                                        Notary Public.

AFFIDAVIT OF ATTENDING PHYSICIAN OR MID-WIFE.

UNITED STATES OF AMERICA, Indian Territory,
    Western   DISTRICT.

    I, Bettie Thomas , a mid-wife , on oath state that I attended on Mrs. Hunter Harjo , wife of Dickey Harjo on the 1st day of January , 1902 ; that there was born to her on said date a female child; that said child was living March 4, 1905, and is said to have been named Lesta Harjo

                                          her
                                Bettie x Thomas
Witnesses To Mark: mark
    DC Skaggs
    Alex Posey

Subscribed and sworn to before me this 26 day of October   , 1905.

                                        Drennan C Skaggs
                                        Notary Public.

N.C. 1039

                              Muskogee, Indian Territory, October 24, 1905.

Hunter Scott,
    Care Teke,
        Morse, Indian Territory.

Dear Madam:

    In the matter of the application for the enrollment of your minor child, Leester Harjo, said to have been born subsequent to May 25, 1901, as a citizen by blood of the Creek Nation, this office desires your affidavit and affidavit of the midwife or physician in attendance at the birth of said child and a blank for that purpose is enclosed herewith.

    In the event that there was no physician or midwife in attendance when said child was born, it will be necessary for you to furnish this office with the affidavits of two disinterested witnesses relative to her birth. Said affidavits must set forth said child's name, the date of her birth, the names of her parents and whether or not she was living on March 4, 1905.

                                Respectfully,
AG-1039   Commissioner.

Applications for Enrollment of Creek Newborn
Act of 1905   Volume XIII

BIRTH AFFIDAVIT.

DEPARTMENT OF THE INTERIOR.
COMMISSION TO THE FIVE CIVILIZED TRIBES.

IN RE APPLICATION FOR ENROLLMENT, as a citizen of the Creek Nation, of Jessie Deer, born on the 9 day of May, 1904

Name of Father: Pinkey Deer   a citizen of the   Creek   Nation.
Name of Mother: Linda Harjo (nee) Deer   a citizen of the   Creek   Nation.

Postoffice   Bearden Ind. Ter.

AFFIDAVIT OF MOTHER.

UNITED STATES OF AMERICA, Indian Territory,
Western   DISTRICT.

I, Linda Harjo (nee) Deer, on oath state that I am 23 years of age and a citizen by blood, of the Creek Nation; that I am the lawful wife of Pinkey Deer, who is a citizen, by blood of the Creek Nation; that a male child was born to me on 9 day of May, 1904, that said child has been named Jessie Deer, and was living March 4, 1905.

                             Linda Harjo nee Deer

Witnesses To Mark:

Subscribed and sworn to before me this 31 day of March, 1905.

my com exp. Aug 19-1908   Tupper Dunn
                                     Notary Public.

AFFIDAVIT OF ATTENDING PHYSICIAN OR MID-WIFE.

UNITED STATES OF AMERICA, Indian Territory,
Western   DISTRICT.

I, Louisa Harjo nee Simmer, a midwife, on oath state that I attended on Mrs. Linda Harjo (nee) Deer, wife of Pinkey Deer on the 9 day of May, 1904; that there was born to her on said date a male child; that said child was living March 4, 1905, and is said to have been named Jessie Deer

                                         her
                             Louisa x Harjo (nee) Simmer
                                   mark

Applications for Enrollment of Creek Newborn
Act of 1905 Volume XIII

Witnesses To Mark:
{ Tupper Dunn
  Pinkey Deer

Subscribed and sworn to before me this 31 day of March , 1905.

my com exp. Aug 19-1908   Tupper Dunn
                                      Notary Public.

NC 1040

OCH
JCL

DEPARTMENT OF THE INTERIOR,
COMMISSIONER TO THE FIVE CIVILIZED TRIBES.

In the matter of the application for the enrollment of Jessie Deer as a citizen by blood of the Creek Nation.

DECISION.

The record in this case shows that on May 23, 1905, application was made, in affidavit form, for the enrollment of Jessie Deer, as a citizen by blood of the Creek Nation, under the provisions of the Act of Congress approved March 3, 1905, (33 Stats.,L 1048).

The evidence and the records of this office show that said Jessie Deer is the child of Linda Deer, whose name appears as Linda Harjo, upon a schedule of citizens by blood of the Creek Nation; and Pinkey Deer whose name appears as Pinky Deer, upon a schedule of citizens by blood of the Creek Nation, approved by the Secretary of the Interior, March 28, 1902, opposite numbers 8954 and 6178 respectively.

The evidence shows that said Jessie Deer was born May 9, 1904 and was living March 4, 1905.

Although the application herein was not made within the time specified by the provisions of the Act of Congress approved March 3, 1905, (33 Stats. L., 1048), jurisdiction to consider the same under said act was given to this office and the Department by the provisions of Section one, of the Act of Congress approved April 26, 1906, (34 Stats. L. 137)

It is, therefore, ordered and adjudged that the said Jessie Deer is entitled to be enrolled as a citizen by blood of the Creek Nation under the provisions of the Act of Congress approved March 3, 1905 (33 Stats. L., 1048) and the application for his enrollment as such is accordingly granted.

Tams Bixby   COMMISSIONER.

Muskogee, Indian Territory.
FEB 18 1907

Applications for Enrollment of Creek Newborn
Act of 1905 Volume XIII

NC. 1040.

Muskogee, Indian Territory, June 21, 1906.

Linda Harjo, formerly Linda Deer,
    Bearden, Indian Territory.

Dear Madam:

    In the matter of the application for the enrollment of your minor child, Jessie Deer, as a citizen by blood of the Creek Nation, you are advised that it is required that you furnish this office with the affidavits of yourself and the midwife, who attended you at the birth of said child, said affidavits showing the name of the child, the names of its parents, the date of birth, and whether said child was living March 4, 1906, and for this purpose there is herewith enclosed, a blank affidavit. This matter should receive your immediate attention.

    You are further advised that this office is unable to identify you or Pinkey Deer, the father of said child, upon its rolls of citizens of the Creek Nation, and it will be necessary that your[sic] furnish this office with your maiden name, the names of your parents and other members of your family, the Creek Indian town to which you belong, the name and roll number as same appear on your deed or allotment certificates to land in the Creek Nation, and any other information that will enable this office to identify you and Pinkey Deer on its records.

                        Respectfully,

1 BA   Commissioner.

                                                                    JWH

N C 1040

                        Muskogee, Indian Territory, March 9, 1907.

Linda Deer,
    % Pinky Deer,
        Bearden, Indian Territory.

Dear Madam :--

    You are hereby advised that on March 2, 1907, the Secretary of the Interior approved the enrollment of your minor child, Jessie Deer, as a citizen by blood of the Creek Nation, and that the name of said child appears upon the roll of new born citizens by blood of the Creek Nation, enrolled under the Act of Congress approved March 3, 1905, as number 1274.

    This child is now entitled to allotment and application therefor should be made without delay at the Creek Land Office, Muskogee, Indian Territory.

                                      Respectfully,

                                                    Commissioner.

Applications for Enrollment of Creek Newborn
Act of 1905 Volume XIII

AFFIDAVIT

(Creek Equalization)

State of Oklahoma
     ss.   In re William Jones
Muskogee County   Cr 9022

  Albert Jones, a Creek citizen, of lawful age, being duly sworn according to law, deposes and says:
  That his post-office address is Pierce, Oklahoma;
  That he is a full brother of William Jones, deceased Creek citizen roll No. 9022; that Siah Jones, is a half brother of said William Jones;
  That the said William Jones died about the year 1906, without issue; that the said William Jones, never had any children, and was never married but once, to Mary Jones who died prior to the death of said William Jones;
  That I am informed that the enrollment records recite that said William Jones was the father of Caddo Jones, whose mother was Sallie Casey;
  Said William Jones and said Sallie Casey were never married and if said William Jones was the father of said child, said child was illegitimate.   Right
                                 (thumb print)
(Illegible) Fife   Albert Jones   *(thumb print)*
Interpreter   Thumb
  Subscribed and sworn to before me this 24th of April, 1915.
Witness   R.P. Harrison Clerk US Dist Court
BS Baugh   By AGW Miller Deputy
                ~~Notary Public~~

    My Com Exp

DEPARTMENT OF THE INTERIOR,
COMMISSION TO THE FIVE CIVILIZED TRIBES.
Near Wetumka, I.T. April 25, 1905.

  In the matter of the application for new born children concerning whose enrollment, No affidavits could be obtained in time.

  James Smith, being duly sworn, testified as follows testified as follows:
Through Alex Posey Official Interpreter:

Examination by the Commission:
Q What is your name? A AJames Smith[sic]. I am king of Pukontallahassee.
Q What is your age? A 66.
Q What is your post office address? A Carson.

Applications for Enrollment of Creek Newborn
Act of 1905 Volume XIII

Statement: I have heard Willie Jones of Tookpafka Town and Sallie Casey of Weogufky have a child about three years old, who is living. It is a girl named <u>Caddo or Caddie Jones</u>. Their post-office is Carson.

Henry G. Hains, being duly sworn, on his oath, states that the above and foregoing is a true and correct transcript of his stenographic notes as taken in said cause on said date.

Henry G. Hains

Subscribed and sworn to before me this 10th day of May, 1905.

Drennan C Skaggs
Notary Public.

BIRTH AFFIDAVIT.

DEPARTMENT OF THE INTERIOR.
COMMISSION TO THE FIVE CIVILIZED TRIBES.

IN RE APPLICATION FOR ENROLLMENT, as a citizen of the Creek Nation, of Caddo Jones, ~~born on the~~ sometime in ~~day of~~ June, 1903

Name of Father: Willie Jones   a citizen of the   Creek   Nation.
Tokpafka Town
Name of Mother: Sallie Casey   a citizen of the   Creek   Nation.
Weogufke Town

Postoffice   Carson, I.T.

AFFIDAVIT OF MOTHER.

Child is present

UNITED STATES OF AMERICA, Indian Territory, ⎫
    Western   DISTRICT.   ⎭

I, Sallie Casey , on oath state that I am over 30 years of age and a citizen by blood , of the Creek Nation; that I am not the lawful wife of Willie Jones , who is a citizen, by blood of the Creek   Nation; that a   female   child was ~~born to me on~~ sometime in ~~day of~~ June , 1903 , that said child has been named Caddo Jones , and is now living. and was living March 4, 1905. That no one attended on me at the birth of the said child

her
Sallie x Casey
mark

Witnesses To Mark:
  { DC Skaggs
    Alex Posey

Applications for Enrollment of Creek Newborn
Act of 1905   Volume XIII

Subscribed and sworn to before me this 12   day of   June , 1905.

          Drennan C Skaggs
          Notary Public.

AFFIDAVIT OF ATTENDING PHYSICIAN OR MID-WIFE.

UNITED STATES OF AMERICA, Indian Territory,
  Western   **DISTRICT.**

                  we are personally acquainted with
~~I~~, We, the undersigned   , ~~a~~ *(blank)* , on oath state that ~~I attended on Mrs~~. Sallie Casey , ~~wife of~~ *(blank)*   ~~on the   day of   , 1~~ ; that there was born to her in June, 1903 a female child; that said child is now living and was living March 4, 1905 and is said to have been named Caddo Jones

          Louisie Bruner
            his
Witnesses To Mark: Linty x Bruner
 { DC Skaggs   mark
   Alex Posey

Subscribed and sworn to before me this 12   day of   June , 1905.

          Drennan C Skaggs
          Notary Public.

DEPARTMENT OF THE INTERIOR,
COMMISSION TO THE FIVE CIVILIZED TRIBES.
NEAR WEELETKA[sic], I.T. April 20, 1905.

In the matter of the application for the enrollment of certain new born children of "Snake" parents.

  Totkis Harjo, being duly sworn, testified as follows,
Through Official Interpreter Alex Posey.

Examination by the Commission:
Q What is your name? A Totkis Harjo.
Q How old are you? A About 60.

Applications for Enrollment of Creek Newborn
Act of 1905 Volume XIII

Q What is your post office address? A Weeletka[sic].

Statement: I have a grandchild named Emma, the father named Artus Hopiye, the mother Sudie, both of Alabama Town. <u>Emma Hopiye</u> is about a year and three months old, born about this time last year. She is living now, their post office is Weeletka[sic] or Wetumka.

Henry G. Hains, being duly sworn, on his oath, states that the above and foregoing is a true and correct transcript of his stenographic notes as taken in said cause on said date.

Henry G. Hains

Subscribed and sworn to before me this 11th day of May, 1905.

Drennan C Skaggs
Notary Public.

N.C. 1042.

DEPARTMENT OF THE INTERIOR,
COMMISSIONER TO THE FIVE CIVILIZED TRIBES.

In the matter of the application for the enrollment of Emma Hopiye as a citizen by blood of the Creek Nation.

ARTUS HOPIYE (alias Cooper Johnson) being duly sworn, testified as follows:

Through Alex Posey Official Interpreter:

BY THE COMMISSIONER:
Q What is your name? A Artus Hopiye is my Indian name and the name by which I am generally known. My English name and the name under which I think I am enrolled is Cooper Johnson.
Q What is your post office address? A Wetumka.
Q How old are you? A I am about fifty.
Q Are you a citizen of the Creek Nation? A Yes, sir.
Q To what town do you belong? A Alabama.
Q What is your wife's name? A Judy.
Q To what town does she belong? A Alabama.
Q Have you a child named Emma? A Yes, sir, but she is not now living.
Q When did she die? A I do not remember the exact date of her death but she died in September of last year.
Q September of 1905? A Yes, sir.
Q When was Emma born? A On the 15th day of September in the year preceeding[sic] her death.
Q September 15, 1904? A Yes, sir, she was just a year old when she died.

Applications for Enrollment of Creek Newborn
Act of 1905 Volume XIII

Q Since you are enrolled as Cooper Johnson you desire to have your child, Emma, enrolled as Emma Johnson do you not? A Yes, sir, but now that she is dead I do not care whether she is enrolled or not. The allotment God has given her in the grave yard is all that she is entitled to and I do not care to claim for her more land than she has already. I myself am not entitled to more land than my grave-house will cover but the Commission has given me 160 acres. I am opposed to laying perpetual claim to any gift of God.

---oooOOOooo---

I, D. C. Skaggs, on oath state that the above and foregoing is a full and true transcript of my stenographic notes as taken in said cause on said date.

D. C. Skaggs

Subscribed and sworn to before me this 24 day of April 1906.

Alex Posey
Notary Public.

Indian Territory I
                I ss
Western District I

We, the undersigned, on oath state that we are personally acquainted with Judy Johnson wife of Cooper Johnson ; that on or about the 15 day of September , 1904 , a female child was born to them and ~~has~~ had been named Emma Johnson ; that said child was living March 4, 1905.

We further state that we have no interest in the above case.

Witnesses to mark: her
  Alex Posey   Louisa x Gray
                         mark

                         her
  DC Skaggs   Annie x Gray
                         mark

Subscribed and sworn to before me this 18 day of April, 1906.

Alex Posey
Notary Public.

Applications for Enrollment of Creek Newborn
Act of 1905 Volume XIII

DEPARTMENT OF THE INTERIOR.
COMMISSION TO THE FIVE CIVILIZED TRIBES.

In the matter of the death of Emma Johnson a citizen of the Creek Nation, who formerly resided at or near Wetumka , Ind. Ter., and died ~~on the~~ in ~~day of~~ September , 1905

AFFIDAVIT OF RELATIVE.

UNITED STATES OF AMERICA, Indian Territory,
Western DISTRICT.

I, Cooper Johnson , on oath state that I am about 50 years of age and a citizen by blood , of the Creek Nation; that my postoffice address is Wetumka , Ind. Ter.; that I am father of Emma Johnson who was a citizen, by blood , of the Creek Nation and that said Emma Johnson died ~~on the~~ in ~~day of~~ September , 1905

                                                  his
                                  Cooper x Johnson
Witnesses To Mark: mark
  Alex Posey
  DC Skaggs

Subscribed and sworn to before me this 18 day of April, 1906.

                                        Alex Posey
                                        Notary Public.

BIRTH AFFIDAVIT.

DEPARTMENT OF THE INTERIOR.
COMMISSION TO THE FIVE CIVILIZED TRIBES.

IN RE APPLICATION FOR ENROLLMENT, as a citizen of the Creek Nation, of Emma Johnson , born on the 15 day of Sept , 1904

Name of Father: Cooper Johnson   a citizen of the   Creek   Nation.
Name of Mother: Judy Johnson   a citizen of the   Creek   Nation.

                                  Postoffice   Wetumka Ind. Ter.

Applications for Enrollment of Creek Newborn
Act of 1905   Volume XIII

Father
AFFIDAVIT OF ~~MOTHER~~.

UNITED STATES OF AMERICA, Indian Territory,
Western   DISTRICT.

    I, Cooper Johnson, on oath state that I am about 50 years of age and a citizen by blood, of the Creek Nation; that I am the lawful ~~wife~~ husband of Judy Johnson, who is a citizen, by blood of the Creek Nation; that a female child was born to ~~me~~ her on 15 day of September, 1904, that said child has been named Emma Johnson, and was living March 4, 1905.

his
Cooper x Johnson
mark

Witnesses To Mark:
- Alex Posey
- DC Skaggs

    Subscribed and sworn to before me this 18" day of April, 1905.

Alex Posey
Notary Public.

(The above Birth Affidavit given again.)

(The Death Affidavit, above, given again.)

NC 1042.

Muskogee, Indian Territory, October 24, 1905.

Judy Johnson,
    Care Totkis Harjo,
        Weleetka, Indian Territory.

Dear Madam:

    In the matter of the application for the enrollment of your minor child, Emma Johnson, said to have been born subsequent to May 25, 1901, as a citizen by blood of the Creek Nation, this office desires your affidavit and affidavit of the midwife or physician in attendance at the birth of said child and a blank for that purpose is enclosed herewith.

    In the event that there was no physician or midwife in attendance when said child was born, it will be necessary for you to furnish this office with the affidavits of two disinterested witnesses relative to her birth. Said affidavits must set forth said child's name, the date of her birth, the names of her parents and whether or not she was living on March 4, 1905.

Applications for Enrollment of Creek Newborn
Act of 1905   Volume XIII

AG-1042.
Respectfully,
Commissioner.

(The two letters below belong with case #546, Applications for Enrollment of Creek Newborn Act of 1905 Volume VII, page 168.)

Muskogee, Indian Territory, December 8, 1905.

McKennon & Willmott,
    Wewoka, Indian Territory.

Gentlemen:

    Receipt is acknowledged of your letter of December 5, 1905, in which you state that George Colonel of Earlsboro, Oklahoma, desires to know if any further evidence is needed in the matter of the enrollment of Arra and Freeman Colonel, as citizens of the Seminole or Creek Nations.

    In reply you are advised application was made for the enrollment of said children as citizens of the Creek Nation on April 1, 1905.

    You are further advised that the name of said child is given variously as Arra and Harry and the surname of said children is given in affidavits in this case as Kernel and Kernells and that of the father of said children is enrolled as a citizen of the Creek Nation under the name of George Kernel.

    It is required that the affidavit of the parents be furnished this office, giving the correct names of said children.

Respectfully,
Acting Commissioner.

NC 546.
Muskogee, Indian Territory, August 8, 1905.

Arretta Kernel,
    Earlsboro, Oklahoma Territory.

Dear Madam:

    In the matter of the application for the enrollment of your minor children Harry Kernel and Freeman Kernel, as citizens by blood of the Creek Nation You are advised that it will be necessary for you to furnish this office with evidence of your marriage to George Kernel, the father of said children.

Applications for Enrollment of Creek Newborn
Act of 1905   Volume XIII

It will also be necessary for you to furnish this office with the affidavits of said George Kernel as to the birth of said children and two blanks for that purpose which have been filled out are inclosed herewith. You are requested to have the said George Kernel appear before a notary public and swear to said affidavits and return the same to this office in the inclosed envelope together with the evidence of marriage above referred to.

Respectfully,

Acting Commissioner.

CTD-35
Env.

NC 1042.

Wetumka, Indian Territory, April 24, 1906.

Commissioner to the Five Civilized Tribes,
    Muskogee, Indian Territory.

Sir:

There are herewith enclosed affidavits and testimony in the matter of the application for the enrollment of Emma Hopiye as a citizen by blood of the Creek Nation.

Respectfully,
Signed Alex Posey,
In Charge Creek Field Party.

N.C. 1042

Muskogee, Indian Territory, April 26, 1906.

Alex Posey,
    Clerk in Charge Creek Enrollment Field Party,
        Holdenville, Indian Territory.

Dear Sir:

Receipt is acknowledged of your letter of April 24, 1906, inclosing affidavits and testimony of Cooper Johnson in the matter of the application for the enrollment of his minor child, Emma Johnson, as a citizen of the Creek Nation.

You are advised that the affidavit of Judy Johnson, mother of said child, is desired in said case.

Respectfully,
Commissioner.

Applications for Enrollment of Creek Newborn
Act of 1905   Volume XIII

REFER IN REPLY TO THE FOLLOWING:
N.C. 1042

DEPARTMENT OF THE INTERIOR,
COMMISSIONER TO THE FIVE CIVILIZED TRIBES.

Muskogee, Indian Territory, August 9, 1906.

Commissioner to the Five Civilized Tribes,
    Muskogee, Indian Territory.

Sir:

    In the matter of the application for the enrollment of Emma Johnson, deceased, as a citizen by blood of the Creek Nation, I have the honor to report that Judy Johnson refuses to give testimony or to execute affidavits relative to the birth and death of said Emma Johnson.

                    Respectfully,
                          Alex Posey
                    Clerk in Charge Creek Field Party.

NC 1042.   EK

                    Muskogee, Indian Territory, March 1, 1907.

Judy Johnson,
    c/o Cooper Johnson,
        Wetumka, Indian Territory.

Dear Madam:

    You are hereby advised that on February 15, 1907, the Secretary of the Interior approved the enrollment of your deceased minor child, Emma Johnson, as a citizen by blood of the Creek Nation, and that the name of said child appears upon the roll of new born citizens by blood of the Creek Nation, enrolled under the act of Congress approved March 3, 1905, as number 1201.

    This child is now entitled to allotment and application therefor should be made without delay at the Creek Land Office, Muskogee, Indian Territory.

                    Respectfully,
                                      Commissioner.

Applications for Enrollment of Creek Newborn
Act of 1905   Volume XIII

DEPARTMENT OF THE INTERIOR,
COMMISSION TO THE FIVE CIVILIZED TRIBES.
NEAR WEELETKA[sic], I.T. April 20, 1905.

In the matter of the application for the enrollment of certain new born children of "Snake" parents.

Minta Baker, being duly sworn, testified as follows, through official interpreter, Alex Posey.

Examination by the Commission:
Q What is your name? A Minta Baker.
Q What is your age? A About 45.
Q What is your post office address? [sic] Weleetka.

X   Statement: Louisa a daughter of Hillis Harjo, and the wife of Legusie, have a girl child that is just crawling, Louisa belongs to Thlopthlocco and Legusie to Alabama, the child is living, the child is named Emma-- their post office is Weeletka[sic].

There is also another woman named Polly, the daughter of Nathlocco Harjo of Alabama Town, has a child, the father is unknown. Jimmie is it's[sic] name, it is a boy. It is a young child and I think the child was born sometime last summer.

Willeya Fish of Alabama Town and Mellogee Fish of Kialigee I think, have a child I think that is just beginning to walk and has not been named yet. I think it is a girl. It is living now, Wetumka is the post office.

The above testimony was participated in by Jacob Sandy.

Q What is your name? A Jacob Sandy.
Q How old are you? A 28.
Q What is your post office address? A Wetumka.

Statement: I am a member of Kialigee Town, I think Williya and Mellogee Fish have another child about three years old, named George Fish and living. I have advised the parents to make application for them but they won't do it. Williya is here now himself and runs away.

A Statement by Jacob Sandy: Arlinga Faction Snakes are now making a roll of new borns which they are going to send to Washington.

Henry G. Hains, being duly sworn, on his oath, states that the above and foregoing is a true and correct transcript of his stenographic notes as taken in said cause on said date.

                                            Henry G. Hains

Applications for Enrollment of Creek Newborn
Act of 1905 Volume XIII

Subscribed and sworn to before me this 11th day of May, 1905.

                                           Drennan C Skaggs
                                           Notary Public.

Indian Territory I
                 I ss
Western District I

     We, the undersigned, on oath state that we are personally acquainted with Louisa Harjo wife of Legus Harjo ; that on or about the 28 day of May ,1902 , a female child was born to them and has been named Emma Harjo ; that said child was living March 4, 1905.

     We further state that we have no interest in the above case.

                                       her
Witnesses to mark: Lena x Yahola
    Alex Posey   mark

                                       his
    DC Skaggs   Massey x Harjo
                                         mark

Subscribed and sworn to before me this 21 day of April, 1906.

                                         Alex Posey
                                         Notary Public.

BIRTH AFFIDAVIT.
DEPARTMENT OF THE INTERIOR.
COMMISSION TO THE FIVE CIVILIZED TRIBES.

     IN RE APPLICATION FOR ENROLLMENT, as a citizen of the Creek Nation, of Emma Harjo , born on the 28 day of May , 1902

Name of Father: Legus Harjo	a citizen of the Creek	Nation.
Alabama Town		
Name of Mother: Louisa Harjo	a citizen of the Creek	Nation.
Thlop thlocco Town		

                         Postoffice   Weleetka Ind Ter

Applications for Enrollment of Creek Newborn
Act of 1905 Volume XIII

AFFIDAVIT OF MOTHER.

UNITED STATES OF AMERICA, Indian Territory, ⎱
  Western   DISTRICT.   ⎰

I, Louisa Harjo, on oath state that I am about 25 years of age and a citizen by blood, of the Creek Nation; that I am the lawful wife of Legus Harjo, who is a citizen, by blood of the Creek Nation; that a female child was born to me on 28 day of May, 1902, that said child has been named Emma Harjo, and was living March 4, 1905.

                                  her
                              Louisa x Harjo
Witnesses To Mark: mark
 ⎰ Alex Posey
 ⎱ DC Skaggs

Subscribed and sworn to before me this 21 day of April, 1906.

                                        Alex Posey
                                        Notary Public.

NC 1043

                          Muskogee, Indian Territory, October 24, 1905.

Louisa Harjo,
    Minta Baker,
        Weleetka, Indian Territory.

Dear Madam:

In the matter of the application for the enrollment of your minor child, Emma Harjo, said to have been born subsequent to May 25, 1901, as a citizen by blood of the Creek Nation, this office desires your affidavit and affidavit of the midwife or physician in attendance at the birth of said child and a blank for that purpose is enclosed herewith.

In the event that there was no physician or midwife in attendance when said child was born, it will be necessary for you to furnish this office with the affidavits of two disinterested witnesses relative to her birth. Said affidavits must set forth said child's name, the date of her birth, the names of her parents and whether or not she was living on March 4, 1905.

                        Respectfully,
                                        Commissioner.

AG-1043

Applications for Enrollment of Creek Newborn
Act of 1905 Volume XIII

DEPARTMENT OF THE INTERIOR,
COMMISSION TO THE FIVE CIVILIZED TRIBES.
NEAR WEELETKA[sic], I.T. April 20, 1905.

In the matter of the application for the enrollment of certain new born children of "Snake" parents.

Minta Baker, being duly sworn, testified as follows, through official interpreter, Alex Posey.

Examination by the Commission:
Q What is your name? A Minta Baker.
Q What is your age? A About 45.
Q What is your post office address? [sic] Weleetka.

Statement: Louisa a daughter of Hillis Harjo, and the wife of Legusie, have a girl child that is just crawling, Louisa belongs to Thlopthlocco and Legusie to Alabama, the child is living, the child is named Emma-- their post office is Weeletka[sic].

There is also another woman named Polly, the daughter of Nathlocco Harjo of Alabama Town, has a child, the father is unknown. Jimmie is it's[sic] name, it is a boy. It is a young child and I think the child was born sometime last summer.

Willeya Fish of Alabama Town and Mellogee Fish of Kialigee I think, have a child I think that is just beginning to walk and has not been named yet. I think it is a girl. It is living now, Wetumka is the post office.

The above testimony was participated in by Jacob Sandy.

Q What is your name? A Jacob Sandy.
Q How old are you? A 28.
Q What is your post office address? A Wetumka.

Statement: I am a member of Kialigee Town, I think Williya and Mellogee Fish have another child about three years old, named George Fish and living. I have advised the parents to make application for them they won't do it. Williya is here now himself and runs away.

A Statement by Jacob Sandy: Arlinga Faction Snakes are now making a roll of new borns which they are going to send to Washington.

Henry G. Hains, being duly sworn, on his oath, states that the above and foregoing is a true and correct transcript of his stenographic notes as taken in said cause on said date.

Henry G. Hains

Applications for Enrollment of Creek Newborn
Act of 1905   Volume XIII

Subscribed and sworn to before me this 11th day of May, 1905.

                                                  Drennan C Skaggs
                                                  Notary Public.

2457-B.

DEPARTMENT OF THE INTERIOR,
COMMISSIONER TO THE FIVE CIVILIZED TRIBES.
NEAR WELEETKA, INDIAN TERRITORY,
NOVEMBER 23, 1906.

In the matter of the application for the enrollment of Jimmie Harjo, a minor child of Polly Harjo, as a citizen by blood of the Creek Nation.

POLLY HARJO, being first duly sworn, by and examined through Alex Posey, a Notary Public, and Official Interpreter, testified as follows:

BY THE COMMISSIONER:

Q What is your name? A Polly Harjo.
Q How old are you? A About 30.
Q What is your postoffice address? A Weleetka, Indian Territory but I have never received any mail there.
Q Are you a citizen of the Creek Nation? A Yes sir.
Q To what Creek town do you belong? A Alabama.
Q Have you a minor child named Jimmie Harjo? A Yes sir, there is the child there.
Q Who is the father of the child? A Jonas Fish of Alabana town.
Q Is he your lawful husband? A No sir.
Q The child is illegitimate, child[sic], is it? A Yes sir.
Q When was the child born? A In the Fall of the year, in cotton picking time. The child is a little over two years old.
Q Have you made application for the enrollment of this child? A Yes sir, I fixed out some papers at Weleetka last year with reference to the child's enrollment.
Q Did you make application for the child as Jimmie Fish, or Jimmie Harjo?
A As Jimmie Fish.
Q You are positive, are you, that you have already made application for the enrollment of this child? A Yes sir.
Q Under what name are you enrolled? A As Polly Harjo, I suppose, because my father was Nathlocco Harjo.

James B. Myers, being first duly sworn, states, that as stenographer to the Commissioner to the Five Civilized Tribes, he recorded the testimony in the foregoing proceedings, and that the above is a true, and correct transcript of his stenographic notes thereof.

Applications for Enrollment of Creek Newborn
Act of 1905   Volume XIII

James B Myers

Subscribed and sworn to before me,
this 10 day of Dec, 1906.

Alex Posey
Notary Public.

NC 1044   OCH
                                                                                               CM

DEPARTMENT OF THE INTERIOR,
COMMISSIONER TO THE FIVE CIVILIZED TRIBES.

In the matter of the application for the enrollment of Jimmie Harjo as a citizen by blood of the Creek Nation.

DECISION

The records of this office show that on April 20, 1905 testimony was offered "in the matter of the application for the enrollment of certain new borns" as citizens by blood of the Creek Nation, which embraced the name of Jimmie, a child of Polly Harjo.

The record further show that on November 16, 1905 application was made, in affidavit form, for the enrollment of Jimmie Harjo, a child of Polly Harjo. A supplemental affidavit was filed January 5, 1906. Further proceedings were had November 23, 1906.

The testimony first above mentioned is herein considered an original application for the enrollment of Jimmie Harjo as a citizen by blood of the Creek Nation under the provisions of the Act of Congress approved March 3, 1905 (33 Stat. L. 1048).

The evidence and the records of this office show that said Jimmie Harjo is the child of Polly Harjo, whose name appears upon a schedule of citizens by blood of the Creek Nation approved by the Secretary of the Interior March 28, 1902, opposite No. 5116. The name of the father of said child is not established by the evidence.

The said affidavit filed January 4, 1905 contains a statement signed by Polly Harjo to the effect that said Jimmie Harjo died in July, 1902, but it does not appear that the same was made under oath. She stated in her testimony given November 23, 1906 that said child was living and present at that time.

The evidence is conflicting as to the exact date of birth of said child, but a preponderance of the evidence establishes such date as sometime subsequent to May 25, 1901, and prior to March 4, 1905, and shows that he was living November 23, 1906.

It is, therefore ordered and adjudged that the said Jimmie Harjo is entitled to be enrolled as a citizen by blood of the Creek Nation, under the provisions of the Act of Congress approved March 3, 1905 (33 Stat. L. 1048), and the application for his enrollment as such is accordingly granted.

Tams Bixby   COMMISSIONER.

Muskogee, Indian Territory,
    FEB 11 1907

Applications for Enrollment of Creek Newborn
Act of 1905   Volume XIII

BIRTH AFFIDAVIT.

DEPARTMENT OF THE INTERIOR.
COMMISSION TO THE FIVE CIVILIZED TRIBES.

IN RE APPLICATION FOR ENROLLMENT, as a citizen of the Creek Nation, of Jimmie Harjo, born on the 5th day of May, 1902

Name of Father: Neharyar Yaholar   a citizen of the   Creek   Nation.
Name of Mother: Polly Yaholar   a citizen of the   Creek   Nation.

         Postoffice   Weleetka IT

AFFIDAVIT OF MOTHER.

UNITED STATES OF AMERICA, Indian Territory,
     Western Judicial   DISTRICT.

     I, Polly Yaholar, on oath state that I am 25 years of age and a citizen by Birth, of the Creek Nation; that I am the lawful wife of Neharyar Yaholar, who is a citizen, by Birth of the Creek Nation; that a Male child was born to me on 5th day of May, 1902, that said child has been named Jimmie Harjo, and is now living.

                                         her
                            Polly Yaholar x
Witnesses To Mark: mark
   Chas Coachman
   JW Crawford

     Subscribed and sworn to before me this 14th day of Nov, 1905.

My Commission Exp Aug 15, 1906   B.H. Mills
                                         Notary Public.

AFFIDAVIT OF ATTENDING PHYSICIAN OR MID-WIFE.

UNITED STATES OF AMERICA, Indian Territory,
     Western Judicial   DISTRICT.

     I, Betsey Yaholar, a mid wife, on oath state that I attended on Mrs. Polly Yaholar, wife of Neharyar Yaholar on the 5th day of May, 1902; that there was born to her on said date a male child; that said child is now living and is said to have been named Jimmie Harjo   her
                             Betsey Yaholar x
                                     mark

Applications for Enrollment of Creek Newborn
Act of 1905   Volume XIII

Witnesses To Mark:
{ Chas Coachman
{ JW Crawford

Subscribed and sworn to before me this 14th day of   Nov   , 1905.

My Commission Exp Aug 15, 1906   B.H. Mills
                                                                            Notary Public.

BIRTH AFFIDAVIT.

DEPARTMENT OF THE INTERIOR.
COMMISSION TO THE FIVE CIVILIZED TRIBES.

IN RE APPLICATION FOR ENROLLMENT, as a citizen of the Creek Nation, of Jimmie Harjo, born on the 5 day of April , 1901

Kiliagee[sic] Town

Name of Father: Connuggee Harjo   a citizen of the   Creek   Nation.
Name of Mother: Polly Harjo Roll No 5116   a citizen of the   Creek   Nation.

Postoffice   Weleetka I.T.

AFFIDAVIT OF MOTHER.

UNITED STATES OF AMERICA, Indian Territory, }
     Western Judicial   DISTRICT.

I, Polly Harjo of Alabama Town , on oath state that I am 30 years of age and a citizen by Blood , of the Creek Nation; that I am the lawful wife of Connuggee Harjo, who is a citizen, by Birth of the Creek Nation; that a male child was born to me on 5 day of April , 1901, that said child has been named Jimmie Harjo , and was living March 4, 1905.

(Signature given below)

Witnesses To Mark:
{ Chas. Coachman
{ Thomas Ryan

Subscribed and sworn to before me this 26 day of December   , 1905.
                                    her
                            Polly x Harjo
                                    mark   Notary Public.

Applications for Enrollment of Creek Newborn
Act of 1905   Volume XIII

AFFIDAVIT OF ATTENDING PHYSICIAN OR MID-WIFE.

UNITED STATES OF AMERICA, Indian Territory, ⎱
   Western Judicial   DISTRICT. ⎰

    I, Betsey Yaholar , a   Mid Wife , on oath state that I attended on Mrs. Polly Yahola , wife of Connuggee Harjo on the 5 day of April , 1901 ; that there was born to her on said date a male child; that said child was living March 4, 1905, and is said to have been named Jimmie Harjo
                                        her
                                Betsey x Yarhola[sic]

Witnesses To Mark: mark
  ⎰ Chas. Coachman
  ⎱ Thomas Ryan

    Subscribed and sworn to before me this 26 day of Dec , 1905.
                                    her
                              Polly x Harjo
                                mark   Notary Public.

NC-1044.

                              Muskogee, Indian Territory, October 23, 1905.

Polly Harjo,
    c/o Nechthlocco Harjo,
        Weleetka, Indian Territory.

Dear Madam:

    In the matter of the application for the enrollment of your minor child, Jimmie Harjo, said to have been born subsequent to May 25, 1901, as a citizen by blood of the Creek Nation, this office requires your affidavit and the affidavit of the physician or midwife who attended at his birth and a blank for that purpose is inclosed herewith.

    In having the same executed be careful to see that all blank spaces are properly filled, all names written in full and that the notary public, before whom the affidavits are sworn to, attaches his name and seal to each affidavit, in case any signature is by mark the same must be attested by two disinterested witnesses.

    If there was no physician or midwife in attendance when said child was born it will be necessary for you to furnish this office with the affidavits of two disinterested persons relative to the birth of said Jimmie Harjo. Said affidavits to set forth said child's name, the date of his birth, the names of his parents and whether or not he was living March 4, 1905.

                              Respectfully,

B C   Commissioner.
Env.

Applications for Enrollment of Creek Newborn
Act of 1905 Volume XIII

N.C. 1044

Muskogee, Indian Territory, December 19, 1905.

Polly Yaholar,
    Care Neharyar Yaholar,
        Weleetka, Indian Territory.

Dear Madam:

    In the matter of the application for the enrollment of your minor child, Jimmie Harjo, as a citizen by blood of the Creek Nation, this office is unable to identify you or Neharyar Yaholar, the father of said child, on its final roll of citizens by blood of the Creek Nation. You are requested to state your maiden name, the names of your parents, the Creek Indian town to which you belong and your roll number as the same appears on your deeds and allotment certificate.

    If the correct surname of the father of said child is Yaholar it necessarily follows that Yaholar is the surname of said child. As you in your affidavit, gave Harjo as the surname of said child, it will be necessary for you to execute a new affidavit giving his correct surname and a blank for that purpose is enclosed herewith.

                          Respectfully,

BA   Commissioner.
Env.

                                                                JWH

N C 1044

Muskogee, Indian Territory, March 9, 1907.

Polly Harjo,
    Weleetka, Indian Territory.

Dear Madam :--

    You are hereby advised that on March 2, 1907, the Secretary of the Interior approved the enrollment of your minor child, Jimmie Harjo, as a citizen by blood of the Creek Nation, and that the name of said child appears upon the roll of new born citizens by blood of the Creek Nation, enrolled under the Act of Congress approved March 3, 1905, as number 1275.

    This child is now entitled to allotment and application therefor should be made without delay at the Creek Land Office, Muskogee, Indian Territory.

Applications for Enrollment of Creek Newborn
Act of 1905 Volume XIII

Respectfully,

Commissioner.

N.C. 1045.

DEPARTMENT OF THE INTERIOR,
COMMISSIONER TO THE FIVE CIVILIZED TRIBES.
Wetumka, I. T., April 16, 1906.

In the matter of the application for the enrollment of two minor children of Wileya and Nellie Fish as citizens by blood of the Creek Nation.

NELLIE FISH, being duly sworn, testified as follows:

Through Alex Posey Official Interpreter:

BY THE COMMISSIONER:

Q What is your name? A Nellie Fish.
Q How old are you? A I am over thirty.
Q Is your name Mellogee Fish or Nellie Fish? A My name is Nellie Fish.
Q What is your post office address? A Wetumka.
Q To what Creek Town do you belong? A Kialigee.
Q Have you two new born children which you not yet enrolled? A Yes, sir.
Q What are their names? A George and Nache.
Q When was George born? A In the month of September. He will be four years old next September.
Q Is Nache a girl? A Yes, sir.
Q When was she born? A In February, last year.
Q What time in February? A In the latter part of the month.
Q Are you sure it was not in March? A Yes, sir, the child was born in February.
Q Who is the father of these two children? A Wileya Fish.
Q To what town does he belong? A Alabana.
Q Is he your lawful husband? A Yes, sir
Q How long have you and Wileya Fish been married? A A long time.
Q As much as ten years? A More than that.

Witness refuses to be examined further.

---oooOOOooo---

Applications for Enrollment of Creek Newborn
Act of 1905   Volume XIII

I, D. C. Skaggs, on oath state that the above and foregoing is a full and true transcript of my stenographic notes as taken in said cause on said date.

D. C. Skaggs

Subscribed and sworn to before me this 20 day of April, 1906.

Alex Posey
Notary Public.

DEPARTMENT OF THE INTERIOR,
COMMISSION TO THE FIVE CIVILIZED TRIBES.
NEAR WEELETKA[sic], I.T. April 20, 1905.

In the matter of the application for the enrollment of certain new born children of "Snake" parents.

Minta Baker, being duly sworn, testified as follows, through official interpreter, Alex Posey.

Examination by the Commission:
Q What is your name? A Minta Baker.
Q What is your age? A About 45.
Q What is your post office address? [sic] Weleetka.

Statement: Louisa a daughter of Hillis Harjo, and the wife of Legusie, have a girl child that is just crawling, Louisa belongs to Thlopthlocco and Legusie to Alabama, the child is living, the child is named Emma-- their post office is Weeletka[sic].

There is also another woman named Polly, the daughter of Nathlocco Harjo of Alabama Town, has a child, the father is unknown. Jimmie is it's[sic] name, it is a boy. It is a young child and I think the child was born sometime last summer.

Willeya Fish of Alabama Town and Mellogee Fish of Kialigee I think, have a child I think that is just beginning to walk and has not been named yet. I think it is a girl. It is living now, Wetumka is the post office.

The above testimony was participated in by Jacob Sandy.

Q What is your name? A Jacob Sandy.
Q How old are you? A 28.
Q What is your post office address? A Wetumka.

Statement: I am a member of Kialigee Town, I think Williya and Mellogee Fish have another child about three years old, named George Fish and living. I

Applications for Enrollment of Creek Newborn
Act of 1905   Volume XIII

have advised the parents to make application for them they won't do it. Williya is here now himself and runs away.

A Statement by Jacob Sandy: Arlinga Faction Snakes are now making a roll of new borns which they are going to send to Washington.

Henry G. Hains, being duly sworn, on his oath, states that the above and foregoing is a true and correct transcript of his stenographic notes as taken in said cause on said date.

Henry G. Hains

Subscribed and sworn to before me this 11th day of May, 1905.

Drennan C Skaggs
Notary Public.

Indian Territory I
                 I ss
Western District I

We, the undersigned, on oath state that we are personally acquainted with Nellie Fish wife of Wileya Fish ; that ~~on or about the~~ sometime in ~~day of~~ February, 1905, a female child was born to them and has been named Nache Fish ; and that said child was living March 4, 1905.

We further state that we have no interest in the above case.

Witnesses to mark:
   Alex Posey
   D C Skaggs

                                his
                          Massey x Harjo
                                mark
                                his
                                Legus x Harjo
                                mark

Subscribed and sworn to before me this 31 day of April, 1906.

Alex Posey
Notary Public.

Applications for Enrollment of Creek Newborn
Act of 1905   Volume XIII

BIRTH AFFIDAVIT.

DEPARTMENT OF THE INTERIOR.
COMMISSION TO THE FIVE CIVILIZED TRIBES.

IN RE APPLICATION FOR ENROLLMENT, as a citizen of the Creek Nation, of Nache Fish, born ~~on the~~ in ~~day of~~ February, 1905

Name of Father: Wileya Fish   a citizen of the   Creek   Nation.
Alabama Town
Name of Mother: Nellie Fish   a citizen of the   Creek   Nation.
Kialigee Town

                Postoffice   Wetumka Ind. Ter.

AFFIDAVIT OF MOTHER.

UNITED STATES OF AMERICA, Indian Territory,
     Western   DISTRICT.

     I, Nellie Fish , on oath state that I am over 30 years of age and a citizen by blood , of the Creek Nation; that I am the lawful wife of Wileya Fish , who is a citizen, by blood of the Creek Nation; that a female child was born to me ~~on~~ in ~~day of~~ February , 1905 , that said child has been named Nache Fish , and was living March 4, 1905.
                                               her
                                Nellie x Fish
Witnesses To Mark: mark
   { Alex Posey
   { Jas. P. Atkins

     Subscribed and sworn to before me this 16 day of   April   , 1906.

                                           Alex Posey
                                           Notary Public.

Indian Territory I
           I ss
Western District I

     We, the undersigned, on oath state that we are personally acquainted with Nellie Fish wife of Wileya Fish ; that ~~on or about the~~ sometime in ~~day of~~ September , 1902 , a male child was born to them and has been named George Fish ; and that said child was living March 4, 1905.

     We further state that we have no interest in the above case.

Applications for Enrollment of Creek Newborn
Act of 1905 Volume XIII

Witnesses to mark:
   Alex Posey
   D C Skaggs
_____
_____

                    his
          Massey x Harjo
              mark
                  his
          Legus x Harjo
              mark

    Subscribed and sworn to before me this 31 day of April, 1906.

                                      Alex Posey
                                      Notary Public.

_____

BIRTH AFFIDAVIT.

DEPARTMENT OF THE INTERIOR.
COMMISSION TO THE FIVE CIVILIZED TRIBES.

_____

    IN RE APPLICATION FOR ENROLLMENT, as a citizen of the Creek Nation, of George Fish, born ~~on the~~ in ~~day of~~ September, 1902

Name of Father: Wileya Fish   a citizen of the   Creek   Nation.
Alabama Town
Name of Mother: Nellie Fish   a citizen of the   Creek   Nation.
Kialigee Town
                            Postoffice   Wetumka Ind. Ter.

_____

AFFIDAVIT OF MOTHER.

UNITED STATES OF AMERICA, Indian Territory, ⎫
     Western   DISTRICT. ⎭

    I, Nellie Fish, on oath state that I am over 30 years of age and a citizen by blood, of the Creek Nation; that I am the lawful wife of Wileya Fish, who is a citizen, by blood of the Creek Nation; that a male child was born to me ~~on~~ in ~~day of~~ September, 1902, that said child has been named George Fish, and was living March 4, 1905.
                                              her
                                      Nellie x Fish
Witnesses To Mark: mark
  { Alex Posey
  { Jas. P. Atkins

    Subscribed and sworn to before me this 16 day of   April, 1906.

                                      Alex Posey
                                        Notary Public.

Applications for Enrollment of Creek Newborn
Act of 1905   Volume XIII

HGH

REFER IN REPLY TO THE FOLLOWING:
NC-1045.

DEPARTMENT OF THE INTERIOR,
COMMISSIONER TO THE FIVE CIVILIZED TRIBES.

Muskogee, Indian Territory, October 23, 1905.

Mellogee Fish,
 c/o Willeya Fish,
  Wetumka, Indian Territory.

Dear Madam:

 In the matter of the application for the enrollment of your minor children George Fish and -- --- Fish, the given name of said latter child being unknown to this office, said to have been born subsequent to May 25, 1901, you are advised that it will be necessary for you to furnish this office with your affidavits and the affidavits of the physician or midwife who attended at the birth of said children and blanks for that purpose are inclosed herewith.

 In having the same executed be careful to see that all blank spaces are properly filled, all names written in full and that the notary public, before whom the affidavits are sworn to, attaches his name and seal to each affidavit. In case any signature is by mark it must be attested by two disinterested witnesses.

 You are further advised that this office is unable to identify you upon the final roll of citizens by blood of the Creek Nation. You are therefore requested to state the name under which you were finally enrolled, the names of your parents and other members of your family, the Creek Indian town to which you belong and your final roll number as the same appears upon your allotment certificate and deeds.

      Respectfully,
         Tams Bixby
           Commissioner.

2 B C
Env.

Applications for Enrollment of Creek Newborn
Act of 1905 Volume XIII

N.C. 1046.

DEPARTMENT OF THE INTERIOR,
COMMISSIONER TO THE FIVE CIVILIZED TRIBES.
Wetumka, I. T., April 13, 1906.

In the matter of the application for the enrollment of two unnamed minor children of Jacob and Rhoda Cubbie as citizens by blood of the Creek Nation.

JACOB CUBBIE, being duly sworn, testified as follows:

Through Alex Posey Official Interpreter:

BY THE COMMISSIONER:
Q What is your name? A Jacob Cubbie.
Q How old are you? A Forty-six.
Q What is your post office address? A Weleetka.
Q Are you a citizen of the Creek Nation. A Yes, sir.
Q To what town do you belong? A Alabama.
Q Application has been made for the enrollment of two new born children of yours. Have you such children? A Yes, sir.
Q What are their names? A Liza and Daniel Cubbie.
Q When was Liza born? A In October. I do not know in what year.
Q How old is she? A She will be five years old next October.
Q Are you positive of that? A Yes, sir.
Q When was Daniel born? A In the same month and will be three years old next October. Both children were born in the latter part of October but I do not know on what day. I am positive that Liza will be five years old and that Daniel will be three years old next October.
Q Are they both living? A Yes, sir.
Q What is the name of their mother? A Rhoda Cubbie.
Q To what Creek Town does she belong? A Alabama.
Q Have you any other children besides Liza and Daniel? A Yes, sir, I have a boy between nine and ten years old named John Cubbie. I think he was enrolled by Charlie Coachman and I have been told that land has been allotted him arbitrarily by the Commission.

---oooOOOooo---

I, D. C. Skaggs, on oath state that the above and foregoing is a full and true transcript of my stenographic notes as taken in said cause on said date.

D. C. Skaggs

Subscribed and sworn to before me this 20 day of April, 1906.

Alex Posey
Notary Public.

Applications for Enrollment of Creek Newborn
Act of 1905   Volume XIII

DEPARTMENT CF THE INTERIOR,
COMMISSION TO THE FIVE CIVILIZED TRIBES.
NEAR WEELETKA[sic], I.T. April 20, 1905.

In the matter of the application for the enrollment of certain new born children of "Snake" parents.

W.T. Young, being duly sworn, testified as follows

Examination by the Commission.
Q What is your name? A W.T. Young. I am a white man and tenant of Cubby.
Q What is your age? A About 50.
Q What os[sic] your post office? A Weeletka[sic]. Jacob Cubby and Rhoda Cubby live right over there across the road, they are not at home. He has gone to a Snake meeting at Alabama Town. They have two children whose names I do not know. One will be four years old next fall and the other was a year old last Xmas. The oldest one is a girl and the youngest is a ----I don't know the sex--Their post office is Weeletka[sic]. They are Snakes, both of the children are living.

Henry G. Hains, being duly sworn, on his oath, states that the above and foregoing is a true and correct transcript of his stenographic notes as taken in said cause on said date.

Henry G. Hains

Subscribed and sworn to before me this 11th day of May, 1905.

Drennan C Skaggs
Notary Public.

Indian Territory I
                I ss
Western District I

We, the undersigned, on oath state that we are personally acquainted with Rhoda Cubbie   wife of   Jacob Cubbie ; that ~~on or about the~~ sometime in ~~day of~~ October , 1901 , a   female   child was born to them and has been named   Liza Cubbie ; and that said child was living March 4, 1905.

We further state that we have no interest in the above case.

Witnesses to mark: Zarah Young
  Alex Posey   her
  Jas. P. Atkins   Mrs. M. A. x Young
                                            mark

Applications for Enrollment of Creek Newborn
Act of 1905 Volume XIII

Subscribed and sworn to before me this 16 day of April, 1906.

Alex Posey
Notary Public.

(The above Birth Affidavit given again.)

BIRTH AFFIDAVIT.

DEPARTMENT OF THE INTERIOR.
COMMISSION TO THE FIVE CIVILIZED TRIBES.

IN RE APPLICATION FOR ENROLLMENT, as a citizen of the Creek Nation, of Daniel Cubbie, born ~~on the~~ in ~~day of~~ October, 1903

Name of Father: Jacob Cubbie	a citizen of the	Creek	Nation.
Name of Mother: Rhoda Cubbie	a citizen of the	Creek	Nation.

Postoffice   Weleetka, Ind. Ter.

AFFIDAVIT OF MOTHER.

UNITED STATES OF AMERICA, Indian Territory, ⎱
    Western   DISTRICT. ⎰

I, Rhoda Cubbie, on oath state that I am about 34 years of age and a citizen by blood, of the Creek Nation; that I am the lawful wife of Jacob Cubbie, who is a citizen, by blood of the Creek Nation; that a male child was born to me ~~on~~ in ~~day of~~ October, 1903, that said child has been named Daniel Cubbie, and was living March 4, 1905.

her
Rhoda x Cubbie
mark

Witnesses To Mark:
  { Alex Posey
  { Jas. P. Atkins

Subscribed and sworn to before me this 16 day of   April, 1906.

Alex Posey
Notary Public.

(The above Birth Affidavit given again.)

Applications for Enrollment of Creek Newborn
Act of 1905   Volume XIII

BIRTH AFFIDAVIT.

DEPARTMENT OF THE INTERIOR.
COMMISSION TO THE FIVE CIVILIZED TRIBES.

IN RE APPLICATION FOR ENROLLMENT, as a citizen of the Creek Nation, of Liza Cubbie, born ~~on the~~ in ~~day of~~ October, 1901

Name of Father: Jacob Cubbie   a citizen of the   Creek   Nation.
Name of Mother: Rhoda Cubbie   a citizen of the   Creek   Nation.

Postoffice   Weleetka, Ind. Ter.

AFFIDAVIT OF MOTHER.

UNITED STATES OF AMERICA, Indian Territory, ⎱
    Western   DISTRICT.   ⎰

I, Rhoda Cubbie , on oath state that I am about 34 years of age and a citizen by blood , of the Creek Nation; that I am the lawful wife of Jacob Cubbie , who is a citizen, by blood of the Creek Nation; that a female child was born to me ~~on~~ in ~~day of~~ October , 1901 , that said child has been named Liza Cubbie , and was living March 4, 1905.

                                                her
                                 Rhoda x Cubbie
Witnesses To Mark: mark
  { Alex Posey
    Jas. P. Atkins

Subscribed and sworn to before me this 16 day of   April , 1906.

                                    Alex Posey
                                    Notary Public.

NC-1046.

                            Muskogee, Indian Territory, October 23, 1905.

Rhoda Cubbie,
    c/o W. T. Young,
        Weleetka, Indian Territory.

Dear Madam:

    In the matter of the application for the enrollment of your two minor children, whose names are unknown to this office, said to have been born subsequent to May 25, 1901, as citizens by blood of the Creek Nation, you are advised that it will be necessary

Applications for Enrollment of Creek Newborn
Act of 1905   Volume XIII

for you to furnish this office with your affidavits and the affidavits of the physician or midwife who attended at the birth of said children, relative to their birth and blanks for that purpose are inclosed herewith.

In having the same executed be careful to see that all blank spaces are properly filled, all names written in full and that the notary public, before whom the affidavits are sworn to, attaches his name and seal to each affidavit. In case any signature is by mark it must be attested by two disinterested witnesses.

In the event that there was no physician or midwife in attendance when said children were born, it will be necessary for you to furnish this office with the affidavits of two disinterested witnesses relative to the birth of said children. Said affidavits to set forth said children's names, the dates of their birth, the names of their parents and whether or not they were living March 4, 1905.

        Respectfully,

               Commissioner.

2 BC
Env.

NC 1046

        Muskogee, Indian Territory, March 1, 1907.

Rhoda Cubbie,
  Care Jacob Cubbie,
    Weleetka, Indian Territory.

Dear Madam:

You are hereby advised that on February 15, 1907, the Secretary of the Interior approved the enrollment of your minor children, Liza and Daniel Cubbie, as citizens by blood of the Creek Nation, and that the names of said children appear upon the roll of new born citizens by blood of the Creek Nation, enrolled under the Act of Congress approved March 3, 1905, as numbers 1202 and 1203 respectively.

These children are now entitled to allotment and application therefor should be made without delay at the Creek Land Office, Muskogee, Indian Territory.

        Respectfully,

               Commissioner.

Applications for Enrollment of Creek Newborn
Act of 1905 Volume XIII

DEPARTMENT OF THE INTERIOR,
COMMISSIONER TO THE FIVE CIVILIZED TRIBES.
Near Weeletka[sic], I.T. April 20, 1905.

In the matter of the application for certain new born children of "snake" parents.

Sam Buckley being duly sworn, testified as follows:
Through Official Interpreter, Alex Posey:

Examination by the Commission:
Q What is your name? A Sam Buckley.
Q What is your age? A Over 50 years old.
Q What is your post office address? A Weeletka[sic].

Statement: I am a former member of the House of Warriros, I belong properly to Thlewarthle Town, but am probably enrolled in the Alabama Town. Ceasar Buckley, my son and Betsey Buckley-- I don't know its name, it was born about the 20th of February this year. Ceasar belongs to Alabama and his wife to Kialigee. The child is living. Post Office, Weeletka[sic]. it[sic] is a girl.
Q Was it last month this child was born or was it the month before? A It was born in February. This is April, last month was March. The child was born in February.
Q Is the child about two months old? A Yes sir, it is a right smart child now.

Henry G. Hains, being duly sworn, on his oath, states that the above and foregoing is a true and correct transcript of his stenographic notes as taken in said cause on said date.

Henry G. Hains

Subscribed and sworn to before me this 11th day of May, 1905.

Drennan C Skaggs
Notary Public.

NC 1047   WSC
                                                                                                 CM

DEPARTMENT OF THE INTERIOR,
COMMISSIONER TO THE FIVE CIVILIZED TRIBES.

In the matter of the application for the enrollment of Cora Buckley as a citizen by blood of the Creek Nation.

DECISION

The record in this case shows that on April 20, 1905 the testimony of Sam Buckley was taken by a Creek enrollment field party from this office "in the matter of the

Applications for Enrollment of Creek Newborn
Act of 1905 Volume XIII

application for certain new born children of Snake parents", and that in said proceeding the said Sam Buckley testified relative to an unnamed female child of Ceasar Buckley and Betsey Buckley. Said action is considered as an original application for the enrollment of said child as a citizen by blood of the Creek Nation under the provisions of the Act of Congress approved March 3, 1905 (33 Stats. 1048). Inasmuch as the given name of said child does not appear from an examination of the records of the Enrollment Division that any application has been made for the enrollment of as a citizen of the Nation. the evidence and for the purpose of securing clearness in the record further reference will be made to her under the name of Cora Buckley. The said Ceasar Buckley and Betsey Buckley are identified from the evidence and the records in the possession of this office as the Ceasar Buckley and Betsey Buckley whose names appear on a schedule of citizens by blood of the Creek Nation approved by the Secretary of the Interior March 28, 1902 opposite Nos. 5112 and 5113 respectively.

The evidence shows that the aforesaid persons are members of the so called Snake faction, from whom it is almost impossible to obtain any information relative to enrollment matters. Diligent efforts have been made by this office through field parties to obtain information relative to the given name of the applicant herein but without success. However, it can be said that the evidence shows that the applicant is the child of the aforesaid Ceasar and Betsey Buckley, and that she was born February 25, 1905, and was living at the time the said Sam Buckley testified herein, viz. April 20, 1905.

It is, therefore, ordered and adjudged that the applicant, Cora Buckley, is entitled to be enrolled as a citizen by blood of the Creek Nation under the provisions of the Act of Congress approved March 3, 1905 (33 Stats. 1048), and the application for her enrollment as such is accordingly granted.

Tams Bixby COMMISSIONER.

Muskogee, Indian Territory,
    FEB 18 1907

NC-1047

Muskogee, Indian Territory, October 24, 1905

Betsey Buckley,
    Ceasar Buckley,
        Weleetka, Indian Territory.

Dear Madam:

In the matter of the application for the enrollment of your minor child, whose given name is unknown to this office, said to have been born subsequent to May 25, 1901, as a citizen by blood of the Creek Nation, this office desires your affidavit and affidavit of the midwife or physician in attendance at the birth of said child and a blank for that purpose is enclosed herewith.

In the event that there was no physician or midwife in attendance when said child was born, it will be necessary for you to furnish this office with the affidavits of two disinterested witnesses relative to its birth. Said affidavits must set forth said child's

Applications for Enrollment of Creek Newborn
Act of 1905   Volume XIII

name, the date of its birth, the names of its parents and whether or not it was living on March 4, 1905.

Respectfully,

AG-1047
Commissioner.

NC 1047

Muskogee, Indian Territory, January 10, 1907.

M. L. Mott,
    Attorney for the Creek Nation,
        Muskogee, Indian Territory.

Dear Sir:

    There is herewith inclosed a copy of the record in the matter of the application for the enrollment of _____ Buckley, child of Caesar and Betsy Buckley.

    Your attention is invited to the fact that while the evidence is incomplete and unsatisfactory there is not enough proof at present to deny the enrollment. Repeated efforts have been made to obtain further evidence and you are requested to use every effort in your power to complete the proof in this case prior to February 1, 1907.

Respectfully,
Commissioner.

CM-NC-1047.

NC 1047.

Muskogee, Indian Territory, January 10, 1907.

Betsey Buckley,
    Care of Ceasar Buckley,
        Weleetka, Indian Territory.

Dear Madam:

    In the matter of the application for the enrollment of your minor child, whose name is unknown to this office, said to have been born subsequent to May 25, 1901, as a citizen by blood of the creek[sic] nation[sic], this office requires your affidavit and affidavit of the midwife or physician in attendance at the birth of said child. Said affidavits must set forth said child's name, the date of his birth, the names of his parents and whether or not he was living on March 4, 1905. A blank for that purpose is herewith enclosed.

Applications for Enrollment of Creek Newborn
Act of 1905 Volume XIII

It is desires also that you furnish this office with the correct name of said child and state whether or not it is still living. You will be allowed 10 days within which to furnish said information, from date hereof.

In the event that there was no physician or midwife in attendance when said child was born, it will be necessary for you to furnish this office with the affidavits of two disinterested witnesses relative to its birth. Said affidavits must set forth said child's name, the date of its birth, the names of its parents and whether or not it was living on March 4, 1905.

Respectfully,

Enc.-2 BA.   Commissioner.

JWH

NC 1047

Muskogee, Indian Territory, March 9, 1907

Betsey Buckley,
    % Ceasar Buckley,
        Weleetka, Indian Territory.

Dear Madam :--

You are hereby advised that on March 2, 1907, the Secretary of the Interior approved the enrollment of your minor child, Cora Buckley, as a citizen by blood of the Creek Nation, and that the name of said child appears upon the roll of new born citizens by blood of the Creek Nation, enrolled under the Act of Congress approved March 3, 1905, as number 1276.

This child is now entitled to allotment and application therefor should be made without delay at the Creek Land Office, Muskogee, Indian Territory.

Respectfully,

Commissioner.

Applications for Enrollment of Creek Newborn
Act of 1905   Volume XIII

2461 B
#3 - C 1049

DEPARTMENT OF THE INTERIOR,
COMMISSION TO THE FIVE CIVILIZED TRIBES.
EUFAULA, I.T. April 19, 1905.

In the matter of the application for the enrollment of certain new born children concerning whom no application could be obtained except through testimony.

Jimsey Fish and William Givens, being duly sworn, testified as follows testified as follows, through Official Interpreter, Alex Posey.

Examination by the Commission:
Q What is your name? A Jimsey Fish.
Q How old are you? A I have never been able to determine my age. (Witness appears to be about 48).
Q What is our post office? A Mellette, I.T.
Q Do you know of some new born children whose parents are unwilling to have them enrolled? A Yes sir.
Q Those about whom you and Mr. Givens are testifying are children all born since May 25, 1901? And for whom application could only be made in this way? A Yes sir.

Q What is your name? A William Givens
Q How old are you? A I am 25.
Q What is your post office address? A Mellette.

Statement: Nocus Ela has two children--his white name is Jim Davis--he belongs to Kialigee Town--I don't know the name of his wife, but she belongs to Kialigee town; one of them is walking and the other is younger. The one that is walking is a boy, don't know the sex of the other. The oldest is named Johnny, don't know the other's name. Both are living. They are both new born children and Nocus said the other day that he had never enrolled them-the post office is Hanna.

Bob and Mahala Bender have two children--these people belong to Tuckabatchee and Hillabee Towns respectively--one of the children is Thomas and the other is Easma--Thomas is just beginning to talk and Easma is older than Thomas. Their post office is Mellette. These children are new borns also.

Josie and Mahala Roberts have two children--the parents belong to Hutchechuppa and Kialigee respectively-- I don't [sic] the names of the children-- one is walking and the other is a baby yet a small child.
Q Were both of them born since May 25, 1901? A Yes sir. The oldest is a girl and I don't know the sex of the youngest. Both are living. Their post office is Indianola.

Thompson Fields and Susie Fields--he is of Okchiye or Fish Pond, I don't know which, and Susie belongs to Hutchechuppa; they have one child born since May 25,

Applications for Enrollment of Creek Newborn
Act of 1905   Volume XIII

1901, I don't know but I think the ~~gi~~ child is a girl. It is living, the child is not able to crawl but can sit up.

   Earnest and Nicey Gouge, of Hickory Ground and Hillabee Towns respectively--- had two children the last time I was at their house--both were born since May 25, don't know the names, both boys I think, both living, post office, Hanna.

   Connie Hawkins of Hillabee Town and Sybilla Hawkins of Fish Pong (?) I don't know her town' they had one child at the time I was at their house; I was at their house last summer 1904, don't know whether a boy or girl, born after May 25, 1901, it was a small child at that time, it is living. Post Office, Hanna.

   Micco Emarthla, his white name is Neddie Walker, and Sallie Emarthla, both parents belong to Kialigee, have one child names Walter born since May 25, 1901, and living. Post Office, Indianola.

   Wiley Fish of Tuckabatchee and Hettie Fish of Kialigee, post office, Mellette, Indian Territory have two children, but one is probably too old being about seven years old, but the field party last year failed to get that old one. The youngest was probably born since May 25, 1901. It is a boy and living. The oldest one is named John I don't know the other.

   Noah Roberts of Kialigee and Hannah Roberts of Hillabee post office, Mellette, Indian Territory have one child name not known, born since May 25, 1901. Don't now the sex, it is living. Noah also has a step-son about seven years old that has never been enrolled named Walter Starr.

Questions addressed to both witnesses:
Q These statements which you have made are for the purpose of getting enrolled the new born children of parents belonging to the Snake Faction? A Yes sir.
Q Neither of you are related to them? A I Jimsey am related to Wiley Fish, who is the son of my brother and that's all.

   Henry G. Hains, being duly sworn, on his oath, states that the above and foregoing is a true and correct transcript of his stenographic notes as taken in said cause on said date.

              (signed) Henry G. Hains

Subscribed and sworn to before me this 11th day of May, 1905.

              (Signed) Drennan C Skaggs
              Notary Public.

   I, Anna Garrigues, on oath state that I copied the above testimony from the original on the 18th day of July, 1906 and that it is a true and correct copy of same.

              Anna Garrigues

Applications for Enrollment of Creek Newborn
Act of 1905   Volume XIII

Subscribed and sworn to before me this 18th day of July 1905.

                                                        Edw C Griesel
                                                        Notary Public.

BIRTH AFFIDAVIT.

DEPARTMENT OF THE INTERIOR.
COMMISSION TO THE FIVE CIVILIZED TRIBES.

IN RE APPLICATION FOR ENROLLMENT, as a citizen of the Creek Nation, of Thomas Bender, born on the *(blank)* day of *(blank)* , 1*(blank)*

Name of Father: Robert Bender   a citizen of the   Creek   Nation.
Tuckabatche
Name of Mother: Jennie Bender   a citizen of the   Creek   Nation.
Hillabee
                            Postoffice   Mellette, I.T.

AFFIDAVIT OF MOTHER.

UNITED STATES OF AMERICA, Indian Territory,
    Western   **DISTRICT.**

     I, Jennie Bender , on oath state that I am about 37 years of age and a citizen by blood , of the Creek Nation; that I am the lawful wife of Robert Bender , who is a citizen, by blood of the Creek Nation; that a male child was born to me on the 8th day of March , 1902 , that said child has been named Thomas Bender , and is now was living. on March 4, 1905.
                                            her
                                    Jennie x Bender
Witnesses To Mark: mark
    { DC Skaggs
      Alex Posey

     Subscribed and sworn to before me this 25 day of   May   , 1905.

                                         Drennan C Skaggs
                                            Notary Public.

Applications for Enrollment of Creek Newborn
Act of 1905   Volume XIII

AFFIDAVIT OF ATTENDING PHYSICIAN OR MID-WIFE.

UNITED STATES OF AMERICA, Indian Territory,
  Western   DISTRICT.

                                                                              my wife
I, Robert Bender , a (blank) , on oath state that I attended on ^ Mrs. Jennie Bender , wife of *(blank)* on the day of sometime in March, 1902 ; that there was born to her on said date a   male   child; that said child is now was living on March 4, 1905, and is said to have been named Thomas Bender

                                his
                    Robert x Bender
Witnesses To Mark: mark
 { DC Skaggs
   Alex Posey

   Subscribed and sworn to before me this   25   day of   May , 1905.

                                Drennan C Skaggs
                                Notary Public.

BIRTH AFFIDAVIT.

DEPARTMENT OF THE INTERIOR.
COMMISSION TO THE FIVE CIVILIZED TRIBES.

   IN RE APPLICATION FOR ENROLLMENT, as a citizen of the *(blank)* Nation, of Daniel Bender , born on or about the 28 day of Nov, 1900

Name of Father: Robert Bender   a citizen of the   Creek   Nation.
Tuckabatche
Name of Mother: Jennie Bender   a citizen of the   Creek   Nation.
Hillabee
                    Postoffice   Mellette, I.T.

AFFIDAVIT OF ATTENDING PHYSICIAN OR MID-WIFE.

UNITED STATES OF AMERICA, Indian Territory,
  Western   DISTRICT.

                                    are personally acquainted with
   We, the undersigned   , a , on oath state that I we attended on Mrs. Jennie Bender , wife of   Robert Bender on the day of , 1 ; that there was born to her on or about the 28 day of Nov. 1900 said date a male child; that said child was living March 4, 1905, and is said to have been named Daniel Bender

                                John Bright
                                Lumber Bright

219

Applications for Enrollment of Creek Newborn
Act of 1905   Volume XIII

Witnesses To Mark:
{

    Subscribed and sworn to before me 11 day of   September   , 1905.

                                Drennan C Skaggs
                                Notary Public.

BIRTH AFFIDAVIT.

DEPARTMENT OF THE INTERIOR.
COMMISSION TO THE FIVE CIVILIZED TRIBES.

IN RE APPLICATION FOR ENROLLMENT, as a citizen of the *(blank)* Nation, of Thomas Bender , born on or about the 9 day of March, 1902

Name of Father: Robert Bender   a citizen of the   Creek   Nation. Tuckabatche

Name of Mother: Jennie Bender   a citizen of the   Creek   Nation. Hillabee

                      Post office   Mellette, I.T.

AFFIDAVIT OF ATTENDING PHYSICIAN OR MID-WIFE.

UNITED STATES OF AMERICA, Indian Territory,
    Western   DISTRICT.

                                are personally acquainted with
   We, the undersigned   , ~~a~~, on oath state that ~~I~~ we ~~attended on~~ Mrs. Jennie Bender , wife of   Robert Bender ~~on the   day of   , 1~~ ; that there was born to her on said date a male child; that said child was living March 4, 1905, and is said to have been named Thomas Bender

                              John Bright
Witnesses To Mark: Lumber Bright
{

    Subscribed and sworn to before me 11 day of   September   , 1905.

                                Drennan C Skaggs
                                Notary Public.

Applications for Enrollment of Creek Newborn
Act of 1905   Volume XIII

C. 1049.

DEPARTMENT OF THE INTERIOR,
COMMISSIONER TO THE FIVE CIVILIZED TRIBES.
Melette[sic], I.T., September 13, 1905.

In the matter of the application for the enrollment of Easma Bender as a citizen by blood of the Creek Nation.

JENNIE BENDER, being duly sworn, testified as follows:

Through Alex Posey Official Interpreter:

BY COMMISSIONER:
Q What is your name? A Jennie Bender.
Q How old are you? A Something like forty years old.
Q What is your post office address? A Melette[sic].
Q Are you a citizen of the Creek Nation? A Yes, sir.
Q To what town do you belong? A Hillabee.
Q Have you a child named Easma? A Yes, sir. This is the child here. (indicating a little boy)
Q Have you two other children named Daniel and Thomas? A Yes, sir, but Daniel is the same as Easma. He is known by both names. I have only two new born children and they are Daniel and Thomas.

---oooOOOooo---

I, D. C. Skaggs, on oath state that the above and foregoing is a full and true transcript of my stenographic notes as taken in said cause on said date.

D. C. Skaggs

Subscribed and sworn to before me this 16 day of Oct. 1905.

Edw C Griesel
Notary Public.

Applications for Enrollment of Creek Newborn
Act of 1905 Volume XIII

NC 1049.

OCH
CM

DEPARTMENT OF THE INTERIOR,
COMMISSIONER TO THE FIVE CIVILIZED TRIBES.

In the matter of the application for the enrollment of Daniel Benton and Thomas Benton as a citizen by blood of the Creek Nation.

DECISION.

The records of this office show that on April 19, 1905, testimony was offered "in the matter of the application for the enrollment of certain new born children" which embraced Thomas and Easma, children of "Bob and Mahala Bender"; which is herein considered as an original application for the enrollment of said children as citizens of the Creek Nation. Affidavits in the matter of the birth of said children were filed May 29, 1905, and October 17, 1905. Further proceedings were had September 13, 1905.

It appears from the evidence and the records of this office that the correct names of the father and mother of said children are Robert Benton and Jennie Benton, and that said Easma is also known by the name, Daniel. Reference will hereinafter be made to said Easma and Thomas under the names Daniel Benton and Thomas Benton respectively.

The evidence and the records of this office show that said Daniel Benton and Thomas Benton are the children of Jennie Benton and Robert Benton, whose names appear upon a schedule of citizens by blood of the Creek Nation approved by the Secretary of the Interior March 28, 1902, opposite Nos. 8367 and 8070 respectively.

The evidence further shows that said Daniel Benton was born November 28, 1900; that said Thomas Benton was born March 9, 1902; and that both of said children were living March 4, 1905.

Although the application herein for the enrollment of said Daniel Benton was not made within the time designated by the Secretary of the Interior under authority in him vested by the provisions of the Act of Congress approved March 3, 1901 (31 Stat. L. 1010), jurisdiction to consider the same under the Act of Congress approved June 30, 1902 (32 Stat. L. 500) was given to this office and the Department by the provisions of Section 1 of the Act of Congress approved April 26, 1906 (34 Stat. L. 137).

It is, therefore, ordered and adjudged that the said Daniel Benton is entitled to be enrolled as a citizen by blood of the Creek Nation, under the provisions of the Act of Congress approved June 30, 1902 (32 Stat. L. 500); that Thomas Benton is entitled to be enrolled as a citizen by blood of the Creek Nation, in accordance with the provisions of law above quoted, and the application for his enrollment as such is accordingly granted.
a citizen by blood of the Creek Nation, under the provisions of the Act of Congress approved March 3, 1905 (33 Stat. L. 1048), and the application for their enrollment as such is accordingly granted.

Tams Bixby COMMISSIONER.

Muskogee, Indian Territory,
FEB 18 1907

Applications for Enrollment of Creek Newborn
Act of 1905   Volume XIII

NC 49

Eufaula I T Sept 2o[sic] 1905

Comr to the 5 civ tribes
    Muskogee I T

Sir:

There is inclosed herewith supplemental proof in the matter of the application for the enrollment of Easma Bender as a citizen by blood of the Creek Nation, together with a copy of New Creek card No. 1o49[sic]

        Respt
            Alex Posey

NC 1049

Muskogee, Indian Territory, October 24, 1905.

Jennie Benton,
    Care Robert Benton,
        Melette[sic], Indian Territory,.

Dear Madam:

In the matter of the application for the enrollment of your minor child, Thomas Benton, born March 9, 1902, as a citizen by blood of the Creek Nation, you spell your surname, the surname of said child and the surname of your husband, Bender.

Your husband, the father of said child, has been identified on the final roll of citizens by blood of the Creek Nation, as Robert Benton and it necessarily follows, if you are as stated his lawful wife, your name is also Benton as is also that of the child, he having been born in lawful wedlock.

In the affidavit of John and Jumbo Bright relative to the birth of said child, they failed to state the date of the birth of said child. Affidavit properly filled out is herewith enclosed and, if it correctly states the facts, you are requested to have same executed before a notary public and return to this office.

This office is unable to identify you on its roll of citizens by blood of the Creek Nation; you are requested to state your maiden name, the names of your parents, the Creek Indian town to which you belong and your roll number as the same appears on your deeds and allotment certificate.

        Respectfully,
                Commissioner.

AG-1049

Applications for Enrollment of Creek Newborn
Act of 1905 Volume XIII

N.C. 1049

Muskogee, Indian Territory, January 9, 1907.

Jennie Bender,
    C/o Robert Bender,
        Melette[sic], Indian Territory

Dear Madam:

    In the matter of the application for the enrollment of your minor children, Daniel and Thomas Bender, as citizens of the Creek Nation, you are hereby advised that there is not sufficient information before this office upon which to identify either you or the said Robert Bender, and you are notified that you will be allowed ten days within which to appear, together with such other witnesses as you May desire, to introduce, for the purpose of testifying in this matter.

                Respectfully,

                                Commissioner.

JWH

NC 1049

Muskogee, Indian Territory, March 9, 1907.

Jennie Benton,
    % Robert Benton,
        Mellette, Indian Territory.

Dear Madam :--

    You are hereby advised that on March 2, 1907, the Secretary of the Interior approved the enrollment of your minor child, Thomas Benton, as a citizen by blood of the Creek Nation, and that the name of said child appears upon the roll of new born citizens by blood of the Creek Nation, enrolled under the Act of Congress approved March 3, 1905, as number 1277.

    This child is now entitled to allotment and application therefor should be made without delay at the Creek Land Office, Muskogee, Indian Territory.

                Respectfully,

                                Commissioner.

Applications for Enrollment of Creek Newborn
Act of 1905   Volume XIII

2461 B
#3 - C 1050

DEPARTMENT OF THE INTERIOR,
COMMISSION TO THE FIVE CIVILIZED TRIBES.
EUFAULA, I.T. April 19, 1905.

In the matter of the application for the enrollment of certain new born children concerning whom no application could be obtained except through testimony.

Jimsey Fish and William Givens, being duly sworn, testified as follows testified as follows, through Official Interpreter, Alex Posey.

Examination by the Commission:
Q What is your name? A Jimsey Fish.
Q How old are you? A I have never been able to determine my age. (Witness appears to be about 48).
Q What is our post office? A Mellette, I.T.
Q Do you know of some new born children whose parents are unwilling to have them enrolled? A Yes sir.
Q Those about whom you and Mr. Givens are testifying are children all born since May 25, 1901? And for whom application could only be made in this way? A Yes sir.

Q What is your name? A William Givens.
Q How old are you? A I am 25.
Q What is your post office address? A Mellette.

Statement: Nocus Ela has two children--his white name is Jim Davis--he belongs to Kialigee Town--I don't know the name of his wife, but she belongs to Kialigee town; one of them is walking and the other is younger. The one that is walking is a boy, don't know the sex of the other. The oldest is named Johnny, don't know the other's name. Both are living. They are both new born children and Nocus said the other day that he had never enrolled them-the post office is Hanna.

Bob and Mahala Bender have two children--these people belong to Tuckabatchee and Hillabee Towns respectively--one of the children is Thomas and the other is Easma--Thomas is just beginning to talk and Easma is older than Thomas. Their post office is Mellette. These children are new borns also.

Josie and Mahala Roberts have two children--the parents belong to Hutchechuppa and Kialigee respectively-- I don't [sic] the names of the children-- one is walking and the other is a baby yet a small child.

Q Were both of them born since May 25, 1901? A Yes sir. The oldest is a girl and I don't know the sex of the youngest. Both are living. Their post office is Indianola.

Applications for Enrollment of Creek Newborn
Act of 1905 Volume XIII

Thompson Fields and Susie Fields--he is of Okchiye or Fish Pond, I don't know which, and Susie belongs to Hutchechuppa; they have one child born since May 25, 1901, I don't know but I think the gi child is a girl. It is living, the child is not able to crawl but can sit up.

Earnest and Nicey Gouge, of Hickory Ground and Hillabee Towns respectively--- had two children the last time I was at their house--both were born since May 25, don't know the names, both boys I think, both living, post office, Hanna.

Connie Hawkins of Hillabee Town and Sybilla Hawkins of Fish Pong (?) I don't know her town' they had one child at the time I was at their house; I was at their house last summer 1904, don't know whether a boy or girl, born after May 25, 1901, it was a small child at that time, it is living. Post Office, Hanna.

Micco Emarthla, his white name is Neddie Walker, and Sallie Emarthla, both parents belong to Kialigee, have one child names Walter born since May 25, 1901, and living. Post Office, Indianola.

Wiley Fish of Tuckabatchee and Hettie Fish of Kialigee, post office, Mellette, Indian Territory have two children, but one is probably too old being about seven years old, but the field party last year failed to get that old one. The youngest was probably born since May 25, 1901. It is a boy and living. The oldest one is named John I don't know the other.

Noah Roberts of Kialigee and Hannah Roberts of Hillabee post office, Mellette, Indian Territory have one child name not known, born since May 25, 1901. Don't now the sex, it is living. Noah also has a step-son about seven years old that has never been enrolled named Walter Starr.

Questions addressed to both witnesses:
Q These statements which you have made are for the purpose of getting enrolled the new born children of parents belonging to the Snake Faction? A Yes sir.
Q Neither of you are related to them? A I Jimsey am related to Wiley Fish, who is the son of my brother and that's all.

Henry G. Hains, being duly sworn, on his oath, states that the above and foregoing is a true and correct transcript of his stenographic notes as taken in said cause on said date.

(signed) Henry G. Hains

Subscribed and sworn to before me this 11th day of May, 1905.

(Signed) Drennan C Skaggs
Notary Public.

I, Anna Garrigues, on oath state that I copied the above testimony from the original on the 18th day of July, 1906 and that it is a true and correct copy of same.

Applications for Enrollment of Creek Newborn
Act of 1905   Volume XIII

Anna Garrigues
Subscribed and sworn to before me this 18th day of July 1905.

Edw C Griesel
Notary Public.

NC 1050   CM

DEPARTMENT OF THE INTERIOR,
COMMISSIONER TO THE FIVE CIVILIZED TRIBES.
Muskogee, Indian Territory, January 19, 1907.

In the matter of the application for the enrollment of MILLIE ROBERTS as a citizen by blood of the Creek Nation.

WILLIAM MCCOMBS, being first duly sworn by Edward Merrick, a Notary Public, testifies as follows:

BY THE COMMISSIONER:

Q What is your name? A William McCombs.
Q How old are you? A 62.
Q What is your postoffice address? A Muskogee.
Q Are you a citizen of the Creek tribe of Indians? A Yes sir.
Q What official position do you now hold? A National interpreter.
Q Are you acquainted with one Josie or Joe Roberts? A Yes sir.
Q Does he sometimes go by the name of Joe Roberts? A He carries three names.
Q What are they? A Joseph Roberts, Josie Roberts, or Joe Roberts.
Q Do you know what Creek Indian town he belongs to? A I am not certain, but he belongs to either Kialigee or Hutchechuppa, possibly he May be a Tuckabatchee.
Q Are you acquainted with his wife? A No sir.
Q Mr. McCombs, there is on file in this office affidavits in the matter of the application of Millie Roberts, in which affidavit it appears that Mary Roberts is the mother of said Millie and that Joe Roberts of Kialigee town is the father; in your opinion, do you think that the Joe Roberts mentioned in this affidavit is the same as Joseph or Josie Roberts? A Yes sir.
Q The postoffice address of these people in the affidavits referred to is given as Melette[sic], Indian Territory, while the postoffice address of Josie Roberts or Joe Roberts, the father, is given as Indianola, Indian Territory; I will ask you if Indianola and Mellette are one? A Well Indianola is nearer your office than Mellette.

It appears from the records of the Commissioner that Josie Roberts is enrolled on Creek Indian card, field No. 3026, opposite roll No. 8257, and that he is a member of Hutchechuppa town.

Applications for Enrollment of Creek Newborn
Act of 1905   Volume XIII

Q Mr. McCombs, you are then satisfied that Joe Roberts and Josie Roberts are one and the same person are you? A Yes sir.
Q I will ask you Mr. McCombs if Josie Roberts is a member of what is know[sic] as the Snake faction of the Creeks? A Yes sir.

WITNESS EXCUSED.

Core Moore, being first duly sworn, states that as stenographer to the Commissioner to the Five Civilized Tribes she reported the proceedings had in the above entitled cause on January 19, 1907, and that the above and foregoing is a true and correct transcript of her stenographic notes taken in said cause on said date.

Core Moore

Subscribed and sworn to before me January 25, 1907.

Edward Merrick
Notary Public.

N.C. 1050.   FHW
                                                                                                            AG

DEPARTMENT OF THE INTERIOR,
COMMISSIONER TO THE FIVE CIVILIZED TRIBES.

In the matter of the application for the enrollment of Millie Roberts and Sister Roberts as citizens by blood of the Creek Nation.

DECISION.

The record in this case shows that on April 19, 1905, Jimsey Fish and William Givens appeared before a Creek enrollment field party at Eufaula, Indian Territory, and being duly sworn testified "in the matter of the application for the enrollment of certain new born children concerning whom no application could be obtained except through testimony", in which proceeding appears the following statement:

> "Josie and Mahala Roberts have two children--the parents belong to Hutchechuppa and Kialigee respectively--I don't know the names of the children--one is walking and the other is a baby yet a small child."

In connection with subsequent evidence and the records of this office, said statement is herein considered an original application for the enrollment of Millie and Sister Roberts, in order that their citizenship rights be protected. Supplemental affidavits as to the birth of said applicants filed on May 29, September 11 and September 21, 1905, are attached to and made a part of the record herein. Further proceedings were had on January 19, 1907.

Applications for Enrollment of Creek Newborn
Act of 1905 Volume XIII

The evidence and the records in the possession of this office show that Millie and Sister Roberts are the children of Josie Roberts and Mahala Roberts, whose names appear on a partial schedule of citizens by blood of the Creek Nation, approved by the Secretary of the Interior March 28, 1902, opposite roll numbers 8257 and 7752 respectively.

The evidence is conflicting as to the date of the birth of the said Millie Roberts but the weight of the evidence establishes the said date as May 22, 1901.

The evidence further shows that the applicant, Sister Roberts, was born November 27, 1902, and that both of said applicants were living March 5, 1905.

Although the application of the said Millie Roberts was not made within the time designated by the Secretary of the Interior, under the authority in him vested by the provisions of the Act of Congress approved March 3, 1901 (31 Stats. 1910), jurisdiction to consider the same under the Act of June 30, 1902, was given to this office and the Department by the provisions of Section 1 of the Act of Congress approved April 26, 1906 (34 Stats., 137).

It is, therefore, ordered and adjudged that the said Millie Roberts is entitled to be enrolled as a citizen by blood of the Creek Nation, under the provisions of the Act of Congress approved June 30, 1902 (32 Stats. 500), and that said Sister Roberts is entitled to be enrolled as a citizen by blood of the Creek Nation, under the provisions of the Act of Congress approved March 3, 1905 (33 Stats., 1048), and the applications for their enrollment as such are accordingly granted.

Tams Bixby   COMMISSIONER.

Muskogee, Indian Territory,
FEB 5- 1907

BIRTH AFFIDAVIT.

DEPARTMENT OF THE INTERIOR.
COMMISSION TO THE FIVE CIVILIZED TRIBES.

IN RE APPLICATION FOR ENROLLMENT, as a citizen of the Creek Nation, of Sister Roberts, born on the 27 day of November, 1902

Name of Father: Joe Roberts   a citizen of the   Creek   Nation.
Kialigee
Name of Mother: Mary Roberts   a citizen of the   Creek   Nation.
Kialigee

Postoffice   Mellette, I.T.

AFFIDAVIT OF MOTHER.

UNITED STATES OF AMERICA, Indian Territory, ⎫
   Western   DISTRICT.   ⎬

I, Mary Roberts, on oath state that I am about 23 years of age and a citizen by blood, of the Creek Nation; that I am the lawful wife of Joe Roberts, who is a citizen, by blood of the Creek Nation; that a female child was born to me on 27

Applications for Enrollment of Creek Newborn
Act of 1905   Volume XIII

day of November , 1902 , that said child has been named Sister Roberts , and ~~is now~~
was living. on March 4, 1905.   her
                                        Mary x Roberts
Witnesses To Mark: marks
   { DC Skaggs
   { Alex Posey

    Subscribed and sworn to before me this 25 day of   May   , 1905.

                                       Drennan C Skaggs
                                        Notary Public.

AFFIDAVIT OF ATTENDING PHYSICIAN OR MID-WIFE.

UNITED STATES OF AMERICA, Indian Territory, }
    Western   **DISTRICT.**

                                                    my wife
    I, Joe Roberts , ~~a (blank)~~ , on oath state that I attended on ^ Mrs. Mary Roberts,
~~wife of~~ *(blank)* on the 27 day of November , 1902 ; that there was born to her on
said date a   female   child; that said child ~~is now~~ was living on March 4, 1905 and is
said to have been named Sister Roberts   his
                                      Joe x Roberts
Witnesses To Mark: mark
   { DC Skaggs
   { Alex Posey

    Subscribed and sworn to before me this 25 day of   May   , 1905.

                                       Drennan C Skaggs
                                        Notary Public.

BIRTH AFFIDAVIT.
                           DEPARTMENT OF THE INTERIOR.
                COMMISSION TO THE FIVE CIVILIZED TRIBES.

    IN RE APPLICATION FOR ENROLLMENT, as a citizen of the *(blank)* Nation, of Sister
Roberts , born on or about the 27 day of Nov , 1902

Name of Father: Joe Roberts   a citizen of the   Creek   Nation.
Hutchechuppa
Name of Mother: Mary Roberts   a citizen of the   Creek   Nation.
Kialigee
                              Postoffice   Melette[sic], I.T.

Applications for Enrollment of Creek Newborn
Act of 1905   Volume XIII

AFFIDAVIT OF ATTENDING PHYSICIAN OR MID-WIFE.

UNITED STATES OF AMERICA, Indian Territory,
  Western   DISTRICT.

are personally acquainted with We, the undersigned , a——, on oath state that I we attended on Mrs. Mary Roberts , wife of Joe Roberts on the day of , 1 ; that there was born to her on or about the 27 day of Nov 1902 said date a female child; that said child was living March 4, 1905, and is said to have been named Sister Roberts

Witnesses To Mark:
{

John Bright
Lumber Bright

Subscribed and sworn to before me 11 day of   Sept.   , 1905.

Drennan C Skaggs
Notary Public.

NC-1050

Muskogee, Indian Territory, December 21, 1905.

Alex Posey,
    Clerk in Charge, Creek Enrollment Field Party,
        Boynton, Indian Territory.

Dear Sir:

April 19, 1905, Jimsey Fish and William Givens appeared before the Commission to the Five Civilized Tribes at Eufaula, Indian Territory, and gave testimony as follows:

"Josie and Mahala Roberts have two children--the parents belong to Hutchechuppa and Kialigee respectively--I don't know the names of the children--one is walking and the other is a baby yet, a small child."

Subsequent to that date, you secured and forwarded to this Office the affidavits of Mary Roberts, John Bright and Lumber Bright relative to the birth of said children. In the affidavits referred to, the mother signed her name as Mary Roberts, and states that she is the lawful wife of Joe Roberts. There is nothing in the affidavits to show that said Mary and Joe Roberts are the same persons as Josie and Mahala Roberts referred to in the testimony of April 19, 1905, and who are identified under those names on the final rolls of citizens by blood of the Creek Nation.

You are therefore instructed to secure new affidavits relative to the births of Millie Roberts, born May 22, 1901, and Sister Roberts, born November 27, 1902, who, it appears, are the children referred in said testimony. You will see to it that the mother

Applications for Enrollment of Creek Newborn
Act of 1905   Volume XIII

signs her correct name, and that she gives the correct name of her husband, the father of said children.

The postoffice address of the parents of said children is given as Mellette, Indian Territory.

Respectfully,
Commissioner.

NC 1050 Millie Roberts

Her father is Joe or Josie Roberts & her mother is Mary or Mahala Roberts. When I called at Joe Roberts house every one was absent but I obtained the above information from neighbors. Millie is now living.

P.B. Ewing

N C 1050.

Muskogee, Indian Territory, March 7, 1907.

Mary Roberts,
    Care of Joe Roberts,
        Mellette, Indian Territory.

Dear Madam:

You are hereby advised that on March 2, 1907 the Secretary of the Interior approved the enrollment of your minor child, Sister Roberts, as a citizen by blood of the Creek Nation, and that the name of said child appears upon the roll of new born citizens by blood of the Creek Nation enrolled under the Act of Congress approved March 3, 1905, as number 1250.

This child is now entitled to allotment and application therefor should be made without delay at the Creek Land Office, Muskogee, Indian Territory.

Respectfully,
Commissioner.

Applications for Enrollment of Creek Newborn
Act of 1905   Volume XIII

2461 B
#4 - C 1051

DEPARTMENT OF THE INTERIOR,
COMMISSION TO THE FIVE CIVILIZED TRIBES.
EUFAULA, I.T. April 19, 1905.

In the matter of the application for the enrollment of certain new born children concerning whom no application could be obtained except through testimony.

Jimsey Fish and William Givens, being duly sworn, testified as follows testified as follows, through Official Interpreter, Alex Posey.

Examination by the Commission:
Q What is your name? A Jimsey Fish.
Q How old are you? A I have never been able to determine my age. (Witness appears to be about 48).
Q What is our post office? A Mellette, I.T.
Q Do you know of some new born children whose parents are unwilling to have them enrolled? A Yes sir.
Q Those about whom you and Mr. Givens are testifying are children all born since May 25, 1901? And for whom application could only be made in this way? A Yes sir.

Q What is your name? A William Givens.
Q How old are you? A I am 25.
Q What is your post office address? A Mellette.

Statement: Nocus Ela has two children--his white name is Jim Davis--he belongs to Kialigee Town--I don't know the name of his wife, but she belongs to Kialigee town; one of them is walking and the other is younger. The one that is walking is a boy, don't know the sex of the other. The oldest is named Johnny, don't know the other's name. Both are living. They are both new born children and Nocus said the other day that he had never enrolled them-the post office is Hanna.

Bob and Mahala Bender have two children--these people belong to Tuckabatchee and Hillabee Towns respectively--one of the children is Thomas and the other is Easma--Thomas is just beginning to talk and Easma is older than Thomas. Their post office is Mellette. These children are new borns also.

Josie and Mahala Roberts have two children--the parents belong to Hutchechuppa and Kialigee respectively-- I don't [sic] the names of the children-- one is walking and the other is a baby yet a small child.

Q Were both of them born since May 25, 1901? A Yes sir. The oldest is a girl and I don't know the sex of the youngest. Both are living. Their post office is Indianola.

Applications for Enrollment of Creek Newborn
Act of 1905 Volume XIII

✓Thompson Fields and Susie Fields--he is of Okchiye or Fish Pond, I don't know which, and Susie belongs to Hutchechuppa; they have one child born since May 25, 1901, I don't know but I think the child is a girl. It is living, the child is not able to crawl but can sit up.

Earnest and Nicey Gouge, of Hickory Ground and Hillabee Towns respectively--- had two children the last time I was at their house--both were born since May 25, don't know the names, both boys I think, both living, post office, Hanna.

Connie Hawkins of Hillabee Town and Sybilla Hawkins of Fish Pong (?) I don't know her town' they had one child at the time I was at their house; I was at their house last summer 1904, don't know whether a boy or girl, born after May 25, 1901, it was a small child at that time, it is living. Post Office, Hanna.

Micco Emarthla, his white name is Neddie Walker, and Sallie Emarthla, both parents belong to Kialigee, have one child names Walter born since May 25, 1901, and living. Post Office, Indianola.

Wiley Fish of Tuckabatchee and Hettie Fish of Kialigee, post office, Mellette, Indian Territory have two children, but one is probably too old being about seven years old, but the field party last year failed to get that old one. The youngest was probably born since May 25, 1901. It is a boy and living. The oldest one is named John I don't know the other.

Noah Roberts of Kialigee and Hannah Roberts of Hillabee post office, Mellette, Indian Territory have one child name not known, born since May 25, 1901. Don't now the sex, it is living. Noah also has a step-son about seven years old that has never been enrolled named Walter Starr.

Questions addressed to both witnesses:
Q These statements which you have made are for the purpose of getting enrolled the new born children of parents belonging to the Snake Faction? A Yes sir.
Q Neither of you are related to them? A I Jimsey am related to Wiley Fish, who is the son of my brother and that's all.

Henry G. Hains, being duly sworn, on his oath, states that the above and foregoing is a true and correct transcript of his stenographic notes as taken in said cause on said date.

signed Henry G. Hains

Subscribed and sworn to before me this 11th day of May, 1905.

Signed Drennan C Skaggs
Notary Public.

I, Anna Garrigues, on oath state that I copied the above testimony from the original on the 18th day of July, 1906 and that it is a true and correct copy of same.

Applications for Enrollment of Creek Newborn
Act of 1905 Volume XIII

Anna Garrigues

Subscribed and sworn to before me this 18th day of July 1905.

Edw C Griesel
Notary Public.

N.C. 1051.
DEPARTMENT OF THE INTERIOR,
COMMISSIONER TO THE FIVE CIVILIZED TRIBES.
Henna, Indian Territory, December 18, 1906.

In the matter of the application for the enrollment of Lizzie (Fields) Stevens as a citizen by blood of the Creek Nation.

THOMPSON STEVENS, being duly sworn, testified as follows through Jesse McDermott official interpreter.

BY THE COMMISSIONER:

Q What is your name? I have three names. Thompson Fields, Thompson Stepney and Thompson Stevens.
Q Under which one of these names were you enrolled? A I do not know.
Q What is your age? A About 22.
Q What is your postoffice address? A Hanna.
Q Are you a Creek citizen? A Yes.
Q To which Creek Indian Town do you belong? A Fish Pond.
Q Have you filed on your allotment? A No, but the land that the Commissioner arbitrary alloted[sic] to me is located about one-half mile south of the Ft. Smith & Western bridge on the Canadian River.
Q Have you the deeds to that land? A No.
Q What was your wife's name before you married her? A Susie Lowee[sic]
Q To which Creek Indian Town does she belong? A Hutchechuppa.

There is an affidavit on file at the office of the Commissioner to the Five Civilized Tribes in the matter of the application for the enrollment of your child Lizzie, giving her last name as Fields.

Q What reason have you for making the application for enrollment under the name of Lizzie Fields when her right name is Lizzie Stevens? A I did not know that my name was on the roll as Thompson Stevens. They call me Thompson Fields all of the time and I thought that that was my right name.

---oooOOOooo---

Applications for Enrollment of Creek Newborn
Act of 1905   Volume XIII

I, Jesse McDermott, on oath state that the above and foregoing is a full and true transcript of my notes as taken in said cause on said date.

Jesse McDermott

Subscribed and sworn to before me this 27" day of Dec 1906.

W^m F A Gierkes
Notary Public.

My Commission expires
6-29-1908

Department of the Interior,
COMMISSION TO THE FIVE CIVILIZED TRIBES.

In the matter of the death of   Lizzie Stevens   a citizen of the ----- Creek ----- Nation, who formerly resided at or near   Hanna   , Ind. Ter., and died on the   7th day of January , 1906

AFFIDAVIT OF RELATIVE.

UNITED STATES OF AMERICA,
   INDIAN TERRITORY,
  Western   District.

I, Thompson Stevens , on oath state that I am about 22   years of age and a citizen by blood   , of the   Creek   Nation; that my postoffice address is   Hanna   , Ind. Ter.; that I am   the father   of   Lizzie Stevens   who was a citizen, by   blood , of the   Creek   Nation and that said   Lizzie Stevens   died on the   7th day of January   , 1906   his

Thompson x Stevens
mark

Witnesses To Mark:
  { J McDermott
    Jim Cantrell

Subscribed and sworn to before me this 18 day of   December , 1906.

My Commission   J McDermott
Expires July 25" 1907   *Notary Public.*

Applications for Enrollment of Creek Newborn
Act of 1905 Volume XIII

BIRTH AFFIDAVIT.

DEPARTMENT OF THE INTERIOR.
COMMISSION TO THE FIVE CIVILIZED TRIBES.

IN RE APPLICATION FOR ENROLLMENT, as a citizen of the Creek Nation, of Lizzie Fields, born on the day of October, 1904

Name of Father: Thompson Fields   a citizen of the   Creek   Nation. Okchiye Town
Name of Mother: Susie Fields (nee Low)   a citizen of the   Creek   Nation. Hutchechuppa Town
                              Postoffice   Hanna, I.T.

AFFIDAVIT OF MOTHER.

UNITED STATES OF AMERICA, Indian Territory,
   Western   **DISTRICT.**

I, Susie Fields , on oath state that I am about 25 years of age and a citizen by blood , of the Creek Nation; that I am the lawful wife of Thompson Fields , who is a citizen, by blood of the Creek Nation; that a female child was born to me on——day of October, 1904, that said child has been named Lizzie Fields , and is now was living. on March 4, 1905
                                                her
                                        Susie x Fields
Witnesses To Mark: mark
  { Alex Posey
  { DC Skaggs

Subscribed and sworn to before me this 25 day of   May   , 1905.

                        Drennan C Skaggs
                            Notary Public.

AFFIDAVIT OF ATTENDING PHYSICIAN OR MID-WIFE.

UNITED STATES OF AMERICA, Indian Territory,
   Western   **DISTRICT.**

I, Jennie Lasley , a mid-wife , on oath state that I attended on Mrs. Susie Fields, wife of Thompson Fields sometime in October , 1904 ; that there was born to her on said date a female child; that said child is now living and is said to have been named Lizzie Fields
                                                her
                                        Jennie x Lasley
                                            mark

Applications for Enrollment of Creek Newborn
Act of 1905   Volume XIII

Witnesses To Mark:
{ DC Skaggs
  Alex Posey

Subscribed and sworn to before me this 31 day of   May   , 1905.

                                  Drennan C Skaggs
                                  Notary Public.

BIRTH AFFIDAVIT.

DEPARTMENT OF THE INTERIOR.
COMMISSION TO THE FIVE CIVILIZED TRIBES.

IN RE APPLICATION FOR ENROLLMENT, as a citizen of the Creek Nation, of Lizzie (Fields) Stevens, born on the 7th day of Oct, 1904

Name of Father: Thompson Stevens   a citizen of the   Creek   Nation.
Name of Mother: Susie Stevens (nee Lowe) a citizen of the   Creek   Nation.
#8358

                            Postoffice   Hanna, Ind. Ter.

AFFIDAVIT OF MOTHER.

UNITED STATES OF AMERICA, Indian Territory, }
    Western   **DISTRICT.**

    I, Susie Stevens, on oath state that I am about 26 years of age and a citizen by blood, of the Creek Nation; that I am the lawful wife of Thompson Stevens, who is a citizen, by blood of the Creek Nation; that a female child was born to me on 7th day of October, 1904, that said child has been named Lizzie Stevens, and was living March 4, 1905. and died January 7th 1906   her

                                  Susie x Stevens
Witnesses To Mark: mark
{ J McDermott
  Jim Cantrell

Subscribed and sworn to before me this 18 day of December   , 1906.

My Commission   J McDermott
Expires July 25" 1907   Notary Public.

Applications for Enrollment of Creek Newborn
Act of 1905   Volume XIII

AFFIDAVIT OF ATTENDING PHYSICIAN OR MID-WIFE.

UNITED STATES OF AMERICA, Indian Territory, }
    Western   DISTRICT.

I, Jennie Lasley , a midwife , on oath state that I attended on Mrs. Susie Stevens , wife of Thompson Stevens on the 7th day of Oct , 1904 ; that there was born to her on said date a female child; that said child was living March 4, 1905, and is said to have been named Lizzie Stevens

                                          her
                          Jennie x Lasley

Witnesses To Mark: mark
{ J McDermott
  Jim Cantrell

Subscribed and sworn to before me this 18 day of December , 1906.

My Commission   J McDermott
Expires July 25" 1907   Notary Public.

BIRTH AFFIDAVIT.

DEPARTMENT OF THE INTERIOR.
COMMISSION TO THE FIVE CIVILIZED TRIBES.

IN RE APPLICATION FOR ENROLLMENT, as a citizen of the Creek Nation, of Lizzie Fields , born on the *(blank)* day of October , 1904

Name of Father: Thompson Fields   a citizen of the Creek Nation. Okche
Name of Mother: Susie " (nee Low) a citizen of the Creek Nation. Hutchechuppa

                        Postoffice   Hanna, I.Ty

AFFIDAVIT OF MOTHER.

UNITED STATES OF AMERICA, Indian Territory, }
    Western   DISTRICT.

I, Susie Fields , on oath state that I am about 25 years of age and a citizen by blood , of the Creek Nation; that I am the lawful wife of Thompson Fields , who is a citizen, by blood of the Creek Nation; that a female child was born to me on——day of October , 1904 , that said child has been named Lizzie Fields , and was living March 4, 1905.

                                        her
                              Susie x Fields
                                  mark

Applications for Enrollment of Creek Newborn
Act of 1905 Volume XIII

Witnesses To Mark:
{ Alex Posey
{ DC Skaggs

Subscribed and sworn to before me this 25" day of   May   , 1905.

Drennan C Skaggs
Notary Public.

AFFIDAVIT OF ATTENDING PHYSICIAN OR MID-WIFE.

UNITED STATES OF AMERICA, Indian Territory,
Western   DISTRICT.

I, Jennie Lasley, a mid-wife, on oath state that I attended on Mrs. Susie Fields, wife of Thompson Fields sometime in October , 1904 ; that there was born to her on said date a female child; that said child is now living and is said to have been named Lizzie Fields

Jennie Lasley

Witnesses To Mark:
{ DC Skaggs
{ Alex Posey

Subscribed and sworn to before me this *(blank)* day of   *(blank)*   , 190__.

(blank)
Notary Public.

NC 1051.   OCH
                                           EK

DEPARTMENT OF THE INTERIOR,
COMMISSIONER TO THE FIVE CIVILIZED TRIBES.

In the matter of the application for the enrollment of Lizzie Stepney, deceased, as a citizen by blood of the Creek Nation.

DECISION.

The records in the possession of the Commissioner show that on April 19, 1905, testimony was offered "in the matter of the application for the enrollment of certain new born children", as citizens by blood of the Creek Nation, which embraced a child of Thompson Fields and Susie Fields. The record further shows that on May 31, 1905, application was made, in affidavit form, for the enrollment of Lizzie Fields, a child of said persons above named, as a citizen by blood of the Creek Nation. On December 18, 1906, application was made, in affidavit form, for the enrollment of Lizzie Stevens,

Applications for Enrollment of Creek Newborn
Act of 1905 Volume XIII

deceased, a child to Thompson Stevens and Susie Stevens. Further proceedings were had on said date.

It appearing from the evidence and the records of this office that said Lizzie Fields, and said Lizzie Stevens, deceased, is the same person, and the person mentioned in said testimony offered April 19, 1905, and that the correct names of the father and mother of said child are Thompson Stepney and Susie Stepney, the proceeding first mentioned is herein considered an original application for the enrollment of Lizzie Stepney, deceased, as a citizen by blood of the Creek Nation, under the provisions of the Act of Congress approved March 3, 1905 (33 Stat., L. 1048), and reference will hereinafter be made to her accordingly.

The evidence and the records of this office show that said Lizzie Stepney, deceased, was the child of Susie Stepney, whose name appears as "Susie Low" upon a schedule of citizens by blood of the Creek Nation, opposite No. 8358, and Thompson Stepney, whose name appears upon a schedule of citizens by blood of the Creek Nation, opposite No. 8331, approved by the Secretary of the Interior March 28, 1902.

The evidence further shows that said Lizzie Stepney, deceased, was born October 7, 1904, and died January 7, 1906.

It is, therefore, ordered and adjudged that the said Lizzie Stepney, deceased, is entitled to be enrolled as a citizen by blood of the Creek Nation, under the provisions of the Act of Congress approved March 3, 1905 (33 Stat., L. 1048), and the application for her enrollment as such is accordingly granted.

Muskogee, Indian Territory,   Tams Bixby   Commissioner.
     FEB 2- 1907

N.C. 1051

Muskogee, Indian Territory, October 24, 1905.

Susie Fields,
     Care Thompson Fields,
         Hanna, Indian Territory.

Dear Madam:

In the matter of the application for the enrollment of your minor child, Lizzie Fields, born in the month of October 1904, as a citizen by blood of the Creek Nation, this office is unable to identify your husband, whose name you say is Thompson Fields, on the approved roll of citizens by blood of the Creek Nation; you are requested to state the names of his parents, the Creek Indian town to which he belongs, and his roll number as the same appears on his deeds and allotment certificate.

In the event that the correct surname of your husband is not Fields but is in fact some other name, it will necessarily follow that you being his lawful wife and the Lizzie being his daughter born in lawful wedlock, have the same name.

Applications for Enrollment of Creek Newborn
Act of 1905 Volume XIII

In the event, therefore, that his surname is other than Fields, it will be necessary for you to execute a new affidavit relative to the birth of said Lizzie Fields, giving therein the correct surname of yourself, the correct surname of said child and of its father, your said husband.

        Respectfully,

                Commissioner.

BA
Env.

N C 1051.

        Muskogee, Indian Territory, March 7, 1907.

Susie Stepney,
  Care of Thompson Stepney,
    Hanna, Indian Territory.

Dear Madam:

You are hereby advised that on March 2, 1907 the Secretary of the Interior approved the enrollment of your minor child, Lizzie Stepney, as a citizen by blood of the Creek Nation, and that the name of said child appears upon the roll of new born citizens by blood of the Creek Nation enrolled under the Act of Congress approved March 3, 1905, as number 1251.

This child is now entitled to allotment and application therefor should be made without delay at the Creek Land Office, Muskogee, Indian Territory.

        Respectfully,

                Commissioner.

Applications for Enrollment of Creek Newborn
Act of 1905   Volume XIII

BIRTH AFFIDAVIT.

DEPARTMENT OF THE INTERIOR,
COMMISSION TO THE FIVE CIVILIZED TRIBES.

In Re- Application for Enrollment, as a citizen of the Creek Nation, of   Leo E. Wadsworth , born on the 10 day of December , 1902

Name of Father: B W Wadsworth   a citizen of the   Creek   Nation.
Name of Mother: Martha Wadsworth   a citizen of the United States   Nation.

Post-office   Bristow Ind Tey

AFFIDAVIT OF MOTHER.

UNITED STATES OF AMERICA,
   INDIAN TERRITORY,
Western   District.

I,   Martha Wadsworth , on oath state that I am 24 years of age and a citizen by Birth , of the United States   Nation; that I am the lawful wife of   BW Wadsworth , who is a citizen, by Birth of the Creek Nation; that a   Male child was born to me on 10 day of December , 1902 , that said child has been named   Leo E Wadsworth , and is now living.

Martha F Wadsworth

Witnesses To Mark:
{ A E Walker

Subscribed and sworn to before me this 24 day of March, 1905.

E W Sims
Notary Public.

AFFIDAVIT OF ATTENDING PHYSICIAN OR MID-WIFE.

UNITED STATES OF AMERICA,
   INDIAN TERRITORY,
Western   District.

I,   A E Walker , a   Midwife , on oath state that I attended on Mrs. Martha Wadsworth , wife of BW Wadsworth on the 10 day of December , 1902; that there was born to her on said date a Male child; that said child is now living and is said to have been named Leo E Wadsworth

Mrs A E Walker

Applications for Enrollment of Creek Newborn
Act of 1905 Volume XIII

Witnesses To Mark:
  W.J. Lad

Subscribed and sworn to before me this 24 day of March, 1905.

E W Sims
Notary Public.

BIRTH AFFIDAVIT.

DEPARTMENT OF THE INTERIOR.
COMMISSION TO THE FIVE CIVILIZED TRIBES.

IN RE APPLICATION FOR ENROLLMENT, as a citizen of the Creek Nation, of Leo E Wadsworth, born on the 10 day of Dec, 1902

Name of Father: Ben W. Wadsworth   a citizen of the   Creek   Nation.
(Hickory Ground)
Name of Mother: Martha   "   a citizen of the   U. S.   Nation.

Postoffice   Bristow

(Child present)

AFFIDAVIT OF ~~MOTHER~~.
Father

UNITED STATES OF AMERICA, Indian Territory,
  Western   DISTRICT.

I, Ben W. Wadsworth, on oath state that I am 34 years of age and a citizen by blood, of the Creek Nation; that I am the lawful ~~wife~~ Husband of Martha Wadsworth, who is not a citizen, by ——— of the —— Nation; that a male child was born to me on 10 day of December, 1902, that said child has been named Leo E Wadsworth, and is now living.

Ben W Wadsworth

Witnesses To Mark:

Subscribed and sworn to before me this 21 day of April, 1905.

Edw C Griesel
Notary Public.

Applications for Enrollment of Creek Newborn
Act of 1905   Volume XIII

BIRTH AFFIDAVIT.

DEPARTMENT OF THE INTERIOR.
COMMISSION TO THE FIVE CIVILIZED TRIBES.

IN RE APPLICATION FOR ENROLLMENT, as a citizen of the Creek Nation, of Ella E. Wadsworth, born on the 22 day of Aug, 1904

Name of Father: Ben W. Wadsworth   a citizen of the   Creek   Nation.
(Hickory Ground)
Name of Mother: Martha   "   a citizen of the   U. S.   Nation.

Postoffice   Bristow

Father
AFFIDAVIT OF ~~MOTHER~~.
(Child present)

UNITED STATES OF AMERICA, Indian Territory, }
Western   DISTRICT.

I, Ben W. Wadsworth, on oath state that I am 34 years of age and a citizen by blood, of the Creek Nation; that I am the lawful ~~wife~~ Husband of Martha Wadsworth, who is not a citizen, by ——— of the —— Nation; that a female child was born to me on 22 day of Aug, 1904, that said child has been named Ella E Wadsworth, and was living March 4, 1905.

Ben W Wadsworth

Witnesses To Mark:
{

Subscribed and sworn to before me this 21 day of April, 1905.

Edw C Griesel
Notary Public.

BIRTH AFFIDAVIT.

DEPARTMENT OF THE INTERIOR,
COMMISSION TO THE FIVE CIVILIZED TRIBES.

In Re- Application for Enrollment, as a citizen of the Creek Nation, of Ella E. Wadsworth, born on the 22 day of August, 1904

Name of Father: B W Wadsworth   a citizen of the   Creek   Nation.
Name of Mother: Martha Wadsworth   a citizen of the United States   Nation.

Post-office   Bristow Ind Tey

Applications for Enrollment of Creek Newborn
Act of 1905   Volume XIII

AFFIDAVIT OF MOTHER.

UNITED STATES OF AMERICA,
  INDIAN TERRITORY,
  Western   District.

I, Martha Wadsworth, on oath state that I am 21 years of age and a citizen by Birth, of the United States Nation; that I am the lawful wife of BW Wadsworth, who is a citizen, by Birth of the Creek Nation; that a Female child was born to me on 22 day of August, 1904, that said child has been named Ella E Wadsworth, and is now living.

Martha F Wadsworth

Witnesses To Mark:
  A E Walker

Subscribed and sworn to before me this 29 day of March, 1905.

E W Sims
Notary Public.

AFFIDAVIT OF ATTENDING PHYSICIAN OR MID-WIFE.

UNITED STATES OF AMERICA,
  INDIAN TERRITORY,
  Western   District.

I, Omer C Coppedge, a Physician, on oath state that I attended on Mrs. Martha Wadsworth, wife of BW Wadsworth on the 22 day of August, 1904; that there was born to her on said date a Female child; that said child is now living and is said to have been named Ella E Wadsworth

Omer C. Coppedge

Witnesses To Mark:
  F.L.B. Leewell
  J.A. Jackman

Subscribed and sworn to before me this 31st day of March, 1905.
My commission expires
  Dec 12th 1908

William Moore
Notary Public.
St Louis Mo

Applications for Enrollment of Creek Newborn
Act of 1905   Volume XIII

BIRTH AFFIDAVIT.

DEPARTMENT OF THE INTERIOR.
COMMISSION TO THE FIVE CIVILIZED TRIBES.

IN RE APPLICATION FOR ENROLLMENT, as a citizen of the *(blank)* Nation, of Walter Walker, born on the 12 day of February, 1903
(Nattie Walker)

Name of Father: Micco Emarthla   a citizen of the   Creek   Nation.
  Kialigee Town
Name of Mother: Sallie Walker   a citizen of the   Creek   Nation.
  Kialigee Town
                           Postoffice   Indianola, I.T.

AFFIDAVIT OF MOTHER.

UNITED STATES OF AMERICA, Indian Territory, }
    Western   DISTRICT.

I, Sallie Walker, on oath state that I am about 28 years of age and a citizen by blood, of the Creek Nation; that I am the lawful wife of Micco Emarthla, who is a citizen, by blood of the Creek Nation; that a male child was born to me on 12 day of February, 1903, that said child has been named Walter Walker, and ~~is now~~ was living. on March 4, 1905

                                              her
                                    Sallie x Walker
Witnesses To Mark: mark
  { DC Skaggs
  { Alex Posey

Subscribed and sworn to before me this 25 day of   May   , 1905.

                              Drennan C Skaggs
                              Notary Public.

AFFIDAVIT OF ATTENDING PHYSICIAN OR MID-WIFE.

UNITED STATES OF AMERICA, Indian Territory, }
    Western   DISTRICT.

                                                        my wife
I, Micco Emarthla, ~~a (blank)~~, on oath state that I attended on ^ Mrs. Sallie Walker, ~~wife of~~ *(blank)* on the 12 day of February, 1903; that there was born to her on said date a   male   child; that said child ~~is now~~ was living on March 4, 1905 and is said to have been named Walter Walker

                              Micco Emarthla
Witnesses To Mark:
  {

Applications for Enrollment of Creek Newborn
Act of 1905   Volume XIII

Subscribed and sworn to before me this 25 day of   May   , 1905.

Drennan C Skaggs
Notary Public.

N.C. 1055.

OCH.
JWH

DEPARTMENT OF THE INTERIOR,
COMMISSIONER TO THE FIVE CIVILIZED TRIBES.

----o----

In the matter of the application for the enrollment of Walter Emarthla as a citizen by blood of the Creek Nation.

DECISION.

The record in this case shows that on May 29, 1905, application was made, in affidavit form, for the enrollment of Walter Walker, a son of Micco Emarthla and Sallie Walker, as a citizen by blood of the Creek Nation, under the provisions of the Act of Congress approved March 3, 1905 (33 Stat. L. 1048). It appears from the record that said Sallie Walker is the lawful wife of said Micco Emarthla. The correct name of this child then is Walter Emarthla and reference will hereafter be made to him accordingly.

The evidence and the records of this office show that said Walter Emarthla is the child of Micco Emarthla and Sallie Emarthla, whose name are included in a schedule of citizens by blood of the Creek Nation approved by the Secretary of the Interior March 28, 1902, opposite numbers 7760 and 7761, respectively. The evidence further shows that said Walter Emarthla was born February 12, 1903, and was living March 4, 1905.

Although the application herein was not made within the time specified by the provisions of the Act of Congress approved March 3, 1905, (33 Stat., L. 1048), jurisdiction to consider the same under said Act of Congress was given to this office and the Department by the provisions of Section 1, of the Act of Congress approved April 26, 1906, (34 Stat., L. 137).

It is therefore, ordered and adjudged that said Walter Emarthla is entitled to enrollment as a citizen by blood of the Creek Nation in accordance with the provisions of the Act of Congress approved March 3, 1905, (33 Stat., L. 1048), and the application for his enrollment as such is accordingly granted.

Tams Bixby Commissioner.

Muskogee, Indian Territory.
FEB 7- 1907

Applications for Enrollment of Creek Newborn
Act of 1905   Volume XIII

HGH

REFER IN REPLY TO THE FOLLOWING:
N.C. 1055

DEPARTMENT OF THE INTERIOR,
COMMISSIONER TO THE FIVE CIVILIZED TRIBES.

Muskogee, Indian Territory, October 24, 1905.

Sallie Emarthla,
    Care Micco Emarthla, (or Nattie Walker),
        Indianola, Indian Territory.

Dear Madam:

    In the matter of the application for the enrollment of your minor child, Walter Walker, born February 12, 1903, as a citizen by blood of the Creek Nation; you state that your surname and the surname of your said child is Walker and that you are the lawful wife of Micco Emarthla.

    The name of said Micco Emarthla appears upon the final roll of citizens by blood of the Creek Nation, and you are identified on said roll as Sallie Emarthla, the wife of said Micco Emarthla; if the correct name of you husband is Micco Emarthla and you are his lawful wife it necessarily follows that your correct name is Sallie Emarthla and not Sallie Walker and that the correct name of your said child, he having been born in lawful wedlock, is Walter Emarthla and not Walter Walker.

    There is herewith enclosed [sic] form of birth affidavit properly filled and you are requested to execute same before a notary public and return to this office.

    This office desires affidavit of the midwife or physician in attendance at the birth of said child.

    In the event that there was no physician or midwife in attendance when said child was born, it will be necessary for you to furnish this office with the affidavits of two disinterested witnesses relative to his birth. Said affidavits must set forth said child's name, the date of his birth, the names of his parents and whether or not he was living on March 4, 1905.

                           Respectfully,
                                       Tams Bixby
                                          Commissioner.

AG-1055

Applications for Enrollment of Creek Newborn
Act of 1905 Volume XIII

N C 1055

Muskogee, Indian Territory, March 7, 1907.

Sallie Emarthla,
    Care of Micco Emarthla,
        Indianola, Indian Territory.

Dear Madam:

You are hereby advised that on March 2, 1907, the Secretary of the Interior approved the enrollment of your minor child, Walter Emarthla, as a citizen by blood of the Creek Nation, and that the name of said child appears upon the roll of citizens by blood of the Creek Nation enrolled under the Act of Congress approved March 3, 1905, as number 1252.

This child is now entitled to allotment and application therefor should be made without delay at the Creek Land Office, Muskogee, Indian Territory.

                Respectfully,
                            Commissioner.

2461 B

DEPARTMENT OF THE INTERIOR,
COMMISSION TO THE FIVE CIVILIZED TRIBES.
Eufaula, I.T. April 19, 1905.

In the matter of the application for the enrollment of certain new born children concerning whom no application could be obtained except through testimony.

Jimsey Fish and William Givens, being duly sworn, testified as follows testified as follows, through Official Interpreter, Alex Posey.

Examination by the Commission:

Q What is your name? A Jimsey Fish.
Q How old are you? A I have never been able to determine my age. (Witness appears to be about 48).

Applications for Enrollment of Creek Newborn
Act of 1905 Volume XIII

Q What is our post office? A Mellette, I.T.
Q Do you know of some new born children whose parents are unwilling to have them enrolled? A Yes sir.
Q Those about whom you and Mr. Givens are testifying are children all born since May 25, 1901? And for whom application could only be made in this way? A Yes sir.

Q What is your name? A William Givens.
Q How old are you? A I am 25.
Q What is your post office address? A Mellette.

Statement: Nocus Ela has two children--his white name is Jim Davis--he belongs to Kialigee Town--I don't know the name of his wife, but she belongs to Kialigee town; one of them is walking and the other is younger. The one that is walking is a boy, don't know the sex of the other. The oldest is named Johnny, don't know the other's name. Both are living. They are both new born children and Nocus said the other day that he had never enrolled them-the post office is Hanna.

Bob and Mahala Bender have two children--these people belong to Tuckabatchee and Hillabee Towns respectively--one of the children is Thomas and the other is Easma--Thomas is just beginning to talk and Easma is older than Thomas. Their post office is Mellette. These children are new borns also.

Josie and Mahala Roberts have two children--the parents belong to Hutchechuppa and Kialigee respectively-- I don't [sic] the names of the children-- one is walking and the other is a baby yet a small child.

Q Were both of them born since May 25, 1901? A Yes sir. The oldest is a girl and I don't know the sex of the youngest. Both are living. Their post office is Indianola.

Thompson Fields and Susie Fields--he is of Okchiye or Fish Pond, I don't know which, and Susie belongs to Hutchechuppa; they have one child born since May 25, 1901, I don't know but I think the child is a girl. It is living, the child is not able to crawl but can sit up.

Earnest and Nicey Gouge, of Hickory Ground and Hillabee Towns respectively---had two children the last time I was at their house--both were born since May 25, don't know the names, both boys I think, both living, post office, Hanna.

Connie Hawkins of Hillabee Town and Sybilla Hawkins of Fish Pong (?) I don't know her town' they had one child at the time I was at their house; I was at their house last summer 1904, don't know whether a boy or girl, born after May 25, 1901, it was a small child at that time, it is living. Post Office, Hanna.

Micco Emarthla, his white name is Neddie Walker, and Sallie Emarthla, both parents belong to Kialigee, have one child names Walter born since May 25, 1901, and living. Post Office, Indianola.

Applications for Enrollment of Creek Newborn
Act of 1905   Volume XIII

Wiley Fish of Tuckabatchee and Hettie Fish of Kialigee, post office, Mellette, Indian Territory have two children, but one is probably too old being about seven years old, but the field party last year failed to get that old one. The youngest was probably born since May 25, 1901. It is a boy and living. The oldest one is named John I don't know the other.

Noah Roberts of Kialigee and Hannah Roberts of Hillabee post office, Mellette, Indian Territory have one child name not known, born since May 25, 1901. Don't now the sex, it is living. Noah also has a step-son about seven years old that has never been enrolled named Walter Starr.

Questions addressed to both witnesses:
Q These statements which you have made are for the purpose of getting enrolled the new born children of parents belonging to the Snake Faction? A Yes sir.
Q Neither of you are related to them? A I Jimsey am related to Wiley Fish, who is the son of my brother and that's all.

Henry G. Hains, being duly sworn, on his oath, states that the above and foregoing is a true and correct transcript of his stenographic notes as taken in said cause on said date.

signed Henry G. Hains

Subscribed and sworn to before me this 11th day of May, 1905.

Signed Drennan C Skaggs
Notary Public.

I, Anna Garrigues, on oath, states that the above and foregoing is a true copy of the original on file in this office.

Anna Garrigues

Subscribed and sworn to before me this 4th day of August 1905.

Edw C Griesel
Notary Public.

Applications for Enrollment of Creek Newborn
Act of 1905 Volume XIII

DEPARTMENT OF THE INTERIOR.
COMMISSION TO THE FIVE CIVILIZED TRIBES.

In the matter of the death of George Fish   a citizen of the Creek Nation, who formerly resided at or near   Hanna , Ind. Ter., and died on the   26 day of November , 1905

AFFIDAVIT OF RELATIVE.

UNITED STATES OF AMERICA, Indian Territory,
Western   DISTRICT.

I, Wiley Fish , on oath state that I am about 25 years of age and a citizen by blood , of the Creek Nation; that my postoffice address is   Hanna , Ind. Ter.; that I am   the father   of   George Fish   who was a citizen, by blood , of the Creek   Nation and that said   George Fish   died on the   26   day of November , 1905

Wiley Fish

Witnesses To Mark:

Subscribed and sworn to before me this 27 day of February, 1907.

My Commission   J McDermott
Expires July 25" 1907   Notary Public.

BIRTH AFFIDAVIT.

DEPARTMENT OF THE INTERIOR.
COMMISSION TO THE FIVE CIVILIZED TRIBES.

IN RE APPLICATION FOR ENROLLMENT, as a citizen of the Creek Nation, of George Fish , born on the 1 day of December , 1904

Name of Father: Wiley Fish   a citizen of the   Creek   Nation.
  Tuckabatche
Name of Mother: Hettie Fish   a citizen of the   Creek   Nation.
  Kialigee

Postoffice   Mellette, I.T.

Applications for Enrollment of Creek Newborn
Act of 1905 Volume XIII

AFFIDAVIT OF MOTHER.

UNITED STATES OF AMERICA, Indian Territory,
   Western   DISTRICT.

    I, Hettie Fish , on oath state that I am about 25 years of age and a citizen by blood , of the Creek Nation; that I am the lawful wife of Wiley Fish , who is a citizen, by blood of the Creek Nation; that a male child was born to me on 1st day of December , 1904 , that said child has been named George Fish , and is now was living. on March 4, 1905. That no one attended on me as physician or midwife at the birth of the child nor was any person present

Witnesses To Mark:

    Subscribed and sworn to before me this........day of................................., 190....

                                   Notary Public.

BIRTH AFFIDAVIT.

DEPARTMENT OF THE INTERIOR.
COMMISSION TO THE FIVE CIVILIZED TRIBES.

    IN RE APPLICATION FOR ENROLLMENT, as a citizen of the Creek Nation, of George Fish, born on the 1st day of Dec, 1904

Name of Father: Wiley Fish   a citizen of the   Creek   Nation.
Name of Mother: Hattie Fish   a citizen of the   Creek   Nation.

                      Postoffice   Hanna, Ind. Ter.

AFFIDAVIT OF MOTHER.

UNITED STATES OF AMERICA, Indian Territory,
   Western   DISTRICT.

    I, Hattie Fish (nee Wakache), on oath state that I am about 26 years of age and a citizen by blood , of the Creek Nation; that I am the lawful wife of Wiley Fish , who is a citizen, by blood of the Creek Nation; that a male child was born to me on 1st day of December, 1904 , that said child has been named George Fish , and was living March 4, 1905; that one was[sic] present when said child was born

                                  her
                            Hattie x Fish
                               mark

Applications for Enrollment of Creek Newborn
Act of 1905 Volume XIII

Witnesses To Mark:
{ J McDermott
{ Thomas Red

Subscribed and sworn to before me this 27 day of   Feb , 1907.

My Commission   J McDermott
Expires July 25" 1907   Notary Public.

NC 1056.   WSC
                                                                            JCL.
DEPARTMENT OF THE INTERIOR,
COMMISSIONER TO THE FIVE CIVILIZED TRIBES.

In the matter of the application for the enrollment of John and George Fish, as citizens by blood of the Creek Nation.

DECISION.

The record in this case shows that on April 19, 1905, the testimony of Jimsey Fish and William Givens was taken by a Creek enrollment field party, from this office, "in the matter of the application for the enrollment of certain new-born children, concerning whom no application could be obtained except through testimony", and that in said proceeding the said Jimsey Fish and William Givens testified that Wiley Fish of Tuckabatchee Town and Hettie Fish of Kialigee Town, had two male children. Said action is considered as an original application for the enrollment of said children as citizens by blood of the Creek Nation. A partially prepared form for a birth affidavit and a note attached thereto written by Alex Posey, is attached to and made a part of the record herein.

It appears from the evidence and the records of this office that said children are the minor children of Wiley Fish whose name appears on a partial schedule of citizens by blood of the Creek Nation, approved by the Secretary of the Interior March 29, 1902, opposite number 8817 and Hettie Fish, who is identified as the same person as Hettie, whose name appears on a partial schedule of citizens by blood of the Creek Nation approved by the Secretary of the Interior March 28, 1902, opposite number 7734.

It further appears from the evidence that the oldest of said children is named John and that he was born about the year 1898 and that the other child is named George and was born December 1, 1904, and that both of said children were living on March 4, 1905.

It is therefore, ordered and adjudged that the applicants, John Fish and George Fish, are entitled to be enrolled as citizens by blood of the Creek Nation, under the provisions of the Acts of Congress approved March 1, 1901, (31 Stats. 861) and March 3, 1905, (33 Stats. 1048), and the application for their enrollment as such is accordingly granted.

                                        Tams Bixby Commissioner.
Muskogee, Indian Territory.
    FEB 27 1907

Applications for Enrollment of Creek Newborn
Act of 1905   Volume XIII

N.C. 1056.

Muskogee, Indian Territory, January 11, 1907.

Alex Posey,
    Clerk in charge Creek Field Party,
        Braggs, Indian Territory.

Dear Sir:

    In the matter of the application for the enrollment of George ~~and John~~ Fish, children of Wiley and Hettie Fish, Mellette, Indian Territory, as citizens by blood of the Creek Nation, you are advised that it will be necessary that you furnish this office with further information concerning said applicants.

    Copies of the records in this case are herewith enclosed.

Respectfully,

1056 N.C.   Commissioner.

NC 1056.

Muskogee, Indian Territory, March 18, 1907.

Hettie Fish
    c/o Wiley Fish,
        Mellette, Indian Territory.

Dear Madam:

    You are hereby advised that the Secretary of the Interior under date of March 4, 1907, approved the enrollment of your minor child, George Fish, as a citizen by blood of the Creek Nation, and that the name of said child appears upon the roll of new born citizens by blood of the Creek Nation, enrolled under the act of Congress approved March 3, 1905, as number 1291.

    This child is now entitled to allotment and application therefor should be made without delay at the Creek Land Office, Muskogee, Indian Territory.

Respectfully,

Commissioner.

Applications for Enrollment of Creek Newborn
Act of 1905   Volume XIII

C 1057
DEPARTMENT OF THE INTERIOR,
COMMISSION TO THE FIVE CIVILIZED TRIBES.
Okmulgee, I. T., April 11, 1905.

In the matter of the application for the enrollment of Ellen Watson as a citizen by blood of the Creek Nation.

KATY WATSON, being duly sworn, testified as follows

Through Alex Posey Official Interpreter:

BY COMMISSION:
Q What is your name? A Katy Watson.
Q How old are you? A Thirty-three.
Q What is your post office address? A Henryetta.
Q Are you a citizen of the Creek Nation? A Yes, sir.
Q To what town do you belong? A Eufaula Deep Fork.
Q Do you make application for the enrollment of your minor child, Ellen Watson, as a citizen by blood of the Creek Nation? A Yes, sir.
Q What is the name of the child's father? A Garland Grayson.
Q Is he a citizen of the Creek Nation? A No, sir, he is a United States citizen.
Q Is he your lawful husband? A No, sir.
Q Were you ever married to him? A No, sir, we had the license to be married and were about to be married but he went back on me.
Q Is he living? A Yes, sir.
Q What is his post office address? A Henryetta.
Q Does he acknowledge the child as his? A Yes, sir
Q Does he contribute towards the support of the child? A Yes, sir.

---oooOOOooo---

I, D. C. Skaggs, on oath state that the above and foregoing is a full and true transcript of my stenographic notes as taken in said cause on said date.

D. C. Skaggs

Subscribed and sworn to before me this 24 day of July, 1905.

J McDermott
Notary Public.

Applications for Enrollment of Creek Newborn
Act of 1905 Volume XIII

INDIAN TERRITORY
SS
WESTERN JUDICIAL DISTRICT

I Hannah Mitchel being duly sworn do on oath state that I was in attendance on Katie Watson a single woman on the birth of a girl baby on the 23rd day of August 10-3 that the child is now known as Ellen Watson and that Katie Watson is a Creek Citizen To all of which I do hereby Certify
                                                            her
                                           --- Hannah x Mitchel
Witness to mark   mark
H E Breese
Willie Grimes

Subscribed and sworn to before the undersigned a Notary Public for the Western District Indian Territory this 23rd day of March 1905.

                                       E E Shock   Notary Public

                              My Commission expires Jan. 18th 1908.

BIRTH AFFIDAVIT.

DEPARTMENT OF THE INTERIOR.
COMMISSION TO THE FIVE CIVILIZED TRIBES.

IN RE APPLICATION FOR ENROLLMENT, as a citizen of the Creek Nation, of Ellen Watson, born on the 23 day of August, 1903

Name of Father: Garland Grayson   a citizen of the United States Nation.
Name of Mother: Katie Watson   a citizen of the   Creek   Nation.
Eufaula Deep Fork Town

                            Postoffice   Henryetta, Ind. Ter.

AFFIDAVIT OF MOTHER.

UNITED STATES OF AMERICA, Indian Territory,   Child is present
    Western   DISTRICT.

I, Katie Watson , on oath state that I am 33 years of age and a citizen by blood, of the Creek Nation; that I am not the lawful wife of Garland Grayson , who is a citizen, by *(blank)* of the United States Nation; that a female child was born to me on 23 day of August, 1903 , that said child has been named Ellen Watson , and was living March 4, 1905.

                                     Katie Watson

Applications for Enrollment of Creek Newborn
Act of 1905   Volume XIII

Witnesses To Mark:
{

Subscribed and sworn to before me this 11 day of April , 1905.

Drennan C Skaggs
Notary Public.

DEPARTMENT OF THE INTERIOR,
COMMISSION TO THE FIVE CIVILIZED TRIBES.
Eufaula, I.T. April 19, 1905.

In the matter of the application for the enrollment of certain new born children concerning whom no application could be obtained except through testimony.

Jimsey Fish and William Givens, being duly sworn, testified as follows testified as follows, through Official Interpreter, Alex Posey.

Examination by the Commission:

Q What is your name? A Jimsey Fish.
Q How old are you? A I have never been able to determine my age. (Witness appears to be about 48).
Q What is our post office? A Mellette, I.T.
Q Do you know of some new born children whose parents are unwilling to have them enrolled? A Yes sir.
Q Those about whom you and Mr. Givens are testifying are children all born since May 25, 1901? And for whom application could only be made in this way? A Yes sir.

Q What is your name? A William Givens.
Q How old are you? A I am 25.
Q What is your post office address? A Mellette.

5/25/05 Statement: Nocus Ela has two children--his white name is Jim Davis--he belongs to Kialigee Town--I don't know the name of his wife, but she belongs to Kialigee town; one of them is walking and the other is younger. The one that is walking is a boy, don't know the sex of the other. The oldest is named Johnny, don't know the other's name.

Applications for Enrollment of Creek Newborn
Act of 1905   Volume XIII

Both are living. They are both new born children and Nocus said the other day that he had never enrolled them-the post office is Hanna.

5/25/05 Bob and Mahala Bender have two children--these people belong to Tuckabatchee and Hillabee Towns respectively--one of the children is Thomas and the other is Easma--Thomas is just beginning to talk and Easma is older than Thomas. Their post office is Mellette. These children are new borns also.

5/25/05 Josie and Mahala Roberts have two children--the parents belong to Hutchechuppa and Kialigee respectively-- I don't [sic] the names of the children-- one is walking and the other is a baby yet a small child.

Q Were both of them born since May 25, 1901? A Yes sir. The oldest is a girl and I don't know the sex of the youngest. Both are living. Their post office is Indianola.

5/25/05 Thompson Fields and Susie Fields--he is of Okchiye or Fish Pond, I don't know which, and Susie belongs to Hutchechuppa. they have one child born since May 25, 1901, I don't know but I think the child is a girl. It is living, the child is not able to crawl but can sit up.

Earnest and Nicey Gouge, of Hickory Ground and Hillabee Towns respectively---had two children the last time I was at their house--both were born since May 25, don't know the names, both boys I think, both living, post office, Hanna. 6/3/05 Grand father
blank affidavit to be filled of and sent in.

5/23/05 Connie Hawkins of Hillabee Town and Sybilla Hawkins of Fish Pong (?) I don't know her town' they had one child at the time I was at their house; I was at their house last summer 1904, don't know whether a boy or girl, born after May 25, 1901, it was a small child at that time, it is living. Post Office, Hanna.

5/25/05 Micco Emarthla, his white name is Neddie Walker, and Sallie Emarthla, both parents belong to Kialigee, have one child names Walter born since May 25, 1901, and living. Post Office, Indianola.

5/25/05 Wiley Fish of Tuckabatchee and Hettie Fish of Kialigee, post office, Mellette, Indian Territory have two children, but one is probably too old being about seven years old, but the field party last year failed to get that old one. The youngest was probably born since May 25, 1901. It is a boy and living. The oldest one is named John I don't know the other.

Noah Roberts of Kialigee and Hannah Roberts of Hillabee post office, Mellette, Indian Territory have one child name not known, born since May 25, 1901. Don't now the sex, it is living. Noah also has a step-son about seven years old that has never been enrolled named Walter Starr. (See note in back)

Applications for Enrollment of Creek Newborn
Act of 1905   Volume XIII

Questions addressed to both witnesses:
Q These statements which you have made are for the purpose of getting enrolled the new born children of parents belonging to the Snake Faction? A Yes sir.
Q Neither of you are related to them? A I Jimsey am related to Wiley Fish, who is the son of my brother and that's all.

    Henry G. Hains, being duly sworn, on his oath, states that the above and foregoing is a true and correct transcript of his stenographic notes as taken in said cause on said date.

                               Henry G. Hains

Subscribed and sworn to before me this 11th day of May, 1905.

                               Drennan C Skaggs
                               Notary Public.

2461-B.
DEPARTMENT OF THE INTERIOR,
COMMISSIONER TO THE FIVE CIVILIZED TRIBES.
Melette[sic], I. T., September 21, 1905.

    In the matter of the application for the enrollment of Joseph Roberts as a citizen of the Creek Nation.

                   NOAH ROBERTS, being duly sworn, testified as follows:

        Through Alex Posey Official Interpreter:

    BY THE COMMISSIONER:
Q What is your name? A Noah Roberts.
Q How old are you? A About thirty-two.
Q What is your post office address? A Melette[sic], I.T.
Q Are you a citizen of the Creek Nation? A Yes, sir.
Q To what town do you belong? A Kialigee.
Q Have you a new born child for whom you have made no application? A Yes, sir.
Q What is the name of the child? A Joseph Roberts.
Q Do you know when he was born? A April 29, 1902.
Q What is the name of the mother of the child? A Hannah.
Q What was her maiden name? A Hannah Tylor[sic].
Q To what town does she belong? A Hillabee.
Q Have you another new born child? A Yes, sir.
Q What is the name of that child? A Annie.
Q When was Annie born? A April 2, 1905.
Q Are both these children living? A Yes, sir.

Applications for Enrollment of Creek Newborn
Act of 1905   Volume XIII

Q Your wife has stated to the Commissioner that Joseph Roberts was born April, 1901[sic], but refused to give testimony or execute an affidavit? A She was mistaken and probably had reference to Annie.
Q Why did you not go before the Commission and make application for the enrollment of Joseph when the Commission was receiving applications for the enrollment of newborn children at Eufaula? A Because I understood that application had been made for the child by one of my neighbors and did not think it was necessary to make another application.
Q Who attended on your wife at the birth of Joseph? A No one was present when the child was born except myself.

HANNAH ROBERTS, being duly sworn, testified as follows:

Through Alex Posey Official Interpreter:

BY THE COMMISSIONER:
Q What is your name? A Hannah Roberts.
Q How old are you? A About twenty-eight.
Q What is your post office address? A Melette[sic].
Q Are you a citizen of the Creek Nation? A Yes, sir.
Q To what town do you belong? A Hillabee.
Q Have you a child named Joseph Roberts? A Yes, sir, this is the child. (indicating a small boy)
Q When was he born? The child was born April 29, 1902.
Q When the Commission was here making inquiry about your children did you not state that Joseph was born April, 1901? A I did not given any testimony in the case and I don't remember what statement I made to you. The date I have now given is correct.
Q Have you another child named Annie? A Yes, sir.
Q When was she born? A April 2, 1905. That is the child you saw in the swing when you were inquiring about Joseph.
Q Was there a mid-wife in attendance at the birth of Joseph? A No, sir, on one was present except my husband.

I, D. C. Skaggs, on oath state that the above and foregoing is a full and true transcript of my stenographic notes as taken in said cause on said date.

D. C. Skaggs

Subscribed and sworn to before me this 16 day of Oct 1905.

Edw C Griesel
Notary Public.

Applications for Enrollment of Creek Newborn
Act of 1905   Volume XIII

BIRTH AFFIDAVIT.

DEPARTMENT OF THE INTERIOR.
COMMISSION TO THE FIVE CIVILIZED TRIBES.

IN RE APPLICATION FOR ENROLLMENT, as a citizen of the Creek Nation, of Joseph Roberts, born on the 29 day of April, 1902

Name of Father: Noah Roberts   a citizen of the   Creek   Nation.
Kialigee
Name of Mother: Hannah Roberts   a citizen of the   Creek   Nation.
Hillabee

         Postoffice   Melette[sic], I.T.

AFFIDAVIT OF MOTHER.

UNITED STATES OF AMERICA, Indian Territory, }
     Western   DISTRICT.

     I, Hanna Roberts, on oath state that I am about 28 years of age and a citizen by blood, of the Creek Nation; that I am the lawful wife of Noah Roberts, who is a citizen, by blood of the Creek Nation; that a male child was born to me on 29 day of April, 1902, that said child has been named Joseph Roberts, and was living March 4, 1905.

                               her
                      Hannah x Roberts
Witnesses To Mark: mark
  { DC Skaggs
    Alex Posey

     Subscribed and sworn to before me this 21 day of September, 1905.

                     Drennan C Skaggs
                         Notary Public.

AFFIDAVIT OF ATTENDING PHYSICIAN OR MID-WIFE.

UNITED STATES OF AMERICA, Indian Territory, }
     Western   DISTRICT.

                                   are personally acquainted with
   We, the undersigned, a——, on oath state that I we attended on Mrs. Hannah Roberts, wife of Noah Roberts on the day of , 1 ; that there was born to her on or about April 29, 1902, said date a male child; that said child was living March 4, 1905, and is said to have been named Joseph Roberts

                     John Bright
                     Lumber Bright

Applications for Enrollment of Creek Newborn
Act of 1905 Volume XIII

Witnesses To Mark:
{

Subscribed and sworn to before me this 23 day of Sept. , 1905.

Drennan C Skaggs
Notary Public.

REFER IN REPLY TO THE FOLLOWING:

Cr 2461-B

DEPARTMENT OF THE INTERIOR,
COMMISSIONER TO THE FIVE CIVILIZED TRIBES.

Muskogee, Indian Territory, July 19, 1905.

Commissioner to the Five Civilized Tribes,
Muskogee, Indian Territory.

Sir:

In the matter of the application for the enrollment of Joseph Roberts (2461-B), a minor child of Noah and Hannah Roberts, as a citizen by blood of the Creek Nation. I have the honor to report that the mother of said child states that the child was born in April, 1901, but both she and the child's father refuse to execute affidavits or to testify in the case; nor can any evidence be secured about said child from relatives and neighbors.

Respectfully,
Alex Posey
Clerk in Charge Creek Field Party.

DEPARTMENT OF THE INTERIOR,
COMMISSION TO THE FIVE CIVILIZED TRIBES.
NEAR SENORA, I. T. April 21, 1905.

In the matter of the application for the enrollment of certain new born children of "Snake" parents"

Louie Lowe, being duly sworn, testified as follows, through Official Interpreter, Alex Posey.

Applications for Enrollment of Creek Newborn
Act of 1905   Volume XIII

Examination by the Commission:
Q What is your name? A Louie Lowe.
Q What is your age? A 25.
Q What is your post office? A Henryetta.
Q Are you a citizen of the Creek Nation? A I am a member of the Okchiye Town and Fish Pond Town.

Statement: Lijah Toney, of Hickory Ground and Losanna Lowe, of Kialigee Town, have a child named <u>Foley Toney,</u> living, it is two years two months and twenty five days old. Their Post Office if Henryetta.

Peter Sloan a Seminole, and Lodie of Weogufky Town, have a child near three years old, and the youngest about a year old; the older named <u>Lillie</u> and the <u>other's name</u> is not know[sic], but it is a boy, both are living. Their post office is Henryetta.

I think Cakochee of Thlewarthle and Lucinda, of Eufaula Canadian, have a child that hasn't been filed for yet, it is about a year old, don't know it's[sic] name, it is a <u>boy</u> and living. Their Post Office is Senora but he nevers[sic] goes after his mail, it is usually returned.

Willie Harjo of Weogufky, and Sukie Harjo of Kialigee have one child, was born in either January or February of this year, and is now living. It's[sic] mother is dead, I don't know it's name but it is under the custody of Joe and Cinda Yahdihka, whose post office is Dustin.

Letka Chupco and Jenely, Leetka is of Fish Pond or Greenleaf and Jenely of Kialigee Town; they have three children, one set of <u>twins,</u> both boys nearly three years old, and the youngest child is a girl born last October, the twins are named <u>John and Johnson,</u> and I don't know the name of the little girl; all three are living, post office, Senora. I think you have now all the children in this neighborhood except those that will be born tonight;

(The above testimony was partly given by Lewis Harjo, of Senora, about 35 years of age, who was duly sworn, through Official Interpreter).

Henry G. Hains, being duly sworn, on his oath, states that the above and foregoing is a true and correct transcript of his stenographic notes as taken in said cause on said date.   Henry G. Hains

Subscribed and sworn to before me this 11th day of May, 1905.

Drennan C Skaggs
Notary Public.

Applications for Enrollment of Creek Newborn
Act of 1905   Volume XIII

Dick Marshall or Tulmarsey of Kialigee town and Eliza Marshall of Tilledega[sic], have a daughter seven or eight years old, named Emma. I do not think she has ever been enrolled. Dick Marshall or Tulmarsey is identified opposite Creek Indian Toll number 7811 as Dickey Tolomase. Eliza Marshall is identified as Eliza Tolomase opposite Creek Indian Roll number 7812.

Sam Emarthla and his wife, Letha, both of Hickory Grounds town, have a child born sometime last year. I don't know the child's name or sex.

Hillis Harjo of Alabama and his wife, Mary Harjo, of Hickory Ground, have a boy child, a year old or over--I don't know its name. They have another child--a boy, and older, but I think you got information about it last year. Hillis Harjo is identified opposite Creek Indian Roll number 7650. Mary Harjo is identified opposite Creek Indian Roll number 7651.

I, Alex Posey, being duly sworn, states[sic] that the above and foregoing is a true and correct transcript of his notes as taken in said cause on said date.

Alex Posey

Subscribed and sworn to before me this 31st day of July, 1906.

Edward Merrick
Notary Public.

N.C. 1059.

DEPARTMENT OF THE INTERIOR,
COMMISSIONER TO THE FIVE CIVILIZED TRIBES.
Senora, I. T., March 15, 1906.

In the matter of the application for the enrollment of Foley Toney as a citizen by blood of the Creek Nation.

WASHINGTON RED, being duly sworn, testified as follows:

Through Alex Posey official interpreter:

BY THE COMMISSIONER:
Q What is your name? A Washington Red.
Q How old are you? A I do not know how old I am but I remember I put up a good fight during the war--in the confederate army. I was arrested during the Snake Uprising and taken to Muskogee and the jailer looked at me and prophesied that I was about sixty-five years old.
Q Are you a citizen of the Creek Nation? A Yes, sir.
Q To what town do you belong? A Hutchechuppa.

Applications for Enrollment of Creek Newborn
Act of 1905 Volume XIII

Q Do you know Losanna Lowe, who is a member of your town? A Yes, sir, but she ought to be enrolled as Lowisa Sloan. And she does not belong to my town but to Kialigee. She May be enrolled simply as Lowisa, I am not certain.
Q Was she ever married to a man named Lijah Toney? A Yes, sir, she was once married to Rogers Toney, in stead of Lijah Toney. There is no such person as Lijah Toney that I know of.
Q To what town did he belong? A Hickory Ground.
Q Did she have a child by him named Foley? A Yes, sir.
Q What was the name of Lowisa's mother? A Wetsey.
Q To what town did she belong? A Kialigee.
Q To what town does Peter Sloan, her father, belong to? A He is a Seminole.

---oooOOOooo---

I, D. C. Skaggs, on oath state that the above and foregoing is a full and true transcript of my stenographic notes as taken in said cause on said date.

D. C. Skaggs

Subscribed and sworn to before me this 21 day of March, 1906.

Alex Posey
Notary Public.

N.C. 1059.

DEPARTMENT OF THE INTERIOR,
COMMISSIONER TO THE FIVE CIVILIZED TRIBES.
Henryetta, I. T., March 17, 1906.

In the matter of the application for the enrollment of Foley Toney as a citizen by blood of the Creek Nation.

LOUISA LOWE, being duly sworn, testified as follows:

Through Alex Posey official interpreter:

BY THE COMMISSIONER:
Q What is your name? A Louisa Lowe. I am enrolled simply as Losanna.
Q How old are you? A I was a small child during the Isparhecher War.
Q What is your post office address? A Henryetta.
Q What is the name of your father? A Peter Sloan.
Q Is he a citizen of the Creek Nation? A He is a Seminole.
Q Is he known by any other name? A No, sir.
Q Is he enrolled in the Seminole Nation under the name of Peter Sloan? A Yes, sir.
Q What is the name of your mother? A Wetsey. She belonged to Kialigee town.

Applications for Enrollment of Creek Newborn
Act of 1905   Volume XIII

Q Did you draw money at the 14 dollar payment as Losanna? A Yes, sir. When I appeared before the Commission in Muskogee I was identified on the Roll as Losanna.
Q Did your mother draw the $14.00 Payment? A Yes, sir.
Q Does your name appear with hers on the roll? A Our names appear together on the Kialigee Roll, I think with Lucy and Lydia, who were my sisters.
Q Are they living? A Lydia is dead but Lucy is living.
Q Have you a child named Foley Toney? A Yes, sir.
Q Who is the father of Foley? A Lijah or Logers or Rogers Toney. (It is difficult for the witness to pronounce "Rogers" correctly)
Q Is he living? A No, sir, he is dead.
Q To what town did he belong? A I do not know.
Q Had he made selection of land when he died? A Yes, sir, he is enrolled and had made selection of land when he died.
Q Was he your lawful husband? A Yes, sir.

---oooCOOooo---

I, D. C. Skaggs, on oath state that the above and foregoing is a full and true transcript of my stenographic notes as taken in said cause on said date.

D. C. Skaggs

Subscribed and sworn to before me this 21 day of March, 1906.

Alex Posey
Notary Public.

BIRTH AFFIDAVIT.

DEPARTMENT OF THE INTERIOR.
COMMISSION TO THE FIVE CIVILIZED TRIBES.

IN RE APPLICATION FOR ENROLLMENT, as a citizen of the Creek Nation, of Foley Toney, born on the 5 day of March, 1903

Name of Father: Lijah Toney   a citizen of the   Creek   Nation.
Hickory Ground   (formerly Toney)
Name of Mother: Losanna Lowe   a citizen of the   Creek   Nation.
Kigligee[sic] Town

Postoffice   Henrietta[sic], I.T.

Applications for Enrollment of Creek Newborn
Act of 1905   Volume XIII

AFFIDAVIT OF MOTHER.

UNITED STATES OF AMERICA, Indian Territory, }
    Western   DISTRICT.

    I, Losanna Lowe, on oath state that I am about 25 years of age and a citizen by blood, of the Creek Nation; that I ~~am~~ was formerly the lawful wife of Lijah Toney, who is a citizen, by blood of the Creek Nation; that a male child was born to me on 5 day of March, 1903, that said child has been named Foley Toney, and was living March 4, 1905.

                                                    her
                                        Losanna x Lowe
Witnesses To Mark: mark
{ DC Skaggs
{ Alex Posey

    Subscribed and sworn to before me this 16 day of June, 1905.

                                          Drennan C Skaggs
                                          Notary Public.

AFFIDAVIT OF ATTENDING PHYSICIAN OR MID-WIFE.

UNITED STATES OF AMERICA, Indian Territory, }
    Western   DISTRICT.

    I, Christie Harjo, a mid-wife, on oath state that I attended on Mrs. Losanna Lowe, the former wife of Lijah Toney on the 5 day of March, 1903; that there was born to her on said date a male child; that said child was living March 4, 1905, and is said to have been named Foley Toney

                                               her
                                        Christie x Harjo
Witnesses To Mark: mark
{ DC Skaggs
{ Alex Posey

    Subscribed and sworn to before me 22 day of June, 1905.

                                          Drennan C Skaggs
                                          Notary Public.

Applications for Enrollment of Creek Newborn
Act of 1905   Volume XIII

NC. 1059

Muskogee, Indian Territory, October 24, 1905.

Losanna Lowe,
    Henryetta, Indian Territory.

Dear Madam:

    In the matter of the application for the enrollment of your minor child, Foley Toney, born January 27[sic], 1903, as a citizen by blood of the Creek Nation, this office is unable to identify you or Lijah Lowe, the father of said child, on its roll of citizens by blood of the Creek Nation; you are requested to state if your husband was ever known by the name of Rogers Toney, also state your maiden name, the names of your parents, the Creek Indian town to which you belong, and your roll number as the same appears on your deeds and allotment certificates.

                            Respectfully,

                                          Commissioner.

BIRTH AFFIDAVIT.

DEPARTMENT OF THE INTERIOR.
COMMISSION TO THE FIVE CIVILIZED TRIBES.

    IN RE APPLICATION FOR ENROLLMENT, as a citizen of the Creek Nation, of Ima Ware, born on the 9th day of August, 1904

Name of Father: Henderson Ware   a citizen of the United States Nation.
Name of Mother: Lula Ware   a citizen of the   Creek   Nation.

                            Postoffice   Wagoner, Indian Territory.

AFFIDAVIT OF MOTHER.

UNITED STATES OF AMERICA, Indian Territory,
Western Judicial District   **DISTRICT.**

    I, Lula Ware, on oath state that I am 26 years of age and a citizen by blood, of the Creek Nation; that I am the lawful wife of Henderson Ware, who is a citizen,

Applications for Enrollment of Creek Newborn
Act of 1905   Volume XIII

~~by~~ *(blank)* of the United States ~~Nation~~; that a female child was born to me on ninth day of August , 1904 , that said child has been named Ima Ware , and was living March 4, 1905.

Lula Ware

Witnesses To Mark:
{

Subscribed and sworn to before me this 8th day of April , 1905.

Ross M. Simpson

Commission expires March 15th, 1908   Notary Public.

AFFIDAVIT OF ATTENDING PHYSICIAN OR MID-WIFE.

UNITED STATES OF AMERICA, Indian Territory, }
Western Judicial District   DISTRICT.

I, S. D. Lyles , a Physician , on oath state that I attended on Mrs. Lula Ware , wife of Henderson Ware on the ninth day of August , 1904 ; that there was born to her on said date a female child; that said child was living March 4, 1905, and is said to have been named Ima Ware

S. D. Lyles M.D.

Witnesses To Mark:
{

Subscribed and sworn to before me tenth day of April , 1905.

Ross M. Simpson
Notary Public.

Applications for Enrollment of Creek Newborn
Act of 1905   Volume XIII

DEPARTMENT OF THE INTERIOR,
COMMISSION TO THE FIVE CIVILIZED TRIBES.
Sonora, I. T., June 16, 1905.

In the matter of the application for the enrollment of Lillie and Loney Sloan as citizens by blood of the Creek Nation.

LODIE SLOAN, being duly sworn, testified as follows:

Through Alex Posey Official Interpreter:

BY COMMISSION:
Q What is your name? A Lodie Sloan.
Q How old are you? A I do not know.

Witness appears to be about twenty-eight years of age.

Q What is your post office address? A Henrietta[sic].
Q Are you a citizen of the Creek Nation? A Yes, sir.
Q To what town do you belong? A Weogufke.
Q Do you make application for the enrollment of your two, children, Lillie and Loney Sloan as citizens by blood of the Creek Nation? A Yes, sir.
Q If it should be found that these two children are entitled to rights in both the Creek and Seminole Nations in which nation do you elect to have them enrolled? A In the Creek Nation.

---oooOOOooo---

I, D. C. Skaggs, on oath state that the above and foregoing is a full and true transcript of my stenographic notes as taken in said cause on said date.

Subscribed and sworn to before me this____day of_____1905.

Notary Public.

N.C. 1061.

DEPARTMENT OF THE INTERIOR,
COMMISSIONER TO THE FIVE CIVILIZED TRIBES.
Senora, I. T., March 20, 1906.

In the matter of the application for the enrollment of Lillie and Loney Sloan as citizens by blood of the Creek Nation.

PETER SLOAN, being duly sworn, testified as follows:

Through Alex Posey Official Interpreter:

Applications for Enrollment of Creek Newborn
Act of 1905 Volume XIII

BY THE COMMISSIONER:
Q What is your name? A Peter Sloan.
Q How old are you? A I was a small boy before the Civil War.
Q What is your post office address? A Senora.
Q Are you a citizen of the Seminole Nation? A Yes, sir. I am enrolled there.
Q Have you two children named Lillie and Loney? A Yes, sir.
Q What is the name of the mother of these children? A Lody (or Rhoda) Sloan.
Q What was her maiden name? A Lody (or Rhoda) Martin.
Q Is she a citizen of the Creek Nation? A I suppose she is a citizen of both the Creek and Seminole Nations. She belongs to Weogufke Town and was carried on the roll of that town by Jim Byrd, when he was Town King.
Q Who were your wife's parents? A They died many years ago and I do not know what their names were, but I know that her father was a Seminole and her mother a Creek. her mother moved from the Creek Nation to the Seminole Nation and my wife was born there. It May be that she is enrolled as a Seminole under the name of Lody (or Rhoda) Martin.
Q Has she any brothers or sisters living? A She had a brother named Nathan Martin, who is dead and who was enrolled as a citizen of the Seminole Nation.
Q Do you know whether or not your wife is enrolled in the Seminole Nation? A She is enrolled and allotted Land in the Seminole Nation though she requested the Commission, through Toney Proctor, Town King, to allot her in the Creek Nation.
Q Do you know under what name she appears on the Weogufke Town Roll? A As Maria Harjo. She was known in Weogufke Town as Maria Harjo and in the Seminole Nation as Lody (or Rhoda) Martin.
Q Do you know whether or not she was enrolled and allotted land in the Creek Nation, under the name of Maria Harjo? A I have never been able to learn and have never investigated the matter.
Q Has your wife received the deeds to her allotment in the Seminole Nation? A She has received the certificate to her allotment but not the deeds.
Q have you that certificate now? A Yes, sir.

Witness presents "Certificate of Homestead Designation", No. 2129, issued to Lott Marty, December 7, 1904, Roll No. 130.

Q Did you wife draw money when the $14.00 Payment was made? A Yes, sir, money was drawn for her by Jim Byrd and sent to her by him while she was living in the Seminole Nation, and she participated in other payments made in the Creek Nation.
Q Was money drawn for her by the town officers of Weogufke Town when the $29.00 Payment was made? A Yes, sir.
Q Under the name of Maria Harjo? A Yes, sir.
Q You[sic] wife's name on the certificate which you present here is given as Lott Marty, is that her correct name? A (Witness examines certificate and consults his wife) This certificate was issued to her child, Lott. My wife says she has lost the certificate issued to herself. Lott is a boy about ten years old. That is a child by her first husband named Sama or Sam Charte.
Q Is your wife's brother, Nathan Martin, also enrolled as a member of Weogufke Town? A Yes, sir.

Applications for Enrollment of Creek Newborn
Act of 1905   Volume XIII

Q Under what name? A As Daniel Harjo.

---oooOOOooo---

    I, D. C. Skaggs, on oath state that the above and foregoing is a full and true transcript of my stenographic notes as taken in said cause on said date.

                               D. C. Skaggs

    Subscribed and sworn to before me this 21 day of March, 1906.

                               Alex Posey
                               Notary Public.

N.C. 1061.

                    DEPARTMENT OF THE INTERIOR,
            COMMISSIONER TO THE FIVE CIVILIZED TRIBES.
            Henryetta, Indian Territory, September 15, 1906.

    In the matter of the application for the enrollment of Lillie and Loney Sloan as citizens by blood of the Creek Nation.
                    PETER SLOAN, being duly sworn, testified as follows: (through Jesse McDermott official interpreter)

BY COMMISSIONER:

Q What is your name? A Peter Sloan.
Q What is your age? A About fifty.
Q What is your postoffice address? A Henryetta.
Q Are you a Creek citizen? A No, I am a Seminole.
Q Are you enrolled in the Seminole Nation? A Yes.
Q Is Rhoda, your wife, enrolled in the Creek Nation? A No, I am almost positive that she enrolled in the Seminole Nation.
Q If she is, under what would she likely to be enrolled? A Rhoda Marty. She would be found on the roll with Nathan Marty.
Q What relation is Nation to her? A Her brother.
Q You made application for the enrollment of your children in the Creek Nation, have you not? A Yes, I did that for the reason that the mother formerly belonged in the Weogufkey[sic] Town. Jim Byrd, the town king, told me she was on the 1895 Pay Roll in that town and I thought that my children would be entitled to enrollment in the Creek Nation as well as the Seminole.

                   STATEMENT BY THE WITNESS.

    I requested the Commissioner through Alex Posey to examine the approved roll of the Creek Nation and advise me whether or not the names Maria Harjo and Daniel

Applications for Enrollment of Creek Newborn
Act of 1905   Volume XIII

Harjo appear thereon. I am under the impression that my wife Rhoda and Nathan Marty were enrolled and arbitrary allotted land under the former names, as I understand that a lot of Creeks are so enrolled and allotted from the mere fact that their names appear on the old pay rolls.

I, Jesse McDermott, on oath state that the above and foregoing is a full and true transcript of my notes as taken in said cause on said date.

Jesse McDermott

Subscribed and sworn to before me this 14th day of November, 1906.

J H Swafford
Notary Public.

My Com Exp 2/26/1910

Copy

BIRTH AFFIDAVIT.

DEPARTMENT OF THE INTERIOR,
COMMISSION TO THE FIVE CIVILIZED TRIBES.

In Re Application for Enrollment, as a citizen of the Creek Nation, of Loney Sloan , born on the 29 day of July, 1904

Name of Father: Peter Sloan   a citizen of the Seminole Nation.
Name of Mother: Lodie Sloan   a citizen of the   Creek   Nation.

Post-office   Henryetta I.T.

AFFIDAVIT OF MOTHER.

(Witness appears to be 28 years of age.)

UNITED STATES OF AMERICA,
   INDIAN TERRITORY,
   Western   District.

I, Lodie Sloan , on oath state that I am   *(blank)* years of age and a citizen by blood , of the Creek Nation; that I am the lawful wife of Peter Sloan , who is a citizen, by blood of the Seminole Nation; that a male child was born to me on 29" day of July , 1904 , that said child has been named Loney Sloan , and ~~is now~~ was living. March 4, 1905   ~~her~~
Lodie x Sloan

WITNESSES TO MARK:

Applications for Enrollment of Creek Newborn
Act of 1905 Volume XIII

Subscribed and sworn to before me this 16 day of June, 1905.

Drennan C Skaggs
NOTARY PUBLIC.

AFFIDAVIT OF ATTENDING PHYSICIAN OR MID-WIFE.

UNITED STATES OF AMERICA, }
INDIAN TERRITORY,
Western District.

I, Losanna Lowe, a midwife, on oath state that I attended on Mrs. Lodie Sloan, wife of Peter Sloan on or about the 29" day of July, 1904; that there was born to her on said date a male child; that said child is now was living March 4, 1905 and is said to have been named Loney Sloan

                        her
                Losanna x Lowe
WITNESSES TO MARK: mark
{ DC Skaggs
{ Alex Posey

Subscribed and sworn to before me this 19 day of June, 1905.

Drennan C Skaggs
NOTARY PUBLIC.

                  Copy
BIRTH AFFIDAVIT.
DEPARTMENT OF THE INTERIOR,
COMMISSION TO THE FIVE CIVILIZED TRIBES.

In Re Application for Enrollment, as a citizen of the Creek Nation, of Lillie Sloan, born on the 6" day of September, 1903

Name of Father: Peter Sloan	a citizen of the Seminole Nation.
Name of Mother: Lodie " Weogufkey	a citizen of the Creek Nation.

                Post-office   Henryetta I.T.

Applications for Enrollment of Creek Newborn
Act of 1905   Volume XIII

AFFIDAVIT OF MOTHER.

UNITED STATES OF AMERICA,
   INDIAN TERRITORY,
   Western   District.

(Witness appears to be at 28 years of age.

I, Lodie Sloan , on oath state that I am   *(blank)*   years of age and a citizen by blood , of the Creek Nation; that I am the lawful wife of Peter Sloan , who is a citizen, by blood of the Seminole Nation; that a male child was born to me on 6 day of September , 1903 , that said child has been named Lillie Sloan , and ~~is now~~ was living. March 4, 1905 that Lydia Martin the midwife in attendance on me at the birth of Lillie is now dead

                                    Lodie Sloan

WITNESSES TO MARK:

{ Subscribed and sworn to before me this 16" day of   June , 1905.

                                  Drennan C Skaggs
                                       NOTARY PUBLIC.

AFFIDAVIT OF ATTENDING PHYSICIAN OR MID-WIFE.

UNITED STATES OF AMERICA,
   INDIAN TERRITORY,
   Western   District.

                                              my wife

I, Peter Sloan , a *(blank)* , on oath state that I attended on ~~Mrs.~~ Lodie Sloan , ~~wife of~~ *(blank)* on the 6 day of September , 1903 ; that there was born to her on said date a male child; that said child ~~is now~~ was living March 4, 1905 and is said to have been named Lillie Sloan   his
                                  Peter x Sloan
WITNESSES TO MARK: mark
{ DC Skaggs
  Alex Posey

Subscribed and sworn to before me this 19" day of   June , 1905.

                                  Drennan C Skaggs
                                       NOTARY PUBLIC.

Applications for Enrollment of Creek Newborn
Act of 1905   Volume XIII

BIRTH AFFIDAVIT.

DEPARTMENT OF THE INTERIOR.
COMMISSION TO THE FIVE CIVILIZED TRIBES.

IN RE APPLICATION FOR ENROLLMENT, as a citizen of the Creek Nation, of Lillie Sloan, born on the 6 day of Sept, 1903

Name of Father: Peter Sloan   a citizen of the Seminole Nation.
Name of Mother: Lody Sloan   a citizen of the Creek Nation.

Postoffice   Senora, I.T.

AFFIDAVIT OF ATTENDING PHYSICIAN OR MID-WIFE.

UNITED STATES OF AMERICA,
    Indian Territory,
Western   DISTRICT.

are personally acquainted with We, the undersigned , a——, on oath state that ~~I~~ we ~~attended on~~ Mrs. Lody Sloan, wife of Peter Sloan ~~on the   day of   , 1~~ ; that there was born to her on or about Sept 6, 1902 ~~said date~~ a male child; that said child ~~is now~~ was living March 4, 1905, and is said to have been named Lillie Sloan

                                   his
                          Lewis x Harjo
Witnesses To Mark: mark
   { DC Skaggs
   { Alex Posey   Annie Ryal

Subscribed and sworn to before me 10" day of   october   , 1905.

                          Drennan C Skaggs
                          Notary Public.

AFFIDAVIT OF MOTHER.

UNITED STATES OF AMERICA, Indian Territory,
    Western   DISTRICT.

I, Washington Riley , on oath state that I am 66 years of age and a citizen by blood , of the Creek Nation; that I ~~am the lawful wife of~~ know Rhoda Salone[sic] , who is a citizen, by blood of the Creek Nation; that a male child was born to me on 6th day of September , 1902 , that said child has been named Lilly Salone , and is now living.   his

                          Washington x Riley
                               mark

Applications for Enrollment of Creek Newborn
Act of 1905   Volume XIII

Witnesses To Mark:
{ Charley W. Powell
{ J L Gary

Subscribed and sworn to before me this 10th day of January , 1907.

J L Gary
Notary Public.

AFFIDAVIT OF ATTENDING PHYSICIAN OR MID-WIFE.

UNITED STATES OF AMERICA, Indian Territory, }
  Western   DISTRICT.

know
I, Sarah Riley , an acquaintance , on oath state that I ~~attended on~~ Mrs. Rhoda Salone , wife of Peter Salone on the 6th day of September , 1902 ; that there was born to her on said date a male child; that said child is now living and is said to have been named Lilly Salone
                                                                her
                                             ~~Washington~~ Sarah x Riley
Witnesses To Mark: mark
  { Charley W. Powell
  { J L Gary

Subscribed and sworn to before me this 10th day of January , 1907.

J L Gary
Notary Public.

NC 1061

Muskogee, Indian Territory, October 24, 1905.

Lodie Sloan,
    Care Peter Sloan,
        Henryetta, Indian Territory.

Dear Madam:

In the matter of the application for the enrollment of your minor children, Lillie Sloan, born September 6, 1903[sic], and Loney Sloan, born July 29, 1904, as citizens by blood of the Creek Nation, this office is unable to identify you on its roll of citizens by blood of the Creek Nation; you are requested to state your maiden name, the names of your parents, the Creek Indian town to which you belong and your roll number as the same appears on your deeds and allotment certificate.

Applications for Enrollment of Creek Newborn
Act of 1905   Volume XIII

Respectfully,
Commissioner.

Nc. 1061.

Muskogee, Indian Territory, January 14, 1907.

Peter Sloan,
Henryetta, Indian Territory.

Dear Sir:

In the matter of the application for the enrollment of your minor children, Lillie and Loney Sloan, as citizens of the Creek or Seminole Nation, you are advised that this office cannot identify you on its final rolls of citizens of the Seminole Nation and you are requested to furnish information as to any other name by which you may be known, the Seminole band to which you belong and, if possible, the roll numbers which appear on your certificates to land in the Seminole Nation.

Respectfully,
Commissioner.

(COPY)

En. 1061

Muskogee, Indian Territory, January 14, 1907.

Peter Sloan,
Henryetta, Indian Territory.

Dear Sir :--

In the matter of the application for the enrollment of your minor children, Lillie and Loney Sloan, as citizens of the Creek or Seminole Nation, you are advised that this office can not identify you on its final rolls of citizens of the Seminole Nation and you are requested to furnish information as to any other name by which you may be known, the Seminole band to which you belong, and if possible, the roll numbers which appear on your certificates to land in the Seminole Nation.

Respectfully,
(Signed) Tams Bixby,
Commissioner.

I appear on Seminole Roll oppiset[sic] No. 1830 by name of Peter   I hold certificate for the following land NW 1/4 of NW 1/4 of Sec 10 & Lot 5 Sec (9) & W 1/2 of SE 1/4 of Sec (2) T & N R 5 E   Containing 120 07 cres[sic]   please advise me at Henrietta[sic] I T   What disposition has ben[sic] made of these filings.
(Signed) Peter

Applications for Enrollment of Creek Newborn
Act of 1905   Volume XIII

AP

REFER IN REPLY TO THE FOLLOWING:

Sem. NB-165

DEPARTMENT OF THE INTERIOR,
COMMISSIONER TO THE FIVE CIVILIZED TRIBES.

Muskogee, Indian Territory, March 6, 1907.

Chief Clerk,
    Creek Enrollment Division:

Dear Sir:-

You are hereby advised that the Commissioner to the Five Civilized Tribes on February 20, 1907, rendered his decision, dismissing the application for the enrollment of Lena Salone as a citizen of the Seminole Nation.

                      Respectfully,
                      Tams Bixby   Commissioner.

Peter Sloan Henryetta I.T. Should be written to asking for identification as a Seminole-- He says he is a Seminole and enrolled but I cant[sic] find him by name Peter Sloan. He is enrolled under a different name. These children should be enrolled as Seminoles.
                      1/11/07   E.M.

W.F.

REFER IN REPLY TO THE FOLLOWING:

NC-1063.

DEPARTMENT OF THE INTERIOR,
COMMISSIONER TO THE FIVE CIVILIZED TRIBES.

Muskogee, Indian Territory, August 5, 1905.

Clerk in Charge Creek Field Party,
    Creek Enrollment Division.

Dear Sir:

In reply to your verbal inquiry of this date as to whether or not an application was ever made to the Commission to the Five Civilized Tribes for the enrollment of Edward

Applications for Enrollment of Creek Newborn
Act of 1905 Volume XIII

S. Brown, born October 5, 1902, child of Stanton Brown, a citizen of the Seminole Nation, and Julia Brown, a citizen of the Creek Nation, as a citizen of the Seminole Nation, you are advised that it does not appear from an examination of the records of this office that any application was ever made for the enrollment of Edward S. Brown as a citizen of the Seminole Nation.

Respectfully,

Tams Bixby
Commissioner.

NC 1063

Muskogee, Indian Territory, November 13, 1906

Chief Clerk,
    Seminole Enrollment Division,
        General Office.

Dear Sir:

    You are hereby advised that Edward S. Brown, born October 5, 1903 to Stanton Brown, an alleged citizen of the Seminole Nation and Julia Brown a citizen by blood of the Creek Nation, is contained in schedule of minor citizens by blood of the Creek Nation, approved by the Secretary of the Interior, September 27, 1905, opposite Roll number 687.

Respectfully,

Commissioner.

BIRTH AFFIDAVIT.

DEPARTMENT OF THE INTERIOR.
COMMISSION TO THE FIVE CIVILIZED TRIBES.

IN RE APPLICATION FOR ENROLLMENT, as a citizen of the Creek Nation, of Edward S. Brown, born on the 5th day of October, 1902

Name of Father: Stanton Brown	a citizen of the Seminole Nation.
Name of Mother: Julia Brown	a citizen of the Creek Nation.

Postoffice   Holdenville, I. T.

Applications for Enrollment of Creek Newborn
Act of 1905   Volume XIII

AFFIDAVIT OF MOTHER.

UNITED STATES OF AMERICA, Indian Territory, }
    Western   DISTRICT.

I, Julia Brown, on oath state that I am 32 years of age and a citizen by birth, of the Creek Nation; that I am the lawful wife of Stanton Brown, who is a citizen, by birth of the Seminole Nation; that a male child was born to me on 5th day of October, 1902, that said child has been named Edward S. Brown, and was living March 4, 1905.

                                          Julia Brown

Witnesses To Mark:
{

    Subscribed and sworn to before me this 25 day of March, 1905.

My commission   V.W. Snider
expires Aug 17th 1908   Notary Public.

AFFIDAVIT OF ATTENDING PHYSICIAN OR MID-WIFE.

UNITED STATES OF AMERICA, Indian Territory, }
    Western   DISTRICT.

I, Lizzie Halsey, a midwife, on oath state that I attended on Mrs. Julia Brown, wife of Stanton Brown on the 5th day of October, 1902; that there was born to her on said date a male child; that said child was living March 4, 1905, and is said to have been named Edward S. Brown

                                        Lizzie Halsey

Witnesses To Mark:
{

    Subscribed and sworn to before me this 25th day of March, 1905.

My commission   V.W. Snider
expires Aug 17th 1908   Notary Public.

Applications for Enrollment of Creek Newborn
Act of 1905   Volume XIII

NC 1083
DEPARTMENT OF THE INTERIOR,
COMMISSIONER TO THE FIVE CIVILIZED TRIBES.
Eufaula, I. T., September 12, 1905.

In the matter of the application for the enrollment of certain new born children as citizens of the Creek Nation.

WICEY ASBURY, being duly sworn, testified as follows:

Through Alex Posey Official Interpreter Posey:

BY THE COMMISSIONER:
Q What is your name? A Wicey Asbury.
Q How old are you? A About thirty.
Q What is your post office address? A Eufaula.
Q Are you a citizen of the Creek Nation? A Yes, sir.
Q To what town do you belong? A Tulladega.
Q Do you know Neda Pologee? A Yes, sir. Her correct name is Lydia Pologee.
Q Is she sometimes known as Lydia Bear? A Yes, sir.
Q To what town does she belong? A Okfuske Canadian.
Q Has she any children? A Yes, sir.
Q How many? A She has three living and one dead.
Q What is he name of the oldest living child? A Cristie Charte, her father was Loney Charte.
Q How old is she? A I think she is about eight years old.
Q Is Loney Charte living or dead? A He is dead.
Q What is the name of the next oldest child? A Its name is Rhoda. I do not know who her father is.
Q How old is Rhoda? A I think she is about four years old. She may be five.
Q What is the name of the next child? A I do not know.
Q Do you know who is the father of it? A Thomas Bear.
Q How old is that child? A About three years old.
Q What is the name of the child that is dead? A I don't know.
Q When did it die? A The child died shortly after the father died and he has been dead about two eyars.
Q How old was the child at the time of its death? A About a year old.

JIMSY ASBURY, being duly sworn, testified as follows:

Through Alex Posey Official Interpreter:

BY THE COMMISSIONER:
Q What is your name? A Jimsy Asbury.
Q How old are you? A I do not know my age, but white people guess my age at about forth-eight.
Q What is your post office address? A Eufaula.

Applications for Enrollment of Creek Newborn
Act of 1905   Volume XIII

Q Are you a citizen of the Creek Nation? A Yes, sir.
Q To what town do you belong? A Tuskegee.
Q Do you know Lydia Pologee or Bear? A Yes, sir.
Q Has she any children? A Yes, sir.
q How many? A She has three. Three girls.
q Do you know the name of her oldest child? A I do not know the names of her children.
q How old is the oldest child? A I think she is at least ten years old.
Q Do you know whether or not land has been selected for her? A I do not know. If she was allotted she was arbitrarilly[sic] filed by the Commission. All of her people were arbitrarilly[sic] filed.
Q What is the name of her father? A Loney Charte.
Q To what town did he belong? A I think he belonged to Eufaula Canadian Town, but I am not positive. Bill McCombs would know because he raised him as an orphan.
Q How old is the next oldest child? A She is between four and five years old.
Q Who is that child's father? A The father is unknown, but it is generally supposed that Ben Kiddo, who is also known as Ben Corser, is the father. He belongs to Cussehta Town.
Q How old is the youngest child? A About three years old.
Q Who is the father of that child? A Thomas Bear.
Q To what town does Thomas Bear belong? A Okfuske Canadian.

---oooOOOooo---

I, D. C. Skaggs, on oath state that the above and foregoing is a full and true transcript of my stenographic notes as taken in said cause on said date.

D. C. Skaggs

Subscribed and sworn to before me this 16 day of October 1905.

Edw C Griesel
Notary Public.

N. C. 1064.

Department of the Interior,
Commissioner to the Five Civilized Tribes.
Eufaula, I. T., August 17, 1906.

In the matter of the application for the enrollment of Rhoda Cato and Lena Bear, as citizens by blood of the Creek Nation.

LYDIA BEAR, being duly sworn testified as follows:

Through Alex Posey, Official Interpreter.

Applications for Enrollment of Creek Newborn
Act of 1905 Volume XIII

BY THE COMMISSIONER:

Q What is your name? A Lydia Bear.
Q How old are you? A About 25.
Q What is your postoffice address? A Eufaula.
Q Are you a citizen of the Creek Nation? A Yes sir.
Q To what Creek town do you belong? A Okfuske Canadian.
Q What was your maiden name? A Lydia Poloke. I am enrolled as Lydia ~~Susie~~ Poloke.
Q Have you a child named Lena Bear? A Yes.
Q When was the child born? A On or about October 15, 1901.
Q Is the child living? A Yes, sir, living.
Q Who is the father of Lena? A Thomas Bear.
Q Is he living? A No sir, he is dead.
Q When did he die? A He died just before Christmas, over two years ago. he will have been dead three years next Christmas.
Q Was he a citizen of the Creek Nation? A Yes sir.
Q To what Creek town did he belong? A Okfuske Canadian.
Q Did he have any other name than Thomas Bear? Was h[sic] A Yes, sir, he was sometimes known as Cussamecha. That was his Indian name, and the name by which he was known until he joined the church. After he became a church member he was named Thomas Bear.
Q Do you know under what name he was enrolled? A I do not.
Q Had he received his allotment of land at the time he died? A Yes, I understood that he was allotted on the land covered by his improvements.
Q Where does that land lie? A I think the land adjoins the allotment selection of Eddie Ross a Creek freedman, and is not far from Eufaula.
Q In what direction? A West. I am not sure this is true, it is what I have heard, he belonged to the Snake Faction and he may have been arbitrarily allotted land by the Commission.
Q Do you know who his parents were? A I do not know who his parents were but he was a brother of Taylor Bear.
Q Where does Taylor Bear live? A Between here and Mellette.
Q Was Thomas Bear your lawful husband? A Yes sir, we were married by Johnson Phillips, a Indian minister of the Gospel, and I have hi our marriage license at home.
Q Who attended on you at the birth of this child? A My mother, Susie Poloke.

Witness is advised that this office requires either the original or certified copy of her marriage license.

Q Have yyou[sic] another child named Rhoda Cato? A Yes sir.
Q When was Rhoda born? A December 31, 1898.
Q Who was her father? A Ben Cato.
Q Is he living? A No sir.
Q When did he die? A He has been dead a number of years; I do not remember the date of his death.
Q Was he a citizen of the Creek Nation? A Yes sir.
Q To what Creek town does he belong? A Cussehta.

Applications for Enrollment of Creek Newborn
Act of 1905   Volume XIII

Q Was Ben Cato your lawful husband? A No sir, but we lived together about two years.
Q Is Rhoda Cato living? A Yes sir.
Q Who attended on you at the birth of Rhoda? A My mother, Susie Poloke.
Q Why is it that you have not made application for the enrollment of this child before now? A I know that the child was entitled to rights, and I wanted her enrolled but my father being a strong Snake sympathizer advised me against making application for the child's enrollment.

James B. Myers, being first duly sworn, states, that as stenographer to the Commissioner to the Five Civilized Tribes, he recorded the testimony in the foregoing proceedings, and that the above is a true, and correct transcript of his stenographic notes thereof.

James B Myers

Subscribed and sworn to before me, this 20 day of August, 1906.

Alex Posey
Notary   Public.

JEM

N. C._____

Department of the Interior,
Commissioner to the Five Civilized Tribes.
Eufaula, I. T., August 18, 1906.

In the matter of the application for the enrollment of Sallie Hill, as a citizen by blood of the Creek Nation.

LYDIA BEAR, being duly sworn testified as follows:

Through Alex Posey, Official Interpreter.
BY THE COMMISSIONER:

Q What is your name? A Lydia Bear.
Q How old are you? A About 25.
Q What is your postoffice address? A Eufaula.
Q Are you a citizen of the Creek Nation? A Yes sir.
Q To what Creek town do you belong? A Okfuske Canadian.
Q Do you know a child named Sallie Hill? A Yes sir.
Q What relation is the child to you? A She is the child of my dead sister, Melindy Hill.
Q Who was the father of the child? A Joh Hill.
Q To what Creek town does he belong? A Okchiye.
Q Is John Hill know by any other name? A The Indians sometimes call him John Tecoxie, and he may be enrolled as John Cox or Coxie.

Applications for Enrollment of Creek Newborn
Act of 1905 Volume XIII

Q Who were his parents? A His mother's name is Soma, his father is known simply as Coxie.
Q Was he lawfully married to you sister Melindy? A They were married by Peter Thlocco, a Creek minister, but had no license from the court.
Q Was Melindy Hill your full sister? A Yes sir, same mother and same father.
Q Who are your parents? A Susie and Tom Poloke, both of Okfuske Canadian town.
Q Do you know under what name Melindy is enrolled? A She was probably enrolled by the Commission as Melindy Poloke. Our proper family name is Deere, but we are all enrolled under the name of Poloke.
Q When did Melindy die? A June 19, 1903.
Q When was Sallie Hill born? A November 17, 1901. She will be five years old the 27th of next November.
Q Who attended on her mother at the birth of this child? A Susie Poloke.
Q Did Melindy have any other child besides Sallie? A She had one other child that died when very small, and before the child was named.
Q Of how many members does your family consist? A Tom and Susie Poloke, myself, Melindy and Israel; Israel is enrolled as Esal.
Q Is Sallie Hill living at this time? A Yes sir.
Q Is John Hill, the father of this child, living? A Yes sir, he has married again and is living somewhere near Hanna.
Q Who has the custody of this child? a My mother has raised the child and now has custody. ~~Her~~ The father never contributed to its support and has never visited the child. He deserted the child on the very day that its mother was burried[sic].

- - - - - - - - - - -

James B. Myers, being first duly sworn, states, that as stenographer to the Commissioner to the Five Civilized Tribes, he recorded the testimony in the foregoing proceedings, and that the above is a true, and correct transcript of his stenographic notes thereof.

James B Myers

Subscribed and sworn to before me this, the 20 day of August, 1906.

Alex Posey
Notary Public.

Applications for Enrollment of Creek Newborn
Act of 1905   Volume XIII

N.C. 1064.   F.H.W.
DEPARTMENT OF THE INTERIOR,
COMMISSIONER TO THE FIVE CIVILIZED TRIBES.

In the matter of the application for the enrollment of Rhoda Cato as a citizen by blood of the Creek Nation.

DECISION.

The record in this case shows that on September 12, 1905, Wicey and Jimsy Asbury, Creek citizens by blood, appeared before a Creek enrollment field party, at Eufaula, Indian Territory, and testified "in the matter of the application for the enrollment of certain new-born children as citizens of the Creek Nation" in which reference is made to Rhoda Cato. The said testimony is herein considered an original application of the said Rhoda Cato in order that the rights of the applicant be protected. A supplemental affidavit filed August 16, 1906, is attached to and made a part of the record herein. Further proceedings were had August 17, 1906. A copy of the transcript of testimony taken in the matter of the application for the enrollment of Sallie Hill as a citizen by blood of the Creek Nation is attached to and made part of the record in this case.

The evidence in this case shows that the said Rhoda Cato is the child of Ben Cato, deceased, and Lydia Bear. The said Ben Cato, deceased, is identified on a partial schedule of citizens by blood of the Creek Nation, approved by the Secretary of the Interior March 28, 1903[sic], opposite roll No. 9280. The said Lydia Bear is identified as Lady Charity on a partial schedule of citizens by blood of the Creek Nation, opposite roll No. 6758, approved by the Secretary of the Interior March 28, 1902.

It further appears in evidence that said Rhoda Cato was born December 31, 1898 and was still living March 4, 1906.

Although the application herein was not made within the time designated by the Secretary of the Interior under the authority in him vested by the provisions of the Act of Congress approved March 3, 1901 (31 Stats., 1010), jurisdiction to consider the same under the Act of June 30, 1902, was given to this office and the Department by the provisions of Section 1 of the Act of Congress approved April 26, 1906 (34 Stats., 137).

It is, therefore, ordered and adjudged that the said Rhoda Cato is entitled to be enrolled as a citizen by blood of the Creek Nation, under the provisions of the Act of Congress approved June 30, 1902 (32 Stats., 500), and the application for her enrollment as such is accordingly granted.

                                                        Tams Bixby   COMMISSIONER.
Muskogee, Indian Territory,
    JAN 18 1907

Applications for Enrollment of Creek Newborn
Act of 1905   Volume XIII

N.C. 1064
BIRTH AFFIDAVIT.

DEPARTMENT OF THE INTERIOR,
COMMISSIONER TO THE FIVE CIVILIZED TRIBES.

ENROLLMENT OF MINORS.   ACT OF CONGRESS, APPROVED APRIL 26, 1906.

IN RE APPLICATION FOR ENROLLMENT, as a citizen of the Creek Nation, of Rhoda Cato, born on the 31 day of December, 1898

Name of Father: Ben Cato deceased, C.F. 4045   a citizen of the   Creek   Nation.
3613
Name of Mother: Lydia Bear (nee Poloke) C.F.   a citizen of the   Creek   Nation.

Tribal enrollment of father   Cussehta   Tribal enrollment of mother   Ofuske Canadian

Postoffice   Eufaula, Indian Territory

AFFIDAVIT OF MOTHER.

UNITED STATES OF AMERICA, Indian Territory,
Western   District.

I, Lydia Bear (nee Poloke), on oath state that I am about 25 years of age and a citizen by blood, of the Creek Nation; that I am not the lawful wife of Ben Cato, who ~~is~~ was a citizen, by blood of the Creek Nation; that a female child was born to me on 31 day of December, 1898, that said child has been named Rhoda Cato, and was living March 4, 1906.

                          her
             Lydia x Bear
WITNESSES TO MARK: mark
{ Alex Posey
  Dan Polk

Subscribed and sworn to before me this 16 day of August, 1906.

                        Alex Posey
                              Notary Public.

AFFIDAVIT OF ATTENDING PHYSICIAN OR MID-WIFE.

UNITED STATES OF AMERICA, Indian Territory,
Western   District.

I, Susie Poloke, a midwife, on oath state that I attended on Lydia Bear not the lawful, wife of Ben Cato on the 31 day of December, 1898; that there was born to

Applications for Enrollment of Creek Newborn
Act of 1905   Volume XIII

her on said date a   female   child; that said child was living March 4, 1906, and is said to have been named Rhoda Cato
her
Susie x Poloke
mark

WITNESSES TO MARK:
{ Alex Posey
{ Dan Polk

Subscribed and sworn to before me this 16   day of   August , 1906.

Alex Posey
Notary Public.

DEPARTMENT OF THE INTERIOR,
COMMISSION TO THE FIVE CIVILIZED TRIBES.
NEAR SENORA, I.T. April 20, 1905.

In the matter of the application for the enrollment of certain new born children of "Snake[sic] parents:

Jim Starr, being duly sworn, testified as follows testified as follows: Through Official Interpreter, Alex Posey:

Examination by the Commission:
Q What is your name? A Jim Starr.
Q What is your age? [sic] About 42.
Q What is your post office address? A Senora.
Q Are you a citizen of the Creek Nation? A I am a member of Arbeka Tulledega, I am a member of the House of Kings of Tulledega Town.

Statement: Ahny Tiger of Hickory Ground and George Tiger, of Wewoka, I think, they have a child about a year old and living. It was born just after last Christmas, it is a girl named not known-

Henry G. Hains, being duly sworn, on his oath, states that the above and foregoing is a true and correct transcript of his stenographic notes as taken in said cause on said date.

Henry G. Hains

Subscribed and sworn to before me this 11th day of May, 1905.

Drennan C Skaggs
Notary Public.

Applications for Enrollment of Creek Newborn
Act of 1905   Volume XIII

N.C. 1065.

DEPARTMENT OF THE INTERIOR,
COMMISSIONER TO THE FIVE CIVILIZED TRIBES.
Senora, I. T., October 10, 1905.

In the matter of the application for the enrollment of an unnamed minor child of Annie Tiger as a citizen by blood of the Creek Nation.

CHRISTIE HARJO, being duly sworn, testified as follows:

Through Alex Posey Official Interpreter:

BY THE COMMISSIONER:
Q What is your name? A Christie Harjo.
Q How old are you? A About sixty.
Q What is your post office address? A Senora.
Q Are you a citizen of the Creek Nation? A Yes, sir.
Q To what town do you belong? A Hickory Ground.
Q Do you know Annie Tiger? A Yes, sir.
Q Has she a new-born child? A Yes, sir.
Q Do you know when it was born? A It was born Christmas day, last year, and will be a year old next Christmas Day.
Q Has Annie Tiger any other name? A No, sir.

LEWIS HARJO, being duly sworn, testified as follows:

Through Alex Posey Official Interpreter:

BY THE COMMISSIONER:
Q What is your name? A Lewis Harjo.
Q How old are you? A About thirty.
Q What is your post office address? A Senora.
Q Are you a citizen of the Creek Nation? A Yes, sir.
Q To what town do you belong? A Hickory Ground.
Q Do you know Annie Tiger? A Yes, sir. I see her every day.
Q Has she a new-born child? A Yes, sir. She has but one child. It was born on last Christmas morning.
Q Do you know the name of the child? A I understand the child has been named Melah.
Q Who is the father of the child? A George Tiger.
Q To what town does he belong? A Wewoka.
Q To what town does Annie Tiger belong? A Hickory Ground.

---oooOOOooo---

Applications for Enrollment of Creek Newborn
Act of 1905   Volume XIII

I, D. C. Skaggs, on oath state that the above and foregoing is a full and true transcript of my stenographic notes as taken in said cause on said date.

D. C. Skaggs

Subscribed and sworn to before me this 16 day of Oct, 1905.

Edw C Griesel
Notary Public.

Copy

BIRTH AFFIDAVIT.

DEPARTMENT OF THE INTERIOR.
COMMISSION TO THE FIVE CIVILIZED TRIBES.

IN RE APPLICATION FOR ENROLLMENT, as a citizen of the Creek Nation, of Melah Tiger, born on the 25" day of Dec., 1904

Name of Father: George Tiger   a citizen of the   Creek   Nation.
Wewoka
Name of Mother: Annie Tiger   a citizen of the   Creek   Nation.
Hickory Ground

Postoffice   Senora I.T.

AFFIDAVIT OF ATTENDING PHYSICIAN OR MID-WIFE.

UNITED STATES OF AMERICA, Indian Territory,
      Western   DISTRICT.

We, the undersigned, personally acquainted with , on oath state that I attended on we are Mrs. Annie Tiger , wife of George Tiger on the day of , 1 ; that there was born to her on said date December 25, 1904 a male child; that said child is now was living March 4, 1905, and is said to have been named Melah Tiger

<table>
<tr><td></td><td>his</td></tr>
<tr><td></td><td>Lewis x Harjo</td></tr>
<tr><td>Witnesses To Mark:</td><td>mark</td></tr>
<tr><td>{ DC Skaggs</td><td>her</td></tr>
<tr><td> Alex Posey</td><td>Christie x Harjo</td></tr>
<tr><td></td><td>mark</td></tr>
</table>

Subscribed and sworn to before me 10 day of   October   , 1905.

Drennan C Skaggs
Notary Public.

Applications for Enrollment of Creek Newborn
Act of 1905 Volume XIII

(The above Birth Affidavit given again.)

REFER IN REPLY TO THE FOLLOWING:
Cr 2463-B

DEPARTMENT OF THE INTERIOR,
COMMISSIONER TO THE FIVE CIVILIZED TRIBES.

Muskogee, I. T. July 19, 1905

Comr. to the Five Civ Tribes
    Muskogee, I T

Sir:

    In the matter of the application for the enrollment of an unnamed minor child of George and Annie Tiger (2463 B) as a citizen by blood of the Creek Nation, I have the honor to report that Semihoye, the grandmother of said child, states that the child is a female and was born December 25, 1904, but she, together with the parents of the child, refuses to execute affidavit or to testify as to the date of the birth of said child. Said child is yet unnamed.

                  Respectfully,

                              Alex Posey

REFER IN REPLY TO THE FOLLOWING:
NC-1065

DEPARTMENT OF THE INTERIOR,
COMMISSIONER TO THE FIVE CIVILIZED TRIBES.

Muskogee, Indian Territory, October 16, 1905.

Commissioner to the Five Civilized Tribes,
    Muskogee, Indian Territory.

Sir:

    There is enclosed herewith supplemental proof in the matter of the application for the enrollment of an unnamed minor child of Annie Tiger as a citizen by blood of the Creek Nation.

    I am unable to secure further evidence in said case.

                  Respectfully,

                            Alex Posey
                  Clerk in Charge, Creek Enrollment Field Party.

Applications for Enrollment of Creek Newborn
Act of 1905   Volume XIII

REFER IN REPLY TO THE FOLLOWING:
N.C. 1065

DEPARTMENT OF THE INTERIOR,
COMMISSIONER TO THE FIVE CIVILIZED TRIBES.

Muskogee, Indian Territory, September 20, 1906.

Commissioner to the Five Civilized Tribes,
    Muskogee, Indian Territory.

Dear Sir:

    In the matter of the application for the enrollment of, Annie[sic] Tiger, as a citizen by blood of the Creek Nation blood of the Creek Nation, I have the honor to report that the parents of said child refuse to execute affidavits relative to her birth or to testify in the case.

                    Respectfully,
                          Jesse McDermott

N.C. 1065

                    Muskogee, Indian Territory, March 1, 1907.

Annie Tiger,
    Care George Tiger,
        Senora, Indian Territory.

Dear Madam:

    You are hereby advised that on February 15, 1907, the Secretary of the Interior approved the enrollment of your minor child, Melah Tiger, as a citizen by blood of the Creek Nation, and that the name of said child appears upon the roll of new born citizens by blood of the Creek Nation, enrolled under the Act of Congress approved March 3, 1905, as number 1204.

    This child is now entitled to allotment and application therefor should be made without delay at the Creek Land Office, Muskogee, Indian Territory.

                    Respectfully,
                          Commissioner.

Applications for Enrollment of Creek Newborn
Act of 1905   Volume XIII

2465-B

DEPARTMENT OF THE INTERIOR,
COMMISSION TO THE FIVE CIVILIZED TRIBES.
Eufaula, I. T., April 14, 1905.

In the matter of the application for the enrollment of Katy and Nicey Gano as citizens by blood of the Creek Nation.

LOUISA GANO, being duly sworn, testified as follows:

Through Alex Posey Official Interpreter:

BY COMMISSIONER:
Q What is your name? A Louisa Gano.
Q What is your age? A I do not know my age.

Witness appears to be about thirty.

Q What is your post office address? A Eufaula.
Q Are you a citizen of the Creek Nation? A Yes, sir.
Q To what town do you belong? A Okfuske Canadian.
Q Do you make application for the enrollment of your children, Katy and Nicey Gano, as citizens by blood of the Creek Nation? A Yes, sir.
Q What is the name of the father of these two children? A George Gano, sometimes known as Mafolate.
Q Is he living? A He died about a year ago.
Q Do you know when Katy was born? A There was no record made of the birth but I think she was born sometime in December, I do not know the year.
Q How many years ago has it been? A About four years.
Q Do you know any one who would know when the child was born? A No, sir. I may be able latter[sic] to ascertain the date of the child's birth by inquiring amon[sic] my neighbors.
Q Do you know whether or not land has been selected for Katy? A I do not think she has been allotted. So far as I know the child has not been enrolled. I have never made application for her.
Q Do you know when Nicey was born? A She was born in the summer when the Indians here were having their "Fish-killing". (The Creek Indians hold their "Fish-killings" during July and August.)
Q How old is the child? A She is going on three years old. She was just beginning to walk at the time her father died.

Nicey is present and appears to be at least two years old.
Kathy is also present and appears to be about four years of age.

---oooOOOooo---

Applications for Enrollment of Creek Newborn
Act of 1905 Volume XIII

I, D. C. Skaggs, on oath state that the above and foregoing is a full and true transcript of my stenographic notes as taken in said cause on said date.

D. C. Skaggs

Subscribed and sworn to before me this 12th day of May, 1905.

Henry G. Hains
Notary Public.

2465-B

DEPARTMENT OF THE INTERIOR,
COMMISSION TO THE FIVE CIVILIZED TRIBES.
Eufaula, I. T., May 18, 1905.

In the matter of the application for the enrollment of Katy and Nicey Gano as citizens by blood of the Creek Nation.

JEANETTA BROOK, being duly sworn, testified as follows:

BY COMMISSION:
Q What is your name? A Jeanetta Brook.
Q How old are you? A Thirty-two.
Q What is your post office address? A Eufaula.
Q Are you a citizen of the Creek Nation? A Yes, sir.
Q To what town do you belong? A Hickory Ground.
Q Do you know Louisa Gano? A Yes, sir.
Q Is she a relative of yours? A No, sir.
Q Is she a neighbor? A No, she lives about a mile and a half or two miles from me.
Q Does she live in the same neighborhood? A Yes, sir.
Q Do you know her children Katy and Nicey Gano? A Yes, sir.
Q How old is Katy? A I don't know just how old she is. I expect she is some where between four and five years old.
Q Do you know about how old Nicey is? A I think she is the youngest She is some where between two and three years old.
Q Who is the father of these children? A George Gano. His Creek name is Mafolate.
Q Is he living? A He is dead.

LOUISA GANO, being duly sworn, testified as follows:

Through Alex Posey Official Interpreter:

BY COMMISSION:
Q What is your name? A Louisa Gano.
Q How old are you? A I don't know my age.

Witness appears to be about thirty years old.

Applications for Enrollment of Creek Newborn
Act of 1905   Volume XIII

Q What is your post office address? a[sic] Eufaula.
Q Are you a citizen of the Creek Nation? A Yes, sir.
Q To what town do you belong? A Okfuske Canadian.
Q Have you fixed the date of the birth of your children Katy and Nicey Gano? A Yes, sir, approximately.
Q When was Katy born? A In December and will be four years old next December. She is just a year older than Nicey.
Q When was Nicey born? A Nicey was born in the summer time and will be three years old this summer.
Q Who attended on you at the birth of Katy? A No one waited on me as mid-wife at the birth of Katy.
Q Did any one attend on you as mid-wife when Nicey was born? A Kizzie Bear attended on me.
Q Where does Kizzie Bear live? A She livest[sic] west of here on Mill Creek.

I, D. C. Skaggs, on oath state that the above and foregoing is a full and true transcript of my stenographic notes as taken in said cause on said date.

(No Signature)

Subscribed and sworn to before me this____day of_____1905.

Notary Public.

C 1066

No. 2465.
DEPARTMENT OF THE INTERIOR,
COMMISSION TO THE FIVE CIVILIZED TRIBES.
Mellette, I. T., May 19, 1905.

Supplemental testimony in the matter of the application for the enrollment of Katy and Nicey Gano as citizens by blood of the Creek Nation.

KIZZIE BEAR, being duly sworn, testified as follows:

Through Alex Posey Official Interpreter:

BY COMMISSION:
Q What is your name? A Kizzie Bear.
Q How old are you? A I am about thirty-six.
Q What is your post office address? A Eufaula.
Q Are you a citizen of the Creek Nation? A Yes, sir.
Q To what town do you belong? A Okchiye.
Q Do you know Louisa and George Gano? A Yes, sir.
Q Are they both living? A George is dead.
Q Do you know their children Katy and Nicey Gano? A Yes, sir.

Applications for Enrollment of Creek Newborn
Act of 1905 Volume XIII

Q Did you attend on Louisa Gano when Nicey was born? A Yes, sir. While attending a meetting[sic] at Okfuske I was called in by George Gano to attend on his wife at the birth of her child.
Q When was that? A In July, three years ago this summer.
Q Will Nicey be three years old next July? A Yes, sir.
Q Do you know when Katy was born? A I do not know.
Q How old was Katy at the time Nicey was born? A She appear to be a little over a year old.

---oooOOOooo---

    I, D. C. Skaggs, on oath state that the above and foregoing is a full and true transcript of my stenographic notes as taken in said cause on said date.

                                  D. C. Skaggs

Subscribed and sworn to before me this 17 day of July 1905.

                                  Edw C Griesel
                                  Notary Public.

C.I. 3142.
N.C. 1066.

                    Department of the Interior,
            Commissioner to the Five Civilized Tribes,
                Eufaula, I. T., August 18, 1906.

    In the matter of the application for the enrollment of Louisa Kano and Wisey Marfoloty, as citizens by blood of the Creek Nation.

    HENRY SCOTT being duly sworn testified as follows:

Through Alex Posey official interpreter.

BY THE COMMISSIONER:

Q What is your name? A Henry Scott.
Q What is your postoffice address? A Eufaula.
Q How old are you? A About 28.
Q Are you a citizen of the Creek Nation? A Yes sir.
Q To what Creek town do you belong? A Hutchechoppa.
Q Are you acquainted with Louisa Kano? A Yes sir.
Q Is she a relative of yours? A She was my wife.
Q Is she dead? A Yes sir.
Q Whene did she die? A May 15, 1906.
Q Were you her second husband? A Yes sir.

Applications for Enrollment of Creek Newborn
Act of 1905   Volume XIII

Q Who was her first husband? A Her former husband was Birdcreek Kano. He was also known as Marfoloty and George Kano.
Q Do you know John Kano? A I am not personally acquainted with John, but he is a brother of Birdcreek Kano and lives somewhere near Hanna.
Q Do you know Janie Kano? A Janie is a daughter of Louisa.
Q Do you know Barney Kano? A Barney was a child of Louisa; he is now dead.
Q Do you know Harty Bear? A Harty was a brother of Louisa and is now dead.
Q Do you know Bamma Bear? A Yes sir, he is also a brother of Louisa.
Q Has Louisa had such child as Wisey? A I do not know anything about her. She never told me that she ever had such child.
Q Was Louisa Kano ever known as Wisey Marfoloty? A No sir, she was known as Louisa Kano.
Q Did Louisa Kano have two other children named Nicey and Katie Kano? A Yes sir.
Q Is Nicey sometimes called Wisey? A No sir, the child is simply Nicey.
Q Are Nicey and Katie living? A The children are both dead.
Q When did Nicey die? A Six days after the mother died.
Q Did the child die on May 21, 1906? A Yes sir.
Q When did Katie die? A The child died in July, this year. I do not know just what time in July, I was absent at the time she died. The child died in the latter part of the month, probably on or about the 20th, I am unable to fix the exact date.
Q How old was Nicey at the time she died? A The child was something like three years old.
Q Do you know the date of her birth? A No sir.
Q How old was Katie at the time she died? A Four and a half or five years old.
Q You do not know anything about Wisey Marfoloty? A No sir.
Q Do you know any one that would be able to give the Commissioner any information about Wisey? A Noah Deere would probably know something about the child.
Q Where does Noah live? A Near the Okfuske church. Noah is a brother of Louisa.

James B. Myers, being first duly sworn, states, that as stenographer to the Commissioner to the Five Civilized Tribes, he recorded the testimony in the foregoing proceedings, and that the above is a true, and correct transcript of his stenographic notes thereof.

James B Myers

Subscribed and sworn to before me this the 23 day of August, 1906.

Alex Posey
Notary Public.

JBM

Applications for Enrollment of Creek Newborn
Act of 1905   Volume XIII

C.I. 3142.
N.C. 1066.

Department of the Interior,
Commissioner to the Five Civilized Tribes,
Eufaula, I. T., August 20, 1906.

In the matter of the enrollment of Louisa Kano and Wisey Marfoloty, as citizens by blood of the Creek Nation.

CHARLES GIBSON, being duly sworn testified as follows:

BY THE COMMISSIONER:

Q What is your name? A Charles Gibson.
Q How old are you? A 59.
Q What is your postoffice address? A Eulaula[sic].
Q You are a citizen of the Creek Nation, are you? A Yes.
Q Were you acquainted with Louisa Kano? A Yes.
Q She is now dead, is she? A Yes.
Q Do you know anything about a child of her's[sic] named Wisey Marfoloty? A No.
Q Did you have a conversation with her relative to a child of that name? A I had a conversation with her about the names Wisey Marfoloty, and she told ---I suspicioned at the time that it was one of her children by that name--and she told me that she did not have a child by that name, Wisey Marfoloty. Then I spoke to her about it and asked her if it could not be possible that it was her that they put down that way, and she said she knowed[sic] it was; tha[sic] she was known as Wisey here among the full blood Indians, I had known her by that name and knowed[sic] it meant Louisa. It is very frequently they change like that from Louisa to Wisey.
Q What was the ossa occasion of your conversation with Louisa about Wisey Marfoloty? A On account of this certificate I had that she turned over to me, I wanted to be certain that it wasn't here before I turned it over to the Commission, and I asked her if she did not have a child by that name dead or alive, and she said she did not.
Q When did you have this conversation with her? A It has been over a year ago. I had this certificate and the dead a good while before I returned it, it was while I was talking about this that she gave it to me and said she didn't need it and she ought not to have it, that "I have the deed to my land and have it leased out already and in cultivation", and I asked her who she had it leased to and she said to Turner and I went in and asked Turner about it and he said yes, it was all right.
Q She stated positively that the certificate did not belong to any member of her family? A She stated positively that it did not belong to her, that she had the deed to her land and had it in cultivation. She said "They don't get but a 160 acres a piece, do they", and I said no, and then she said "It is not mine, I guess they have filed me twice".
Q Do you know her husband? A Yes.
Q What was his name? A He had two names; Marfoloty was his boy and Indian name, and lots of people knew him as Marfoloty.
Q And he had another name? A He had an English name of George Marfoloty.

Applications for Enrollment of Creek Newborn
Act of 1905   Volume XIII

Q Was he ever known as Bird Creek Kano? A The Dawes Commission gave him that name, that is his war name that was given him at the Busk.
Q Louisa Kano is now dead, is she? A Yes sir

James B. Myers, being first duly sworn, states, that as stenographer to the Commissioner to the Five Civilized Tribes, he recorded the testimony in the foregoing proceedings, and that the above is a true, and correct transcript of his stenographic notes thereof.

James B. Myers

Subscribed and sworn to before me this the 28 day of August, 1906.

Alex Posey
Notary Public.

C.I. 3142.
N.C. 1066.

DEPARTMENT OF THE INTERIOR,
COMMISSIONER TO THE FIVE CIVILIZED TRIBES,
EUFAULA, I. T., AUGUST 20, 1906.

In the matter of the enrollment of Louisa Kano and Wisey Marfoloty as citizens by blood of the Creek Nation.

NOAH DEERE being duly sworn testified as follows:

Through Alex Posey Official Interpreter.

BY THE COMMISSIONER:

Q What is your name? A Noah Deere.
Q What is your age? A I do not know my age. (The witness appears to be about 35).
Q What is your postoffice address? A Eufaula.
Q Are you a citizen of the Creek Nation? A Yes sir.
Q To what Creek town do you belong? A Okfuske Canadian.
Q Did you know a member of this town named Louisa Kano? A Yes sir.
Q Was she any relation of yours? A She was my sister.
Q Is she living? A No sir, she is dead.
Q When did she die? A About the 15th of May.
Q This year? A Yes sir.
Q Who was her husband? A Her former husband was George Kano or Marfoloty.
Q Was George Kano or Marfoloty ever known as Bird Creek Kano? A Yes sir
Q Was your sister Louisa married more than once? A Yes sir.

Applications for Enrollment of Creek Newborn
Act of 1905   Volume XIII

Q To whom was she married at the time of her death? A Henry Scott.
Q Did she have any children by her first husband, George Kano? A Yes sir.
Q Can you name them? A A boy named Barney and two daughters named Nicey and Katie. She had another boy that died, I do not know what the child's name was.
Q How old was that child when it died? A I do not know, but the child I think was able to sit up and crawl.
Q Did she have any other children? A Yes sir, she had a daughter named Jennie by another man.
Q Do you know the child's father? A Jennie was supposed to be an illegitimate child of Frank Ross, sometimes called Falumke among the Indians, who dies many years ago.
Q Was Jennie her oldest child? A Yes sir, she had the child before she was married to George Kano.
Q Our records show that one Oscar Kano was the father of Jennie, who was a brother of George Kano, was the father of the child, but the mother said Frank Ross or Falunke, was the child's father.
Q Did Louisa have any other children besides Jennie, Barney, Nicey, and Katie Kano, and the dead child whose name you do not know? A No sir, she only had five children.
Q Did she not have a child named Wisey Marfoloty? A I know of no such child, she had no children other than those I have named.
Q How many children did Louisa have at the time the 1895 Creek Payment was made? A I do not know.
Q Are you positive that she had no such child as Wisey Marfoloty? A Yes sir.
Q Are any of her children living? A No sir. They are every one dead.
Q When did Jennie die? A I am unable to say when she died, she has been dead probably about six years.
Q When did Barney die? A I do not know, but Barney died after Jennie died.
Q When did Nicey die? A The child died recently.
Q In what month? A May, this year. I do not know the date of the month.
Q When did Katie die? A Katie died sometime in July.
Q This year? A Yes. The mother and the children died one after the other, the mother dying first and the two children following. If there is such a child as Wisey Marfoloty enrolled it is a mistake for Louisa never had such child, of that I am positive.

. . . . . .

JOHN KELLEY being duly sworn testified as follows:

Through Alex Posey, Official Interpreter.

BY THE COMMISSIONER:

Q What is your name? A John Kelley.
Q How old are you? A I am unable to state exactly how old I am, but I am something like 50 years old.
Q What is your postoffice? A Eufaula.
Q Are you a citizen of the Creek Nation? A Yes sir.
Q To what Creek town do you belong? A Okfuske.

Applications for Enrollment of Creek Newborn
Act of 1905   Volume XIII

Q Are you acquainted with a member of your town named Louisa Kano? A Yes sir.
Q Is she living? A She is now dead.
Q When did she die? A She died in May of this year, I am unable to give you the exact date.
Q Did you know the members of her family? A Yes sir.
Q How many children did she have? A She had five children, I think.
Q Can you name them? A I do not know the names of all of them.
Q Do you know a child of hers named Jennie? A Yes sir. Jennie was her oldest child.
Q Is Jennie living? A She is dead, she has been dead, I think, between six and seven years. She was living at the time the people began filing upon their allotments, I do not know how long ago that has been.
Q Did you know another child of hers named Barney? A I do not recall the name.
Q Did she have a child named Nicey? A She had two children that died recently, but I only know the name of ne, Katie. Louisa had five children all together. She lost a young child years ago, I did not know the name of the child.
Q Did she have a child named Wisey Marfoloty? A No sir, there is no such child in her family. I have lived near neighbor to Louisa a long time, eleven or twelve years, and knew her intimately, she had no such child as Wisey. Both Nicey and Katie are dead, having died but recently. The grave records will show just when they died, also the date of their mother's death.
Q Where are Louisa Kano and her children burried[sic]? A Right down there in the field.

The graves of Louisa, Nicey and Katie Kano are visited and the following records are found upon the head-boards of said graves.

"Louisa departed this life at two o'clock May 15, 1906".

"Okfuske, in Memory of Nicy Gayno, died May 22, 1906, age 4 years".

"Katie Kano departed this life on the 12th day of August, 1906, and was burried[sic] in the 13th".

James B. Myers, being first duly sworn, states, that as stenographer to the Commissioner to the Five Civilized Tribes, he recorded the testimony in the foregoing proceedings, and that the above is a true, and correct transcript of his stenographic notes thereof.

James B. Myers

Subscribed and sworn to before me this the 28 day of August, 1906.

Alex Posey
Notary Public.

Applications for Enrollment of Creek Newborn
Act of 1905 Volume XIII

BIRTH AFFIDAVIT.

DEPARTMENT OF THE INTERIOR.
COMMISSION TO THE FIVE CIVILIZED TRIBES.

IN RE APPLICATION FOR ENROLLMENT, as a citizen of the Creek Nation, of Nicey Gano, born ~~on the day of~~ the latter part of July, 1903

Name of Father: George Gano   a citizen of the Creek Nation.
Hillabee Town
Name of Mother: Louisa Gano   a citizen of the Creek Nation.
Okfuske Canadian Town

             Postoffice   Eufaula, I.T.

AFFIDAVIT OF ATTENDING PHYSICIAN OR MID-WIFE.

UNITED STATES OF AMERICA, Indian Territory,
     Western   DISTRICT.

     I, Kizzie Bear, a mid-wife, on oath state that I attended on Mrs. Louisa Bear, wife of George Bear ~~on the day of~~ the latter part of July, 1903; that there was born to her on said date a female child; that said child ~~is now~~ was living on March 4, 1905 and is said to have been named Nicey Gano

                                      her
                            Kizzie x Bear
Witnesses To Mark: mark
   { DC Skaggs
     Alex Posey

     Subscribed and sworn to before me this 19 day of   May, 1905.

                           Drennan C Skaggs
                              Notary Public.

N.C. 1066.

DEPARTMENT OF THE INTERIOR,
COMMISSIONER TO THE FIVE CIVILIZED TRIBES.

     In the matter of the application for the enrollment of Nicey and Katy Kano, both deceased, as citizens by blood of the Creek Nation.

DECISION.

     The record in this case shows that on April 14, 1905, Louisa Kano appeared before a Creek enrollment field party at Eufaula, Indian Territory, and made application for the enrollment of her minor children, Nicey and Katy Kano, as citizens by blood of

Applications for Enrollment of Creek Newborn
Act of 1905   Volume XIII

the Creek Nation. Further proceedings were had May 18, and May 19, 1905, and August 18, and August 20, 1906. A supplemental affidavit, filed May 20, 1905, is attached to and made a part of the record herein.

The evidence in this case shows that the said Nicey and Katy Kano, both deceased, were children of Bird Creek Kano and Louisa Kano, whose names appear on a partial schedule of citizens by blood of the Creek Nation, approved by the Secretary of the Interior March 28, 1902, opposite roll numbers 8389 and 8391, respectively. The surname of the said applicants appears variously spelled in the testimony and the supplemental affidavit, but, inasmuch as the father is identified as Bird Creek Kano, the said applicants are herein considered as Katy and Nicey Kano.

The evidence further shows that the said Nicey Kano was born in July 1903, and died May 22, 1906, and that Katy Kano was born in December 1901, and died August 12, 1906.

The Act of Congress approved March 3, 1905, (33 Stats., 1048), provides in part as follows:

> "That the Commission to the Five Civilized Tribes is authorized for sixty days after the date of the approval of this act to receive and consider applications for enrollment, of children, born subsequent to May twenty-fifth, nineteen hundred and one, and prior to March fourth, nineteen hundred and five, and living on said latter date, to citizens of the Creek tribe of Indians whose enrollment has been approved by the Secretary of the Interior prior to the approval of this act; and to enroll and make allotments to such children."

It is, therefore, ordered and adjudged that the said Nicey and Katy Kano, both deceased, are entitled to enrollment as citizens by blood of the Creek Nation, in accordance with the provisions of the Act of Congress above quoted, and the application for their enrollment as such is accordingly granted.

Muskogee, Indian Territory,   Tams Bixby   COMMISSIONER.
JAN 17 1907

C 1066

Dustin, Indian Territory, June 3, 1905.

Commission to the Five Civilized Tribes,
   Muskogee, Indian Territory.

Gentlemen:

I return herewith copies of testimony taken in the following cases, as I find it impossible to secure further evidence:

Sarty, Enrollment No. 520.
Chepe and Folle Homahta, Creek Indian Card Field No. 2871.

Applications for Enrollment of Creek Newborn
Act of 1905   Volume XIII

✓ Katy and Nicey Gano, No. 2465 B.
William Tiger, No. ____ B.
Amy Kelly, No. 2467 B.
Heliswa and Kaska Beaver, No. 2466 B.
Lena Bear, No. ____ B.
Setepake Scott, No. 2447 B.
Mahlahsee Mitchell, No. 2447 B.
Susanna and Onate Johnson, No. 2468 B.

Respectfully,
(Signed) Alex Posey,
Clerk in Charge Creek Field Party.

REFER IN REPLY TO THE FOLLOWING:
NC 1066.

DEPARTMENT OF THE INTERIOR,
COMMISSIONER TO THE FIVE CIVILIZED TRIBES.

Muskogee, Indian Territory, June 21, 1906.

Louisa Gano,
    Eufaula, Indian Territory.

Dear Madam:

    In the matter of the application for the enrollment of your minor children, Nicey and Katy Gano, as citizens of the Creek Nation, you are advised that it is required that you furnish this office with the affidavits of yourself and the midwife, who attended you at the birth of said child, said affidavits showing the name of the child, the names of its parents, the date of birth, and whether said child was living March 4, 1906, and for this purpose there is herewith enclosed a blank affidavit. This matter should receive your immediate attention.

    You are further advised that this office is unable to identify you or George Gano, the father of said children, upon its rolls of citizens of the Creek Nation, and it will be necessary that you furnish this office with your maiden name, the names of your parents and other members of your family, the Creek Indian town to which you belong, the name and roll number as same appear on your deeds or allotment certificates to land in the Creek Nation, and any other information which will enable this office to identify you and said George Gano on its records.

Respectfully,
Tams Bixby
Commissioner.

1 BA.

Applications for Enrollment of Creek Newborn
Act of 1905   Volume XIII

N C 1066.

Muskogee, Indian Territory, March 7, 1907.

Noah Deere,
    Care of Charles Gibson,
        Eufaula, Indian Territory.

Dear Sir:

You are hereby advised that on March 2, 1907 the Secretary of the Interior approved the enrollment of Nicey and Katy Kano, deceased minor children of Louisa Kano, deceased, and George Kano, deceased, and that the names of said children appear upon the roll of new born citizens by blood of the Creek Nation enrolled under the Act of Congress approved March 3, 1905, as numbers 1253 and 1254, respectively.

These children are now entitled to allotments and application therefor should be made by the duly appointed administrator without delay at the Creek Land Office, Muskogee, Indian Territory.

                Respectfully,
                          Commissioner.

2468 B

DEPARTMENT OF THE INTERIOR,
COMMISSION TO THE FIVE CIVILIZED TRIBES.
Eufaula, I. T., April 14, 1905.

In the matter of the application for the enrollment of Susanna and Onate Johnson as citizens by blood of the Creek Nation.

JOHNSON LEWIS, being duly sworn, testified as follows:

Through Alex Posey Official Interpreter:

BY COMMISSION;
Q What is your name? A Johnson Lewis.
Q How old are you? A Forty-five.
Q What is your post office address? A Eufaula.

Applications for Enrollment of Creek Newborn
Act of 1905   Volume XIII

Q Are you a citizen of the Creek Nation? A Yes, sir.
Q To what town do you belong? A Eufaula Canadian Town.
Q Do you know Sam and Leda Johnson? A Yes, sir.
Q Do you know their children Susanna and Onate Johnson? A Yes, sir.
Q Do you know whether or not the parents of these children have made application for their enrollment? A They have not.
Q Do you know why? A They have refused to make application because they are members of the Snake Faction and are opposed to allotment of land in severalty.
Q Do you know how old Susanna is? A She is between four and five years old.
Q Do you know whether or not she was born prior to May 25, 1901 or subsequent to that date? A I do not know positively but I think she was living on that date. A man of the name of Milam, I remember, has endevored[sic] to have them make application for the child and was in this neighborhood making inquiries as to the child's name and age.
Q Do you know how old Onate is? A She is a little older than that girl there (indicating a little child in the yeard[sic]) who will be two years old in May.
Q How much older is Onate than the little girl indicated by you? A think Onate is about three years old.
Q Was she born before or after May 25, 1901? A She was born after.
Q Are both of these children living? A Yes, sir, they are living.
Q To what Creek towns do the parents of these children belong? A The father belongs to Okfuske Town and the mother belongs to Eufaula Canadian Town.

---oooOOOooo---

I, D. C. Skaggs, on oath state that the above and foregoing is a full and true transcript of my stenographic notes as taken in said cause on said date.

D. C. Skaggs

Subscribed and sworn to before me this 12th day of May, 1905.

Henry G Hains
Notary Public.

N.C. 1067.

DEPARTMENT OF THE INTERIOR,
COMMISSIONER TO THE FIVE CIVILIZED TRIBES.
Eufaula, I. T., September 30, 1905.

In the matter of the application for the enrollment of Susanna and Onate Johnson as citizens by blood of the Creek Nation.

LUCINDA LEWIS, being duly sworn, testified as follows:

Through Alex Posey Official Interpreter:

Applications for Enrollment of Creek Newborn
Act of 1905   Volume XIII

BY THE COMMISSIONER:
Q What is your name? A Lucinda Lewis.
Q How old are you? A Over thirty.
Q What is your post office address? A Eufaula.
Q Are you a citizen of the Creek Nation? A Yes, sir.
Q To what town do you belong? A Okfuske Canadian.
Q Do you know Sam and Leda Johnson? A Yes, sir. Sam is my uncle.
Q Do you know their children Susanna and Onate? A Yes, sir.
Q Do you know when Susanna was born? A I do not know, but the mother told me the other day that the child was four years old.
Q Did she state whether or not it was over four years old? A No sir, she just simply stated that the child was four years old. The mother herself does not know what month or year the child was born.
Q How old do you think Susanna is? A The child is about four years old.
Q Do you think it is over four years old? A It may be a little over four years old.
Q Do you know when Onate was born? A The mother said Onate was born the day before Christmas and would be three years old next Christmas.

---oooOOOooo---

I, D. C. Skaggs, on oath state that the above and foregoing is a full and true transcript of my stenographic notes as taken in said cause on said date.

D. C. Skaggs

Subscribed and sworn to before me this 16 day of Oct 1905.

Edw C Griesel
Notary Public.

N.C. 1067.

DEPARTMENT OF THE INTERIOR,
COMMISSIONER TO THE FIVE CIVILIZED TRIBES.
Eufaula, I. T., September 30, 1905.

In the matter of the application for the enrollment of Susanna and Onate Johnson as citizens by blood of the Creek Nation.

SALLIE JOHNSON, being duly sworn, testified as follows:

Through Alex Posey Official Interpreter:

BY THE COMMISSIONER:
Q What is your name? A Sallie Johnson.
Q How old are you? A About sixty.
Q What is your post office address? A Eufaula.

Applications for Enrollment of Creek Newborn
Act of 1905 Volume XIII

Q Are you a citizen of the Creek Nation? A Yes, sir.
Q To what town do you belong? A Okfuske Canadian.
Q Do you know Sam and Leda Johnson? A Yes, sir.
Q What relation are they to you? A Sam is my brother.
Q Do you know their children, Susanna and Onate? A Yes, sir.
Q Do you know when Susanna was born? A I do not know (1902) the date of her birth.
Q How old is she? A She is about four years old.
Q In what season of the year was she born? A I think she was born in the Fall of the year.
Q Do you know when Onate was born? A I do not know whether she was born in the Fall or the Spring of the year but the child is about two years old or over. The child is just beginning to talk a little.
Q Are you sure that Onate is not three years old? A Yes, sir.
Q Are you sure that Susanna is not over four years old? A She is just about four years old.
Q Have Sam and Leda any other children? A They have three other children. Sallie, who was named for me, Edmund and another child who is a girl. I think she is called Tullegee. She was raised up in Nuyaka. These three children are by a different woman. Their mother's name is Millie.
Q What is her sir-name[sic]? A I do not know.
Q Has Leda any children by Sam besides Susanna and Onate? A She has another child named Claudie *(illegible)*. She has only three children by Sam. Claudie has several nicknames, Roman, Jimmie, Wilsoche and Cheparne, but his correct name is Claudie.
Q Have they a child named Wouman? A that is the same as Roman.

JOHNSON LEWIS, being duly sworn, testified as follows:

Through Alex Posey Official Interpreter:

BY THE COMMISSIONER;
Q What is your name? A Johnson Lewis.
Q How old are you? A Forty-five.
Q What is your post office address? A Eufaula.
Q Are you a citizen of the Creek Nation? A Yes, sir.
Q To what town do you belong? A Eufaula Canadian.
Q You have heretofore given testimony in this case have you not? A Yes, sir.
Q Have you been able to fix the dates of the births of Susanna and Onate Johnson? A I have made repeated inquired but have not been able to learn when the two children were born. The parents would give me no information. The mother of the children, as I stated in my former testimony, belongs to Eufaula Canadian Town, and is enrolled in that town but I received a letter, not long ago, from Noah Gregory (Sapulpa) stating that that she was enrolled as an Eucha.
Q Did she ever belong to Eucha Town? A She was born and raised among the Euches and speaks the Euche Language but she is not an Euche by blood. Her mother belonged to Eufaula Canadian Town and her father may have been an Euche.
Q Did Noah Gregory state in his letter the name under which you are finally enrolled, the names of your parents and other members of your family, the Creek Indian town to which

Applications for Enrollment of Creek Newborn
Act of 1905   Volume XIII

you belong and your final roll number as the same appears upon your allotment certificate and deeds. she was enrolled in Euche Town? A He said just as Leda.
Q Are either Susanna or Onate known by any other name? A No, sir.
Q Do you still think that Susanna was born prior to May 25, 1901? A I still think the child was born prior to that time.
Q How old do you judge her to be? A I think she is fully five years old and Onate is over two years old.

---oooCOOooo---

I, D. C. Skaggs, on oath state that the above and foregoing is a full and true transcript of my stenographic notes as taken in said cause on said date.

D. C. Skaggs

Subscribed and sworn to before me this 16 day of Oct. 1905.

Edw C Griesel
Notary Public.

C 1066

Dustin, Indian Territory, June 3, 1905.

Commission to the Five Civilized Tribes,
    Muskogee, Indian Territory.

Gentlemen:

I return herewith copies of testimony taken in the following cases, as I find it impossible to secure further evidence:

Sarty, Enrollment No. 520.
Chepe and Folle Homahta, Creek Indian Card Field No. 2871.
Katy and Nicey Gano, No. 2465 B.
William Tiger, No. ____ B.
Amy Kelly, No. 2467 B.
Heliswa and Kaska Beaver, No. 2466 B.
Lena Bear, No. ____ B.
Setepake Scott, No. 2447 B.
Mahlahsee Mitchell, No. 2447 B.
<u>Susanna and Onate</u> Johnson, No. 2468 B.

Respectfully,
(Signed) Alex Posey,
Clerk in Charge Creek Field Party.

Applications for Enrollment of Creek Newborn
Act of 1905 Volume XIII

N.C. 1067.

Dustin, Indian Territory, October 12, 1905.

Commissioner to the Five Civilized Tribes,
    Muskogee, Indian Territory.

Sir:

There is enclosed herewith testimony taken September 30, 1905, in the matter of the application for the enrollment of Susanna and Onate Johnson as citizens by blood of the Creek Nation, together with a copy of New Creek card number 1067 and a copy of testimony heretofore taken in said case.

I am unable to secure further evidence in said case.

                Respectfully,
                Alex Posey
                Clerk in Charge Creek Field Party.

N.C. 1067.   F.H.W.
DEPARTMENT OF THE INTERIOR,
COMMISSIONER TO THE FIVE CIVILIZED TRIBES.

In the matter of the application for the enrollment of Susanna Johnson and Onate Johnson as citizens by blood of the Creek Nation.

DECISION.

The record in this case shows that on April 14, 1905, Johnson Lewis appeared before a Creek enrollment field party, at Eufaula, Indian Territory, and gave testimony in the matter of the application for the enrollment of said Susanna and Onate Johnson as citizens by blood of the Creek Nation, which testimony is herein considered an application for the enrollment of the said applicants. Further proceedings were had on September 30, 1905. Copies of letters from Alex Posey, clerk in charge of a Creek field party, bearing date of June 3, 1905, and October 12, 1905, are attached to and made part of the record herein.

The evidence shows that the parents of the said Susanna and Onate Johnson are members of the Snake or disaffected faction of Creek Indians and that this office was unable to obtain birth affidavits executed in the regular form although efforts were made so to do through Alex Posey, clerk in charge Creek field party. It is, however, sufficiently clear from the records of this office, examined in connection with the testimony, that said Susanna and Onate Johnson are the children of Sam and Lydia Johnson, whose names appear on a partial schedule of citizens by blood of the Creek Nation approved by the Secretary of the Interior March 28, 1902, opposite roll Nos. 8724 and 8725, respectively.

Applications for Enrollment of Creek Newborn
Act of 1905   Volume XIII

It appears that the Leda Johnson to whom reference is made in the testimony is identified as Lydia Johnson.

The evidence appears conflicting as to the date of the birth of said Susanna Johnson but the weight of evidence establishes said date as some time in the autumn of 1901.

It further appears that the said Onate Johnson was born December 24, 1902, and that both applicants were living on April 14, 1906.

The Act of Congress approved March 3, 1905, (33 Stats. 1048) provides in part as follows:

"That the Commission to the Five Civilized Tribes is authorized for sixty days after the date of the approval of this act to receive and consider applications for enrollment, of children, born subsequent to May twenty-fifth, nineteen hundred and one, and prior to March fourth, nineteen hundred and five, and living on said latter date, to citizens of the Creek tribe of Indians whose enrollment has been approved by the Secretary of the Interior prior to the approval of this act; and to enroll and make allotments to such children."

It is, therefore, ordered and adjudged that the said Susanna Johnson and Onate Johnson are entitled to be enrolled as citizens by blood of the Creek Nation, in accordance with the provisions of law above quoted, and the application for their enrollment as such is accordingly granted.

Muskogee, Indian Territory,   Tams Bixby   COMMISSIONER.
JAN 25 1907

NC 1067.

Muskogee, Indian Territory, March 7, 1907.

Leda Johnson,
    Care of Sam Johnson,
        Eufaula, Indian Territory.

Dear Madam:

You are hereby advised that on March 2, 1907 the Secretary of the Interior approved the enrollment of your minor children, Susanna and Onate Johnson, as citizens by blood of the Creek Nation, and that the names of said children appear upon the roll of new born citizens by blood of the Creek Nation enrolled under the Act of Congress approved March 3, 1905, as numbers 1255 and 1256, respectively.

These children are now entitled to allotments and application therefor should be made without delay at the Creek Land Office, Muskogee, Indian Territory.

                Respectfully,
                          Commissioner.

Applications for Enrollment of Creek Newborn
Act of 1905   Volume XIII

DEPARTMENT OF THE INTERIOR,
COMMISSION TO THE FIVE CIVILIZED TRIBES.
NEAR SENORA, I.T. April 21, 1905.

In the matter of the application for the enrollment of certain new born children of "Snake" parents:

Asaf Jones, being duly sworn, testified as follows, through Alex Posey, Official Interpreter: Also by Maria Kelley, and Sam Kelley.
Examination by the Commission:
Q What is your name? A Asaf Jones.
Q What is your age? [sic] About 23.
Q What is your post office address? A Weeletka[sic]. I am a citizen of the Creek Nation.

What is your name? A Maria Kelley.
Q What is your age? A About 35.
Q What is your post office address? A Senora.
Q Are you a citizen of the Creek Nation? A No sir, Seminole Nation.

What is your name? A Sam Kelley.
Q What is your age? A I am over 30.
Q What is your post office address? A Senora, Indian Territory
Q Are you a citizen of the Creek Nation? A Yes sir.

Statement: Hillis Harjo of Alabama Town, and Mary Harjo of Hickory Ground have a child about three years old between two and three years--it is a girl--- we saw it--don't know it's[sic] name.

Sam Emarthla and Leechie, whose maiden name was Taylor, have two children--both boys and living--both under three years old--don't know their names, both parents are of Hickory Ground town.

Roley Taylor and Arcichky of Hickory ground[sic] has one child not a year old. It is a girl and living--don't know it's[sic]. (The child appears later one but parents are unwilling to testify)
Q (To Maria) Have you some children you want to make application for? A Yes sir, two.
Q What is the name of the oldest one? A Sallie. She is here.
Q How old is she? A three years old.
Q What is the name of the next one? A David, this baby here.
Q When was David born? A The 25th of February, this year.
Q Do you know when the other was born? A March 10, 1902.
Q What is the name of the father of the child? A Sam Kelley.
Q Is he a citizen of the Creek Nation? A Yes sir.

Applications for Enrollment of Creek Newborn
Act of 1905   Volume XIII

Q If it should be found that these children have rights in both the Creek and Seminole Nations, in which Nation do you now elect for them to make their allotment? A In the Creek Nation.

Q (To Sam) What Creek Indian Town do you belong to Sam? A Arbeka North Fork.
Q If it should be found that these children have rights in both the Creek and Seminole Nations, in which Nation do you now elect for them to take their allotment? A In the Creek Nation.

Statement by Asaf: Some of these children, the parents have not looked after them--I don't know how they stand now, but a while back they were opposed to it--I am a member of Weogufky Town.

Statement by Louisa Riley, about 40 or over, Dustin, Indian Territory, being duly sworn, through Official Interpreter Alex Posey, states: Turner Scott of Artussee Town and Polly Scott a Seminole, have two children both boys, the oldest is about two years and the other is not quite a year old. Both are living, the post office of the parents is Dustin. I am the grandmother the oldest is named Lumber and Luffus the youngest; the parents want to file for the children in the Creek Nation if they can. I know that, thats[sic] what they told me just the other day.

Statement by Louisa Riley: Sahala Lewis, Indian name Slow Harjo of Hutchechuppa and Annie Lewis, nee Fields, of Kialigee Town, they have two children, the oldest is named Albert, he is about two years old; I don't know the name of the youngest one and don't know it's[sic]age, but the child is not very old. The parents have been wanting to make application but have not been able to go before the Commission--it was born before New Years[sic] I think, I am unable to fix the date, both are living, the post office is Dustin.

Statement by Asaf Jones: George Thompson of Tookpafka Town and Emma Canard, of Tulwarthlocco, have a child named Isreal Thompson, the child is about three years old, the child is living. Senora is the post office. Also Dick Marshall of Kialigee Town and Liza Marshall, of Arbeka North Fork have a child a girl named Emma about three years old, living, post office Senora.

Statement by Sam Kelley: Peter and Mully King both of Arbeka North Fork, have a child named Luila, a girl, about two years old and living, also a girl about a year old named Sallie. Their post office is Senora.

Testimony by Bunny Hicks, who being duly sworn, through Interpreter states:

Q What is your name? A Bunny Hicks.
Q What is your age? A I am about 20.
Q What is your post office? A Senora. Henry Hicks of Quassarte No. 1.(?) and Louisa Hicks of Arbeka, have a child named Joseph over three years old, maybe four years old, don't know the month he was born in, it is living. Joe is my brother. I also have a sister named Kogee Hicks of Quassarte and she and Hagar Thompson of Tookpafka Town,

Applications for Enrollment of Creek Newborn
Act of 1905   Volume XIII

have a child names Newman Thompson, which will be four years old the 24th of this month.

    Henry G. Hains, being duly sworn, on his oath, states that the above and foregoing is a true and correct transcript of his stenographic notes as taken in said cause on said date.

                                    Henry G. Hains

Subscribed and sworn to before me this 11th day of May, 1905.

                                    Drennan C Skaggs
                                    Notary Public.

N.C. 995.

                    DEPARTMENT OF THE INTERIOR,
           COMMISSIONER TO THE FIVE CIVILIZED TRIBES.
                     Senora, I. T., October 10, 1905.

    In the matter of the application for the enrollment of George Harjo as a citizen of the Creek Nation.

           CHRISTIE HARJO, being duly sworn, testified as follows:

    Through Alex Posey Official Interpreter:

BY THE COMMISSIONER:
Q What is your name? A Christie Harjo.
Q How old are you? A About sixty.
Q What is your post office address? A Senora.
Q Are you a citizen of the Creek Nation? A Yes, sir.
Q To what town do you belong? A Hickory Ground.
Q Do you know Helis and Mary Harjo? A Yes, sir.
Q Do you know a child of theirs named George? A Yes, sir.
Q Do you know when that child was born? A No, sir.
Q How old is he? A The child is about three years old. The parents are near neighbors of mine but I don't know the date of the child's birth.

                      ---oooOOOooo---

    I, D. C. Skaggs, on oath state that the above and foregoing is a full and true transcript of my stenographic notes as taken in said cause on said date.

                                    D. C. Skaggs

Applications for Enrollment of Creek Newborn
Act of 1905   Volume XIII

Subscribed and sworn to before me this 16 day of Oct 1905.

          Edw C Griesel
           Notary Public.

REFER IN REPLY TO THE FOLLOWING:
Cr 2464-B

DEPARTMENT OF THE INTERIOR,
COMMISSIONER TO THE FIVE CIVILIZED TRIBES.

      Muskogee, Indian Territory, July 19, 1905.

Commissioner to the Five Civilized Tribes,
  Muskogee, Indian Territory.

Sir:

  In the matter of the application for the enrollment of an unnamed minor child of Hellis and Mary Harjo (2464-B), as a citizen by blood of the Creek Nation. I have the honor to report that the parents refuse to execute affidavits or to testify in the case; nor can any evidence be secured from relatives and neighbors about said child. Said child appears to be about three years of age and is said to be named George Harjo.

         Respectfully,
           Alex Posey
        Clerk in Charge Creek Field Party.

REFER IN REPLY TO THE FOLLOWING:
1068
NC-~~995~~

DEPARTMENT OF THE INTERIOR,
COMMISSIONER TO THE FIVE CIVILIZED TRIBES.

      Muskogee, Indian Territory, October 16, 1905.

Commissioner to the Five Civilized Tribes,
  Muskogee, Indian Territory.
Sir:

  There is enclosed herewith supplemental proof in the matter of the application for the enrollment of application for the enrollment of George Harjo as a citizen by blood of the Creek Nation.

  I am unable to secure further evidence in said case.

         Respectfully,
          Alex Posey
      Clerk in Charge Creek Enrollment Field Party.

Applications for Enrollment of Creek Newborn
Act of 1905 Volume XIII

N.C. 1068.

F.H.W.

DEPARTMENT OF THE INTERIOR,
COMMISSIONER TO THE FIVE CIVILIZED TRIBES.

In the matter of the application for the enrollment of George Harjo as a citizen by blood of the Creek Nation.

DECISION.

The record in this case shows that on April 21, 1905, Asaf Jones, Maria Kelley and Sam Kelley appeared before a Creek enrollment field party at Senora, Indian Territory, and testified "in the matter of the application for the enrollment of certain newborns, children is Snake parents." In the said testimony appears the following statement:
"Hillis Harjo of Alabama Town, and Mary Harjo of Hickory Ground
have a child about three years old between two and three years--it is a girl---
we saw it--don't know it's[sic] name."

This statement of the above mentioned witnesses is herein considered an application for the enrollment of the said George Harjo in order that the rights of the said applicant be protected. Further proceedings were had on October 10, 1905. Copies of letters to the commissioner, bearing dates of July 19 and October 16, 1905, are attached to and made part of the record herein.

The evidence shows that the parents of the applicant are members of the Sake or disaffected faction of Creek Indians, that the commissioner made every effort to have birth affidavits executed in the regular form but such efforts were unsuccessful.

The evidence further shows that George Harjo is the child of Hillis and Mary Harjo, whose names appear on a partial schedule of citizens by blood of the Creek Nation approved by the Secretary of the Interior March 28, 1902, opposite roll Nos. 7650 and 7651 respectively.

It further appears that the said George Harjo was born some time during the year 1902 and was living on the date of the last proceedings herein.

The Act of Congress approved March 3, 1905, (33 Stats. 1048) provides in part as follows:

"That the Commission to the Five Civilized Tribes is authorized for sixty days after the date of the approval of this act to receive and consider applications for enrollment, of children, born subsequent to May twenty-fifth, nineteen hundred and one, and prior to March fourth, nineteen hundred and five, and living on said latter date, to citizens of the Creek tribe of Indians whose enrollment has been approved by the Secretary of the Interior prior to the approval of this act; and to enroll and make allotments to such children."

It is, therefore, ordered and adjudged that the said George Harjo is entitled to be enrolled as a citizen by blood of the Creek Nation, in accordance with the provisions of law above quoted, and the application for her[sic] enrollment as such is accordingly granted.

Applications for Enrollment of Creek Newborn
Act of 1905 Volume XIII

Muskogee, Indian Territory,   Tams Bixby   COMMISSIONER.
JAN 18 1907

NC 1068.

Muskogee, Indian Territory, March 7, 1907.

Mary Harjo,
    Care of Hillis Harjo,
        Senora, Indian Territory.

Dear Madam:

You are hereby advised that on March 2, 1907 the Secretary of the Interior approved the enrollment of your minor child, George Harjo, as a citizen by blood of the Creek Nation, and that the name of said child appears upon the roll of new born citizens by blood of the Creek Nation enrolled under the Act of Congress approved March 3, 1905, as number 1257.

This child is now entitled to allotment and application therefor should be made without delay at the Creek Land Office, Muskogee, Indian Territory.

                Respectfully,
                        Commissioner.

DEPARTMENT OF THE INTERIOR,
COMMISSION TO THE FIVE CIVILIZED TRIBES.
NEAR SENORA, I.T. April 21, 1905.

In the matter of the application for the enrollment of certain new born children of "Snake" parents:

Asaf Jones, being duly sworn, testified as follows, through Alex Posey, Official Interpreter: Also by Maria Kelley, and Sam Kelley.
Examination by the Commission:
Q What is your name? A Asaf Jones.
Q What is your age? [sic] About 23.
Q What is your post office address? A Weeletka[sic]. I am a citizen of the Creek Nation.

Applications for Enrollment of Creek Newborn
Act of 1905   Volume XIII

What is your name? A Maria Kelley.
Q What is your age? A About 35.
Q What is your post office address? A Senora.
Q Are you a citizen of the Creek Nation? A No sir, Seminole Nation.

What is your name? A Sam Kelley.
Q What is your age? A I am over 30.
Q What is your post office address? A Senora, Indian Territory
Q Are you a citizen of the Creek Nation? A Yes sir.

      Statement: Hillis Harjo of Alabama Town, and Mary Harjo of Hickory Ground have a child about three years old between two and three years--it is a girl--- we saw it-- don't know it's[sic] name.

✓ Sam Emarthla and Leechie, whose maiden name was Taylor, have two children-- both boys and living--both under three years old--don't know their names, both parents are of Hickory Ground town.

      Roley Taylor and Arcichky of Hickory ground[sic] has one child not a year old. It is a girl and living--don't know it's[sic]. (The child appears later one but parents are unwilling to testify)
Q (To Maria) Have you some children you want to make application for? A Yes sir, two.
Q What is the name of the oldest one? A Sallie. She is here.
Q How old is she? A three years old.
Q What is the name of the next one? A David, this baby here.
Q When was David born? A The 25th of February, this year.
Q Do you know when the other was born? A March 10, 1902.
Q What is the name of the father of the child? A Sam Kelley.
Q Is he a citizen of the Creek Nation? A Yes sir.
Q If it should be found that these children have rights in both the Creek and Seminole Nations, in which Nation do you now elect for them to make their allotment? A In the Creek Nation.

Q (To Sam) What Creek Indian Town do you belong to Sam? A Arbeka North Fork.
Q If it should be found that these children have rights in both the Creek and Seminole Nations, in which Nation do you now elect for them to take their allotment? A In the Creek Nation.

      Statement by Asaf: Some of these children, the parents have not looked after them--I don't know how they stand now, but a while back they were opposed to it--I am a member of Weogufky Town.

      Statement by Louisa Riley, about 40 or over, Dustin, Indian Territory, being duly sworn, through Official Interpreter Alex Posey, states: Turner Scott of Artussee Town and Polly Scott a Seminole, have two children both boys, the oldest is about two years and the other is not quite a year old. Both are living, the post office of the parents

Applications for Enrollment of Creek Newborn
Act of 1905   Volume XIII

is Dustin. I am the grandmother the oldest is named Lumber and Luffus the youngest; the parents want to file for the children in the Creek Nation if they can. I know that, thats[sic] what they told me just the other day.

Statement by Louisa Riley: Sahala Lewis, Indian name Slow Harjo of Hutchechuppa and Annie Lewis, nee Fields, of Kialigee Town, they have two children, the oldest is named Albert, he is about two years old; I don't know the name of the youngest one and don't know it's[sic]age, but the child is not very old. The parents have been wanting to make application but have not been able to go before the Commission--it was born before New Years[sic] I think, I am unable to fix the date, both are living, the post office is Dustin.

Statement by Asaf Jones: George Thompson of Tookpafka Town and Emma Canard, of Tulwarthlocco, have a child named Isreal Thompson, the child is about three years old, the child is living. Senora is the post office. Also Dick Marshall of Kialigee Town and Liza Marshall, of Arbeka North Fork have a child a girl named Emma about three years old, living, post office Senora.

Statement by Sam Kelley: Peter and Mully King both of Arbeka North Fork, have a child named Luila, a girl, about two years old and living, also a girl about a year old named Sallie. Their post office is Senora.

Testimony by Bunny Hicks, who being duly sworn, through Interpreter states:

Q What is your name? A Bunny Hicks.
Q What is your age? A I am about 20.
Q What is your post office? A Senora. Henry Hicks of Quassarte No. 1.(?) and Louisa Hicks of Arbeka, have a child named Joseph over three years old, maybe four years old, don't know the month he was born in, it is living. Joe is my brother. I also have a sister named Kogee Hicks of Quassarte and she and Hagar Thompson of Tookpafka Town, have a child names Newman Thompson, which will be four years old the 24th of this month.

Henry G. Hains, being duly sworn, on his oath, states that the above and foregoing is a true and correct transcript of his stenographic notes as taken in said cause on said date.

                              Henry G. Hains

Subscribed and sworn to before me this 11th day of May, 1905.

                              Drennan C Skaggs
                              Notary Public.

Applications for Enrollment of Creek Newborn
Act of 1905   Volume XIII

DEPARTMENT OF THE INTERIOR,
COMMISSION TO THE FIVE CIVILIZED TRIBES.
NEAR SENORA, I.T. April 21, 1905.

In the matter of the application for the enrollment of certain new born children of "Snake" parents:

Asaf Jones, being duly sworn, testified as follows, through Alex Posey, Official Interpreter: Also by Maria Kelley, and Sam Kelley.
Examination by the Commission:
Q What is your name? A Asaf Jones.
Q What is your age? [sic] About 23.
Q What is your post office address? A Weeletka[sic]. I am a citizen of the Creek Nation.

What is your name? A Maria Kelley.
Q What is your age? A About 35.
Q What is your post office address? A Senora.
Q Are you a citizen of the Creek Nation? A No sir, Seminole Nation.

What is your name? A Sam Kelley.
Q What is your age? A I am over 30.
Q What is your post office address? A Senora, Indian Territory
Q Are you a citizen of the Creek Nation? A Yes sir.

Statement: Hillis Harjo of Alabama Town, and Mary Harjo of Hickory Ground have a child about three years old between two and three years--it is a girl--- we saw it-- don't know it's[sic] name.

Sam Emarthla and Leechie, whose maiden name was Taylor, have two children-- both boys and living--both under three years old--don't know their names, both parents are of Hickory Ground town.

Roley Taylor and Arcichky of Hickory ground[sic] has one child not a year old. It is a girl and living--don't know it's[sic]. (The child appears later one but parents are unwilling to testify)
Q (To Maria) Have you some children you want to make application for? A Yes sir, two.
Q What is the name of the oldest one? A Sallie. She is here.
Q How old is she? A three years old.
Q What is the name of the next one? A David, this baby here.
Q When was David born? A The 25th of February, this year.
Q Do you know when the other was born? A March 10, 1902.
Q What is the name of the father of the child? A Sam Kelley.
Q Is he a citizen of the Creek Nation? A Yes sir.

Applications for Enrollment of Creek Newborn
Act of 1905   Volume XIII

Q If it should be found that these children have rights in both the Creek and Seminole Nations, in which Nation do you now elect for them to make their allotment? A In the Creek Nation.

Q (To Sam) What Creek Indian Town do you belong to Sam? A Arbeka North Fork.
Q If it should be found that these children have rights in both the Creek and Seminole Nations, in which Nation do you now elect for them to take their allotment? A In the Creek Nation.

Statement by Asaf: Some of these children, the parents have not looked after them--I don't know how they stand now, but a while back they were opposed to it--I am a member of Weogufky Town.

Statement by Louisa Riley, about 40 or over, Dustin, Indian Territory, being duly sworn, through Official Interpreter Alex Posey, states: Turner Scott of Artussee Town and Polly Scott a Seminole, have two children both boys, the oldest is about two years and the other is not quite a year old. Both are living, the post office of the parents is Dustin. I am the grandmother the oldest is named Lumber and Luffus the youngest; the parents want to file for the children in the Creek Nation if they can. I know that, thats[sic] what they told me just the other day.

Statement by Louisa Riley: Sahala Lewis, Indian name Slow Harjo of Hutchechuppa and Annie Lewis, nee Fields, of Kialigee Town, they have two children, the oldest is named Albert, he is about two years old; I don't know the name of the youngest one and don't know it's[sic]age, but the child is not very old. The parents have been wanting to make application but have not been able to go before the Commission--it was born before New Years[sic] I think, I am unable to fix the date, both are living, the post office is Dustin.

Statement by Asaf Jones: George Thompson of Tookpafka Town and Emma Canard, of Tulwarthlocco, have a child named Isreal Thompson, the child is about three years old, the child is living. Senora is the post office. Also Dick Marshall of Kialigee Town and Liza Marshall, of Arbeka North Fork have a child a girl named Emma about three years old, living, post office Senora.

Statement by Sam Kelley: Peter and Mully King both of Arbeka North Fork, have a child named Luila, a girl, about two years old and living, also a girl about a year old named Sallie. Their post office is Senora.

Testimony by Bunny Hicks, who being duly sworn, through Interpreter states:

Q What is your name? A Bunny Hicks.
Q What is your age? A I am about 20.
Q What is your post office? A Senora. Henry Hicks of Quassarte No. 1.(?) and Louisa Hicks of Arbeka, have a child named Joseph over three years old, maybe four years old, don't know the month he was born in, it is living. Joe is my brother. I also have a sister named Kogee Hicks of Quassarte and she and Hagar Thompson of Tookpafka Town,

Applications for Enrollment of Creek Newborn
Act of 1905   Volume XIII

have a child names Newman Thompson, which will be four years old the 24th of this month.

Henry G. Hains, being duly sworn, on his oath, states that the above and foregoing is a true and correct transcript of his stenographic notes as taken in said cause on said date.

(Signed) Henry G. Hains

Subscribed and sworn to before me this 11th day of May, 1905.

(Signed) Drennan C Skaggs
Notary Public.

I, Anna Garrigues, on oath state that the above and foregoing is a true and correct copy of the original on file in the office of the commissioner[sic] to the Five Civilized Tribes.

Anna Garrigues

Subscribed and sworn to before me this 23 day of October 1905

J McDermott
Notary Public.

N.C. 1069.

DEPARTMENT OF THE INTERIOR,
COMMISSIONER TO THE FIVE CIVILIZED TRIBES.
Senora, I. T., October 10, 1905.

In the matter of the application for the enrollment of Sandy and Sarty Emarthla as citizens by blood of the Creek Nation.

CHRISTIE HARJO, being duly sworn, testified as follows:

Through Alex Posey Official Interpreter:

BY THE COMMISSIONER:
Q What is your name? A Christie Harjo.
Q How old are you? A About sixty.
Q What is your post office address? A Senora.
Q Are you a citizen of the Creek Nation? A Yes, sir.
Q To what town do you belong? A Hickory Ground.
Q Do you know Sam Emarthla and his wife, Leechie? A Yes, sir. They almost live in my yard.
Q Do you know their children, Sandy and Sarty? A Yes, sir.
Q Do you know when Sandy was born? A According to the mother's statement he was born January 5, and was three years old last January.
Q Do you know when Sarty was born? A I do not know.
Q How old is the child? A The child is over two years old.

Applications for Enrollment of Creek Newborn
Act of 1905   Volume XIII

Q Both children are living are they? A Yes, sir. Sam Emarthla may be enrolled as Sam Fry.
Q To what town do the parents belong? A They both belong to Hickory Ground.

---oooOOOooo---

I, D. C. Skaggs, on oath state that the above and foregoing is a full and true transcript of my stenographic notes as taken in said cause on said date.

D. C. Skaggs

Subscribed and sworn to before me this 16 day of Oct 1905.

Edw C Griesel
Notary Public.

REFER IN REPLY TO THE FOLLOWING:
N.C. 1069

**DEPARTMENT OF THE INTERIOR,
COMMISSIONER TO THE FIVE CIVILIZED TRIBES.**

Henryetta, Indian Territory, September 18, 1906.

Commissioner to the Five Civilized Tribes,
   Muskogee, Indian Territory

Dear Sir:

In the matter of the application for the enrollment of Sandy and Sarty (Emarthla) Fry, as citizens by blood of the Creek Nation, I have the honor to report that the parents of said children refuse to execute affidavits relative to their birth or to testify in the case.

Respectfully,
Jesse McDermott
In Charge.

Applications for Enrollment of Creek Newborn
Act of 1905 Volume XIII

N.C. 1069.

F.H.W.
A.G.

DEPARTMENT OF THE INTERIOR,
COMMISSIONER TO THE FIVE CIVILIZED TRIBES.

In the matter of the application for the enrollment of Sandy and Sarty Fry as citizens by blood of the Creek Nation.

DECISION.

The record in this case shows that on April 21, 1905, Asaf Jones, Mary Kelly and Sam Kelly, citizens of the Creek Nation, appeared before a Creek enrollment field party near Senora, Indian Territory, and gave testimony "in the matter of the application for the enrollment of certain new-born children of Snake parents", in which testimony appears the following statement:

"Sam Emarthla and Leechie, whose maiden name was Taylor, have two children--both boys and living--both under three years old--don't know their names, both parents are of Hickory Ground town."

The said statement is herein considered an original application for the enrollment of Sandy and Sarty Fry as citizens by blood of the Creek Nation blood of the Creek Nation, inasmuch as the father is identified under the surname "Fry" and in order that the interests of the applicants be protected. Further proceedings were had at Senora, Indian Territory, October 10, 1905.

The evidence shows that the parents of said applicants were members of the "Snake" or disaffected faction of Indians and that frequent unsuccessful efforts were made by this office to secure birth affidavits executed in the regular form.

It appears from the evidence and records in the possession of this office that said Sandy and Sarty Fry are the children of Sam and Leechie (Emarthla) or Fry, whose names appear as Sam Fry and Leechie Taylor in a partial schedule or[sic] citizens by blood of the Creek Nation, approved by the Secretary of the Interior March 28, 1902, opposite Nos. 8488 and 8442 respectively.

It appears from the evidence that the parents of the applicants as above identified are sometimes known as Sam and Leechie Emarthla.

It further appears that said Sandy Fry was born January 5, 1902, that Sarty Fry was born some time in the year 1903 or 1904, and that both were living on the date of the last proceedings herein.

It is, therefore, ordered and adjudged that said Sandy and Sarty Fry are entitled to be enrolled as citizens by blood of the Creek Nation, in accordance with the provisions of the Act of Congress approved March 3, 1905 (33 Stats., 1048), and the application for their enrollment as such is accordingly granted.

Tams Bixby COMMISSIONER.

Muskogee, Indian Territory,
JAN 29 1907

Applications for Enrollment of Creek Newborn
Act of 1905 Volume XIII

REFER IN REPLY TO THE FOLLOWING:
Cr 2464 B

DEPARTMENT OF THE INTERIOR,
COMMISSIONER TO THE FIVE CIVILIZED TRIBES.

Muskogee, Indian Territory, July 19, 1905.

Comr to the Five Civ Tribes
    Muskogee, I T

Sir:

In the matter of the application for the enrollment of two unnamed minor children is Sam and Leechie Emarthla (2464-B), as citizens by blood of the Creek Nation, I have the honor to report that the mother is said children states that the children are named Sandy and Sarty Emarthla and are two and three years old respectively, but both she and the father of the children refuse to execute affidavits or to testify in the case; nor can any evidence be secured from relatives and neighbors about said children

        Respectfully
           Alex Posey

N C 1069.

        Muskogee, Indian Territory, March 7, 1907.

Leechie Fry,
    Care of Sam Fry,
        Senora, Indian Territory.

Dear Madam:

You are hereby advised that on March 2, 1907 the Secretary of the Interior approved the enrollment of your minor children, Sandy and Sarty Fry, as citizens by blood of the Creek Nation, and that the names of these children appear upon the roll of new born citizens by blood of the Creek Nation enrolled under the Act of Congress approved March 3, 1905, as numbers 1258 and 1259, respectively.

These children are now entitled to allotments and application therefor should be made without delay at the Creek Land Office, Muskogee, Indian Territory.

        Respectfully,
           Commissioner.

Applications for Enrollment of Creek Newborn
Act of 1905   Volume XIII

DEPARTMENT OF THE INTERIOR,
COMMISSION TO THE FIVE CIVILIZED TRIBES.
NEAR SENORA, I.T. April 21, 1905.

In the matter of the application for the enrollment of certain new born children of "Snake" parents:

Asaf Jones, being duly sworn, testified as follows, through Alex Posey, Official Interpreter: Also by Maria Kelley, and Sam Kelley.
Examination by the Commission:
Q What is your name? A Asaf Jones.
Q What is your age? [sic] About 23.
Q What is your post office address? A Weeletka[sic]. I am a citizen of the Creek Nation.

What is your name? A Maria Kelley.
Q What is your age? A About 35.
Q What is your post office address? A Senora.
Q Are you a citizen of the Creek Nation? A No sir, Seminole Nation.

What is your name? A Sam Kelley.
Q What is your age? A I am over 30.
Q What is your post office address? A Senora, Indian Territory
Q Are you a citizen of the Creek Nation? A Yes sir.

Statement: Hillis Harjo of Alabama Town, and Mary Harjo of Hickory Ground have a child about <u>three years old</u> between two and three years--it is a girl--- we saw it-- don't know it's[sic] name.

Sam Emarthla and Leechie, whose maiden name was Taylor, have two children-- <u>both boys</u> and living--both under three years old--don't know their names, both parents are of Hickory Ground town.

Roley Taylor and Arcichky of Hickory ground[sic] has one child not a year old. It is a <u>girl</u> and living--don't know it's[sic]. (The child appears later one but parents are unwilling to testify)
Q (To Maria) Have you some children you want to make application for? A Yes sir, two.
Q What is the name of the oldest one? A <u>Sallie</u>. She is here.
Q How old is she? A three years old.
Q What is the name of the next one? A <u>David</u>, this baby here.
Q When was David born? A The 25th of February, this year.
Q Do you know when the other was born? A March 10, 1902.
Q What is the name of the father of the child? A Sam Kelley.
Q Is he a citizen of the Creek Nation? A Yes sir.

Applications for Enrollment of Creek Newborn
Act of 1905   Volume XIII

Q If it should be found that these children have rights in both the Creek and Seminole Nations, in which Nation do you now elect for them to make their allotment? A In the Creek Nation.

Q (To Sam) What Creek Indian Town do you belong to Sam? A Arbeka North Fork.
Q If it should be found that these children have rights in both the Creek and Seminole Nations, in which Nation do you now elect for them to take their allotment? A In the Creek Nation.

Statement by Asaf: Some of these children, the parents have not looked after them--I don't know how they stand now, but a while back they were opposed to it--I am a member of Weogufky Town.

Statement by Louisa Riley, about 40 or over, Dustin, Indian Territory, being duly sworn, through Official Interpreter Alex Posey, states: Turner Scott of Artussee Town and Polly Scott a Seminole, have two children both boys, the oldest is about two years and the other is not quite a year old. Both are living, the post office of the parents is Dustin. I am the grandmother the oldest is named Lumber and Luffus the youngest; the parents want to file for the children in the Creek Nation if they can. I know that, thats[sic] what they told me just the other day.

Statement by Louisa Riley: Sahala Lewis, Indian name Slow Harjo of Hutchechuppa and Annie Lewis, nee Fields, of Kialigee Town, they have two children, the oldest is named Albert, he is about two years old; I don't know the name of the youngest one and don't know it's[sic]age, but the child is not very old. The parents have been wanting to make application but have not been able to go before the Commission--it was born before New Years[sic] I think, I am unable to fix the date, both are living, the post office is Dustin.

Statement by Asaf Jones: George Thompson of Tookpafka Town and Emma Canard, of Tulwarthlocco, have a child named Isreal Thompson, the child is about three years old, the child is living. Senora is the post office. Also Dick Marshall of Kialigee Town and Liza Marshall, of Arbeka North Fork have a child a girl named Emma about three years old, living, post office Senora.

Statement by Sam Kelley: Peter and Mully King both of Arbeka North Fork, have a child named Luila, a girl, about two years old and living, also a girl about a year old named Sallie. Their post office is Senora.

Testimony by Bunny Hicks, who being duly sworn, through Interpreter states:

Q What is your name? A Bunny Hicks.
Q What is your age? A I am about 20.
Q What is your post office? A Senora. Henry Hicks of Quassarte No. 1.(?) and Louisa Hicks of Arbeka, have a child named Joseph over three years old, maybe four years old, don't know the month he was born in, it is living. Joe is my brother. I also have a sister named Kogee Hicks of Quassarte and she and Hagar Thompson of Tookpafka Town,

Applications for Enrollment of Creek Newborn
Act of 1905   Volume XIII

have a child names <u>Newman Thompso</u>n, which will be four years old the 24th of this month.

    Henry G. Hains, being duly sworn, on his oath, states that the above and foregoing is a true and correct transcript of his stenographic notes as taken in said cause on said date.

                                          Henry G. Hains

Subscribed and sworn to before me this 11th day of May, 1905.

                                        Drennan C Skaggs
                                        Notary Public.

Indian Territory)
) SS
Western District)

                                                                        were

    We, the undersigned, on oath state that we ~~are~~ personally acquainted with Nellie Taylor, deceased   wife of   Roley Taylor   ; and that on or about the 20 day of May 1904 , a female   child was born to them and has been named   Judy Taylor; and that said child was living March 4, 1905.

    We further state that we have no interest in the above case.

                                                  his
                                      Lewis x Harjo
                                          mark
                                          her
                                     Christy x Harjo
                                          mark

Witnesses to mark:
  Alex Posey
  DC Skaggs

Subscribed and sworn to before me this 15 day of March 1906.

                                          Alex Posey
                                          Notary Public.

Applications for Enrollment of Creek Newborn
Act of 1905 Volume XIII

BIRTH AFFIDAVIT.

DEPARTMENT OF THE INTERIOR.
COMMISSION TO THE FIVE CIVILIZED TRIBES.

    IN RE APPLICATION FOR ENROLLMENT, as a citizen of the Creek Nation, of Judy Taylor, born on the 20 day of May, 1904

Name of Father: Roley Taylor   a citizen of the   Creek   Nation.
Hickory Ground Town   (nick-name *(Illegible)*
Name of Mother: Nellie Taylor   a citizen of the   Creek   Nation.
Hickory Ground Town

         Postoffice   Senora, Ind. Terr.

             Father
AFFIDAVIT OF MOTHER.

UNITED STATES OF AMERICA, Indian Territory, ⎫
    Western   **DISTRICT.** ⎭

    I, Roley Taylor, on oath state that I am over 30 years of age and a citizen by blood, of the Creek Nation; that I ~~am~~ was the lawful ~~wife~~ husband of Nellie Taylor, deceased, who ~~is~~ was a citizen, by blood of the Creek Nation; that a female child was born to me on 20" day of May, 1904, that said child has been named Judy Taylor, and was living March 4, 1905.
                                      his
                              Roley x Taylor
Witnesses To Mark: mark
  { DC Skaggs
     Alex Posey

    Subscribed and sworn to before me this 6 day of July, 1905.

                       Drennan C Skaggs
                       Notary Public.

AFFIDAVIT OF ATTENDING PHYSICIAN OR MID-WIFE.

UNITED STATES OF AMERICA, Indian Territory, ⎫
    Western   **DISTRICT.** ⎭

    I, Semahoye, a mid-wife, on oath state that I attended on Mrs. Nellie Taylor, wife of Roley Taylor ~~on the~~ sometime in ~~day of~~ May, 1904; that there was born to her on said date a female child; that said child was living March 4, 1905, and is said to have been named Judy Taylor
                               her
                          x Semahoye
                          mark

Applications for Enrollment of Creek Newborn
Act of 1905   Volume XIII

Witnesses To Mark:
{ DC Skaggs
 Alex Posey

Subscribed and sworn to before me this 6 day of   July   , 1905.

Drennan C Skaggs
Notary Public.

NC 1070.

Muskogee, Indian Territory, July 12, 1905.

Roley Taylor,
    Senora, Indian Territory.

Dear Sir:

In the matter of the application for the enrollment of your minor child, Judy Taylor , as a citizen by blood of the Creek Nation, you are advised that the affidavit of the mother of said child is required.

There is herewith enclosed blank form of birth affidavit, and in executing same care should be exercised to see that all blanks are properly filled, all names written in full and in the event that either of the persons signing the affidavit is unable to write, signature by mark must be attested by two witnesses. The affidavit must be executed before a Notary Public and the notarial seal and signature of the officer must be attached to the affidavit.

Respectfully,

Commissioner.

1 BA.

NC-1070.

Muskogee, Indian Territory, October 23, 1905.

Roley Taylor,
    Senora, Indian Territory.

Dear Sir:

In the matter of the application for the enrollment of your minor child, Judy Taylor, born May 20, 1904, as a citizen by blood of the Creek Nation, you are advised that it will be necessary for you to furnish this office with the affidavits of two disinterested witnesses relative to the birth of said child. Said affidavits must set forth

Applications for Enrollment of Creek Newborn
Act of 1905   Volume XIII

said child's name, the date of her birth, the names of her parents and whether or not she was living on March 4, 1905.

You state in your affidavit, executed July 6, 1905, that you are not the husband of Nellie Taylor, deceased. You are requested to advise this office whether you intended to state that said Judy Taylor is an illegitimate child or that you were formerly the lawful husband of said Nellie Taylor, deceased.

Respectfully,
Commissioner.

NC-1070.

Muskogee, Indian Territory, December 21, 1905.

Roley Taylor,
    Senora, Indian Territory.

Dear Sir:

In the matter of the application for the enrollment of your minor child, Judy Taylor, born May 20, 1904, as a citizen by blood of the Creek Nation, you are again advised that it will be necessary for you to furnish this Office with the affidavits of two disinterested persons relative to the birth of said child, and a blank for that purpose is herewith enclosed. In having same executed, be careful to see that all blanks are properly filled out, all names written in full, and in the event that either of the affiants is unable to write, a signature by mark must be attested by two witnesses must be attested by two witnesses who are able to write. The notary public must date, sign and seal the affidavit.

This matter should receive your immediate attention.

Respectfully,
Commissioner.

Dis

N.C. 1070.

Muskogee, Indian Territory, March 1, 1907.

Nellie Taylor,
    Care Roley Taylor,
        Senora, Indian Territory.

Dear Madam:

You are hereby advised that on February 15, 1907, the Secretary of the Interior approved the enrollment of your minor child, Judy Taylor, as a citizen by blood of the

Applications for Enrollment of Creek Newborn
Act of 1905 Volume XIII

Creek Nation, and that the name of said child appears upon the roll of new born citizens by blood of the Creek Nation, enrolled under the act of Congress approved March 3, 1905, as number 1205.

This child is now entitled to allotment and application therefor should be made without delay at the Creek Land Office, Muskogee, Indian Territory.

        Respectfully,

                    Commissioner.

N.C. 1071
DEPARTMENT OF THE INTERIOR,
COMMISSION TO THE FIVE CIVILIZED TRIBES.
Near Senora, I.T. April 21, 1905.

In the matter of the application for the enrollment of certain new born children of "Snake" parents:

Asaf Jones, being duly sworn, testified as follows, through Alex Posey, Official Interpreter: Also by Maria Kelley, and Sam Kelley.
Examination by the Commission:
Q What is your name? A Asaf Jones.
Q What is your age? [sic] About 23.
Q What is your post office address? A Weeletka[sic]. I am a citizen of the Creek Nation.

What is your name? A Maria Kelley.
Q What is your age? A About 35.
Q What is your post office address? A Senora.
Q Are you a citizen of the Creek Nation? A No sir, Seminole Nation.

What is your name? A Sam Kelley.
Q What is your age? A I am over 30.
Q What is your post office address? A Senora, Indian Territory
Q Are you a citizen of the Creek Nation? A Yes sir.

Applications for Enrollment of Creek Newborn
Act of 1905   Volume XIII

Statement: Hillis Harjo of Alabama Town, and Mary Harjo of Hickory Ground have a child about three years old between two and three years--it is a girl--- we saw it-- don't know it's[sic] name.

Sam Emarthla and Leechie, whose maiden name was Taylor, have two children-- both boys and living--both under three years old--don't know their names, both parents are of Hickory Ground town.

Roley Taylor and Arcichky of Hickory ground[sic] has one child not a year old. It is a girl and living--don't know it's[sic]   (The child appears later one but parents are unwilling to testify)
Q (To Maria) Have you some children you want to make application for? A Yes sir, two.
Q What is the name of the oldest one? A Sallie. She is here.
Q How old is she? A three years old.
Q What is the name of the next one? A David, this baby here.
Q When was David born? A The 25th of February, this year.
Q Do you know when the other was born? A March 10, 1902.
Q What is the name of the father of the child? A Sam Kelley.
Q Is he a citizen of the Creek Nation? A Yes sir.
Q If it should be found that these children have rights in both the Creek and Seminole Nations, in which Nation do you now elect for them to make their allotment? A In the Creek Nation.

Q (To Sam) What Creek Indian Town do you belong to Sam? A Arbeka North Fork.
Q If it should be found that these children have rights in both the Creek and Seminole Nations, in which Nation do you now elect for them to take their allotment? A In the Creek Nation.

Statement by Asaf: Some of these children, the parents have not looked after them--I don't know how they stand now, but a while back they were opposed to it--I am a member of Weogufky Town.

Statement by Louisa Riley, about 40 or over, Dustin, Indian Territory, being duly sworn, through Official Interpreter Alex Posey, states: Turner Scott of Artussee Town and Polly Scott a Seminole, have two children both boys, the oldest is about two years and the other is not quite a year old. Both are living, the post office of the parents is Dustin. I am the grandmother the oldest is named Lumber and Luffus the youngest; the parents want to file for the children in the Creek Nation if they can. I know that, thats[sic] what they told me just the other day.
Statement by Louisa Riley: Sahala Lewis, Indian name Slow Harjo of Hutchechuppa and Annie Lewis, nee Fields, of Kialigee Town, they have two children, the oldest is named Albert, he is about two years old; I don't know the name of the youngest one and don't know it's[sic]age, but the child is not very old. The parents have been wanting to make application but have not been able to go before the Commission--it was born before New Years[sic] I think, I am unable to fix the date, both are living, the post office is Dustin.

Applications for Enrollment of Creek Newborn
Act of 1905   Volume XIII

Statement by Asaf Jones: George Thompson of Tookpafka Town and Emma Canard, of Tulwarthlocco, have a child named Isreal Thompson, the child is about three years old, the child is living. Senora is the post office. Also Dick Marshall of Kialigee Town and Liza Marshall, of Arbeka North Fork have a child a girl named Emma about three years old, living, post office Senora.

Statement by Sam Kelley: Peter and Mully King both of Arbeka North Fork, have a child named Luila, a girl, about two years old and living, also a girl about a year old named Sallie. Their post office is Senora.

Testimony by Bunny Hicks, who being duly sworn, through Interpreter states:

Q What is your name? A Bunny Hicks.
Q What is your age? A I am about 20.
Q What is your post office? A Senora. Henry Hicks of Quassarte No. 1.(?) and Louisa Hicks of Arbeka, have a child named Joseph over three years old, maybe four years old, don't know the month he was born in, it is living. Joe is my brother. I also have a sister named Kogee Hicks of Quassarte and she and Hagar Thompson of Tookpafka Town, have a child names Newman Thompson, which will be four years old the 24th of this month.

Henry G. Hains, being duly sworn, on his oath, states that the above and foregoing is a true and correct transcript of his stenographic notes as taken in said cause on said date.
(Signed) Henry G. Hains
Subscribed and sworn to before me this 11th day of May, 1905.
(Signed) Drennan C Skaggs
Notary Public.

I, Anna Garrigues, on oath state that the above and foregoing is a true and correct copy of the original on file in the office of the commissioner[sic] to the Five Civilized Tribes.

Anna Garrigues
Subscribed and sworn to before mt[sic] shis[sic] 14 day of December 1905

J McDermott
Notary Public.

Applications for Enrollment of Creek Newborn
Act of 1905 Volume XIII

NC-1071
Cr I-1434
Department of the Interior,
Commissioner to the Five Civilized Tribes.
Muskogee, Indian Territory, December 11, 1905

In the matter of the application for the enrollment of Sallie and David Kelley as citizens by blood of the Creek Nation.

Sam Kelley, being duly sworn, testified as follows testified as follow s(through Jesse McDermott, Official Interpreter):

EXAMINATION BY THE COMMISSIONER:
Q What is your name? Sam Kelley; I am enrolled as Simon Killer.
Q What is the name of your father? A Ahe-fo-lo-ka.
Q What is the name of your mother? A Louina. They were taking the names and the parties did not know how to write, they got me down Simon Killer; I think that's [sic] way I was finally enrolled. I have here a certificate covering my allotment, giving the name Simon Killer, by my right name is Kelley.
Q Have you a brother enrolled under the name Kelley? A Yes sir.
Q What is his first name? A Wadly.
Q His are the same parents as yours? A Yes sir.
Q To what Town do you belong? A Arbeka Tullidiga.

The Interpreter explains that the people of Arbeka and Tullidiga Towns living about the same settlement have some confusion among them as to the names of the Towns.
It appears from notations on cards of the records of this Office that said Louina Kelley is of Tilledega and said Ahe-fo-lo-ka is of Arbeka.

Q How old are you? A About 40.
Q What is your postoffice address? A Senora.
Q Did you get your deeds? A No, sir.
Q What is your correct name? A Sam Kelley.
Q The way your brother enrolled? that is the way it should be, should it? A Yes sir.
Q The certificate is wrong then--Simon Killer? A Yes sir.
Q And your enrollment on the card as "Simon Killer;" that is wrong too, is it? A Yes sir.
Q Your correct name is Sam Kelley? A Yes sir.

THE COMMISSIONER: (To the Interpreter) Now, Mr. McDermott, explain to the man that his name will have to be changed on the final roll, and that will require a great deal of time and trouble, and if "Kelley" is correct, then the enrollment of his children will stand under names Sallie and David Kelley.

A The way the name is down on the roll is incorrect. I desire same to changed to Kelley and my children, I desire them to be named under the same name.

Applications for Enrollment of Creek Newborn
Act of 1905   Volume XIII

Q Have you two children by the names Sallie and David Kelley? A Yes sir.
Q What is the name of their mother? A Mariah Kelley.
Q Is she living? A Yes sir.
Q Is she a citizen of the Creek Nation? A No.
Q Seminole? A She is Seminole.
Q Has application ever been made for these children as citizens of the Seminole Nation? A We made an attempt to have them enrolled in the Seminole Nation, but they refused. They were not there when Posey One was in our settlement we made application before him.
Q At that time you and Mariah both said you wanted them enrolled in the Creek Nation? A Yes sir.
Q When was Sallie Kelley born? A I am not positive, but I think it was born in March. She was three years old last March.
Q March, 1902? A Yes sir.
Q Is Sallie living? A Yes sir.
Q When was your child, David, born? A Born in February.
Q What year? A February, last year.
Q This is 1905; was it 1905 or 1904? A Yes, 1904.
Q It was a year old this last February, then? A Yes sir.
Q We have Mariah Kelley's affidavit, stating that it was born on the 25th day of February, 1905; is that correct? A Mistaken, it was 1904.

The witness is advised that this Office requires the affidavit of Mariah Kelley, stating the correct date of the birth of this child and a blank for that purpose is handed him.

Q David Kelley living? A Yes sir.
Q And the midwife who attended says it was the 25th day of February 1904; is it correct? A Yes, that was the correct date.
Q Do you insist on having your name changed from Simon Killer, as it is on the final roll, to Sam Kelley, knowing all the difficulties and delays that will be thereby occasioned? A Yes sir.

Witnessed has in his certificates of Simon Killer, opposite Roll No. 4549, enrolled on Creek Indian card 1434.
Wadly Kelly, before referred to as his brother, is identified on Creek Indian card, Field No. 397, roll No. 1275.

Q Here is another trouble in these affidavits made out before Posey and Skaggs. The name is spelled by the notary "Kelley" and it is signed by mark; whereas your brother Wadly's name on the final roll is spelled "Kelly;" which of these two is correct? A The name should be spelled as Kelly.
Q The notary public made a mistake in putting the "ey"? A Yes sir.
Q What are the correct names of these two children? A Sallie and David Kelly.

Applications for Enrollment of Creek Newborn
Act of 1905   Volume XIII

INDIAN TERRITORY, Western District.
   I, J. Y. Miller, a stenographer to the Commissioner to the Five Civilized Tribes, do hereby certify that the above and foregoing is a true and complete translation of my notes as same appear in my stenographic report of this case.

JY Miller

Sworn to and subscribed before me
   this the 16th day of December,
1905.

J McDermott
Notary Public.

NC 1071.   OCH.
DEPARTMENT OF THE INTERIOR,
COMMISSIONER TO THE FIVE CIVILIZED TRIBES.

In the matter of the application for the enrollment of Sallie Kelly and David Kelly, as citizens by blood of the Creek Nation.

DECISION.

The record in this case shows that on April 21, 1905, application was made for the enrollment of Sallie Kelley and David Kelley, children of Maria and Sam Kelley, as citizens by blood of the Creek Nation, under the provisions of the act of Congress approved March 3, 1905 (33 Stats. L., 1048). Affidavits in the matter of the birth of said children were filed July 1, 1905, and December 11, 1905. Further proceedings were had on December 11, 1905. Supplemental affidavit was filed December 21, 1905.
   In appearing from the evidence and the records of this office that the correct names of the father and mother of said children are Sam Kelly and Maria Kelly, reference hereinafter will be made to said children in the names Sallie Kelly and David Kelly.
   The evidence and the records of his office show that said Sallie Kelly and David Kelly are the children of Maria Kelly, a citizen of the Seminole Nation, and Sam Kelly, whose enrollment was approved under the name "Simon Killer" on a schedule of citizens by blood of the Creek Nation , approved by the Secretary of the Interior March 13, 1902, opposite number 4549.
   The records of this office further show that the name of the father of said children was changed upon said approved roll from Simon Killer to Sam Kell, upon his petition and by authority of the Department.
   The evidence further shows that said Sallie Kelly was born March 10, 1902; that said David Kelly was born February 25, 1904; and that both of said children were living on December 11, 1905.
   The records of this office show that neither of said children are enrolled as citizens of the Seminole Nation, and that no application has ever been made for their enrollment, or either of them, as such.
   The evidence shows that the father and mother of said Sallie Kelly and David Kelly elect to have them enrolled as citizens by blood of the Creek Nation.

Applications for Enrollment of Creek Newborn
Act of 1905   Volume XIII

It is, therefore, ordered and adjudged that said Sallie Kelly and David Kelly are entitled to be enrolled as a citizen by blood of the Creek Nation under the provisions of the act of Congress approved March 3, 1905 (33 Stats. L., 1048), and the application for their enrollment as such is accordingly granted.

Muskogee, Indian Territory   Tams Bixby   COMMISSIONER.
FEB 7- 1907

BIRTH AFFIDAVIT.

DEPARTMENT OF THE INTERIOR.
COMMISSION TO THE FIVE CIVILIZED TRIBES.

IN RE APPLICATION FOR ENROLLMENT, as a citizen of the Creek Nation, of Sallie Kelly, born on the 10" day of Mch , 1902

Name of Father: Sam Kelly   a citizen of the   Creek   Nation.
Name of Mother: Maria "   a citizen of the Seminole   Nation.

Postoffice   Senora, I.T.

AFFIDAVIT OF MOTHER.

UNITED STATES OF AMERICA, Indian Territory,
    Western   DISTRICT.

I, Sam Kelly , on oath state that I am 40 years of age and a citizen by blood, of the Creek Nation; that I am the lawful ~~wife~~ husband of Maria Kelly , who is a citizen, by blood of the Seminole Nation; that a female child was born to me on 10" day of Mch , 1902 , that said child has been named Sallie Kelly , and was living March 4, 1905.

                                        Sam Kelly
Witnesses To Mark:
{

Subscribed and sworn to before me this 11th day of December , 1905.

                                        J McDermott
                                            Notary Public.

Applications for Enrollment of Creek Newborn
Act of 1905   Volume XIII

BIRTH AFFIDAVIT.

DEPARTMENT OF THE INTERIOR.
COMMISSION TO THE FIVE CIVILIZED TRIBES.

IN RE APPLICATION FOR ENROLLMENT, as a citizen of the Creek Nation, of David Kelly, born on the 25" day of Feb, 1904

Name of Father: Sam Kelly   a citizen of the   Creek   Nation.
Name of Mother: Maria "   a citizen of the Seminole   Nation.

Postoffice   Senora, I.T.

AFFIDAVIT OF MOTHER.

UNITED STATES OF AMERICA, Indian Territory,
Western   DISTRICT.

I, Sam Kelly, on oath state that I am 40 years of age and a citizen by blood, of the Creek Nation; that I am the lawful ~~wife~~ husband of Maria Kelly, who is a citizen, by blood of the Seminole Nation; that a male child was born to me on 25" day of Feb, 1904, that said child has been named David Kelly, and was living March 4, 1905.

Sam Kelly

Witnesses To Mark:

Subscribed and sworn to before me this 11th day of December, 1905.

J McDermott
Notary Public.

BIRTH AFFIDAVIT.

DEPARTMENT OF THE INTERIOR.
COMMISSION TO THE FIVE CIVILIZED TRIBES.

IN RE APPLICATION FOR ENROLLMENT, as a citizen of the Creek Nation, of Sallie Kelley, born on the for 10 day of March, 1902

Name of Father: Sam Kelley   a citizen of the   Creek   Nation.
Tulladega Town
Name of Mother: Maria Kelley   a citizen of the Seminole   Nation.

Postoffice   Sonora, Ind. Terr.

Applications for Enrollment of Creek Newborn
Act of 1905   Volume XIII

AFFIDAVIT OF MOTHER.

Child is present.

UNITED STATES OF AMERICA, Indian Territory, ⎫
    Western   DISTRICT.   ⎬

I, Maria Kelley, on oath state that I am about 35 years of age and a citizen by blood, of the Seminole Nation; that I am the lawful wife of Sam Kelley, who is a citizen, by blood of the Creek Nation; that a female child was born to me on 10 day of March, 1902, that said child has been named Sallie Kelley, and was living March 4, 1905.

                              her
                       Maria x Kelley

Witnesses To Mark: mark
  ⎰ DC Skaggs
  ⎱ Alex Posey

Subscribed and sworn to before me this 26 day of   June, 1905.

                              Drennan C Skaggs
                              Notary Public.

AFFIDAVIT OF ATTENDING PHYSICIAN OR MID-WIFE.

UNITED STATES OF AMERICA, Indian Territory, ⎫
    Western   DISTRICT.   ⎬

I, Lowisa Riley, a mid-wife, on oath state that I attended on Mrs. Maria Kelley, wife of Sam Kelley on the 8th or 10th day of March, 1902; that there was born to her on said date a female child; that said child was living March 4, 1905, and is said to have been named Sallie Kelley

                              her
                       Lowisa x Riley

Witnesses To Mark: mark
  ⎰ DC Skaggs
  ⎱ Alex Posey

Subscribed and sworn to before me this 21 day of   June, 1905.

                              Drennan C Skaggs
                              Notary Public.

Applications for Enrollment of Creek Newborn
Act of 1905   Volume XIII

BIRTH AFFIDAVIT.

DEPARTMENT OF THE INTERIOR.
COMMISSION TO THE FIVE CIVILIZED TRIBES.

IN RE APPLICATION FOR ENROLLMENT, as a citizen of the Creek Nation, of David Kelley, born on the for 25 day of February, 1904

Name of Father: Sam Kelley   a citizen of the   Creek   Nation.
Tuladega Town
Name of Mother: Maria Kelley   a citizen of the Seminole   Nation.

Postoffice   Sonora, Ind. Terr.

AFFIDAVIT OF MOTHER.

Child is present.

UNITED STATES OF AMERICA, Indian Territory, }
    Western   DISTRICT.

I, Maria Kelley, on oath state that I am about 35 years of age and a citizen by blood, of the Seminole Nation; that I am the lawful wife of Sam Kelley, who is a citizen, by blood of the Creek Nation; that a male child was born to me on 25 day of February, 1905[sic], that said child has been named David Kelley, and was living March 4, 1905.

                                    her
                            Maria x Kelley
Witnesses To Mark: mark
 { DC Skaggs
 { Alex Posey

Subscribed and sworn to before me this 26 day of   June, 1905.

                            Drennan C Skaggs
                            Notary Public.

AFFIDAVIT OF ATTENDING PHYSICIAN OR MID-WIFE.

UNITED STATES OF AMERICA, Indian Territory, }
    Western   DISTRICT.

I, Lowisa Riley, a mid-wife, on oath state that I attended on Mrs. Maria Kelley, wife of Sam Kelley on the 25 day of February, 1904; that there was born to her on said date a male child; that said child was living March 4, 1905, and is said to have been named David Kelley
                                    her
                            Lowisa x Riley
                                   mark

Applications for Enrollment of Creek Newborn
Act of 1905   Volume XIII

Witnesses To Mark:
{ DC Skaggs
  Alex Posey

Subscribed and sworn to before me this 21 day of June , 1905.

Drennan C Skaggs
Notary Public.

BIRTH AFFIDAVIT.

DEPARTMENT OF THE INTERIOR.
COMMISSION TO THE FIVE CIVILIZED TRIBES.

IN RE APPLICATION FOR ENROLLMENT, as a citizen of the Creek Nation, of David Kelly , born on the for 25" day of Feb , 1904

Name of Father: Sam Kelly   a citizen of the   Creek   Nation.
Name of Mother: Maria "   a citizen of the Seminole   Nation.

Postoffice   Sonora, I.T.

AFFIDAVIT OF MOTHER.

UNITED STATES OF AMERICA, Indian Territory,
    Western   DISTRICT.

I, Maria Kelly , on oath state that I am 35 years of age and a citizen by blood , of the Seminole Nation; that I am the lawful wife of Sam Kelly , who is a citizen, by blood of the Creek Nation; that a Male child was born to me on 25" day of February ,1904 , that said child has been named David Kelly , and was living March 4, 1905.

                             her
                          Maria x Kelly
Witnesses To Mark: mark
{ John W Likowiki
  Daniel Colbert

Subscribed and sworn to before me this 13th day of December , 1905.

My Commission Expires July 13th 1908.   J. W. Fowler
                                        Notary Public.

Applications for Enrollment of Creek Newborn
Act of 1905 Volume XIII

NC-1071.

Muskogee, Indian Territory, October 23, 1905.

Maria Kelley,
    c/o Sam Kelley,
        Senora, Indian Territory.

Dear Madam:

In the matter of the application for the enrollment of your minor children, Sallie Kelley, born March 10, 1902, and David Kelley, born February 25, 1905[sic], as citizens by blood of the Creek Nation, it appears from your affidavits, relative to the birth of said children, that you are a citizen of the Seminole Nation.

You are therefore requested to furnish this office with the joint affidavit of yourself and husband, Sam Kelley, electing whether you will have the said Sallie King[sic] and David King[sic] enrolled as citizens of the Creek or Seminole Nation.

You are advised that this office is unable to identify Sam Kelley, the father of said children, upon the final roll of citizens by blood of the Creek Nation. You are requested to state the name under which he was finally enrolled, the names of his parents and other members of his family, his age, the Creek Indian town to which he belongs and his final roll number as the same appears upon his allotment certificate and deeds.

Please give the matter herein mentioned your immediate attention.

                Respectfully,
                              Commissioner.

NC-1071.

Muskogee, Indian Territory, December 12, 1905.

Clerk in Charge,
    Seminole Enrollment Division.

Dear Sir:

April 21, 1905, application was made to the Commission to the Five Civilized Tribes for the enrollment of Sallie Kelley, born March 10, 1902, and David Kelley, born February 25, 1904, as citizens by blood of the Creek Nation. It appears that the mother of said children is enrolled as Maria Kelley, a citizen of the Seminole Nation, and the father of said children, Simon Killer (or Sam Kelley), a citizen of the Creek Nation.

You are requested to advise the Creek Enrollment Division whether or not application has been made for the enrollment of said children as citizens of the Seminole Nation, and if so, what disposition was made of such application.

Applications for Enrollment of Creek Newborn
Act of 1905 Volume XIII

Respectfully,

Acting Commissioner.

NC-1071.

Muskogee, Indian Territory, December 21, 1905.

Clerk in Charge,
    Seminole Enrollment Division.

Dear Sir:

April 21, 1905, application was made to the Commission to the Five Civilized Tribes for the enrollment as citizens by blood of the Creek Nation of Sallie Kelley, born March 10, 1902, and David Kelley, born February 25, 1904, children of Maria Kelley, said to be a citizen of the Seminole Nation, and Sam Kelley (or Simon Killer), a citizen by blood of the Creek Nation.

You are requested to advise the Creek Enrollment Division whether or not application has been made for the enrollment of said children, or either of them, as citizens by blood of the Creek Nation blood of the Seminole Nation, and if so, what disposition has been made of same.

An early reply is requested.

Respectfully,

Commissioner.

REFER IN REPLY TO THE FOLLOWING:

**DEPARTMENT OF THE INTERIOR,
COMMISSIONER TO THE FIVE CIVILIZED TRIBES.**

Muskogee, Indian Territory, December 21, 1905.

Chief Clerk,
    Creek Enrollment Division,
        General Office.

Dear Sir:

Replying to letter of the Acting Commissioner, dated December 12, 1905, I have to advise you that the Seminole Enrollment records do not show that any application was made for the enrollment of the children of Maria Kelly, who it seems to be a citizen of the Seminole Nation.

Respectfully,
HCF Hackbusch
Clerk in charge Seminole Division

Applications for Enrollment of Creek Newborn
Act of 1905 Volume XIII

NC 1071.

Muskogee, Indian Territory, March 7, 1907.

Sam Kelly,
    Senora, Indian Territory.

Dear Sir:

    You are hereby advised that on March 2, 1907 the Secretary of the Interior approved the enrollment of your minor children, Sallie and David Kelly, as citizens by blood of the Creek Nation, and that the names of these children appear upon the roll of new born citizens by blood of the Creek Nation enrolled under the Act of Congress approved March 3, 1905, as numbers 1260 and 1261, respectively.

    These children are now entitled to allotments and application therefor should be made without delay at the Creek Land Office, Muskogee, Indian Territory.

                        Respectfully,
                          Commissioner.

NC-1072
DEPARTMENT OF THE INTERIOR,
COMMISSIONER TO THE FIVE CIVILIZED TRIBES.

Muskogee, Indian Territory, December 15, 1905.

    In the matter of the application for the enrollment of Lumber and Rufus[sic] Scott as citizens by blood of the Creek Nation.

    Turner Scott, being duly sworn, testified as follows (through Jesse McDermott, Official Interpreter):

EXAMINATION BY THE COMMISSIONER:
Q What is your name? A Truner[sic] Scott.
Q What is the name of your father? A Lambert Scott.
Q What is the name of our mother? A Wisey.
Q How old are you? A About 29 years of age.
Q What is your postoffice address? A Weleetka. Before it was established I used to get my mail at Watsonville; never did get my mail at Dustin.

Applications for Enrollment of Creek Newborn
Act of 1905   Volume XIII

Q What has become of your wife, Lucinda? A We have separated. She is married to another man.
Q How long ago did you separate? A I cannot tell you it has been some time.
Q Have you two children by the names Lumber and Luffus Scott? A Yes sir.
Q What is the name of their mother? A Polly.
Q Is she a citizen of the Creek Nation? A No, she is a Seminole citizen.
Q She is living? A Yes sir.
Q Were you married to her before you had these children? A Yes sir.
Q Both of these children are living now? A Yes sir.
Q The oldest's name is what? A Lumber.
Q When was Lumber born? A February 25, 1903; will be three years old this coming February.
Q The next child, what is its name? A Rufus. The grandmother of the child made the first application and she was unable to call his name the correct way, and the man who took the application spelled it according to her pronunciation, which made Luffus.
Q The right way is the English pronunciation? A Yes sir.
Q These are both your children, are they? A Yes, they are both mine.
Q When was Rufus born? A He will be one year old the 17th of this month.
Q Turner, if it should be found that these two children of yours are entitled to be enrolled in either the Creek or Seminole Nations, in which Nation do you desire to have them enrolled and take their land? A They are really citizens of the Seminole Nation and I made an effort to have them enrolled over there but they refused to take our application. I think they still refuse to take them over there. I will have to have them enrolled in the Creek Nation.
Q You had better get him to make a positive answer. We have a letter from the Seminole Division which says that Thomas Palmer, the band chief states--testifies about a child named Lumpa Scott, born February 25, 1903; is that your oldest child? you think it refers to your oldest child, Lumber? A I wrote him shortly after the child was born, and by that I suppose he had reference to the same child.
Q Tell him, then, if he prefers to have them enrolled in the Creek Nation we would like to have his election; we do not care which he takes. The Seminole mother has already elected in the Creek Nation. A I desire to have them enrolled in the Creek and Take their allotments in the same Nation.
Q You elect for them in the Creek Nation, then, do you? A Yes sir.
Q You havn't[sic] a copy of the marriage license of the marriage to this Seminole woman? A I had been written about the marriage license some time ago and I answered the letter stating that we were not married according to United States law.

INDIAN TERRITORY, Western District.
    I, J. Y. Miller, a stenographer to the Commissioner to the Five Civilized Tribes, do hereby certify that the above and foregoing is a true and complete translation of my notes as same appear in my stenographic report of this case.

                                               JY Miller

Sworn to and subscribed before me
   this the 19th day of December,   J McDermott
   1905.   Notary Public.

Applications for Enrollment of Creek Newborn
Act of 1905 Volume XIII

DEPARTMENT OF THE INTERIOR,
COMMISSION TO THE FIVE CIVILIZED TRIBES.
Sonora, I. T., June 19, 1905.

In the matter of the application for the enrollment of Lumber and Rufus Scott as citizens by blood of the Creek Nation.

POLLIE SCOTT, being duly sworn, testified as follows:
Through Alex Posey Official Interpreter:

BY COMMISSION:
Q What is your name? A Pollie Scott.
Q How old are you? A About thirty.
Q What is your post office address? A Soncra.
Q Are you a citizen of the Seminole Nation? A Yes, sir.
Q Do you make application for the enrollment of your minor children, and , as citizens by blood of the Creek Nation, and that the names of these children appear upon the roll of new born citizens by blood of the Creek Nation enrolled under the Act of Congress approved March 3, 1905, as numbers Lumber and Rufus Scott, as citizens by blood of the Creek Nation bloood[sic] of the Creek Nation? A Yes, sir.
Q If it should be found that these two children are entitled to rights in both the Creek and Seminole Nation[sic] in which nation do you elect to have them enrolled? A In the Creek Nation.

---oooOOOooo---

I, D. C. Skaggs, on oath state that the above and foregoing is a full and true transcript of my stenographic notes as taken in said cause on said date.
D. C. Skaggs
Subscribed and sworn to before me this 30 day of Dec 1905.
Edw C Griesel
Notary Public.

BIRTH AFFIDAVIT.

DEPARTMENT OF THE INTERIOR.
COMMISSION TO THE FIVE CIVILIZED TRIBES.

IN RE APPLICATION FOR ENROLLMENT, as a citizen of the Creek Nation, of Rufus Scott, born on the 17 day of December, 1904

Name of Father: Turner Scott   a citizen of the   Creek   Nation.
    Artussee Town
Name of Mother: Pollie Scott   a citizen of the Seminole   Nation.

Applications for Enrollment of Creek Newborn
Act of 1905   Volume XIII

Postoffice   Sonora, I.T.

AFFIDAVIT OF MOTHER.

UNITED STATES OF AMERICA, Indian Territory,
   Western   DISTRICT.

I, Pollie Scott , on oath state that I am about 30 years of age and a citizen by blood , of the Seminole Nation; that I am the lawful wife of Turner Scott , who is a citizen, by blood of the Creek Nation; that a male child was born to me on 17 day of December , 1904 , that said child has been named Rufus Scott , and was living March 4, 1905.

                                             her
                                    Pollie x Scott

Witnesses To Mark: mark
  { DC Skaggs
    Alex Posey

Subscribed and sworn to before me this 19 day of June , 1905.

                                    Drennan C Skaggs
                                    Notary Public.

AFFIDAVIT OF ATTENDING PHYSICIAN OR MID-WIFE.

UNITED STATES OF AMERICA, Indian Territory,
   Western   DISTRICT.

I, Sarah Riley , a mid-wife , on oath state that I attended on Mrs. Pollie Scott , wife of Turner Scott on the 17 day of December , 1904 ; that there was born to her on said date a male child; that said child was living March 4, 1905, and is said to have been named Rufus Scott

                                             her
                                    Sarah x Riley

Witnesses To Mark: mark
  { DC Skaggs
    Alex Posey

Subscribed and sworn to before me this 19 day of June , 1905.

                                    Drennan C Skaggs
                                    Notary Public.

Applications for Enrollment of Creek Newborn
Act of 1905 Volume XIII

BIRTH AFFIDAVIT.

DEPARTMENT OF THE INTERIOR.
COMMISSION TO THE FIVE CIVILIZED TRIBES.

IN RE APPLICATION FOR ENROLLMENT, as a citizen of the Creek Nation, of Lumber Scott, born on the 25 day of February, 1903

Name of Father: Turner Scott   a citizen of the   Creek   Nation.
  Artussee Town
Name of Mother: Pollie Scott   a citizen of the Seminole   Nation.

Postoffice   Sonora, I.T.

AFFIDAVIT OF MOTHER.

UNITED STATES OF AMERICA, Indian Territory, }
   Western   DISTRICT.

I, Pollie Scott, on oath state that I am about 30 years of age and a citizen by blood, of the Seminole Nation; that I am the lawful wife of Turner Scott, who is a citizen, by blood of the Creek Nation; that a male child was born to me on 25 day of February, 1903, that said child has been named Lumber Scott, and was living March 4, 1905.

                                        her
                                Pollie x Scott
Witnesses To Mark: mark
  { DC Skaggs
    Alex Posey

Subscribed and sworn to before me this 19 day of   June   , 1905.

                                    Drennan C Skaggs
                                    Notary Public.

AFFIDAVIT OF ATTENDING PHYSICIAN OR MID-WIFE.

UNITED STATES OF AMERICA, Indian Territory, }
   Western   DISTRICT.

I, Lowisa Riley, a mid-wife, on oath state that I attended on Mrs. Pollie Scott, wife of Turner Scott on the 25 day of February, 1903 ; that there was born to her on said date a male child; that said child was living March 4, 1905, and is said to have been named Lumber Scott
                                    her
                                Sarah x Riley
                                  mark

Applications for Enrollment of Creek Newborn
Act of 1905   Volume XIII

Witnesses To Mark:
{ DC Skaggs
  Alex Posey

    Subscribed and sworn to before me this 21 day of   June   , 1905.

                                Drennan C Skaggs
                                Notary Public.

NC-1072.

                        Muskogee, Indian Territory, October 23, 1905.

Clerk in Charge,
    Seminole Enrollment Division.

Dear Sir:

    Application was made to the Commission to the Five Civilized Tribes for the enrollment of Lumber Scott, born February 25, 1903, and Rufus Scott, born December 17, 1904, children of Turner Scott a citizen of the Creek Nation, and Polly Scott, a citizen of the Seminole Nation, as citizens by blood of the Creek Nation.

    You are requested to inform the Creek Enrollment Division as to whether application has been made for the enrollment of said children as citizens of the Seminole Nation and if so what disposition has been made of same.

                        Respectfully,
                                    Commissioner.

NC-1072.

                        Muskogee, Indian Territory, October 23, 1905.

Polly Scott,
    Senora, Indian Territory.

Dear Madam:

    In the matter of the application for the enrollment of your minor children, Lumber Scott, born February 25, 1903, and Rufus Scott, born December 17, 1904, as citizens by blood of the Creek Nation, you are advised that it will be necessary for you to furnish this office with evidence of your marriage to Turner Scott, the father of said children.

    Such evidence may consist of either the original or a certified copy of your marriage license and certificate.

Applications for Enrollment of Creek Newborn
Act of 1905   Volume XIII

REFER IN REPLY TO THE FOLLOWING:

DEPARTMENT OF THE INTERIOR,
COMMISSIONER TO THE FIVE CIVILIZED TRIBES.

Muskogee, Indian Territory, October 28, 1905.

Clerk in Charge,
    Creek Enrollment Division.

Dear Sir:

    Receipt is hereby acknowledged of your letter of the 23rd instant, in which you request to be informed whether or not application has been made for the enrollment of Lumber Scott, born February 25, 1903, and Rufus Scott born December 17, 1904, children of Turner Scott, a citizen of the Creek Nation and Polly Scott, a citizen of the Seminole Nation, and as to what disposition has been made of same.

    In reply you are advised that no application has been for the enrollment of Rufus Scott as a citizen of the Seminole Nation, but an application for the enrollment of Lumpa Scott as a citizen of the Seminole Nation was made on May 31, 1905, by Thomas Palmer, a Band Chief of the Seminole Nation.

    Testimony of Thomas Palmer taken on above date, shows that Lumpa Scott was born February 25, 1903, is on the Band Chiefs[sic] roll, and that the parents of Lumpa Scott are "snake Indians" and refuse to apply for the enrollment of their child.

    The names of Lumpa Scott's parents were not given at the time the application was made but Thomas Palmer said that he would send in these names, which has not been done.

    Lumpa Scott has not been finally enrolled as a citizen of the Seminole Nation.

Respectfully,
Tams Bixby   Commissioner.

Applications for Enrollment of Creek Newborn
Act of 1905   Volume XIII

C 1072
~~N.C. 904~~

Muskogee, Indian Territory, October 30, 1905.

Chief Clerk,
    Seminole Enrollment Division.

Dear Sir:

    Receipt is acknowledged of your communication of October 28, 1905, replying to the communication of the Creek Enrollment Division of October 23, 1905, relative to the application for the enrollment of Lumber Scott as a citizen by blood of the Creek Nation.

    You state that application has been made for the enrollment of Lumpa Scott, who is now identified as the same person as said Lumber Scott, as a citizen by blood of the Seminole Nation.

    There is herewith enclosed copy of testimony taken June 19, 1905 in the matter of the application for the enrollment of said Lumber Scott as a citizen by blood of the Creek Nation in which an election is made by the mother of said child for his enrollment in the Creek Nation. Said testimony was taken at Senora, Indian Territory, by the Creek Enrollment field party and is not yet signed and sworn to. When the same has been properly signed and sworn to, another copy will be sent to your office.

                      Respectfully,

                                          Commissioner.

AG-5o

N.C. 1072

Muskogee, Indian Territory, November 28, 1905.

Turner Scott,
    Weleetka, Indian Territory.

Dear Sir:

    Receipt is acknowledged of your letter of November 19, 1905, relative to the right to enrollment of your minor children, Lumber and Luffus (or Rufus) Scott, as citizens of the Creek Nation; you ask when you can file for said children. You are advised that on April 21, 1905, Louisa Riley appeared before the Commission Creek enrollment field party and testified relative to the enrollment of Lumber and Luffus Scott, children of Turner and Polly Scott; she stated at that time that both you and the Seminole mother of said children desired them to be enrolled in the Creek Nation.

    June 29, 1905, affidavits of Polly Scott were filed in the matter of the application for the enrollment of Lumber and Rufus Scott; on the same day said Polly Scott under

Applications for Enrollment of Creek Newborn
Act of 1905   Volume XIII

oath testified that she desired said Lumber and Rufus Scott enrolled as citizens of the Creek Nation.

You are advised that in order to correct the discrepancies in the name and to determine in which nation, Creek or Seminole, said children should be enrolled, you will be required to appear before the office of the Commissioner to the Five Civilized Tribes, for the purpose of being examined under oath. If it should be impossible for you to appear in person, you should furnish this office with your affidavit electing in which nation you desire said children to be enrolled, state the correct name of said Rufus or Luffus and the dates of the birth of both children. Said affidavits should be duly executed before a notary public and should state whether said children were living March 4, 1905.

This matter should receive your immediate attention.

Respectfully,

Acting Commissioner.

W^{m}OB

REFER IN REPLY TO THE FOLLOWING:

Sem. N B 175

DEPARTMENT OF THE INTERIOR,
COMMISSIONER TO THE FIVE CIVILIZED TRIBES.

Muskogee, Indian Territory, December 29, 1905.

Chief Clerk,
  Creek Enrollment Division,

Dear Sir:

On May 31, 1905, application was made for the enrollment of Lumpa Scott minor child of Pollie Scott, as a citizen of the Seminole Nation. Subsequently on June 19, 1905, Pollie Scott appeared before the enrollment party at Sonora, Indian Territory, and elected for her child, Lumpa (Lumber) Scott to be enrolled as a citizen of the Creek Nation.

You are therefore requested to advise the Seminole Enrollment Division the status of the application for the enrollment of Lumpa (Lumber) Scott as a citizen of the Creek Nation; whether he has been enrolled as a citizen of said nation and if so his roll number and the date of the approval of his enrollment by the Department.

Respectfully,
Tams Bixby Commissioner.

Applications for Enrollment of Creek Newborn
Act of 1905   Volume XIII

Sem. NB-175.
NBC-1072.

Muskogee, Indian Territory, January 2, 1906.

Chief Clerk of Seminole Enrollment Division,
    Muskogee, Indian Territory.

Dear Sir:

    Receipt is acknowledged of your letter of December 29, 1905 in which you ask to be advised as to the status of the application for the enrollment of Lumpa (Lumber) Scott, minor child of Polly Scott, a citizen of the Seminole Nation, as a citizen of the Creek Nation.

    In reply you are advised that the matter of the application for the enrollment of Lumber Scott, child of said Polly Scott, is pending, and that when final action is had in the matter you will be duly notified.

                               Respectfully,
                                           Commissioner.

N.C. 1072

Muskogee, Indian Territory, March 1, 1907.

Turner Scott,
    Dustin, Indian Territory.

Dear Sir:

    You are hereby advised that on February 15, 1907, the Secretary of the Interior approved the enrollment of your minor children, Lumber and Rufus Scott, as citizens by blood of the Creek Nation, and that the names of said children appear upon the roll of new born citizens by blood of the Creek Nation, enrolled under the act of Congress approved March 3, 1905, as numbers 1206 and 1207 respectively.

    These children are now entitled to allotments and application therefor should be made without delay at the Creek Land Office, Muskogee, Indian Territory.

                               Respectfully,
                                         Commissioner.

Applications for Enrollment of Creek Newborn
Act of 1905 Volume XIII

REFER IN REPLY TO THE FOLLOWING:
Sem-NB-175

DEPARTMENT OF THE INTERIOR,
COMMISSIONER TO THE FIVE CIVILIZED TRIBES.

Muskogee, Indian Territory, March 8, 1907.

Chief Clerk,
    Creek Enrollment Division,

Dear Sir:

You are hereby notified that the Commissioner to the Five Civilized Tribes, on February 20, 1907, rendered his decision dismissing the application for the enrollment of Lumpa (Lumber) Scott as a citizen of the Seminole Nation.

Respectfully,

Tams Bixby Commissioner.

BIRTH AFFIDAVIT.

DEPARTMENT OF THE INTERIOR.
COMMISSION TO THE FIVE CIVILIZED TRIBES.

IN RE APPLICATION FOR ENROLLMENT, as a citizen of the Creek Nation, of John Lewis, born on or about the 10 day of December, 1904

Name of Father: Sahala Lewis   a citizen of the   Creek   Nation.
Hutchechuppa Town
Name of Mother: Annie Lewis   a citizen of the   Creek   Nation.
Hutchechuppa Town

                    Postoffice   Henryetta, I.T.

Applications for Enrollment of Creek Newborn
Act of 1905   Volume XIII

AFFIDAVIT OF MOTHER.

UNITED STATES OF AMERICA, Indian Territory, }
   Western   DISTRICT.

    I, Annie Lewis , on oath state that I am about 22 years of age and a citizen by blood , of the Creek Nation; that I am the lawful wife of Sahala Lewis , who is a citizen, by blood of the Creek Nation; that a male child was born to me on or about 10th day of December , 1904 , that said child has been named John Lewis , and was living March 4, 1905. That no one attended on me as physician or midwife at the birth of the child.

                                                  her
                                      Annie x Lewis
Witnesses To Mark: mark
  { DC Skaggs
    Alex Posey

    Subscribed and sworn to before me this 21 day of   June   , 1905.

                                  Drennan C Skaggs
                                      Notary Public.

AFFIDAVIT OF ATTENDING PHYSICIAN OR MID-WIFE.

UNITED STATES OF AMERICA, Indian Territory, }
   Western   DISTRICT.

                                                are personally acquainted with
    We, the undersigned   , ~~a~~ , on oath state that ~~I~~ we ~~attended on~~ Mrs. Annie Lewis , wife of Sahala Lewis ~~on the   day of   , 1~~ ; that there was born to her on or about the 10th day of December 1904 ~~said date~~ a male child; that said child was living March 4, 1905, and is said to have been named John Lewis

                                        her
                                  Lowisa x Riley
Witnesses To Mark: mark
  { DC Skaggs   her
    Alex Posey   Sarah x Riley
                                      mark

Subscribed and sworn to before me this 21 day of   June   , 1905.

                                  Drennan C Skaggs
                                      Notary Public.

Applications for Enrollment of Creek Newborn
Act of 1905 Volume XIII

BIRTH AFFIDAVIT.

DEPARTMENT OF THE INTERIOR.
COMMISSION TO THE FIVE CIVILIZED TRIBES.

IN RE APPLICATION FOR ENROLLMENT, as a citizen of the Creek Nation, of Albert Lewis, born ~~on the day of~~ January, 1903

Name of Father: Sahala Lewis Hutchechuppa   a citizen of the Creek Nation.
Name of Mother: Annie Lewis (nee Fields) Hutchechuppa   a citizen of the Creek Nation.

Postoffice Henryetta, I.T.

AFFIDAVIT OF MOTHER.

UNITED STATES OF AMERICA, Indian Territory,
Western DISTRICT.

I, Annie Lewis, on oath state that I am about 22 years of age and a citizen by blood, of the Creek Nation; that I am the lawful wife of Sahala Lewis, who is a citizen, by blood of the Creek Nation; that a male child was born to me ~~on day of~~ January, 1903, that said child has been named Albert Lewis, and was living March 4, 1905. That no one attended on me as physician or midwife at the birth of the child.

                          her
                      Annie x Lewis

Witnesses To Mark: mark
  DC Skaggs
  Alex Posey

Subscribed and sworn to before me this 21 day of June, 1905.

                    Drennan C Skaggs
                    Notary Public.

AFFIDAVIT OF ATTENDING PHYSICIAN OR MID-WIFE.

UNITED STATES OF AMERICA, Indian Territory,
Western DISTRICT.

are personally acquainted with We, the undersigned, ~~a~~, on oath state that ~~I~~ we ~~attended on~~ Mrs. Annie Lewis, wife of Sahala Lewis ~~on the day of , 1~~ ; that there was born to her ~~on the day of~~ January 1903 ~~said date~~ a male child; that said child was living March 4, 1905, and is said to have been named Albert Lewis

                        her
                    Lowisa x Riley
                      mark

Applications for Enrollment of Creek Newborn
Act of 1905 Volume XIII

Witnesses To Mark:
{ DC Skaggs
{ Alex Posey

her
Sarah x Riley
mark

Subscribed and sworn to before me this 21 day of June , 1905.

Drennan C Skaggs
Notary Public.

DEPARTMENT OF THE INTERIOR,
COMMISSION TO THE FIVE CIVILIZED TRIBES.
NEAR SENORA, I.T. April 21, 1905.

In the matter of the application for the enrollment of certain new born children of "Snake" parents:

Asaf Jones, being duly sworn, testified as follows, through Alex Posey, Official Interpreter: Also by Maria Kelley, and Sam Kelley.
Examination by the Commission:
Q What is your name? A Asaf Jones.
Q What is your age? [sic] About 23.
Q What is your post office address? A Weeletka[sic]. I am a citizen of the Creek Nation.

What is your name? A Maria Kelley.
Q What is your age? A About 35.
Q What is your post office address? A Senora.
Q Are you a citizen of the Creek Nation? A No sir, Seminole Nation.

What is your name? A Sam Kelley.
Q What is your age? A I am over 30.
Q What is your post office address? A Senora, Indian Territory
Q Are you a citizen of the Creek Nation? A Yes sir.

Statement: Hillis Harjo of Alabama Town, and Mary Harjo of Hickory Ground have a child about three years old between two and three years--it is a girl--- we saw it-- don't know it's[sic] name.

Applications for Enrollment of Creek Newborn
Act of 1905 Volume XIII

Sam Emarthla and Leechie, whose maiden name was Taylor, have two children--both boys and living--both under three years old--don't know their names, both parents are of Hickory Ground town.

Roley Taylor and Arcichky of Hickory ground[sic] has one child not a year old. It is a girl and living--don't know it's[sic]. (The child appears later one but parents are unwilling to testify)
Q (To Maria) Have you some children you want to make application for? A Yes sir, two.
Q What is the name of the oldest one? A Sallie. She is here.
Q How old is she? A three years old.
Q What is the name of the next one? A David, this baby here.
Q When was David born? A The 25th of February, this year.
Q Do you know when the other was born? A March 10, 1902.
Q What is the name of the father of the child? A Sam Kelley.
Q Is he a citizen of the Creek Nation? A Yes sir.
Q If it should be found that these children have rights in both the Creek and Seminole Nations, in which Nation do you now elect for them to make their allotment? A In the Creek Nation.

Q (To Sam) What Creek Indian Town do you belong to Sam? A Arbeka North Fork.
Q If it should be found that these children have rights in both the Creek and Seminole Nations, in which Nation do you now elect for them to take their allotment? A In the Creek Nation.

Statement by Asaf: Some of these children, the parents have not looked after them--I don't know how they stand now, but a while back they were opposed to it--I am a member of Weogufky Town.

Statement by Louisa Riley, about 40 or over, Dustin, Indian Territory, being duly sworn, through Official Interpreter Alex Posey, states: Turner Scott of Artussee Town and Polly Scott a Seminole, have two children both boys, the oldest is about two years old and the other is not quite a year old. Both are living, the post office of the parents is Dustin. I am the grandmother the oldest is named Lumber and Luffus the youngest; the parents want to file for the children in the Creek Nation if they can. I know that, thats[sic] what they told me just the other day.

Statement by Louisa Riley: Sahala Lewis, Indian name Slow Harjo of Hutchechuppa and Annie Lewis, nee Fields, of Kialigee Town, they have two children, the oldest is named Albert, he is about two years old; I don't know the name of the youngest one and don't know it's[sic]age, but the child is not very old. The parents have been wanting to make application but have not been able to go before the Commission--it was born before New Years[sic] I think, I am unable to fix the date, both are living, the post office is Dustin.

Statement by Asaf Jones: George Thompson of Tookpafka Town and Emma Canard, of Tulwarthlocco, have a child named Isreal Thompson, the child is about three

Applications for Enrollment of Creek Newborn
Act of 1905 Volume XIII

years old, the child is living. Senora is the post office. Also Dick Marshall of Kialigee Town and Liza Marshall, of Arbeka North Fork have a child a girl named Emma about three years old, living, post office Senora.

Statement by Sam Kelley: Peter and Mully King both of Arbeka North Fork, have a child named Luila, a girl, about two years old and living, also a girl about a year old named Sallie. Their post office is Senora.

Testimony by Bunny Hicks, who being duly sworn, through Interpreter states:

Q What is your name? A Bunny Hicks.
Q What is your age? A I am about 20.
Q What is your post office? A Senora. Henry Hicks of Quassarte No. 1.(?) and Louisa Hicks of Arbeka, have a child named Joseph over three years old, maybe four years old, don't know the month he was born in, it is living. Joe is my brother. I also have a sister named Kogee Hicks of Quassarte and she and Hagar Thompson of Tookpafka Town, have a child names Newman Thompson, which will be four years old the 24th of this month.

Henry G. Hains, being duly sworn, on his oath, states that the above and foregoing is a true and correct transcript of his stenographic notes as taken in said cause on said date.
(Signed) Henry G. Hains
Subscribed and sworn to before me this 11th day of May, 1905.
(Signed) Drennan C Skaggs
Notary Public.

I, Anna Garrigues, on oath state that the above and foregoing is a true and correct copy of the original on file in the office of the commissioner[sic] to the Five Civilized Tribes.

Anna Garrigues
Subscribed and sworn to before me this 23 day of October 1905

J McDermott
Notary Public.

No. 2464-B.　　　　　　　　　　　　　　　　　　NC 1076
DEPARTMENT OF THE INTERIOR,
COMMISSION TO THE FIVE CIVILIZED TRIBES.
Senora, I. T., June 26, 1905.

In the matter of the application for the enrollment of Luella King as a citizen by blood of the Creek Nation.

PETER KING, being duly sworn, testified as follows:

Applications for Enrollment of Creek Newborn
Act of 1905   Volume XIII

Through Alex Posey Official Interpreter:

BY COMMISSION:
Q What is your name? A Peter King.
Q How old are you? A About thirty.
Q What is your post office address? A Senora.
Q To what town do tou[sic] belong? A Arbeka Tuladega.
Q Have you a child named Luella? A Yes, sir.
Q What is the name of her mother? A Mullie (Mollie) King.
Q To what town does your wife belong? A Arbeka Tuladega.
Q Do you know when Luella was born? A March 14, 1900.
Q Have you a record of her birth? A Yes, sir.

Witness presents a small memorandum book in which the following entry, written in the Creek Language, is found: "Luella was born March 14, 1900 and the other child was born April 26, 1904."

Q Did you make this record? A Yes, sir.
Q Do you know whether or not Luella was enrolled? A She was enrolled by the Town Officers, but I do not know under what name. The child was a baby at the time the enrollment was made and yet unnamed. The Town Officers gave her a name at the time they enrolled her but I do not know what it was.
Q Who do you mean by "the other child" referred to in the record which you have presented? A Sallie, my youngest child.

---oooOOOooo---

I, D. C. Skaggs, on oath state that the above and foregoing is a full and true transcript of my stenographic notes as taken in said cause on said date.

D. C. Skaggs

Subscribed and sworn to before me this___ day of   JUL 17 1905   1905

Edw C Griesel
Notary Public.

(The above Birth Affidavit given again.)

Applications for Enrollment of Creek Newborn
Act of 1905   Volume XIII

NC 1076   FHW

DEPARTMENT OF THE INTERIOR,
COMMISSIONER TO THE FIVE CIVILIZED TRIBES.

In the matter of the application for the enrollment of Luila King, as a citizen by blood of the Creek Nation.

DECISION.

The record in this case shows that on April 21, 1905, Sam Kelley testified before a Creek enrollment field party, near Senora, Indian Territory in the matter of the application for the enrollment of certain new born childred[sic] of "Snake" parents, in which testimony appears the following statement: "Peter and Mully King, both of Arkena, North Fork, have a child named Luila, a girl, about 2 years old and living". The said statement is herein considered an original application for the enrollment of Luila King, as a citizen by blood of the Creek Nation, in order that the rights of the said applicant be protected. Further proceedings were had June 26, 1905, a supplemental affidavit filed December 8, 1906, as to the birth of said applicant is attached to and made a part of the record herein.

The evidence in this case and the records of this office show that the said Luila King is a child of Peter King and Mollie King. The said Peter King is identified on a partial schedule of citizens by blood of the Creek Nation, approved by the Secretary of the Interior March 28, 1902, opposite roll No. 7979. The said Mollie (or Mully) King is identified as Millie Perryman, whose name appears on a partial schedule of citizens by blood of the Creek Nation, approved by the Secretary of the Interior, March 13, 1902, opposite roll No. 4761.

It further appears in the evidence that the said Luila King was born March 14, 1900, and was still living on December 5, 1906.

Although the application herein was not made within the time designated by the Secretary of the Interior, under the authority in him vested by the provisions of the Act of Congress approved March 3, 1901, (31 Stat. 1010) jurisdiction to consider the same under the act of June 30, 1902, was given to this office and the Department by the provisions of Section One, of the Act of Congress approved April 26, 1906, (34 Stat., 137).

It is, therefore, ordered and adjudged that the said Luila King is entitled to be enrolled as a citizen by blood of the Creek Nation, under the provisions of the Act of Congress approved June 30, 1902, (32 Stats. 500) and the application for her enrollment as such is accordingly granted.

                                                            Tams Bixby   COMMISSIONER.

Muskogee, Indian Territory,
JAN 22 1907

Applications for Enrollment of Creek Newborn
Act of 1905   Volume XIII

BIRTH AFFIDAVIT.

DEPARTMENT OF THE INTERIOR.
COMMISSION TO THE FIVE CIVILIZED TRIBES.

IN RE APPLICATION FOR ENROLLMENT, as a citizen of the Creek Nation, of Luila King, born on the 14 day of March, 1900

Name of Father: Peter King   a citizen of the   Creek   Nation.
Name of Mother: Mollie King (nee Starr)   a citizen of the   Creek   Nation.

Postoffice   Senora, I.T.

AFFIDAVIT OF MOTHER.

UNITED STATES OF AMERICA, Indian Territory, }
    Western   DISTRICT.

    I, Mollie King (nee Starr), on oath state that I am about 23 years of age and a citizen by blood, of the Creek Nation; that I am the lawful wife of Peter King, who is a citizen, by blood of the Creek Nation; that a female child was born to me on 14 day of March, 1900, that said child has been named Luila King, and was living March 4, 1905. and is now living.

                                          her
                                  Mollie x King
Witnesses To Mark: mark
  { J McDermott
     Thomas Harjo

    Subscribed and sworn to before me this 5" day of December, 1906.

My Commission   J McDermott
Expires July 25" 1907   Notary Public.

AFFIDAVIT OF ATTENDING PHYSICIAN OR MID-WIFE.

UNITED STATES OF AMERICA, Indian Territory, }
    Western   DISTRICT.

    I, Annie King, a midwife, on oath state that I attended on Mrs. Mollie King, wife of Peter King on the 14" day of March, 1900; that there was born to her on said date a female child; that said child was living March 4, 1905, and is said to have been named Luila King and is now living

                                          her
                                  Annie x King
Witnesses To Mark: mark
  { J McDermott
     Thomas Harjo

Applications for Enrollment of Creek Newborn
Act of 1905 Volume XIII

Subscribed and sworn to before me this 5" day of December , 1906.

My Commission
Expires July 25" 1907

J McDermott
Notary Public.

NC 1076.

Muskogee, Indian Territory, July 25, 1906.

Millie King,
    c/o Peter King,
        Senora, Indian Territory.

Dear Madam:

    In the matter of the application for the enrollment of your minor children Luila and Sallie King, you are advised that you should appear at this office at an early date with the midwife or physician who attended you at the birth of these children for the purpose of being examined.[sic] under oath.

                Respectfully,
                        Commissioner.

NC 1076.

Muskogee, Indian Territory, March 7, 1907.

Mully King,
    Care of Peter King,
        Senora, Indian Territory.

Dear Madam:

    You are hereby advised that on March 2, 1907 the Secretary of the Interior approved the enrollment of your minor child, Luila King, as a citizen by blood of the Creek Nation, and that the name of said child appears upon the roll of new born citizens by blood of the Creek Nation enrolled under the Act of Congress approved March 3, 1905, as number 1262.

    This child is now entitled to allotment and application therefor should be made without delay at the Creek Land Office, Muskogee, Indian Territory.

                Respectfully,
                        Commissioner.

Applications for Enrollment of Creek Newborn
Act of 1905   Volume XIII

2466 N

DEPARTMENT OF THE INTERIOR,
COMMISSION TO THE FIVE CIVILIZED TRIBES.
Eufaula, I. T., April 14, 1905.

In the matter of the application for the enrollment of Heliswa and Kaska Beaver as citizens by blood of the Creek Nation.

JOHNSON LEWIS, being duly sworn, testified as follows:

Through Alex Posey Official Interpreter:

BY COMMISSION:
Q What is your name? A Johnson Lewis.
Q How old are you? A Forty-five.
Q What is your post office address? A Eufaula.
Q Are you a citizen of the Creek Nation? A Yes, sir.
Q To what town do you belong? A Eufaula Canadian.
Q Do you know Willie and Annie Beaver? A Yes, sir.
Q To what Creek Towns do they belong? A Willie belongs to Okfauke Canadian and Annie belongs to Hickory Ground.
Q What was Annie's name before her married[sic] to Willie Beaver? A Annie Johnson.
Q Do you know their children, <u>Heliswa</u> and <u>Kaska</u> Beaver? A Yes, sir.
Q Which of the two is the oldest? A The girl, Kaska.
Q How old is she? A I do not know but I think she was enrolled and arbitrarily filed by the Commission. I am quite certain that the child is six or seven years old. The mother has had two children since that child was born.
Q How old is Heliswa? A The child is over a year old but I do not think it is two years old.
Q Do you know whether it was born prior to May 25, 1901, or subsequent to that date? A It was born after May 25, 1901.
Q Are both of these children living? A Yes, sir.

---oooOOOooo---

I, D. C. Skaggs, on oath state that the above and foregoing is a full and true transcript of my stenographic notes as taken in said cause on said date.
D. C. Skaggs
Subscribed and sworn to before me this 12th day of May, 1905.
Henry G Hains
Notary Public.

Applications for Enrollment of Creek Newborn
Act of 1905   Volume XIII

No. 2466.

DEPARTMENT OF THE INTERIOR,
COMMISSION TO THE FIVE CIVILIZED TRIBES.
Eufaula, I. T., May 16, 1905.

In the matter of the application for the enrollment of Heliswa and Kaska Beaver as citizens by blood of the Creek Nation.

MARY SMITH, being duly sworn, testified as follows:

Through Alex Posey Official Interpreter:

BY COMMISSION:
Q What is your name? A Mary Smith.
Q How old are you? A Twenty-three.
Q What is your post office address? A Eufaula.
Q Are you a citizen of the Creek Nation? A Yes, sir.
Q To what town do you belong? A Okfuske Canadian.
Q Do you know Willie and Annie Beaver? A Yes, sir.
Q What relation, if any, are they to you? A Annie is my cousin.
Q Do you know two children of theirs named Heliswa and Kaska Beaver? A Yes, sir. Heliswa is also known as Legus Beaver and Kaska is also know[sic] as Leah Beaver.
Q To what town do the parents of these children belong? A The mother belongs to Hickory Ground and the father to Okfuske Canadian.
Q Do you know whether or not they have made application for the enrollment of these children? A They have made no application.
Q Do you know why? A They belong to the Snzke[sic] Faction.
Q Do you know how old Heliswa or Legus Beaver is? A He is something over a year old.
Q Is he as much as two years old? A No, sir.
Q Do you know about what time of the year he was born? A In the spring of last year.
Q Do you know the age of Kaska or Leah Beaver? A The child will be four years old next September. Kaska is a week older than my child (indicating a small boy who is standing down the corn row) and my child was born on the nineth[sic] of September 1901 and will be four years old next September.
Q Are both of these children living? A Yes, sir.

---oooOOOooo---

I, D. C. Skaggs, on oath state that the above and foregoing is a full and true transcript of my stenographic notes as taken in said cause on said date.   DC Skaggs

Subscribed and sworn to before me this 18" day of July 1905.
Edw C Griesel
Notary Public.

Applications for Enrollment of Creek Newborn
Act of 1905   Volume XIII

No. 2466.

DEPARTMENT OF THE INTERIOR,
COMMISSION TO THE FIVE CIVILIZED TRIBES.
Eufaula, I. T., May 18, 1905.

In the matter of the application for the enrollment of Heliswa and Kaska Beaver as citizens by blood of the Creek Nation.

ADELINE WHITE, being duly sworn, testified as follows:

BY COMMISSION:
Q What is your name? A Adeline White.
Q How old are you? A I couldn't tell my age.

Witness appears to be about fifty years of age.

Q What is your post office address? A Eufaula.
Q Are you a citizen of the Creek Nation? A Yes, sir.
Q To what town do you belong? A Tuskegee.
Q Do you know Willie and Annie Beaver? A Yes, sir.
Q Do you know their children Heliswa and Kaska Beaver? A Yes, sir.
Q Do you know when Heliswa was born? A I know but I couldn't tell just exactly the date.
Q About how old is the child? A A little over a year old.
Q Did you attend on Annie Beaver at the time Heliswa was born? A Yes, sir.
Q Do you know in what time of the year the child was born? A I don't know.
Q You are positive that the child is not two years old? A No, sir it is not two years old.
Q Is it over a year old? A Yes, sir.
Q Do you know how old Kaska is? A I wasn't with her when Kaska was born. That is the oldest one.
Q How old would you judge the child to be? A I guess she is about four years old.
Q Both children are living are they? A Yes, sir.

---oooOOOooo---

I, D. C. Skaggs, on oath state that the above and foregoing is a full and true transcript of my stenographic notes as taken in said cause on said date.   DCSkaggs

Subscribed and sworn to before me this 15" day of July 1905.
Edw C Griesel
Notary Public.

Applications for Enrollment of Creek Newborn
Act of 1905   Volume XIII

No. 2466.

DEPARTMENT OF THE INTERIOR,
COMMISSION TO THE FIVE CIVILIZED TRIBES.
Eufaula, I. T., May 18, 1905.

In the matter of the application for the enrollment of Heliswa and Kaska Beaver as citizens by blood of the Creek Nation.

JEANETTA BROOK, being duly sworn, testified as follows:

BY COMMISSION:
Q What is your name? A Jeanetta Brook.
Q How old are you? A Thirty-two.
Q What is your post office address? A Eufaula.
Q Are you a citizen of the Creek Nation? A Yes, sir.
Q To what town do you belong? A Hickory Ground.
Q Do you know Willie and Annie Beaver? A Yes, sir.
Q Are they any relation of yours? A Annie's mother is my half-sister.
Q Have they two children named Heliswa and Kaska Beaver? A Yes, sir.
Q Do you know when Heliswa was born? A I don't remember whether it was in February of whether it was in March, but it was in one of those months and it is a year old. That would have been in 1904.
Q Are you sure that it was in either February or March? A Yes, sir, it was in 1904, either the last of February or the first of March.
Q Do you know who attended on her as mid-wife when Heliswa was born? A Adeline White.
Q Is Heliswa a boy or girl? A Boy.-
Q Do you know when Kaska was born? A She was born in August.
Q How old will she be next August? A She will be four years old next August.
Q Kaska is a girl is she? A Yes, sir.
Q Both children are living are they? A Yes, sir.

---oooOOOooo---

I, D. C. Skaggs, on oath state that the above and foregoing is a full and true transcript of my stenographic notes as taken in said cause on said date.

DC Skaggs

Subscribed and sworn to before me this 18 day of July 1905.

Edw C Griesel
Notary Public.

Applications for Enrollment of Creek Newborn
Act of 1905 Volume XIII

N.C. 1079.　　　　　　　　　　　　　　　　　　　　　　　　　　　　F.H.W.
DEPARTMENT OF THE INTERIOR,
COMMISSIONER TO THE FIVE CIVILIZED TRIBES.

In the matter of the application for the enrollment of Kaska and Heliswa Beaver as citizens by blood of the Creek Nation.

DECISION.

The record in this case shows that on April 14, 1905, Johnson Lewis appeared before a Creek enrollment field party, at Eufaula, Indian Territory, and testified in the above entitled cause, which testimony will be considered an application for the enrollment of Kaska and Heliswa Beaver in order that the rights of the said applicants be protected.

Supplemental affidavits filed May 17 and 18, 1905, are attached to and made part of the record herein. Further proceedings were had May 16 and 18, 1905.

The evidence shows that the parents of said applicants are members of the Snake or disaffected faction of Creek Indians and that all the efforts of the Commission to secure birth affidavits in the regular form were unsuccessful. It is, however, clearly shown in evidence that the said Kaska and Heliswa are the children of Willie and Annie Beaver, whose names appear on a partial schedule of citizens by blood of the Creek Nation approved by the Secretary of the Interior November 14, 1902, opposite roll Nos. 9344 and 9345 respectively.

It appears further that the evidence is not definite or specific as to the exact date of the birth of the said applicants but it is clearly established that the Kaska Beaver was born some time in September, 1901 and that the said Heliswa Beaver was born in February or March, 1904.

The evidence further shows that both of said children were living on the date of the last proceedings herein.

The Act of Congress approved March 3, 1905, (33 Stats., 1048) provides in part as follows:

> "That the Commission to the Five Civilized Tribes is authorized for sixty days after the date of the approval of this act to receive and consider applications for enrollment, of children, born subsequent to May twenty-fifth, nineteen hundred and one, and prior to March fourth, nineteen hundred and five, and living on said latter date, to citizens of the Creek tribe of Indians whose enrollment has been approved by the Secretary of the Interior prior to the approval of this act; and to enroll and make allotments to such children."

It is, therefore, ordered and adjudged that the said Kaska and Heliswa Beaver are entitled to be enrolled as citizens by blood of the Creek Nation, in accordance with the provisions of law above quoted, and the application for their enrollment as such is accordingly granted.

　　　　　　　　　　　　　　　　　　　　　Tams Bixby　COMMISSIONER.
Muskogee, Indian Territory,
　　January 17, 1907

Applications for Enrollment of Creek Newborn
Act of 1905   Volume XIII

BIRTH AFFIDAVIT.

DEPARTMENT OF THE INTERIOR.
COMMISSION TO THE FIVE CIVILIZED TRIBES.

IN RE APPLICATION FOR ENROLLMENT, as a citizen of the Creek Nation, of Kaska Beaver (Leah) , born on the *(blank)* day of September , 1901

Name of Father: Willie Beaver   a citizen of the   Creek   Nation.
Okfuske Canadian Town
Name of Mother: Annie Beaver   a citizen of the   Creek   Nation.
Hickory Ground Town

Postoffice   Eufaula, I.T.

relative
AFFIDAVIT OF ~~MOTHER~~.

UNITED STATES OF AMERICA, Indian Territory,
    Western   DISTRICT.

I, Mary Smith , on oath state that I am 23 years of age and a citizen by blood , of the Creek Nation; ~~that I am the lawful wife of~~   , that I am a cousin of Annie Beaver who is a citizen, by blood of the Creek Nation; that a female child was born to ~~me~~ her on *(blank)* day of September , 1901 , that said child has been named Kaska Beaver , and ~~is now living~~. was living on March 4, 1905.

                                        Mary Smith
Witnesses To Mark:
{

Subscribed and sworn to before me this 16 day of   May   , 1905.

                                        Drennan C Skaggs
                                        Notary Public.

Applications for Enrollment of Creek Newborn
Act of 1905   Volume XIII

BIRTH AFFIDAVIT.

DEPARTMENT OF THE INTERIOR.
COMMISSION TO THE FIVE CIVILIZED TRIBES.

  IN RE APPLICATION FOR ENROLLMENT, as a citizen of the Creek Nation, of Hiliswa[sic] Beaver, born on the *(blank)* day of *(blank)*, 190....

Name of Father: Willie Beaver   a citizen of the   Creek   Nation.
 Okfuske Canadian Town
Name of Mother: Annie Beaver   a citizen of the   Creek   Nation.
 Hickory Ground Town

        Postoffice   Eufaula, I.T.

AFFIDAVIT OF ATTENDING PHYSICIAN OR MID-WIFE.

UNITED STATES OF AMERICA, Indian Territory,
  Western   DISTRICT.

  I, Adeline White, a mid-wife, on oath state that I attended on Mrs. Annie Beaver, wife of Willie Beaver ~~on the   day of , 1~~ ; a little over a year ago that there was born to her on said date a male child; that said child ~~is now~~ was living on March 4, 1905 and is said to have been named Heliswa Beaver

           her
        Adeline x White
Witnesses To Mark: mark
 { DC Skaggs
  Alex Posey

  Subscribed and sworn to before me this 18 day of   May   , 1905.

        Drennan C Skaggs
        Notary Public.

N.C. 1079.

       Muskogee, Indian Territory, March 1, 1907.

Annie Beaver,
  Care Willie Beaver,
    Eufaula, Indian Territory.

Dear Madam:

  You are hereby advised that on February 15, 1907, the Secretary of the Interior approved the enrollment of your minor children, Kaska and Heliswa Beaver, as a citizen

Applications for Enrollment of Creek Newborn
Act of 1905   Volume XIII

by blood of the Creek Nation, and that the name of said children appear upon the roll of new born citizens by blood of said nation, enrolled under the act of Congress approved March 3, 1905, as numbers 1208 and 1209 respectively.

    These children are now entitled to allotments and application therefor should be made without delay at the Creek Land Office, Muskogee, Indian Territory.

                        Respectfully,

                                                Commissioner.

Index

AHE-FO-LO-KA 338
AHOYATHLEE
    Louina 7
    Lovina 4
ALLEN
    H L 171
ANDERSON
    D D 27,31
    Lucy 103,114
ANGELL
    W H 18
ARHOLOKOCHE
    Maggie 143
ARSOY
    Lobina 7
ARSOYALEE
    Lovina 5,6
ASBURY
    Jimsy 284,289
    Wicey 284,289
ATKINS
    Jas P 204,205,208,209,210

BAKER
    Minta 191,193,194,202
BARLOW
    Billy 74
BARNETT
    Austin 28
    Jennie 74
    Martin 28
    Millie 28
BAUGH
    B S 181
BEAR
    Bamma 300
    Fannie 77
    George 305
    Kizzie 298,305
    Lena 285,286,307,312
    Louisa 305
    Lydia ... 284,285,286,287,289,290
    Sarah 113
    Taylor 286
    Thomas 284,285
BEARFOOT
    Nocus Elle 113
BEAVER
    Annie 368,369,370,371,
    372,373,374
    Barney 34,35
    Heliswa 307,312,368,369,370,
    371,372,374
    Hiliswa 374
    Kaska 307,312,368,369,370,
    371,372,373,374
    Leah 369,373
    Legus 369
    Willie 368,369,370,371,
    372,373,374
BENDER
    Bob 70,72,216,222,225,
    233,251,260
    Daniel 219,221,224
    Easma 70,72,216,221,222,
    223,225,233,251,260
    Jennie 218,219,220,221,224
    Mahala 70,72,216,222,225,
    233,251,260
    Robert 218,219,220,224
    Thomas 70,72,216,218,219,
    220,221,222,224,225,233,251,260
BENNIE 19
BENTON
    Daniel 222
    Easma 222
    Homas 224
    Jennie 222,223,224
    Robert 222,223,224
    Thomas 222,223
BETTIE 17,22
BIG JACK 17,19,21,22
BIG WILLIAM 2,10,14,23,67
BIXBY
    Mr 153
    Tams 17,34,53,55,56,58,63,

Index

76,85,125,127,136,152,156,158, 165,169,179,196,206,213,222,229, 241,248,249,255,280,281,282,289,306,307,314,320,327,341,354, 356,358,365,372
BOLEY 86,87,94,102,106
BREESE
   H E 258
   Harry E 97,98
BRIGHT
   John 219,220,223,231,263
   Jumbo 223
   Lumber 219,220,231,263
BROOK
   Jeanetta 297,371
BROWN
   Edward S 281,282,283
   Julia 282,283
   Stanton............................ 282,283
BRUNER
   Addie 101,112
   Linty 183
   Louisie 183
   Maggie 113
   Mary 101,112
   Nicey 113
   Susie 101,112
   Willie 101,112
BRUSTER
   C R 97
BUCKLEY
   Betsey 212,213,214,215
   Caesar 214
   Ceasar 212,213,214,215
   Cora 212,213,215
   Sam.................................. 212,213
BUCKNER
   Jack 2,11,14,24,68,69
   Lizzie 69
   Susie 2,11,14,24,68,69
   Wiley 2,11,14,24,68,69
BULLET
   Hannah 1,10,14,23,67
   Jacob.......................1,10,14,23,67
   Maxey.....................1,10,14,23,67
BUNNER
   Arlie 138
   Mosey 136,137,138,139
   Ollie 136,137,139
   Susie 136,137,139
BUNNY
   Arlie 129,135,136,140,145,153
   Moser .. 129,135,136,140,145,153
   Susie 136
BUTLER
   Myron 74
   Sam 74
BYRD
   Jim 273,274

CAKOCHEE 265
CANARD
   Emma ..316,322,324,330,337,362
   Felix 119,125
CANTRELL
   Jim 7,236,238,239
CASEY
   Sallie 181,182,183
CATO
   Ben 286,287,289,290
   Rhoda ..285,286,287,289,290,291
CHARTE
   Cristie 284
   Loney 284,285
   Sam 273
   Sama 273
CHEEK
   Maggie 141,142
CHUPCO
   Jenely 265
   John 265
   Johnson 265
   Leetka 265
   Letka 265
CLARK
   Nichols 21

Index

COACHMAN
  Charlie 207
  Chas 198,199
COBBS
  E A 98
COLBERT
  Daniel 345
COLONEL
  Arra 188
  Freeman 188
  George 188
  Harry 188
COPPEDGE
  Omer C 246
CORSER
  Ben 285
COX
  John 28,287
COXEY 28
COXIE 287,288
CRAWFORD
  D M 27,31
  J W 198
CUBBIE
  Daniel 207,209,211
  Jacob 207,208,209,210,211
  John 207
  Liza 207,208,210,211
  Rhoda 207,208,209,210,211
CUBBY
  Jacob 208
  Rhoda 208
CULLER 28
CUSSAMECHA 286

DAVIS
  Jim 70,72,74,216,225,233, 251,259
  Johnny 70,72,75,216,225,233, 251,259
DEER
  Jessie 178,179,180
  Linda 178,179,180

Minnie 150
Pinkey 178,179,180
Pinky 179,180
Sophia 150
Sparny 150
DEERE 288
  Edmund 146,147,148,151,152
  Isparney 129,131,135,140,145, 146,147,148,149,151,154
  Linda 141
  Malinda 28
  Minnie 129,131,135,140,145, 148,149,150,151,152,154
  Noah 300,302,308
  Pinkey 141
  Sophie 151
  Sophy 129,135,137,140,145, 146,147,148,149,150,151,152,154
  Sparny 152
DEO
  Jennie 36,40,42
  Louina 3,7
  Lovina 4,5
  Nancy 2,11,14,24,68
  Nasa 42
  Thomas 2,11,14,24,37,68
  Thompson 4
DUNN
  Tupper 178,179

ELA
  Johnny 70,72,216,225,233, 251,259
  Nocus 70,72,77,216,225,233, 251,259,260
ELLE
  Nocus 75,80,81
EMARTHLA
  Leechid 325
  Leechie 315,321,323,327,328,329,336,362
  Letha 266

Micco............71,73,217,226,234,
247,248,249,250,251,260
Sallie.......71,73,217,226,234,248,
249,250,251,260
Sam............266,315,321,323,325,
326,327,328,329,336,362
Sandy.............................. 325,328
Sarty 325,328
Walter............71,73,217,226,234,
248,249,250,251
ESAL 288
EWING
   P B... 232

FAIRFIELD
   H L 107
FALUNKE............................... 303
FEARS
   W T....................................... 45,50
FIELDS
   Annie...............316,322,324,330,
   336,360,362
   Dicey 59
   George 80
   Lizzie...............235,237,238,239,
   240,241,242
   Lydia 74
   Susie 70,72,216,226,234,237,
   239,240,241,251,260
   Thompson......70,72,216,226,234,
   235,237,239,240,241,251,260
FIFE
   Nellie 128
   Nettie 119,126,127,128
   Nixie 119,126
FISH
   George 191,194,201,202,204,
   205,206,253,254,255,256
   Hattie 254
   Hettie 71,73,217,226,234,252,
   253,254,255,256,260
   Jimmie 195
   Jimsey.......70,72,73,216,217,225,
226,228,231,233,234,250,252,255,
259,261
   John 71,73,226,234,252,
255,256,260
   Mellogee.....191,194,201,202,206
   Nache 201,203,204
   Nellie.................201,203,204,205
   Wiley.............71,73,217,226,234,
252,253,254,255,256,260,261
   Wileya 201,203,204,205
   Willeya.............191,194,202,206
   Williya............................191,203
FISHER
   Lussee.....................1,10,14,23,67
   Willie......................1,10,14,23,67
FIXICO
   Bittie..21
   Chippie.......................................9
   Heneha 21,22
   Henneha 21,22
   Jenetta......................................21
   Lucy 21
   Sally 21
   Siah..21
   Tummie 120
FOLEY
   Melinda 2,10,14,23,67
   Taylor 2,10,14,23,67
FOLOTKOKEE..........2,10,14,23,67
FOWLER
   J W 345
FRANCIS
   John 45,50
FRY
   Leechie 327,328
   Sam..........................326,327,328
   Sandy.......................326,327,328
   Sarty 326,327,328

GANO
   George.296,297,298,299,305,307
   Katy.....296,297,298,299,307,312
   Louina 7

Louisa 296,297,299,305,307
Lovina 4
Nicey 296,297,298,299,
305,307,312
GARRIGUES
Anna 73,89,217,226,227,
234,235,252,325,337,363
GARY
J L.. 279
GAYNO
Nicy.. 304
GEORGE
Nellie 2,11,14,23,67
Timonthluppy 2,11,14,23,67
GIBSON
Charles............................ 301,308
Wilson 37
GIELDS
George....................................... 79
GIERKES
Wm F A 236
GIVENS
Charter................................ 45,50
Mr.. 251
William...........70,72,216,225,228,
231,233,250,255,259
GOUGE
Earnest............71,73,217,226,234,
251,260
Nicey 71,73,217,226,234,
251,260
GRAY
Annie 185
Jimmie 78,79,80,81
Jimmy 75,76,77,78,82
Johnnie ..75,76,77,78,79,80,81,82
Louisa 185
Mandy 75,76,77,79,80,81,82
Nancy 75,76,77,78,79,80,81,82
GRAYSON
Garland........................... 257,258
GREEN
Bennie 21,22

Bettie 2,11,14,16,24,68
Bittie..22
Jacob..............2,11,14,16,19,24,68
Lucy 19,21,22
Sally 22
GREGORY
Noah......................................311
GRIESEL
Edw 310
Edw C..........2,3,4,11,15,24,68,74,
75,83,85,88,95,103,107,176,218,
221,227,235,244,245,252,262,285,
293,299,312,318,326,350,364,369
,370,371
GRIMES
Willie......................................258
GRISHOLM
Martha 99
GUY
J E......................134,141,147,148

HACKBUSCH
H C F 347
HAINS
H G 27,51,89
Henry G 71,73,86,87,88,94,95,
101,102,103,106,107,112,117,119,
126,129,135,140,145,154,161,175
,182,184,191,194,203,208,212,
217,226,234,252,261,265,291,297,
309,317,322,325,331,337,363,368
HALE
Billie 143
Billy..............................141,142,144
Edmund 147
Jasper.................141,142,143,144
Maggie 141,142,143,144
Ollie................................136,148
HALL
Ollie..138
HALSEY
Lizzie......................................283
HARJO

381

Adam 115
Alex 133
Chofolop 176
Christie 269,292,293,317,325
Christy 331
Connuggee 198,199
Daniel 274,275
Dickey 161,175,176,177
Eliza 120
Emma 191,192,193,194,202
George 317,318,319,320
Hasty 34
Helis 317
Hellis 318
Hillis 191,194,202,266,315, 319,320,321,323,329,336,361
Houster 34
Houston 28,29,32
Hunda 161,175
Hunter 175,176,177
Huston 27,31
Jimmie 191,194,195,196,197, 198,199,200,202
Keepsey 134
Leester 161,175,177
Legus 192,193,203,205
Legusie 191,194,202
Lesta 175,176,177
Lewis 265,278,292,293,331
Linda 178,179,180
Losanna 161,169,175
Lottie 168
Louina 120,123,124
Louisa .. 178,191,192,193,194,202
Maria 273,274
Mary 266,315,317,318,319, 320,321,323,329,336,361
Massey 192,203,205
Millie 34
Miss Houston 33
Nathlocco 191,194,195,202
Polly 191,194,195,196,198, 199,200,202

Sallie 35
Selina 120
Slow 316,322,324,330,336,362
Sukie 265
Suntulle 120
Thomas 366
Totkis 183,187
Willie 265
HAR-JOC-CHE 165
HAR-JO-CHE 168
HARJOCHE
    Adam 161,165,170,175
    Losana 168
    Lottie 168
    Martha 161,165,170,175
    Yahdehka 161,175
    Yarteka 165,168
HARJOCHEE
    Adam 163,164,166,169
    Losan 169
    Losana 165,170
    Losanna 162,163,164,165,166, 167,170
    Lottie 167,168,169,170
    Martha 162,164,169
    Yahdehka 170
    Yardeka 162,163,164,165, 166,167
    Yarteka 169,170
HARJOS
    Lottie 161,175
HARRED
    Adam 101,112
    Davis 101,112,117
    Liza 101,112,117
    Sarah 101,112,115,116,117
    Sarney 101,112,115,116,117
    Tarpie 101,112,117
HARRISON
    R P 181
    W H 84
    Wilson 84
HARROD

Sarnie.................................... 100
HARRY
   Peggie.................................. 99
HAWKINS
   Conie 226
   Connie 1,10,14,23,67,71,73, 217,234,251
   Sabella.................... 1,10,14,23,67
   Sybilla 71,73,217,226,234,251
HAYNES
   Jim 2,10,14,23,67
   Joe 2,10,14,23,67
HELELT
   Adam 114
HELLET
   Adam 113,114,115,116
   Sam............ 100,101,104,112,113, 114,115,117
HELLETT
   Sam...................................... 100
HERROD
   Aman 113
   David 100,103,104,105,113
   Eliza............ 100,103,104,105,113
   Sarah........................ 113,114,115
   Sarnie................................... 113
   Tarpie 100,103,104,105
HICKS
   Bunny ..316,322,324,330,337,363
   Henry...316,322,324,330,337,363
   Joe 316,324,330,337,363
   Joseph..316,322,324,330,337,363
   Kogee ..316,322,324,330,337,363
   Louisa 316,322,324,337,363
HILL
   Billie 129,135,140,145,153
   Cindy 118
   J H 22
   Jacob...................................... 28
   James 22
   Jasper 129,135,140,145,153
   John 2,11,14,24,25,26,27,28, 30,31,32,33,35,68,287,288

Lumsey............ 26,27,28,29,30,31, 32,33,34,35
Lunisey 25,26
Melindy 287,288
Millie 2,11,14,24,25,26,27,28, 30,31,32,33,34,35,68
Mr 21
Ollie.. 137
Ramsey 34
Sallie.................... 28,287,288,289
Sampson 28
HOMAHTA
   Chepe 306,312
   Folle 306,312
HOMATKA
   Cotcha 18
HOPIYE
   Artus...................................... 184
   Emma 184
   Jennie 74,120,122
   Judy 184
   Span... 74
   Sudie...................................... 184
HOPIYW
   Emma 189
HOUSTON 29
HOWARD
   James..................................... 171
HULLET
   Sam.. 113
HULLIE 101,112,117
   Dave 86,87,94,102,106
   Davis 104
   Eliza 86,87,94,102,106
   Tarpie 86,87,94,102,106
HUTKEY
   George 19
   Jennetta 19
   Siah... 19

ISRAEL 288

JACKMAN

Index

J A 246
JOHN
Eliza 86,87,94,102,106
JOHNSON 28
Annie 368
Ceasar 86,87,95,96,97,106
Cheparne 311
Claudie 311
Coasar 94
Cooper 184,185,186,187,190
Edmund 311
Eliza 95,96,97
Emma 185,186,187,189,190
Hotukle 86
Hotulke 87,94,96,97,102,106
Jimmie 311
Judy 185,186,187,189,190
Leda 309,310,311,312,314
Lena 59
Lydia 313,314
Onate 307,308,309,310,311, 312,313,314
Roman 311
Sallie 310,311
Sam 308,309,310,311,313,314
Seasar 102
Susanna 307,308,309,310,311, 312,313,314
Tullegee 311
Wesley 86,87,94,95,102,106
Wilsoche 311
Wouman 311
JONES
Albert 181
Asaf 315,316,319,320,321, 322,323,324,327,329,330,335,336, 337,361,362
Caddie 182
Caddo 181,182,183
Hannah 89
Mary 181
Siah 181
William 181
Willie 182
KANO
Barney 300,303,304
Bird Creek 302,306
Birdcreek 300
George 300,302,303,308
Harty 300
Janie 300
Jennie 303,304
John 300
Katie 300,303,304
Katy 305,306,308
Louisa 299,300,301,302,304, 305,306,308
Nicey ... 300,303,304,305,306,308
Oscar 303
Wisey 300
KEITH
Mr 21
KELL
Sam 340
KELLEY
David 321,323,329,336,338, 339,340,344,346,347,362
Davie 315
John 303
Louina 338
Maria 315,319,320,321,323,329,335,340 ,342,343,344,346,347,361,362
Mariah 339
Sallie ... 315,321,323,329,336,338, 339,340,342,343,346,347,362
Sam ..... 315,316,319,320,321,322, 323,324,329,330,335,336,337,338, 339,340,342,343,344,346,347,361 ,362,363,365
KELLY
Amy 307,312
David 339,340,342,345,348
Maria 340,341,342,345,347
Mary 327

Sallie 339,340,341,348
Sam 327,340,341,342,345,348
Skaggs 339
Sukey 9
Wadly 339
KERNEL 188
Arretta 188
Freeman 188
George 188,189
Harry 188
KERNELLS 188
KESSETKA 162,164,166,167
KIDDO
Ben 285
KILLER
Simon 338,339,340,346,347
KING
Annie 366
Caesar 8,9
Cogee 159
David 346
Haney 133,134
Henry 129,130,131,132,135, 140,145,153
Hepsey 130
Jackson 8,9
Janelle 129,135
Janelly 130,131,132,133,134, 140,145,153
Jennie 8,9
Louisa 160
Luella 363,364
Luila 316,322,324,330,337, 363,365,366,367
Millie 367
Mollie 364,365,366
Mullie 364
Mully 316,322,324,330,337, 363,365,367
Peter 316,322,324,330,337, 363,364,365,366,367
Sallie 129,130,131,132,133, 134,135,140,145,153,316,324,330, 337,346,363,364,367
KIZZIE 86,87,94,102,106

LAD
W J 244
LADY CHARITY 289
LARNEY
Bettie 2,11,14,15,16,17,18,19, 21,24,68
Bittie 21,22
Cheparney 15,16,17,18,19,20, 21,22
Jacob 2,11,14,15,16,17,18,19, 21,22,24,68
LASAH
Nettie 163,164,166,168
LASLEY
Jennie 4,5,6,237,239,240
Lizzie 2,10,14,23,67
Sam 2,10,14,23,67
Wisey 2,10,14,23,67
LAVAL
Julia C 75
LEEWELL
F L B 246
LENDER
Barney 103,114
LEWIS
Albert 316,322,324,330,336, 360,362
Annie .. 316,322,324,330,336,358, 359,360,362
John 358,359
Johnson 308,311,313,368,372
Lucinda 309,310
Sahala 316,322,324,330,336, 358,359,360,362
LIKOWIKI
John W 345
LINDSEY
Cilla 2,10,14,23,67
Freeland... 1,2,3,4,5,6,10,14,23,67
Phillip 2,10,14,23,67

Sallie 3
Sarah 3,4,5,6,7
LITTLE
   Sallie 132,133,134
LOSANNA 267,268
LOT
   Thomas 93
LOTT
   Jennie....86,87,88,89,90,91,92,93, 94,102,106
   Lena 89,90,91,92,93
   Lucy 86,87,88,89,91,92,93, 94,102,106
   Tena 86,87,92,94,102,106
   Thomas 88,89,93
   Tommie 86,87,90,91,92, 94,102,106
LOUINA 338
LOUISA 300
LOW
   Susie 237,239,241
LOWE
   Lijah 270
   Losanna 265,267,268,269, 270,276
   Louie 264,265
   Louisa 267
   Susie 238
LOWEE
   Susie 235
LOWELL
   George A 18
LOWISA 267
LUCINDA 265
LUCUS
   Emerline 84
LUCY 268
LUNISEY
   Chippie 9
LYDIA 268
LYLES
   S D 271
   S D, MD 271

MCCOMBS
   Bill 285
   Mr 227,228
   William 227
MCDERMOTT
   J .... 6,7,24,89,107,131,132,133, 134,141,148,236,238,239,253,255, 257,325,337,340,341,342,349,363 ,366,367
   Jesse 18,128,132,133,134, 141,147,148,158,164,235,236,274, 275,295,326,348
   Jesse M 126
   Mr 338
MCINTOSH
   L G 43,44,45,48,50,52
   Lena 52
MCKENNON & WILLMOTT ... 188
MAFOLATE 296,297
MARFOLOTY 300
   George 301
   Wisey ..299,300,301,302,303,304
MARSHALL
   Dick 266,316,322,324,330, 337,363
   Eliza 266
   Emma 266,316,322,324, 330,337,363
   Liza 316,322,324,330,337,363
MARTIN
   Lody 273
   Nathan 273
   Rhoda 273
MARTY
   Lott 273
   Nathan 274,275
   Rhoda 274,275
MAYCHICK
   Maggie Hill 129,135,140,145, 153
MELINDY 288
MERRICK

Edward 20,30,44,49,50,75,155, 227,228,266
Lona..........2,3,11,15,16,24,27,30, 68,74,75,140,154

MILLER
A G W 181
J Y 88,95,103,107,340,349

MILLIE.. 311

MILLS
B H 197,198

MITCHEL
Hannah 258

MITCHELL
Mahlahsee........................ 307,312
Nellie 107
Sam..................................... 107

MOORE
Core 228
William................................ 246

MOTT
M L 214

MYERS
J B.............37,63,103,104,114,115
James B 100,101,113,114,195, 196,287,288,300,302,304

NICHOLS
C 22
Clark 20

NOBLE
E T................................... 172,173

OKCHUNPULLA 19

OXFORD
W H 89

PALMER
J M... 171
Sarah.......................171,172,173
Thomas.....................53,349,354

PANCAKE
Cheparne............................... 120
Cindy 120

Willie.......................................120

PANOSKE
Cheparney 121,122
Cindy...............................123,124
Selina.................120,121,122,123
Willie..................120,121,122,123

PARKER
Gabe E..20

PARNOSKE
Bunkie 119,126
Nuskey 119,126
Selina.........................119,124,126
Willie................................119,126

PARNOSKEY
Bunkie 124
Nuskey 124

PARNOSKY
Cheparney 125
Cindy.....................................125
Salina....................................125
Willie.....................................125

PEETIE....................................19,20

PERRYMAN
Millie 365

PHILLIPS
Johnson.................................286

PIGEON
Cemelane.................................36
Jennie 2,11,14,24,36,37,38,40, 41,42,43,68
Jim..........2,11,14,24,36,37,38,39, 40,41,42,43,68,95
John..36
Mattie......................................36
Nache 36,37,38,39,40,41,42,43

POLK
Dan...............................290,291

POLOGEE
Lydia 285
Lydie 284
Neda 284

POLOKE
Lydia 286,290

Melindy 288
Susie 286,287,288,290,291
Tom 288
POLOKEE
Ludie 28
Tom 28
POSEY...................................... 339
Alex 1,3,5,8,9,10,12,13,15,
17,19,23,25,26,32,34,36,37,38,39,
40,60,61,62,63,65,66,67,69,70,72,
74,76,77,78,79,80,86,87,88,89,90,
91,92,94,95,96,97,100,101,102,103
,104,106,108,109,110,112,113,
114,115,117,118,119,121,122,123,
124,125,129,130,131,135,137,144
,145,146,147,149,150,151,153,
155,158,160,161,162,163,164,166,
167,168,169,174,175,176,177,181
,182,183,184,185,186,187,189,
190,191,192,193,194,195,196,201,
202,203,204,205,207,208,209,210
,212,218,219,221,223,225,230,
231,233,237,238,240,247,256,257,
259,261,262,263,264,266,267,268
,269,272,274,276,278,284,285,
287,288,290,291,292,294,296,297,
299,300,302,304,305,307,308,309
,310,311,312,313,315,316,317,
318,320,321,323,324,325,328,329,
330,331,332,333,335,336,343,344
,345,350,351,352,353,359,360,
361,362,364,368,369,374
POWELL
Charley W 279
PROCTOR
Jaly 1,10,14,23,67
Keeley 29
Nancy 1,2,3,4,10,14,23,67
Sukey......................1,10,14,23,67
T E... 42
Toney..................................... 273

RAIFORD

A E 43,44
Lena...........43,44,45,48,51,53,54,
55,56,57,58
Osie 48
Ossie.........43,44,45,48,49,50,51,
52,54,55,57
Pearl 43,50,51,52,53,54,55,
56,57,58
Selina....43,44,45,48,49,50,51,52,
53,54,55,56
Sosa 53,56
RANDALL
Dicey 58,59,60,61,64
Dicy............................62,64,65,66
Roman 58,59,60,61,64
Sam........58,59,60,61,62,64,65,66
Willie...............61,62,63,64,65,66
RAYFORD
Lena............................45,46,54
Osie 46
Ossie............................45,47,53
Pearl 47,53
Salina...54
Selina........................45,46,47,53
RED
Thomas...................................255
Washington 266
RENTIE
Lewis...................................98,99
Louis....................................97,98
Lucreesey 97,98,99
Peggie..............................97,98,99
RILEY
Louisa.........316,321,322,324,330,
336,355,362
Lowisa 343,344,352,359,360
Sarah..................279,351,359,361
Susanna 28
Washington 278
ROBERTS
Annie...............................261,262
Hannah ...71,73,217,226,234,252,
260,261,262,263,264

388

Joe 227,228,229,230,231,232
Joseph.........227,261,262,263,264
Josie........70,72,216,225,227,228,
229,231,232,233,251,260
Mahala....70,72,216,225,228,229,
231,232,251,260
Malaha................................. 233
Mary 227,229,230,231,232
Millie 227,228,229,231,232
Noah 71,73,217,226,234,252,
260,261,263,264
Sister...........228,229,230,231,232
ROSS
   Eddie 286
   Frank 303
RYAL
   Annie........................82,83,84,278
   L B.................................. 82,83,84
   Mary 84,85
   Willie 83,84
   Willie B 82,83
RYAN
   Thomas 198,199

SALLY 22
SALONE
   Lena............................... 281
   Lillie 278
   Lilly 279
   Peter................................. 279
   Rhoda 278,279
SAMPSON
   Cindy 118
   Katy............147,149,150,151,152
   Wash.................................... 118
   Wiley 118
SANDY
   Jacob..................191,194,202,203
   Jcaob..................................... 194
SANGEE
   Jim 2,10,23,67
   Joe 2,10,14,23,67
SARBE 34

SARTY 306,312
SAUNDERS
   W R 171,173
SCOTT
   Henry...............................299,303
   Hunter..............................175,177
   Lambert 348
   Lucinda..................................349
   Luffus 316,322,324,330,336,
349,355,362
   Lumber 316,322,324,330,336,
348,349,350,352,353,354,355,356,
357,358,362
   Lumpa .349,354,355,356,357,358
   Pollie 350,351,352,356
   Polly 316,321,324,330,336,
349,353,354,355,357,362
   Rufus ..348,349,350,351,353,354,
355,356,357
   Setepake 307,312
   Truner....................................348
   Turner........316,321,324,330,336,
348,350,351,352,353,354,355,357,
362
   Wisey 348
SELVIDGE
   R B 6
SEMAHOYE 332
SEMIHOYE..............................294
SHANAFELT
   Mattie P 20
SHOCK
   E E......................................258
SIMMER 129,135,136,140,145,151,
153,154
   Louisa....................................178
SIMMON
   Charley 35
SIMMONS
   Charlie....................................34
   Chippie 2,11,12,13,14,24,68
   Emma 12,13
   Geo 42

Walter 2,11,12,13,14,24,68
SIMPSON
   Ross M 271
SIMS
   E W..........................243,244,246
SKAGGS
   D C 4,5,8,9,12,13,24,25,26,
   32,34,37,38,40,60,61,62,69,76,77,
   78,79,80,90,91,92,96,97,99,108,
   109,110,118,119,120,121,122,123,
   124,130,131,137,146,147,149,155
   ,160,162,163,164,166,167,168,
   176,177,183,185,186,187,192,193,
   202,203,205,207,218,219,221,230
   ,237,238,240,247,257,262,263,
   267,268,269,272,274,276,277,278,
   285,293,297,298,299,305,309,310
   ,312,317,326,331,332,333,343,
   344,345,350,351,352,353,359,360,
   361,364,368,369,370,371,374
   Drennan C 5,9,12,13,25,26,32,37,
   38,39,40,41,46,47,48,60,61,62,69,
   71,73,76,77,78,79,80,87,88,90,91,
   92,95,96,97,99,100,101,103,107,
   108,109,110,112,117,118,119,120,
   121,122,123,124,126,129,135,137
   ,138,140,142,143,145,146,147,
   149,154,156,160,161,162,163,164,
   166,167,168,174,175,177,182,183
   ,184,192,195,203,208,212,217,
   218,219,220,226,230,231,234,237,
   238,240,247,248,252,259,261,263
   ,264,265,269,276,277,278,291,
   293,305,317,322,325,331,332,333,
   337,343,344,345,351,352,353,359
   ,360,361,363,373,374
SKAGS
   D C 182
SLOAN
   [Eter... 276
   Lillie 265,272,273,274,276,
   277,278,279,280
   Lodie ...265,272,275,276,277,279

   Lody 273,278
   Loney 272,273,274,275,
   276,279,280
   Lowisa...................................267
   Peter 265,267,272,273,274,
   275,276,277,278,279,280,281
   Rhoda 273,274
SMITH
   Annie 154,155,156
   Frank J...................................132
   James......................................181
   Joe......................................27,31
   Mary..............................369,373
SNAKE.........16,71,73,119,126,154,
168,183,191,194,202,203,208,212,
213,217,226,228,234,252,261,264,
266,286,287,291,309,313,315,319,
320,323,327,329,335,354,361,365,
369
SNIDER
   V W 283
SOLOMAN 29
SOMA...................................28,288
SORBE 34
SPANIARD
   James............86,87,92,94,102,106
STARR
   Jim..291
   Mollie 366
   Nancy 75,77
   Walter............71,73,217,226,234,
   252,260
STEPNEY
   Lizzie......................240,241,242
   Susie 241,242
   Thompson......................241,242
STEVENS
   Lizzie...235,236,238,239,240,241
   Susie 238,239,241
   Thompson..........235,238,239,241
   Tompson...............................236
STIDHAM
   Eliza 107,108,109,110,111

Johnny 107,108,110,111
Liza...................86,88,94,102,106
Mattie .86,88,94,102,106,109,110
Timmie 86,88,94,102,106,111
Timmy 108,109,110,111
Tommy 107
SULLINS
   John W 59
   Julia B.. 59
SWAFFORD
   J H 275
SYOKIGEE 79

TAHAKEE................................. 12
TAYLOR
   Arcichky...........315,321,323,329, 336,362
   Judy 331,332,333,334
   Leechie 315,321,323,327,329, 336,362
   Nellie 331,332,334
   Roley 315,321,323,329,331, 332,333,334,336,362
TECOXIE
   John 287
TEKE 175,177
THLOCCO
   Peter.. 288
   William...................2,10,14,23,67
THOMAS
   Bettie 177
   Wesley................................. 43,44
THOMPSON
   Cogee............................... 159,160
   George 316,322,324,330,337, 362
   Hagar 316,322,324,330,337, 363
   Isreal..........316,322,324,330,337, 362
   Manuel............................ 159,160
   Newman 317,322,325,331, 337,363

   Nora.................................159,160
   Stepney......................................235
TIGER
   Ahny...291
   Annie.................292,293,294,295
   Bryan..................171,172,173,174
   Geo W 174
   George........291,292,293,294,295
   George W 171,172,173,174
   Jacob..............................18,21,22
   Joe 19
   Leah..97
   Louisa......................................118
   Melah 292,293,295
   Sarah H....................................173
   Susan 171,173,174
   Susan H 171,172
   Susie 173
   William...........................307,312
TISH
   Meleya.......................................12
TOLOMASE
   Dickey 266
   Eliza 266
TONEY
   Foley....265,266,267,268,269,270
   Lijah 265,267,268,269
   Logers......................................268
   Losanna 268
   Rogers 267,268,270
TYLOR
   Hannah 261

VALLYHON
   J R 59
   James R 59

WADLY 338
WADSWORTH
   B W 243,245,246
   Ben W 244,245
   Ella E................................245,246
   Leo E................................243,244

Martha 243,244,245,246
Martha F 243,246
WAKACHE
　Hattie 254
WALKER
　A E 243,246
　Mrs A E 243
　Nattie 247,249
　Neddie 71,73,217,226,234, 251,260
　Sallie........................247,248,249
　Walter..................71,247,248,249
WARE
　Henderson...................... 270,271
　Ima................................... 270,271
　Lula 270,271
WASHINGTON
　Sukey...................................... 110
WATSON
　Ellen 257,258
　Katie 258
　Katy 257
WESLEY
　Major.. 49
WETSEY 267
WHITE
　Adeline 370,371,374
　George 19
　Jennetta................................... 19
　Siah... 19
WILLIAMS
　Cinda 2,10,14,23,67
WILSON
　Bettie 86,87,94,102
　Bettiew 106
　Charlie 101,112,117
　Minnie 86,87,94,102,106
　Thomas 86,87,94,102,106
　Wicey 147,149,150,151,152
　Wisey................86,87,94,102,106
WOLF
　Annie 155
　Cobler...............129,135,140,145, 154,157
　Cobley 155,159
　Matilda 129,135,140,145,153, 154,155,156,157,158
YAHDIHKA
　Cinda 265
　Joe 265
YAHOLA
　Anne.......................................159
　Annie..129,135,140,145,154,155, 156,157,158
　Della......................................128
　Lena.......................................192
　Polly......................................199
　Roman...................................128
　William.....................161,168,174
　Willie................................154,155
YAHOLAR
　Betsey..............................197,199
　Della...............................127,128
　Neharyar..........................197,200
　Polly 197,200
　Roman 127
YARHOLA
　William..................................165
YOUNG
　Mrs M A................................208
　W T 208,210
　Zarah 208

www.ingramcontent.com/pod-product-compliance
Lightning Source LLC
Chambersburg PA
CBHW020239030426
42336CB00010B/542